LIVING STANDARDS IN LATIN AMERICAN HISTORY

HEIGHT, WELFARE, AND DEVELOPMENT, 1750–2000

Edited by Ricardo D. Salvatore, John H. Coatsworth, and
Amílcar E. Challú

Published by Harvard University David Rockefeller Center for Latin
American Studies

Distributed by Harvard University Press
Cambridge, Massachusetts
London, England
2010

Library of Congress Cataloging-in-Publication Data

Living standards in Latin American history : height, welfare, and development,
1750–2000 / edited by Ricardo D. Salvatore, John H. Coatsworth, and Amílcar
E. Challú.

     p. ; cm.

Includes bibliographical references.
ISBN: 978-0-674-05585-8

1. Cost and standard of living—Latin America—History. 2. Poverty—Latin
America—History. 3. Anthropometry—Latin America. 4. Latin Americans—
Health and hygiene—History. 5. Latin America—Economic conditions—
History. 6. Latin America—Social conditions—History. I. Salvatore, Ricardo
Donato. II. Coatsworth, John H. III. Challú, Amílcar E.

HC130.P6 L58 2010
330.91/7468

Contents

1
Introduction

Ricardo D. Salvatore, John H. Coatsworth, and Amílcar E. Challú

Latin America's widespread poverty and multi-dimensioned inequalities have perplexed and provoked observers since at least the colonial era. Colonial administrators faced periodic famines and epidemics with little to offer beyond religious processions, belated charity, or requisitions of food for the starving. Leaders of popular movements, politicians, and policy makers condemned the appalling living conditions of the masses as early as the independence era, but little changed. Social scientists began studying "the social question" by the turn of the twentieth century, but major advances in the understanding and improvement of human welfare did not occur until the widespread dissemination of germ theory showed that the rich and well-born could not escape infection without major investments in urban sanitation that benefited even the poor. It took a Great Depression and a Second World War to make the broader issue of living standards a more or less continuous preoccupation of scholars as well as governments.

Until recently, economic historians could not contribute much to the discussion of living standards and inequality, because quantitative evidence for earlier eras was lacking. The social and cultural dimensions of inequality studied by historians of the region's slave, caste, class, race, and gender hierarchies nonetheless yielded crucial evidence on the legacies of inequality that still burden Latin American societies. Census data and vital statistics, which began to be collected in Latin America late in the nineteenth century, provided the shocking insight that life expectancy, disease, and morbidity in some countries stood at levels comparable to premodern societies.[1] Governments did not begin systematic efforts to collect data on poverty or income distribution until the 1960s or later. The new data influenced debates over the meaning of "economic development" and demonstrated that Latin America had reached the end of the twentieth century more unequal, and thus with higher poverty rates given its level of GDP per capita, than any other world region.

Since the 1990s, historians, economists, and other social scientists have sought to document and analyze the historical roots of Latin America's high inequality and persistent poverty. This volume brings together some of the most important results of this work: scholarly efforts to measure and explain changes in Latin American living standards as far back as the colonial era. The recent work has focused on physical welfare, often referred to as "biological" well-being. Much of it uses novel measures, such as data on the heights or stature of children and adults (a measure of net nutrition), the Human Development Index (HDI), and other composite "quality of life" indexes.[2] Other works use more conventional measures, such as calculations of real wages, infant mortality, or access to health and education, but bring to the discussion new and more reliable measurements that can be used for comparing countries.[3] As in the case of Europe and the United States, where this kind of work first began, the results have often proved to be unexpected and startling.

Understanding and Measuring Development

For the past half century, economists and other social scientists have debated the contested relationship between productivity advance and welfare. In the early stages of the debate, the arguments centered on issues of definition and measurement. Just as most third-world governments had begun to collect data and produce annual GDP estimates (1950s–60s), many social scientists were already arguing that economic *growth,* conventionally measured by GDP per capita, was too narrow a definition of economic development. GDP per capita says nothing about economic structure or social progress. The definition of economic *development,* it was argued, should include not only productivity increase but also changes in the sectoral distribution of production (more industry, less raw materials exports) and improvements in health, education, income distribution, and poverty rates. The argument for the narrower definition was that without productivity advance (from whatever sector of the economy), social progress could not be achieved. The argument for a broader definition that included investment in "human capital" was that economic growth could not be sustained without "social development."

The proximate origins of the new emphasis on social progress in development economics can be traced back to theorists of social development, many associated with the U.N. Economic Commission for Latin America (now ECLAC) in the 1960s and 1970s, and to work on human capital by Chicago economists Theodore Schultz and Gary Becker. Since 1973, when Nordhaus and Tobin questioned the meaning of traditional measurements of growth and national accounting,[4] scholars began to look for new indicators of welfare while others tried to "improve" on per capita income estimates by introducing corrections for unpaid labor, non-market production, leisure, the quality of goods, and the negative externalities (air and water pollution) associated with economic growth.[5] In contrast, Amartya Sen's influential "capabilities approach" suggested that rather than measuring welfare as a basket of goods and services, experts should look at the most basic components of all human activities: the capacity to produce, consume, and enjoy the benefits of labor.[6]

The diffusion of this notion coincided with efforts to substitute a "quality of life index" for per capita GDP as a measure of economic advance.[7] The ensuing proliferation of composite indexes for measuring the quality of life led development professionals to impose a single new index that sought to adjust estimates of GDP with measures that gauged improvements in longevity and education. The Human Development Index, adopted by the United Nations in 1982, became a staple ingredient in the annual reports of the U.N. Development Program (UNDP) and other U.N. agencies.[8] Economic historians working on the North Atlantic past took up the challenge presented by the U.N.'s embrace of the HDI and used it to reexamine the long-run growth experience of Britain and other European economies.[9] Some recent work on Latin America has employed the HDI and other composite indicators of human welfare.[10] Interestingly, the HDI tends to show less international inequality than conventional measures of income. This is because HDI takes into account increases in social spending, in particular investments in public education and health, which can grow rapidly at little cost when the initial levels are low. As a result, the HDI of relatively poor countries tends to grow faster than the GDP.

Meanwhile, economic historians of the developed economies in the 1980s and 1990s were discovering the importance of living standards, now redefined as "biological well-being," in promoting or constraining economic growth. Robert Fogel, for example, argued in his 1993 Nobel Prize address that the chronic malnutrition that affected substantial portions of the English population at the beginning of the nineteenth century prevented most of the labor force from working at all or from working at modern levels of intensity and productivity.[11] Thus the history of living standards, once assumed by many economists as a mere by-product of economic growth, became central to understanding economic growth itself. Fogel's argument, and those of others who followed him, propelled the study of the biological standard of living to the center of debates over the relationship between social and economic development.

Discussions of social development also took a new turn late in the twentieth century as social scientists rediscovered the significance of political economy in understanding obstacles to economic growth. At first, debates focused on the role of institutional arrangements in promoting or blocking economic growth, an approach pioneered by Douglass North (who shared the 1993 Nobel Prize with Fogel) and consolidated in what came to be called the "new institutional economics." This approach emphasized the importance of clearly defined and efficiently protected property rights for facilitating transactions and promoting investment in productivity-enhancing economic activities.[12] The development debate simultaneously shifted to a discussion of the causal relationship between inequality and economic backwardness. At issue was the significance of inequality for the development of institutions that play a crucial role in promoting or inhibiting economic growth in the long run. Elite-dominated political systems, it was argued, often failed to protect the human and property rights of majorities. In such an environment, economic growth was reduced both by the successful rent-seeking of elite groups and by the high costs and risks faced by most citizens who would otherwise have participated more fully in the economic marketplace.

Biological Well-Being and Human Welfare

The systematic use of adult stature as an indicator of human welfare is relatively recent in historical studies. Borrowing from the insight of physical anthropology that adult height was related to nutritional status in the first years of life, Le Roy Ladurie, Jean Paul Aron, and Nicole Bernageau used the abundant French anthropometric statistics of the conscription cohorts.[13] In the 1970s and particularly the 1980s, the use of adult stature was refined and used more systematically and rigorously in studies of economic history. U.S. scholars engaged in the discussion of the "economics of slavery" used heights to ascertain whether slaves, who had become valuable "human assets," received more or less food as a result of the increasing integration and specialization of the southern plantation economy.[14] This line of inquiry—using human heights to estimate past levels of nutrition and health—matured in the work of Fogel, Margo, and Steckel, and was later extended and expanded to other regions, periods, and issues in the work of Komlos, Floud, and their followers.[15] These scholars transformed a set of intuitions and propositions about biological well-being and economic growth into a productive and innovative field of study called "anthropometric history."[16] By the late 1990s, the sub-discipline was already an international undertaking involving the work of hundreds of practitioners around the globe.[17] The key to this developing literature was the insight, adopted from work in medicine and public health, that the average heights of most human populations is highly correlated with net nutrition in childhood. Net nutrition is defined as the intake of calories and certain key nutrients minus what is used by the individual to maintain basic bodily functions (heartbeat, breathing) and "spent" on work and resisting infection or other environmental assaults. Net nutrition in childhood, especially during the growth spurts that occur before age three and again in adolescence, determines adult height. Except for highly migratory populations, adult heights reflect conditions in the localities and regions in which the child grew up, provided that the samples are large enough to minimize the influence of genetic factors. Hence the importance of this measure as a local and regional indicator of the biological standard of living.

Anthropometric historians report adult heights by birth cohorts. There is still debate, however, on the extent to which children subject to food deprivation in the first three years of life can catch up during adolescence. The adult heights of birth cohorts are negatively correlated with infant mortality rates in the same region, because children with potentially fatal infections in the digestive system cannot properly assimilate the food they consume. But the correlation is not perfect, because adult heights reflect only the well-being of survivors (the children not included in mortality statistics) whose adult heights may reflect adolescent catching up. Moreover, the prevalence of child labor (especially during early adolescence) may also affect adult heights to the extent that work tends to consume nutrients that would otherwise contribute to growth.

Historians have found data on the stature of human populations in the records of army battalions, prisons, passports, identification cards, and other written records as far back as the eighteenth century; earlier data on wages, income, and consumption are generally lacking. The average stature of soldiers, for example, can be estimated (if samples are sufficiently large) with confidence for regions and even localities. The same is not true for per-capita GDP or wages. GDP figures are generally estimated for entire nations or, more recently, for provinces and regions, but are usually constructed by making problematic assumptions about inter-district transfers and migrations. Wages of skilled and semi-skilled workers are usually available only for major cities or industrial areas. Rural wages, in contrast, generally fail to capture the diversity of wage rates across various rural occupations and statuses. In the case of mean stature, however, the records usually indicate exactly the locality in which the soldier was born as well as the locality in which he was recruited.

Another advantage of this measure is that it serves as a direct rather than an indirect indicator of well-being. Public health experts often use measures such as the number of doctors or hospital beds per thousand population. These measures indicate the availability of medical services, but say nothing about their use by the population. Average stature, on the other hand, provides individual information that comes directly from the body of the person being measured. It reflects the "use" that the body has made of nutrients in bodily maintenance, work, fighting disease, and growth.[18]

Scholars have given height data and related indicators a variety of uses. Whereas mean heights can be used to estimate the trend in the evolution of net nutrition of a given population, the coefficient of variation associated with this data can be used as a summary estimate of inequality in the distribution of nutrients over time.[19] This, in turn, can serve as an indicator of economic inequality in a given society. Gaps in average height across population subgroups provide another view of inequality by focusing on the differences in nutritional status across classes and ethnic groups, as well as sex and age groups. Where available, the Body Mass Index (BMI) also provides an important direct measure of the health of a given population.[20] In addition, some authors have worked with the lower ranges of the distribution of heights to estimate "rates of stunting" or malnutrition, using guidelines developed by U.N. experts. The proportion of people suffering from food deficiency is the closest we can get to the notion of a "poverty rate" in past societies for which it is impossible to demarcate a monetary poverty line or estimate how many lived below that line.

Perhaps the single most important finding of anthropometric history has been the discovery of periods of absolute decline in stature (that is, widespread deterioration of conditions of health and nutrition) during industrialization and other periods of economic modernization. This apparent paradox, called the "antebellum puzzle" in the United States (for the period 1820–1860), has also been found in England and most of Western Europe.[21] The overcrowding of working-class tenements, the environmental deterioration of industrial towns, and the rapid spread of infectious disease have been said to account for the anomaly of economic growth with deterioration in nutrition and health. Other influential works have placed the burden of explanation on the integration of the countryside into the larger market economy (often referred to as the commercialization of agriculture), and on the relative rise in the price of food during industrialization.[22] While J. Williamson had understood the phenomenon of "urban disamenities" as the "cost" paid by rural laborers for migrating to secure higher wages in urban industries, the discovery of this decline in biological welfare gave new ammunition to the "pessimists" in the old debate over the standard of living in industrializing England.[23]

These anomalies of rising productivity and falling net nutrition also moved authors to distinguish between "economic" and "biological" welfare.

The former refers to the traditional notion, coined by Pigou following Marshall, that equates welfare with the "satisfaction" that a certain basket of goods and services provides to its possessor and consumer.[24] The notion of "biological welfare," on the other hand, refers to the improvement in the conditions of health and nutrition that may or may not result from economic growth. It relates to the impact of economic change on human bodies, changes that can be measured by mortality, morbidity, adult heights, and physical strength. Economic welfare is determined mainly by income that is more often than not measured in private or individual terms. Biological welfare, on the other hand, is determined in part by environmental factors (including the presence or absence of public goods like sanitation and potable water) that, in combination with market conditions, produce effects on the bodies of people who have little or no choice in the matter (mainly children). Though neo-classical economists have argued that welfare can be purchased with income, or improved with money transfers,[25] the shocks to the biological well-being of children have long-term effects on their lives, affecting their health and their life span, whether they are compensated or not.

Institutions and Inequality

The renewed interest in the links between inequality, institutions, and economic growth began with an essay by U.S. economic historians Stanley Engerman and the late Kenneth Sokoloff,[26] who argued that factor endowments (mainly land and climate) in the colonial period predisposed Latin America and the Caribbean to economic activities where large enterprises predominated (slave plantations and large haciendas). The resulting concentration of wealth made it possible for small elites to dominate institutions and policies to the detriment of majorities whose property and civic rights suffered. The authors contrasted this development to the Mid-Atlantic and New England colonies in British North America, where the predominance of family farms and therefore more egalitarian institutions encouraged broad participation in markets and thus faster economic growth. Daron Acemoglu, Simon Johnson, and James Robinson made a similar argument about the negative effect of elite-dominated economic institutions in an influential essay,[27] but pointed to the exploitative colonial regimes established in Latin America in contrast to the more egalitarian majority-European settlement colonies, rather than factor endowments, as the main cause.

Anthropometric historians have not yet engaged this debate, largely because their empirical findings are not yet sufficiently abundant to uncover region-wide patterns. The first two centuries of Spanish colonization—as far as we know—left no records about population heights, and existing skeletal remains, which have also been used to measure heights, are not numerous enough to make solid inferences. Historical demographers have provided scattered data on general mortality, and for particular cases, such as late eighteenth-century Mexico or Potosí, historians have used indicators of excess deaths to uncover periods of declining health.[28] Recent work on tree rings and other climatic reconstructions has contributed additional evidence on colonial climate, so it is now possible to chronicle the history of natural disasters, famines, and epidemic diseases through laborious archival research.[29] It is still impossible, however, to test directly the Engerman-Sokoloff hypothesis of *economic* inequality for most of the colonial era. Indeed, the entire period from the Conquest to the 1700s seems difficult to integrate to the research agenda of anthropometric history for lack of data.

Nonetheless, a considerable body of recent work on inequality has called into question the empirical basis of the hypothesis that colonial Latin America suffered from an unusually high degree of *economic* inequality. Studies of late colonial and nineteenth-century wealth distribution suggest that wealth distribution was unequal in late colonial or early nineteenth-century Latin America, but probably not more unequal than in the United States or England at the same time.[30] As in British North America, some Spanish colonies were more unequal than others, Moreover, highly unequal slave colonies in the Caribbean had the highest per capita GDP in the Americas.[31] Williamson, Coatsworth, and others have argued that Latin America's unusually high inequality was not a colonial phenomenon, but originated in the late nineteenth century with the onset of export-oriented economic growth.[32] For the late colonial era and the past two centuries, the anthropometric contribution to this debate has been growing steadily in recent years. Work on the eighteenth and nineteenth centuries by Salvatore on Argentina and Challú on Mexico, based on military records, showed that class and regional differences in adult height at the end of the colonial era were significant, but smaller than in most European studies.[33] This work has also contributed new perspectives on economic trends. In Challú's work, for example, the eighteenth century, once thought to be a golden age of prosperity in Mexico, has emerged as an era of long-term deterioration in stature, rising inequality, and declining real income. The independence era (long thought to be economically disastrous), was not accompanied by a fall in living standards. Inequality in net nutrition may have peaked in the mid to late nineteenth century, during the era of export-led growth.[34] Twentieth-century studies have also produced some unexpected results, including periods of stagnation and even decline in heights,[35] though Colombia may have been an exception.[36] Recent work on Brazil has shown persistent regional as well as social inequalities in stature,[37] while Guatemalan data show a similar persistence of stagnation in stature and even severe stunting of children among the indigenous majority of the population (see Rios and Bogin in this book).

The development of germ theory and the massive investments in public health it inspired (better sanitation, drinking water, medical care) in Latin America, along with rising incomes due to economic growth, appear to explain the overall upward trend in stature in most countries in the twentieth century, though inequality and persistent poverty tended to dampen the trend to higher stature. Thus, trends in welfare and inequality measured by stature have reinforced the conclusions reached by more conventional measures of welfare and productivity that show improvement, but at long-term rates well below most other world regions.

The Contributions of This Volume

This volume has two interconnected goals: first, to introduce scholars to new findings on living standards and physical well-being in Latin American history; and second, to revisit, in the light of this new evidence, established interpretations of Latin American economic history. The book presents novel interpretations, based upon new data on the biological well-being of Latin American populations from the colonial period to the present. Geographically, the volume covers eight modern countries (Argentina, Bolivia, Chile, Colombia, Brazil, Guatemala, Mexico, and Uruguay) thus providing a broad assessment of the trajectory of living standards in Latin America over the last three centuries. Most contributions trace changes in average height across generations and social groups, but also add a wide variety of perspectives and approaches, including analysis of infant mortality rates, application of the Human Development Index to earlier eras, the calculation of Gini coefficients using income and wealth data, and the construction of composite indexes of welfare.

While the common concern is to contribute new evidence about the standard of living of workers and other subaltern populations in Latin America, the authors use these indicators to test traditional historical wisdom about matters central to the history of the region. Among them are the integration of markets and the spread of disease in the colonial economy, the relative well-being of elites and working classes during processes of economic growth, the comparative efficacy of authoritarian versus democratic governments in fighting infant mortality, and the persistence of racial inequality in contemporary Central America.

In his essay, Challú provides new evidence on average heights that bridge the late colonial and early national eras in Mexico. We now know from the historiographical advances of the last forty years that the colonial economy in the late eighteenth century entered a period of increasing stress, as a result of the pressures of population growth and the dissolution of traditional entitlements as the economy became more trade-oriented. Challú shows that the commercialization of agriculture and the increasing integration of regional grain markets in this era negatively affected access to food for important population groups and hence shaped the evolution of biological well-being. The chapter by López-Alonso presents findings on average heights of Mexican workers during the period 1850–1950. Her data contradict conclusions based on income and wage data, making López-Alonso's contribution all the more challenging and interesting. She demonstrates, for example, that from 1870 to 1930 the average height of the Mexican working class hardly changed, despite the rapid growth and urbanization of the Porfirian era and a major social revolution.

Meisel and Vega's work provides important insights on a country lacking GDP statistics for the late nineteenth century. Using data from travel passports, the authors estimate the height of elite Colombians between 1870 and 1920. Contrary to common belief, during these fifty years of economic progress the Colombian elite showed no signs of improvement in its biological well-being. Meisel and Vega suggest that the lack of sanitation facilities, particularly the lack of potable water, may have been responsible for this stagnation in heights, for the elite was well fed and quite tall compared to workers in industrialized countries.

In his chapter, Salvatore challenges the traditional economic historiography of Argentina, which presents the period of 1890–1914 as a "golden age" and the following interwar period as a time of economic "retardation" or "great delay." Comparing data on the stature of army recruits with data on per-capita income and wages, he finds that during the export boom of the first decade of the twentieth century, Argentina, a food-rich economy, suffered from nutrition stress. He also finds that external shocks like World War One and the onset of the Great Depression had little impact on food security; in fact, workers tended to be better off in the 1930s than earlier. This finding suggests that the "great delay" and the "deceleration" theses need to be seriously reconsidered.

`The chapter on modern Brazil by Monasterio, Ferreira, and Shikida provides novel evidence on inequalities in nutrition and health. Using a large database generated by a 2002–2003 public health survey, the authors estimate differences in average heights according to income groups, regions, and race. While other indicators show that there has been progress in income distribution and regional convergence in Brazil, this research shows that, when biological welfare is considered, inequality has not declined in the last forty years.

The question of the convergence (or divergence) of developing countries to developed countries has been a topic of discussion for the last twenty years.[38] In much of this literature, Latin America is presented as a region that missed opportunities for catching up created by the world economy in the postwar era. If not in economic terms, was there a catch-up in terms of human development? This is the issue that Bértola and associates address in their chapter on three Mercosur countries (Argentina, Brazil, and Uruguay) in the twentieth century. By introducing an inequality-adjusted HDI, Bértola and coauthors tell a new, compelling story. Argentina converged with the developed countries until 1914, and then it started to lose ground. Uruguay continued to converge, but fell behind after 1945. Brazil slowly but consistently converged until the 1980s.

Between 1960 and 1995, Chile experienced one of the largest and fastest declines in infant mortality in the world. Though part of this achievement can be attributed to the policies of democratic governments, the fall in infant mortality was fastest during the first decade of the military regime headed by General Pinochet (1974–1983). McGuire's essay raises interesting questions about the context and efficacy of public health policies during democratic and authoritarian regimes. The decline in infant mortality from 118 per 1000 to 11 per 1000 occurred during a period that produced sluggish income growth, high inequality of income distribution, and stagnation in poverty levels. He shows that Pinochet's government concentrated on the health of poor infants and mothers while neglecting other areas of public health.

Guatemala has been studied intensively by historians, economists, sociologists, and anthropologists in part because it suffers from extreme inequality in the distribution of income and exceptionally high poverty rates. In the 1980s, Guatemala experienced a period of civil conflict in which government forces carried out a genocidal war against indigenous populations that included widespread massacres, forced resettlement, and mass flight from the country. Ríos and Bogin show that these conditions had an impact on the bodies of Guatemalans, translating into situations of long-term stagnation of adult heights, severe stunting of children, and huge differences in stature by ethnicity and urban-rural residence. Indeed, Ríos and Bogin report, forensic data taken from those killed in the massacres of 1981–82 show an average stature lower than that estimated from skeletal remains of Mayans during the Pre-Classic and Classic eras. The major drivers behind the vast inequality in biological well-being are not found in genetic or geographic determinism: Maya immigrants in the United States did significantly better than those who stayed in Guatemala. Instead, the authors propose that the combined failure of public policies, limited access to resources, and structural socioeconomic pressures explain the high rates of stunting and low height attainment in Guatemala.

The Agenda for Future Research

The chapters of this collection suggest that extending empirical knowledge in this area is likely to yield a high return. What is not known about the history of living standards, however measured, is much greater than what is known. The anthropometric history of Latin America is still in its infancy. The history of assaults on human health from communicable diseases that could be prevented or mitigated, civil and interpersonal violence that causes permanent damage beyond the immediate victims, political and cultural norms that misallocate resources, and public policies that fail to protect citizens from malnutrition or ecological degradation has yet to be thoroughly explored. The history of inequality and its implications for institutional development and thus economic growth will take years of research and analysis to sort out.

What we know about the history of living standards, and particularly what is presented in this volume, both confirms and defies some long-held ideas about poverty and exclusion in the region, their synergies with processes of economic growth, and their relationship with institutions. To some extent, our findings do confirm that Latin America has "fallen behind," not only in economic growth, but also in living standards compared to other regions of the world. Despite improvements in some national experiences, the indicators of living standards and biological well-being from the late nineteenth century on show low to very low standards of living when compared with countries and regions that started out with similar levels *circa* 1800. Certainly new research will be needed both to reconfirm this pattern and to uncover places and times when Latin Americans managed to escape this tragic legacy.

The findings presented here also problematize the expectation that economic modernization results in automatic improvements (even in the long-term) in living standards. In Argentina, the moment of frontier expansion and export-led growth was characterized by a stagnation in average height; Colombia's economic expansion in the early twentieth century was similarly uncorrelated to increases in height among the upper and middle classes. The rapid economic growth attained during the Porfiriato similarly did not correlate with any gain in average height among the Mexican working classes. Even more importantly, the low measures of biological well-being shown in cases such as contemporary Guatemala and Brazil, as well as in Mexico and Colombia in the early twentieth century, show that stunting, malnutrition, and disease exert a toll on the physical capacity to sustain a productive life, hence lowering potential productivity and trapping entire regions and even countries at low levels of economic modernization. These studies, then, heighten the importance of understanding biological (in contrast, say, to cultural) constraints in explaining economic underperformance. Frenchmen and Englishmen in the eighteenth century were taller than present-day lower-class Guatemalans and comparable to present-day Nordestinos from Brazil. Low statures point to low nutritional status during childhood, which constrains the individual's capabilities as an adult, hence reinforcing the cycle of poverty and destitution. The synergies between biological living standards, inequality, and economic performance point to the issue of the role of institutions and social provisioning.

By broadening the definition of development and welfare, the contributions in this volume also engage in the debate on the role of institutions, inequality, and economic growth in Latin America. The seminal work of Sokoloff and Engerman sought to show that differences in inequality ultimately shaped the divergent economic trajectories of the United States and Latin America. While this was a valuable insight, the authors' conclusions hinged on the assumption that inequality has been a constant in Latin American history since the Conquest. By contrast, the height trajectories documented in this volume demonstrate changes in the availability and distribution of resources that refute this assumption. For instance, while Argentina resembles the United States and Canada, heights in that country only increased once the frontier-led, open-space path of development reached an end.

Perhaps more puzzling is the lack of correlation between democratization and improvements in living standards. While insurgency and independence in Mexico brought the involvement of new political actors and the mobilization of peasant communities to defend their interests, biological well-being in Mexico stagnated. A hundred years later, the Mexican Revolution did not produce notable improvements in heights, as would be expected of effective redistributive policies. In Argentina, the "infamous decade" of the 1930s was a period of major improvements in living standards, despite the meltdown of democratic institutions after the 1930 military coup. The most startling example of divergence between democracy and improved living standards is the case of Pinochet's Chile, in which McGuire found reductions in infant mortality in the context of a repressive regime that systematically attacked working-class interests.[39] The steady improvement of average height in twentieth-century Brazil runs against data that show high and persisting rates of poverty; heights continued to improve during the repressive and socially regressive post-1964 military government. The contributions in this volume, then, add a historical dimension and comparative perspective to the recent literature that shows stagnation in living standards despite the strong current of democratization in Latin America in the past two decades.[40]

Notes

* Most chapters in this edited volume were originally presented at a conference entitled "Living Standards in Latin American History," held at the David Rockefeller Center for Latin American Studies, Harvard University, April 8–9, 2005. The editors would like to thank Markus Baltzer, Zephyr Frank, Alejandra Irigoin, Yovanna Pineda, María del Rosario Prieto, Alfonso Quiroz, James Robinson, Richard Steckel, Pamela Surkan, Eduardo Villamor, Jeffrey Williamson, and John Womack, Jr., for their involvement and reviews at different stages of this publication. Elizabeth Becker provided copyediting assistance with bibliographies. Last but not least, the editors are grateful for the support of the David Rockefeller Center for Latin American Studies and its staff, including the coordination and editorial skills of June Erlick and Anna Safran, from the organization of the original conference to the conclusion of this volume.

1. In a recent revision of the issue of life expectancy in ancient Rome and Greece, the author found that the life table derived from early twentieth-century Chile had a better fit than tables derived from European experiences. Woods, "Ancient and Early Modern Mortality."

2. *Historia Agraria*'s special issue on anthropometric history in the Iberian world illustrates the scope of these new approaches, see *Historia Agraria* 47 (April 2009).

3. Dobado González, Gómez Galvarriato and Williamson, "Globalization"; Williamson, "Real Wages"; Astorga, Bergés and FitzGerald, "Standard of Living"; Prados de la Escosura, "When Did Latin America Fall behind?"

4. Nordhaus and Tobin, "Is Growth Obsolete?"

5. Still, neo-classical economists insisted that, if the right vector of prices was found, they could adjust income estimates to reflect all externalities. See Jorgenson, "Aggregate Consumer Behavior."

6. Nussbaum and Sen, *The Quality of Life*; Sen, *Commodities and Capabilities*; Alkire, *Valuing Freedoms*.

7. Morris, *Measuring the Condition*.

8. See, for example, the yearly *Human Development Report* first launched in 1990.

9. Crafts, "Some Dimensions"; Sylla and Toniolo, *Patterns of European Industrialization;* Floud and Harris, "Health, Height and Welfare."

10. Prados de la Escosura, "When Did Latin America Fall Behind?" The HDI has become so popular that it is used not only by professional economists and economic historians of the region, but also by provincial politicians who want to claim that, despite low incomes, their provinces had made "social progress."

11. Fogel, "Economic Growth."

12. North, *Structure and Change in Economic History.*

13. Aron, Dumont and LeRoy Ladurie, *Anthropologie du conscrit;* LeRoy Ladurie and Bergnageau, "Étude sur un Contingent Militaire."

14. Fogel and Engerman, *Time on the Cross.*

15. Steckel, "Slave Height Profiles from Coastwise Manifests"; Margo and Steckel, "Heights of American Slaves"; Fogel, "Nutrition and the Decline"; Tanner, "The Potential of Auxological Data"; Komlos, *Nutrition and Economic Development;* Floud, Gregory and Wachter, *Height.*

16. Steckel, "Stature and the Standard of Living"; Steckel, "Strategic Ideas."

17. Komlos and Baten, *The Biological Standard of Living in Comparative Perspective;* Komlos, *Stature, Living Standards;* Steckel and Floud, *Health and Welfare during Industrialization.* For the most recent survey of the field, see Steckel, "Heights and Human Welfare."

18. The same argument can be applied to neo-classical economists who argue that all well-being, including biological well-being, can be purchased with income. If this is true, to examine nutrition, an estimation of food expenditures of working-class families, in comparison with the prices of food, should be enough. Working-class budgets are an indirect indicator: the nutrients purchased with a given income can be later reduced by methods of cooking, protein and calcium content of the food, and the distribution of meals among husband, wife, and children.

19. Moradi and Baten, "Inequality in Sub-Saharan Africa."

20. On application of this approach in 19th-century Mexico, see Carson, "Mexican Body Mass."

21. Floud, Gregory, and Wachter, *Height;* Steckel and Floud, *Health and Welfare during Industrialization;* Floud, "Height, Weight and Body Mass of the British Population since 1820"; Komlos and Coclanis, "On the Puzzling Cycle"; Komlos and Baten, *The Biological Standard of Living in Comparative Perspective;* Haines, "Growing Incomes, Shrinking People"; Haines, Craig, and Weiss, "The Short and the Dead"; Komlos, *The Biological Standard of Living;* Komlos, "Shrinking in a Growing Economy?"; Brinkman and Drukker, "Does the Early-Economic-Growth-Puzzle Apply to Contemporary Developing Countries?"

22. Cuff, *Hidden Cost.*

23. Floud and Harris, "Health, Height and Welfare: Britain, 1700-1980"; Pollard, "Sheffield and Sweet Auburn"; Williamson, "Urban Disamenities."

24. Pigou, *The Economics of Welfare.*

25. McKenzie, *Measuring Economic Welfare.*

26. Engerman and Sokoloff, "Factor Endowments."
27. Acemoglu, Johnson, and Robinson, "Reversal of Fortune."
28. Rabell, *Población novohispana;* Tandeter, "Población y economía"; Boleda and Tandeter, "Dinámica demográfica."
29. Therrell, "Tree rings and 'El Año del Hambre' in Mexico"; Acuña-Soto et al., "Megadrought and Megadeath in Sixteenth-Century Mexico"; O'Hara and Metcalfe, "Reconstructing the Climate of Mexico from Historical Records"; García-Herrera et al., "Chronology of El Niño Events"; Villalba, "Climatic Fluctuations"; Gil Montero and Villalba, "Tree Rings as a Surrogate for Economic Stress"; Endfield, "Climate and Crisis in Eighteenth Century Mexico"; García Acosta, "Risks and Disasters in the History of the Mexico Basin."
30. See for instance Gelman and Santilli, "Distribución de la riqueza"; Frank, "Wealth Holding"; Johnson and Frank, "Cities and Wealth."
31. Eltis, "Total Product of Barbados"; Coatsworth, "Economic and Institutional Trajectories."
32. Williamson, "Real Wages"; Coatsworth, "Inequality, Institutions and Economic Growth in Latin America."
33. Salvatore, "Heights and Welfare"; Challú, "Grain Markets."
34. López-Alonso, "Growth with Inequality"; Meisel and Vega, "The Biological Standard."
35. Salvatore, "Stature Decline"; López-Alonso, "Growth with Inequality."
36. Meisel and Vega, "The Biological Standard."
37. See Frank, "Stature," and Monasterio's chapter in this volume.
38. Thorp, *Progress, Poverty and Exclusion.*
39. Winn, *Victims.*
40. Skidmore, "Brazil's Persistent Income Inequality"; Haber, *Mexico since 1980;* Albala-Bertrand, "Evolution of Aggregate Welfare."

References

Acemoglu, Johnson, and James Robinson. "Reversal of Fortune: Geography and Institutions in the Making of the Modern World Income Distribution." *Quarterly Journal of Economics* 117 (2002): 1231–1294.

Acuña-Soto, Rodolfo, David W. Stahle, Malcolm K. Cleveland, and Matthew D. Therrell, "Megadrought and Megadeath in Sixteenth-Century Mexico." *Emerging Infectious Diseases* 8, no. 4 (2002): 360–362.

Albala-Bertrand, José Miguel. "Evolution of Aggregate Welfare and Development Indicators in Latin America and the OECD, 1950–85." In *Welfare, Poverty and Development in Latin America*, ed. Ch. Abel, and C. Lewis, 33–48. Houndsmill: Macmillan, 1993.

Alkire, Sabina. *Valuing Freedoms: Sen's Capability Approach and Poverty Reduction.* Oxford: Oxford University Press, 2002.

Aron, Jean Paul, Paul Dumont, and Emmanuel LeRoy Ladurie. *Anthropologie du conscrit français d'après les comptes numériques et sommaires du recrutement de l'armée (1819–1926).* Paris: Mouton, 1972.

Astorga, Pablo, Ame R. Bergés, and Valpy FitzGerald. "The Standard of Living in Latin America during the Twentieth Century." Queen Elizabeth House Working Paper Series 103, Oxford University, 2003.

Boleda, Mario, and Enrique Tandeter. "Dinámica demográfica en los Andes centro-meridionales." *Desarrollo Economico* 42, no. 168 (2003): 589–613.

Brinkman, H. J., and J. W. Drukker. "Does the Early-Economic-Growth-Puzzle Apply to Contemporary Developing Countries?" In *The Biological Standard of Living in Comparative Perspective,* ed. John Komlos and Joerg Baten, 55–89. Stuttgart: Franz Steiner Verlag, 1998.

Carson, Scott Alan. "Mexican Body Mass Index Values in the Late 19th-Century American West." *Economics and Human Biology* 5 (2007): 37–47.

Challú, Amílcar. "Grain Markets, Food Supply Policies and Living Standards in Late Colonial Mexico." Ph.D. Dissertation, Harvard University, 2007.

Coatsworth, John H. "Economic and Institutional Trajectories in Nineteenth-Century Latin America." In *Latin America and the World Economy since 1800,* ed. John H. Coatsworth and Alan M. Taylor, 23–54. Cambridge, MA: Harvard University Press, 1998.

———. "Inequality, Institutions and Economic Growth in Latin America." *Journal of Latin American Studies* 40, no. 3 (2008): 545–569.

Crafts, N. F. R. "Some Dimensions of the 'Quality of Life' during the British Industrial Revolution." *Economic History Review* 50, no. 4 (1997): 617–639.

Cuff, Timothy. *The Hidden Cost of Economic Development: The Biological Standard of Living in Antebellum Pennsylvania.* Burlington: Ashgate Publishing, 2005.

Dobado González, Rafael, Aurora Gómez Galvarriato, and Jeffrey Williamson. "Mexican Exceptionalism: Globalization and De-Industrialization, 1750–1877." *The Journal of Economic History* 68, no. 3 (2008): 758–811.

Eltis, David. "The Total Product of Barbados, 1664–1701." *Journal of Economic History* 55, no. 2 (1995): 321–338.

Endfield, Georgina H. "Climate and Crisis in Eighteenth Century Mexico." *The Medieval History Journal* 10, no. 1–2 (2007): 99–125.

Engerman, Stanley L., and Kenneth L. Sokoloff. "Factor Endowments, Institutions, and Differential Paths of Growth among New World Economies: A View from Economic Historians of the United States." In *How Latin America Fell Behind,* ed. Haber Stephen, 260–304. Stanford: Stanford University Press, 1997.

Floud, Roderick. "Height, Weight and Body Mass of the British Population since 1820." *NBER Working Paper Series on Historical Factors in Long-Run Growth* Historical Paper #108 (1998).

Floud, Roderick, Annabel Gregory, and Kenneth W. Wachter. *Height, Health and History: Nutritional Status in the United Kingdom, 1750–1980.* Cambridge: Cambridge University Press, 1990.

Floud, Roderick, and Bernard Harris. "Health, Height and Welfare: Britain, 1700–1980." In *Health and Welfare during Industrialization,* ed. Richard H. Steckel and Roderick Floud, 91–126. Chicago: University of Chicago Press, 1997.

Fogel, Robert. "Nutrition and the Decline of Mortality since 1700: Some Preliminary Findings." In *Long-term Factors in American Economic Growth*, ed. Stanley Engerman and Robert Gallman, 439–527. Chicago: University of Chicago Press, 1986.

———. "Economic Growth, Population Theory and Physiology." *American Economic Review* 84 (1994): 369–395.

Fogel, Robert, and Stanley L. Engerman. *Time on the Cross: The Economics of American Negro Slavery*. Boston: Little Brown, 1974.

Frank, Zephyr. "Stature in Nineteenth-Century Rio De Janeiro: Preliminary Evidence from Prison Records." *Revista de Historia Económica* 24, no. 3 (2006): 465–489.

———. "Wealth Holding in Southeastern Brazil, 1815–60." *Hispanic American Historical Review* 85, no. 2 (2005): 223–258.

García Acosta, Virginia. "Risks and Disasters in the History of the Mexico Basin: Are They Climatic or Social?" *The Medieval History Journal* 10, no. 1–2 (2007): 127–142.

García-Herrera, Ricardo, Henry F. Díaz, Rolando R. García, María del Rosario Prieto, et al. "A Chronology of El Niño Events from Primary Documentary Sources in Northern Perú." *Journal of Climate* 21, no. 9 (2008): 1948–1962.

Gelman, Jorge, and Daniel Santilli. "Distribución de la riqueza y crecimiento económico. Buenos Aires en la época de Rosas." *Desarrollo Económico* 43, no. 169 (2003): 75–101.

Gil Montero, Raquel, and Ricardo Villalba. "Tree Rings as a Surrogate for Economic Stress–an Example from the Puna of Jujuy, Argentina in the 19th Century." *Dendrochronologia* 22, no. 3 (2005): 141–147.

Haber, Stephen H. *Mexico since 1980*. New York: Cambridge University Press, 2008.

Haines, Michael. "Growing Incomes, Shrinking People – Can Economic Development be Hazardous to Your Health? Historical Evidence for the United States, England, and the Netherlands in the Nineteenth Century." *Social Science History* 28, no. 2 (2004): 249–270.

Haines, Michael R., Lee A. Craig, and Thomas Weiss. "The Short and the Dead: Nutrition, Mortality, and the 'Antebellum Puzzle' in the United States." *The Journal of Economic History* 63, no. 2 (2003): 382–413.

"Human Development Reports (HDR)." United Nations Development Program, http://hdr.undp.org/.

Johnson, Lyman, and Zephyr Frank. "Cities and Wealth in the South Atlantic: Buenos Aires and Rio de Janeiro before 1860." *Comparative Studies in Society and History* 48, no. 3 (2006): 634–668.

Jorgenson, Dale W. "Aggregate Consumer Behavior and the Measurement of Social Welfare." *Econometrica* 58, no. 5 (1990): 1007–1040.

Komlos, John. *Nutrition and Economic Development in the Eighteenth-Century Habsburg Monarchy*. Princeton: Princeton University Press, 1989.

Komlos, John, ed. *Stature, Living Standards, and Economic Development: Essays in Anthropometric History*. Chicago: University of Chicago Press, 1994.

Komlos, John. *The Biological Standard of Living on Three Continents: Further Essays in Anthropometric History.* Boulder: Westview Press, 1995.

————. "Shrinking in a Growing Economy? The Mystery of Physical Stature during the Industrial Revolution." *Journal of Economic History* 58, no. 3 (1998): 779–802.

Komlos, John, and Joerg Baten, eds. *The Biological Standard of Living in Comparative Perspective.* Stuttgart: Franz Steiner Verlag, 1998.

Komlos, John, and Peter Coclanis. "On the Puzzling Cycle in the Biological Standard of Living: The Case of Antebellum Georgia." *Explorations in Economic History* 34, no. 4 (1997): 433–459.

LeRoy Ladurie, Emmanuel, and Nicole Bergnageau. "Étude sur un Contingent Militaire (1868): Mobilité géographique, délinquance et stature, mises en rapport avec d'autres aspects de la situation des conscrits." *Annales de Démographie Historique* 7 (1970): 311–336.

López-Alonso, Moramay. "Growth with Inequality: Living Standards in Mexico, 1850–1950." *Journal of Latin American Studies* 39, no. 1 (2007): 81–105.

Margo, Robert A., and Richard H. Steckel. "The Heights of American Slaves: New Evidence on Slave Nutrition and Health." *Social Science History* 6, no. 4 (1982): 516–18.

McKenzie, George W. *Measuring Economic Welfare.* Cambridge: University of Cambridge Press, 1983.

Meisel, Adolfo, and Margarita Vega. "The Biological Standard of Living (and Its Convergence) in Colombia, 1870–2003." *Economics and Human Biology* 5, no. 1 (2007): 100–122.

Moradi, Alexander, and Joerg Baten. "Inequality in Sub-Saharan Africa: New Data and New Insights from Anthropometric Estimates." *World Development* 33, no. 8 (2005).

Morris, Morris. *Measuring the Condition of the World's Poor: The Physical Quality of Life Index.* New York: Pergamon Press, 1979.

Nordhaus, W. D., and J. Tobin. "Is Growth Obsolete?" In *Economic Growth*, ed. W. D. Nordhaus, and J. Tobin, 1–80. Boston: National Bureau of Economic Research, 1972.

North, Douglass Cecil. *Structure and Change in Economic History.* New York: Norton, 1981.

Nussbaum, Martha C., and Amartya Sen, eds. *The Quality of Life.* World Institute for Development Economics Research, 1993.

O'Hara, Sarah L., and Sarah E. Metcalfe. "Reconstructing the Climate of Mexico from Historical Records." *The Holocene* 5, no. 4 (1995): 485–490.

Pigou, Arthur Cecil. *The Economics of Welfare.* London: Macmillan, 1912.

Pollard, Sidney. "Sheffield and Sweet Auburn—Amenities and Living Standards in the British Industrial Revolution: A Comment." *Journal of Economic History* 41, no. 4 (1981): 902–904.

Prados de la Escosura, Leandro. "When Did Latin America Fall Behind? Evidence from Long-Run International Inequality." In *The Decline of Latin American*

Economies: Growth, Institutions, and Crisis, ed. Sebastian Edwards, Gerardo Esquivel, and Graciela Márquez. Chicago: University of Chicago Press, 2007.

Rabell, Cecilia. *La población novohispana a la luz de los registros parroquiales. Avances y perspectivas de investigación*. Mexico City: Instituto de Investigaciones Sociales, Universidad Nacional Autónoma de Mexico, 1990.

Salvatore, Ricardo. "Heights and Welfare in Late-Colonial and Post-Independence Argentina." In *The Biological Standard of Living in Comparative Perspective*, ed. John Komlos, and Joerg Baten, 97–121. Stuttgart: Franz Steiner Verlag, 1998.

———. "Stature Decline and Recovery in a Food-Rich Export Economy: Argentina 1900–1934." *Explorations in Economic History* 41, no. 3 (2004): 233–255.

Sen, Amartya. *Commodities and Capabilities*. Delhi: Oxford University Press, 1999.

Skidmore, Thomas E. "Brazil's Persistent Income Inequality: Lessons from History." *Latin American Politics and Society* 46, no. 2 (2004): 133–150.

Steckel, Richard H., and Roderick Floud, eds. *Health and Welfare during Industrialization*. Chicago: University of Chicago Press, 1997.

Steckel, Richard H. "Slave Height Profiles from Coastwise Manifests." *Explorations in Economic History* 16, no. 4 (1979): 363–380.

———. "Stature and the Standard of Living." *Journal of Economic Literature* 33, no. 4 (1995): 1903–1940.

———. "Strategic Ideas in the Rise of the New Anthropometric History and Their Implications for Interdisciplinary Research." *Journal of Economic History* 58, no. 3 (1998): 803–821.

———. "Heights and Human Welfare: Recent Developments and New Directions." *Explorations in Economic History* 46, no. 1 (2009): 1–23.

Sylla, Richard, and Gianni Toniolo, eds. *Patterns of European Industrialization: The Nineteenth Century*. London: Routledge, 1991.

Tandeter, Enrique. "Población y economía en el siglo XVIII andino." In *Cambios demográficos en América Latina: la experiencia de cinco siglos*. Córdoba: Universidad Nacional de Córdoba, 1998.

Tanner, James H. "The Potential of Auxological Data for Monitoring Economic and Social Well-Being." *Social Science History* 6, no. 4 (1982): 571–581.

Therrell, Matthew D. "Tree Rings and 'El Año del Hambre' in Mexico." *Dendrochronologia* 22, no. 3 (2005): 203–207.

Thorp, Rosemary. *Progress, Poverty and Exclusion: An Economic History of Latin America in the 20th Century*. Washington, D.C: Inter-American Development Bank, 1998.

Villalba, R. "Climatic Fluctuations in Northern Patagonia during the Last 1000 Years as Inferred From Tree-rings." *Quaternary Research* 34, no. 3 (1990): 346–60.

Williamson, Jeffrey. "Urban Disamenities, Dark Satanic Mills, and the British Standard of Living Debate." *Journal of Economic History* 41, no. 1 (1981): 75–83.

———. "Real Wages, Inequality and Globalization in Latin America before 1940." *Revista de Historia Económica* 17, no. especial (1999): 101–142.

Winn, Peter, ed. *Victims of the Chilean Miracle: Workers and Neoliberalism in the Pinochet Era, 1973–2002.* Durham: Duke University Press, 2004.

Woods, Robert. "Ancient and Early Modern Mortality: Experience and Understanding." *Economic History Review* 60, no. 2 (2007): 373–399.

2

The Great Decline: Biological Well-Being and Living Standards in Mexico, 1730–1840

Amílcar E. Challú

Despite long-standing perceptions that Latin America and Mexico have been endemically riddled with poverty and high inequality, we now know that the population of Mexico experienced important changes in living standards over the course of history, and that these changes were intrinsically connected to economic growth, the development of political and economic institutions, and the balance of power between different social sectors. Still, the picture remains confused and contradictory. We lack fine-grained data suitable for long-run analysis. In the colonial period, we know that human welfare declined as food prices increased, mortality crises became more frequent, and peasants were relegated to lower-quality lands. Still, how did living standards compare with international benchmarks of the day? And even more, how was the decline experienced by people of different economic means? For the early post-independence period, we have conflicting assessments: a traditional thesis proposing a continued decline or stagnation, and a revisionist position that claims that living standards improved as subsistence agriculture gained new strength after the insurgency of the 1810s. We know even less about international comparisons and the decomposition of changes in different groups. Reconstructing the trends in living standards not only provides a missing piece of what we know about everyday material life, but it is also critical to helping understand the most fundamental problems of economic and social history, such as how economic growth (or lack thereof) affects human development, how the persistence of political economic institutions engenders inequality, and what is the problematic relationship between popular mobilization and living conditions.

In this chapter I use soldier heights to trace the trajectory of living standards in the late colonial and early post-independence periods in the central region of Mexico. The major conclusion is that Mexico experienced a long and sustained decline in height that started in the mid-eighteenth century and extended into the first decades after independence. The decline was not only important in absolute terms, but also relative to trends in Europe and elsewhere. I propose that increasing hardship in acquiring basic food staples and harsher climatic conditions contributed to the decline. More importantly, height gaps between social groups increased over this period: height loss was more pronounced among those of a lower socioeconomic status, and in rural areas. The long-run decline in heights and the widening of height gaps across social sectors point to a fundamental continuity in the period.

Living Standards in Mexican History

Material living standards and biological well-being in colonial Mexico were very low compared to present-day standards. Famines and epidemics caused the death of thousands in a single year. In 1785–86, *el año del hambre* ("the year of the famine"), perhaps 15% of the population in the fertile Bajío region died, according to some accounts.[1] The years 1748–50, 1801, and 1808–9 were also marked by famine, while minor agricultural crises occurred regularly throughout the colonial period.[2] Epidemics were another regular presence, often (but not always) associated with malnutrition. Smallpox periodically struck Mexico in the eighteenth century, affecting large sectors of the population, especially children. About 30% of the soldiers recruited from the 1760s to the 1860s showed signs of smallpox. Typhus was another common epidemic; it affected a third of Mexico City's population in 1813. In 1833 cholera also made its first appearance in Mexico, with similar consequences.[3]

As revealing as the records of epidemics and famines are, they conceal the fact that chronic malnutrition and poor living conditions diminished defenses against diseases and resulted in a long-run, high-mortality environment that transcended the occasional short-term crisis. Long, healthy lives were the privilege of a few. Life expectancy at birth in Mexico City in 1832 was thirty-five years. In Parral, Chihuahua, McCaa estimates life expectancy in the 20 to 30 years range for the first half of the nineteenth century. In San Luis Potosí, the median age of death in the 1820s (excluding children under six years) was thirty-seven years.[4] Across the country, infant and child mortality were high as well. Infant mortality was likely in the 35–40% range, to be consistent with the low life expectancy. Almost half of all deaths in Mexico City in 1832 corresponded to children below age five; similar figures are recorded for León (Guanajuato) and San Luis Potosí.[5]

Disease, low life expectancy, and high infant mortality varied widely among socioeconomic groups. In Mexico City, typhoid fever in 1813 and cholera in 1833 hit each area of the city differently, with many more of the poor dying.[6] Soldiers from a poor background were more likely to have signs of smallpox. In the reports on burials of San Luis Potosí, adult women died while seven years younger, on average, than men; child mortality was also higher among females: 30%, compared to 20% among males. In León, Guanajuato, mortality increased seven times from normal to famine years among Indians and other non-Spanish groups, while only twice among the Spanish.[7] The quantity and quality of food, particularly protein intake, also varied along similar lines. Travelers and writers reported that the wealthy consumed an exorbitant amount of meat, but Indians and the urban poor could only rarely afford *frijoles,* and almost never meat.[8]

While it is clear that living standards were low, and that inequality was high, international comparisons and long-term trends (especially those spanning the traditional colonial-national divide) are still controversial. A major reason for this is that we rarely have available a consistent and comparable indicator over a long period of time. Several indicators point to a decline in living standards in the last decades of the colonial regime. Demographic studies based on parish records of births and burials show an increase in the frequency of epidemics, and even demographic loss in some places.[9] Beginning with Florescano's ground-breaking work on the Mexico City granary, studies on corn and wheat prices show an upward trend in the last forty years of colonial domination in Mexico, suggesting scarcity and increased hardship for most of the population, especially the poor.[10] These concurrent signs of deterioration have led historians to identify these decades as a period of frequent subsistence crises.[11] Leading this process was population growth, which increased the labor force and broke up the existing strategies of peasant communities. Landed elites gained greater control over production and labor agreements and pushed peasants to less fertile lands.[12] Similarly, rights to water became more precarious for peasant communities.[13] An emergent revisionism, however, proposes a more optimistic account of the eighteenth century, focusing on per-capita economic growth and growth-fostering institutions.[14] Recent work by Rafael Dobado, moreover, has suggested not only that the state of the economy was healthy but also that living standards compared favorably with those of Europe in the eighteenth century.[15] While there is a clear consensus that conditions deteriorated in the last decades of the colonial period, scholars disagree on the evaluation of the decades after the Hidalgo rebellion. In part the disagreement stems from more precarious data, but also from radically different perspectives on the post-independence period—more specifically, was it a period of economic disarray and depression, or the aborted genesis of an alternative, peasant-oriented order? I refer to the two positions as the "pessimistic" and the "optimistic" views, respectively. The optimistic case is championed by John Tutino and Robert McCaa. In his study of the demography in the nineteenth century, McCaa argued that agricultural crises stopped being as frequent and acute as in the late colonial period, that food production increased, smallpox receded, and that consequently life expectancy improved and the population grew at faster rates.[16] Tutino's work on peasant family economies argues that after the massive mobilization of the 1810s, the hacienda resident population obtained better conditions to access land, and peasant communities gained room to make decisions on production. Under these conditions of rural decompression, overall corn production improved, and subsistence agriculture emerged as an engine of economic growth and material welfare. The post-independence moment was short-lived, as in the 1850s the elites regained power and started to curtail the advances of the subsistence sector.[17]

The pessimistic case is similarly based on demographic and economic evidence, but of different sorts. Brading and Wu's classic study on demographic dynamics of western Bajío in the eighteenth and nineteenth centuries presented a picture of remarkable vulnerability to agricultural crises and demographic instability that extended from the 1760s to the 1860s, suggesting long-term factors that transcended the independence milestone.[18] Studies of the cholera outbreak of 1833 similarly point to critical conditions and social differences not different from the experience of the late colonial era.[19] From an economic perspective, John Coatsworth's "Obstacles to Economic Growth in Mexico" presented the case of economic stagnation before the Porfiriato.[20] Salvucci, in his revision of national income estimates, agreed with Coatsworth, but also pointed out the unwarranted optimism and political motivations behind the economic discourse of the 1830s and early 1840s, on which some of the assessments on food production are based.[21] Last but not least, Chowning's study on Michoacán proposed that a reconfigured *hacendado* elite rebuilt its economic power in the 1830s, suggesting a shorter period in which peasants gained leverage.[22]

Biological Well–Being and Heights: Data and Methodology

Heights are a valuable tool to study living conditions and human welfare. The attainment of height is conditioned by cumulative net nutrition. While at the individual level there is a large variation in heights related to unique circumstances and genetic characteristics, cumulative net nutrition (the balance of nutritional intake and energetic expenditure) influences the process of body growth and the final height the individual attains. Net nutrition in the first three years of life is particularly critical. A malnourished child's body that is fighting against disease or using energy to maintain body temperature in a cold climate has fewer available nutrients and energy to grow. While there are opportunities to partially catch up lost growth potential, the effect of these factors in the first years of life conditions the height that can be attained and reflects in the average height of the population. By examining the trends of average height over time, or across social groups, we can gain an understanding of how economic, environmental, and health conditions affect biological well-being, which is a key component in the development of capabilities of individuals. Heights are particularly good indicators of living standards in pre-industrial societies that were more exposed to shocks in local food supply, epidemics, and poor sanitation. Last but not least, heights provide a mass of data that encompasses vast regions and social groups over a long period of time, which is hard to match in other studies of living standards.

Sources

About 7,500 military records with height and additional information were collected in Mexico's Archivo General de la Nación.[23] More than half of the original entries, however, were excluded because they were in the cavalry, were younger than 18 or older than 40, were born in the northern or southern regions, or had an invalid height.[24] Of the selected cases, 28% correspond to recruits enrolled before 1810, the overwhelming majority in the permanent army and provincial regiments, while 14% were sampled from the 1791–2 census ordered by Viceroy Revillagigedo to create lists of all males eligible for military service. The cases from the independence war (1810–1821) account for 6% of the total; most are from permanent units of the loyalist army, but some were from companies of pardoned Indian insurgents. The remainder of the records (52%) corresponds to men drafted after independence (1821). Of these most were soldiers directly recruited into the permanent army or destined to it through the state reserve corps.

The most common source of information is the *filiación,* a document that identified the soldier and provided information on the conditions of recruitment.[25] Despite numerous organizational changes in the army, particularly after independence, the *filiaciones* share a common core of information: name; town and state of origin; current residence; height, measured in Parisian or Castilian feet, inches, and lines with the date of the measurement included in many cases; age; occupation; marital status; physical traits (skin, eye, and hair color, and other personal traits such as smallpox marks and wounds). While racial categories served as criteria for enrollment in the colonial period, only a few records carry explicit information on the *calidad* (racial standing) of the soldier. After the identification, there is some information on the conditions of recruitment (service term; pay; and whether the subject was a volunteer, drafted by lottery, or redeeming a judiciary sentence), the place of recruitment, and the unit to which the soldier was assigned. The act of enrollment was formalized by the signatures of the recruiting officer, two witnesses, and the recruited man; if the recruit was illiterate, he penned a cross as a sign of consent.[26]

The Height Measurement

Recruiting instructions consistently specified that the recruiting officers were responsible for the measurement. As soon as recruits came in, they were measured in their bare feet. The measurement was taken in feet, inches, and lines (a line being the twelfth part of an inch). Despite the common designation in feet, two different measurement units were actually in use in the period covered in this study, resulting in different height distributions and changing minimum requirements.

In large populations, heights are expected to conform to the normal distribution, which is continuous and symmetrical around a single peak. There is also a strong regularity in the standard deviation of heights, which on average is 6.86 cm. Historical military samples, however, do present significant deviations from the expected distribution due to the minimum height requirement. Moreover, imprecisions in the measurement create "heaping," which is the overabundance of rounded numbers. It is important, then, to discuss how heights are distributed in order to tailor the method used to adjust for the sample deficiencies.

The observed distribution of heights is neither continuous nor symmetrical, as shown in Figure 1. First, it shows that more than 40% of the cases lacked line precision (heaping). This was the likely result of cursory measurement of the soldier's stature at the time of recruiting. The solution is to lump observations at the inch order; it implies losing some detail, but it is necessary for the sake of consistency across records. Cases are also abnormally concentrated in the 60–inch value. This characteristic also derives from the practice of measuring height at the time of recruiting. Since five feet was the customary minimum requirement, stating the minimum needed height was either a shortcut to saying that the soldier fit the minimum requirements, or to disguising a shorter stature.[27] After a unit-by-unit

Figure 1.
Histogram of Height Observations, Entire Dataset.

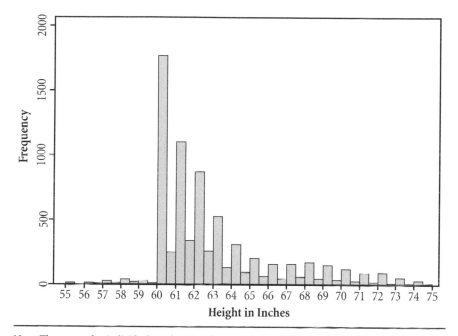

Note: There are a few individuals under 55 and over 75 inches (0.85% of the total).
Source: Anthropometric dataset, see text.

analysis, most of the 60–inch records were eliminated from the analysis, unless the subset of cases conformed to normally distributed values.[28] Two final problems are the lack of symmetry (with a noticeable shortfall to the left of 60 inches), and the existence of more than one peak (noticeably at 60 and 68 inches) that runs against the assumption of one central tendency of a normal distribution. In fact, the dataset contains not one but three distinct height distributions that vary in their mean and truncation points (see Figure 2).[29] Changes in measurement units and different minimum height requirements explain the different height distributions and the apparent increase of height in the early 1840s.

The first subset of cases corresponds to soldiers recruited through the colonial period until 1847; the mode in this group being 61 inches. The measurement standard used for recruits in the colonial and early national periods was the Paris foot, also known as *pie del rey*. While only a handful of *filiaciones* explicitly stated the use of the Paris foot and instructions refer to the measure as "pies," contemporary Spanish publications clearly refer

Figure 2.
Histogram of Height Observations by Army Group.

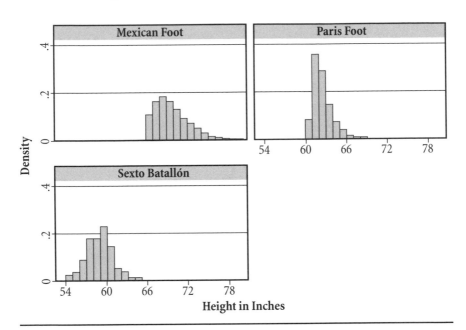

Note: Inches as measured in the original recruitment records.
Source: Anthropometric dataset, see text.
Graphics by Observed Height Distributions

to the use of the *pie del rey* in recruitment and other military measurements. The first Bourbon king of Spain, Philip V, introduced the French measures in the military and they continued to be used until the 1840s both in Spain and in Mexico.[30] A Paris inch was equivalent to 2.71 cm. The height requirement for regular infantry units was 60 inches.[31] Given the low frequency of observations with line precision and the abnormal frequency of five feet observations, the truncation point should be set at 61 inches or 164.7 cm in most units.[32]

The second group includes soldiers recruited from 1842 to the late 1850s. The distinctive characteristic is a much taller height measurement, with a mode of 68 inches. The explanation for the leap in height is that the use of the Mexican inch, based on the Burgos inch, was equivalent to 2.33 cm according to Mexican conversion tables of the mid-century.[33] It was first referred to in the 1838 law that instituted the levy by lottery,[34] but it was not applied until 1842. By 1846 all army units, with the exception of the Sexto Batallón, had a height distribution consistent with the Mexican inch.

The legal minimum requirement changed from the late 1830s on. The 1838 *Ley de Sorteo* established 66 inches as the minimum, but other instructions and laws from 1839, 1853, and 1854 moved that minimum back and forth.[35] Yet it is apparent that recruiters used a lower *de facto* minimum requirement, since it is only under 66 Mexican inches (153.25 cm) that a shortfall is noticeable in the observed distribution of heights of this group.

The third observed distribution includes 130 cases recruited from 1852 to 1854 in the Sexto Batallón (1852–1854). The mode in this group is very low, 59 inches, and there is no apparent truncation point. In fact, a normality test does not refute the hypothesis of a normal distribution,[36] which also demonstrates that the underlying distribution of height in army records follows the expected pattern. While the recruitment sheets do not provide any explicit indication of the measurement used (other than stating it in feet, inches, and lines) it is apparent that the Paris foot was used, even if the resulting average is about 1.5 cm shorter than in other contemporary divisions using the Mexican foot.

To summarize, a few corrections were applied to render these height observations suitable for statistical analysis. The cases with 60 inches (five feet) were eliminated, heights were aggregated at the inch level (e.g., 61.0–61.99 becomes 61.5), and the data were translated into centimeters using Paris inches for the first and third groups of cases, and Mexican inches for the second (with inch equivalencies of 2.7066 and 2.3259 cm, respectively). An ancillary variable records the four observed truncation points: 60 and 61 Paris inches for the first group, 66 Mexican inches for the second, and none for the third.

Demographic and Socioeconomic Characterization

Ethnicity, class, and residence interacted in complex ways to define social networks and differentiate groups in colonial society. The individuals in this dataset can be described as "plebeian," a term used in studies of the eighteenth and nineteenth centuries to characterize the popular classes that live in a fluid world of social and economic relationships.[37] It is certainly not representative of indigenous groups or the upper classes. Still, the degree of socioeconomic differentiation within the plebeian group is significant in terms of the conditions that the individuals experienced early in their lives.

The description of complexion serves as an indicator of social differentiation based on racial *a prioris*.[38] The most common skin colors reported in the *filiaciones* were white (*blanco*), ruddy (*rosado*), tanned or brown (*trigueño*), and black (*pardo, moreno*). Some colonial records report 'light' (*claro)* and 'good' (*bueno*). *Trigueño* is the most frequent description (51%);

followed by *rosado* (17%) and white (12%); black is the least common (1%). This information was simplified in a binary variable, dark or white skin. The overall proportion of the dark- and white-skinned is 63 and 37%, respectively.[39]

Skin color and other physical traits are closely related to other indicators of status and economic opportunities. Of the seven cases with a "don" title, six were of white complexion. Family names associated with *castas* and Indians were significantly more associated with a dark complexion. In the 173 cases in which both complexion and race classification were available, the correlation was strong: soldiers identified as Indians, *castas*, and *castizos* were three times more likely to be described as dark, while 83% of the Spanish were described as white. Those described as white were more likely to be Spanish. A white complexion was also associated with variables related to economic opportunities, such as the ability to sign and skilled occupations.[40]

The second indicator of social differentiation is literacy and is estimated by the soldier's signature (or lack thereof) in the recruitment document. The signature rate was about 25% in urban occupations that required specialized skills (such as artisans and merchants), while it was less than 10% among construction workers, day workers, workshop laborers, and similar low-skill and rural occupations. As historian Mary Kay Vaughan explained, "the more successfully families were integrated in the urban economy, the more accessible and useful literacy became."[41] It is safe to assume, then, that on average those who could sign were more likely to have had the opportunity to learn how to read and write, and were raised in a family with more economic means than someone who did not know how to write.[42] Overall, about 21% of the soldiers signed their forms, a percentage that was higher than the literacy rate in the general population, which was very likely below 15%.[43]

While only literacy and complexion are used in the statistical analysis of heights, a look at occupations permits a better comparison with the population as a whole.[44] According to a simplified version of Cook's tabulations of the Revillagigedo Census (1791–3), about 2% of the entire population with a reported occupation was in commercial or professional activities, 15% in specialized productive activities, and 83% in unskilled occupations. The figures are roughly consistent with a statistical report on the state of Querétaro (which is, overall, representative of the population covered in this study) dated in the mid-nineteenth century. In the anthropometric sample, by contrast, the share of commercial and professional occupations is 6% and 35% for skilled, and 59% for unskilled workers.[45] That is, the sample over-represents more specialized and skilled occupations. The army was particularly more successful at recruiting independent farmers (*labradores*) but failed at recruiting unskilled dependent workers, who were protected by legal means or by the de-facto power of their employers.[46]

The variables of social differentiation (see Table 1) show significant changes in the social composition of the sample. Over time, the proportion of whites and signing soldiers diminished. Before 1810, white-skinned soldiers accounted for 40%; during the insurrection in the 1810s and afterward, the proportion declined to 30%. The different proportions are an indication of the selection bias in the army, not actual changes in the population. Despite the dubious effectiveness of changes in rules that excluded certain groups from recruitment,[47] it is clear that the army brought in more dark-skinned and illiterate soldiers after independence, perhaps as the result of increased use of coercive recruitment. While the skin color and signature variables control for these compositional changes in the sample, possible unaccounted effects are measured in binary variables for different subsets of the sample.

Table 1.
Sociodemographic Characteristics of the Sample by Birth Cohort.

	1730–1750	1751–1780	1781–1810	1811–1821	1822–1840	Total
Complexion						
Dark skin	215 (169)	548 (218)	400 (317)	551 (550)	514 (511)	2,228 (1,765)
Light skin	125 (93)	415 (212)	268 (265)	237 (237)	243 (243)	1,288 (1,050)
Literacy						
No sign.	244 (190)	737 (193)	516 (421)	654 (643)	634 (629)	2,785 (2,076)
Signature	96 (92)	226 (135)	152 (142)	134 (132)	123 (123)	731 (624)
Rural occupation or geographic origin						
No	301	664	426	493	482	2,366
Yes	39	299	242	295	275	1,150
Urban classification						
Towns	75	167	84	100	93	519
Capitals	105	311	216	210	254	1,096
Village and scattered	160	485	368	478	410	1,901
Region						
Northwest	258	343	324	457	268	1,650
Center	68	402	216	277	372	1,335
Southeast	14	218	128	54	117	531
Total	**340**	**963**	**668**	**788**	**757**	**3,516**

Note: The figures under complexion and literacy are obtained from the imputed variables rounded to the integer; the figures in parentheses are the original (non-imputed) frequencies.
Source: Anthropometric dataset, see text.

There is also detailed information on the place of origin that is used to differentiate regions, as well as urban and rural residence. Almost all records identify the soldier as a *vecino* (resident) of a place, and over 80% of the records also identify where he was *natural* (native) of. The information on such places is usually detailed, pointing to villages or towns, although in some cases only the district name (sometimes the *intendencia* or state, but usually a lower-level jurisdiction) is known. The place of origin (*natural*) was preferred to the place of residence, as it is a better indication of the conditions in which an individual grew up; when not available, the place of residence was used.[48] The locational information was simplified in variables describing the region and urban or rural status.

Place of origin was summarized in three regions: Northwest, Center, and Southeast (see Figure 3). Cases from other regions (the far North, as well as Yucatán and Chiapas in the South) were eliminated from the dataset because of the low number of cases. While simple enough that it achieves a high frequency of cases per region, the division also accounts for the well-known north-south height gradient and socioeconomic differences.[49] The sample over-represents the population from the Northwest. The northwest region has 47% of the cases, compared to 30% in population counts *circa* 1800; the center has 39% and 55% in the dataset and population counts, respectively.[50]

Figure 3.
Intendancies and Regions.

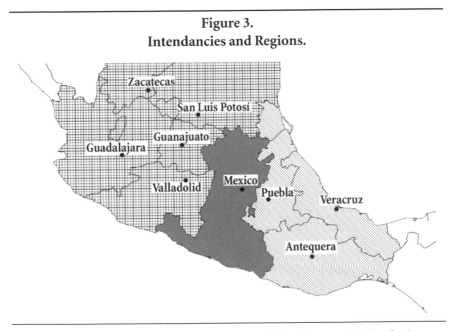

Sources: Intendancy boundaries from 1788 were constructed using Commons, *Las intendencias*; Gerhard, *A Guide*.

Place of origin was also used to identify the rural and urban origin of the individuals. The variable "Capitals" identifies cases from provincial capitals (Guadalajara, Guanajuato, Mexico, Oaxaca, Puebla, Querétaro, San Luis Potosí, Valladolid or Morelia, Veracruz and Zacatecas).[51] As seats of government, provincial capitals had stronger social provisioning; their population ranged from 12,000 (San Luis Potosí) to 150,000 (Mexico City) *circa* 1800. A second variable, labeled "Towns," identifies those from mid-sized towns that had *villa* status (for example Cholula, León, and Zitácuaro, among others).[52] *Villa* status came with demographic and population importance and was associated with a higher degree of autonomy in local governance; while there is no complete population information, the typical *villa* had from 2,000 to 10,000 inhabitants. About a third of the cases were from provincial capitals, 15% from *villas*, and 52% from the remainder—villages and haciendas. By contrast, the proportion of the entire population living in provincial capitals was about 9% of the total. The sum of the population in all towns and capitals (an imperfect approximation to the urban population) was probably around 15%.[53]

Finally, a variable labeled "Rural" captures whether an individual either reported an hacienda as the place of origin, or a rural occupation such as *labrador* (farmer), *gañán* (hacienda worker) and *jornalero* (day worker). Rural provenance is important because it indicates proximity to food. Because the rural variable takes occupation into account, it is possible that a soldier is classified as rural and urban at the same time. About 33% were identified as rural, while the proportion of rural occupations in the entire population was over 80%.[54]

Analysis of Truncated Samples and Assessment of the Technique

The study relies on regression analysis to estimate the effect of one variable, such as literacy or decade of birth, holding the rest constant. An ordinary regression analysis, however, assumes normally distributed data, which is not the case in studies that rely on truncated samples, like this one. Fortunately, the methodology to analyze truncated height distributions is well developed and tested.[55] Human heights have two well-known regularities that help to choose a more suitable technique: they are normally distributed, and the standard deviation is remarkably similar across populations. The histograms are consistent with an underlying normal distribution truncated at the point of the minimum height requirement. Moreover, observed height frequencies in the only division with no enforced minimum requirement, the Sexto Batallón, passed a normality test. A truncated regression (i.e., a maximum-likelihood regression that assumes a truncated normal distribution) is then a suitable technique to reconstruct the heights. In comparison to other techniques (such as the Komlos and Kim regression on truncated samples), it allows the use of multiple truncation points. In practical terms, the use of the truncated regression provides coefficients with accurate standard errors to assess the reliability of the estimate, and makes it possible to use multiple truncation points in the sample and hence to keep a larger number of cases in the analysis.

Table 2 reports the results of the truncated regression of height by decade of birth and sociodemographic controls. The magnitude and sign of the coefficients conform to expected variations in height and attest to the reliability of the data, even if the statistical significance of the coefficients is relatively low.[56] Decadal changes are relatively smooth as expected: very rarely does the average height of a population change more than three centimeters in one decade, and in this sample the greatest variation is 1.41 cm (from the 1760s to the 1770s); moreover, they are in the range of long-run change detected by Komlos and A'Hearn in their studies of eighteenth-century Europe. The coefficients on signature and white complexion are positive and statistically significant, as should be expected given that they indicate a relatively privileged upbringing. The urban-rural location variables lack statistical significance, although it will be shown that this is because the effects changed over the time period. Height varies along the north-south gradient found by other authors (even though the geographic scope excludes the present-day northernmost and southernmost states in Mexico).[57] The northwest region was 0.87 and 1.51 cm taller than the center and south, respectively.

The regression also incorporates dummy variables for specific subsets of the sample to account for possible variations in recruiting and measurement errors.[58] The Manila regiment (Batallón Fixo de Infantería del Rey de Manila) and the Grenadiers companies are the only ones with pronounced and statistically significant effects. The Manila regiment recruited more extensively among vagrants (*vagos*) and had a lower height estimate, almost 3 cm in average, while the Grenadier elite companies (as in Europe) were more than 5 cm taller than regular soldiers. The variable "Insurgents" identifies predominantly indigenous soldiers that received an amnesty from the viceroy in 1817; while they were 1.2 cm shorter, the coefficient has a large statistical error. The army units using the Mexican foot measure are almost one centimeter shorter than Paris-foot divisions, a difference that can be accounted for by the imperfection and deterioration of the measurement standards.[59] The coefficients on the national army and the military census are close to zero and not statistically significant. The age-correction variables

Table 2.
Determinants of Height

Variable	Coefficient	Std. Error	p
Pre-1750	2.52	1.21	0.04
1751–60	1.18	1.33	0.38
1761–1770	2.12	1.26	0.09
1771–1780	0.71	1.24	0.57
1781–1790	0.05	1.20	0.97
1791–1800	Ref.		
1801–1810	−0.63	1.60	0.69
1811–1821	−1.69	1.56	0.28
1822–1830	−1.88	1.59	0.24
1831–1840	−2.13	1.66	0.20
Signature	1.68	0.43	0.00
White	1.98	0.36	0.00
Rural	−0.54	0.38	0.16
Capitals	−0.53	0.39	0.18
Other cities	0.20	0.46	0.67
Central region	Ref.		
Northwest region	0.87	0.36	0.02
South region	−0.64	0.51	0.21
Manila regiment	−2.90	1.15	0.01
Military census	−0.21	0.72	0.77
Insurgents	−1.19	1.46	0.41
National army	0.26	1.76	0.88
Mexican foot	−0.89	0.47	0.06
Grenadiers	5.46	1.17	0.00
18	−1.96	0.61	0.00
19	−1.71	0.67	0.01
20	−1.64	0.56	0.00
21	−0.38	0.77	0.63
22	0.25	0.57	0.67
23+	Ref.		
Constant	162.43	1.20	0.00
Sigma	6.24	0.14	0.00
Observations	3516.00		

Note: Obtained through a Maximum-Likelihood Truncated Regression. All units are in centimeters. The frequency by decade ranges from 161 (1790s) to 787 (1810s). Column p stands for the probability that the coefficient is different than 0, that is, that the effect is null.
Source: Anthropometric dataset, see text.

show that males were experiencing physical growth until they were 22 years old, following expected patterns.[60] Finally, the estimated dispersion term (sigma) is smaller than the accepted 6.86 standard deviation in heights, but it is similar to other findings in high-quality data of historical populations.[61]

General Trends and International Comparisons

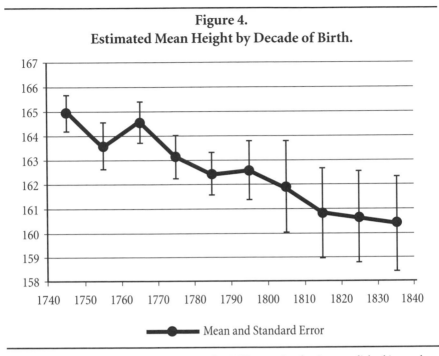

Figure 4.
Estimated Mean Height by Decade of Birth.

Mean and Standard Error

Note: Height measurement in centimeters. Based on Table 2, setting the signature, light skin, rural, capitals, *villas*, northwest, south, age, and army division dummy variables to zero.

Average height by decade of birth declined more than four centimeters (Figure 4) over the century analyzed here. The decline started in the mid-eighteenth century and continued into the early national era. Heights fell from 165 cm in the 1740s to 162.5 in the 1780s, declined to almost 161 cm in the 1810s, and continued to decline half a centimeter in the first two decades after independence. The decline was the steepest from the 1760s to the 1780s and from the 1790s to the 1810s. The vertical lines indicate the standard error of the estimation. After 1800 the estimates have more uncertainty, but the overall decline from the mid-eighteenth century to the 1830s is statistically significant.[62]

The heights of male Mexicans found in this study are in the range of other findings in Mexico and Latin America (Table 3). They are comparable (if not taller) to historical heights in the Maya region, River Plate region, and Latin America in general. In comparison with the other figures in Mexico, heights seemingly improved from the 1830s to the second half of the nineteenth century and the early twentieth century.[63] The lowest point was

Table 3.
Comparison of Male Heights in Mexico, Mesoamerica, and Latin America.

Population	Birth Cohort	Adult height (in centimeters)
1. Mexico		
1.a. Colonial and national armies, central Mexico	1740s–1830s	164.9–160.4
1.b. Federal army (central region as reference)	1870s–1900s	163.5–163.7
1.c. Anthropometric surveys of creoles, mestizos and indigenous people from central Mexico	Early 20th century	161.0–163.5
2. Mesoamerica		
2.a. Skeletal remains of Maya males from Tipu, Belize	Mid-colonial	160.3
2.b. Rural *ladinos*, Guatemala	1905–1920	160.7
2.c. Peasants, IDs from village of Cobán, Guatemala	1917–1932	157.5 *
3. Latin America		
3.a. National army, Argentina (modal)	1785–1839	158.2–160.1
3.b. Long-run trend, Latin America	1600–1750	*c.* 163–162

Sources: 1.a. based on Table 2; 1.b. López-Alonso, chapter in this collection, Table 3, model 1b, using the center region as the reference group; 1.c. Kelly, *Physical Anthropology*, 18; 2.a.–2.c. Ríos and Bogin's chapter in this collection, tables 4 and 5 and figure 15; 3.a. Salvatore, "Heights and Welfare," 107; 3.b. Bogin and Keep, "Eight Thousand Years," 336.

Notes: The original average in 2.c. (155.2–155.7) was for 18-year-old males; I added 2 cm (see coefficient on age 18 in Table 2) to account for height gain.

attained in the 1830s (160.4 cm). From the point of view of secular change, the trend from the 1740s to the 1830s is consistent with Bogin's finding of a very long-run stagnation and even decline in heights from the post-classic to the early twentieth century, but it stands in contrast with the improvements in height in Argentina in a similar period.

Compared to the European Mediterranean population (Figure 5), Mexican males were five or more centimeters shorter than Northern Italians, less than two centimeters shorter than the French in the eighteenth century, and about the same as Southern Spaniards. In terms of secular change, the resemblance to Northern Italy and France in the eighteenth century is remarkable: the three countries peaked in the 1740s or 1760s and then

Figure 5.
Heights in Mexico and European Mediterranean Countries, by Decade of Birth.

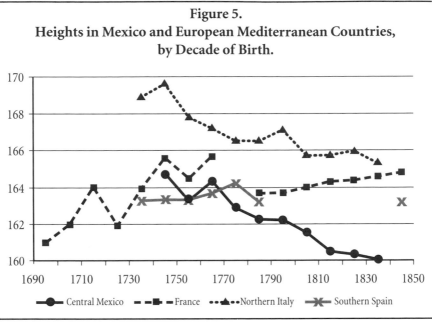

Notes: All measurements in centimeters. Heights standardized to 21 years of age (20–21 in the case of France). The Mexican series is scaled to reflect actual regional weights.

Sources: Cámara, "Long-Term Trends," 68; Komlos, "An Anthropometric History of Early-Modern France," 184; A'Hearn, "Anthropometric Evidence," 364; Weir, "Economic Welfare," 191.

declined until the end of the eighteenth century. The pattern conforms to the overall decline of heights in Europe from the mid-eighteenth century until its end.[64] By contrast, the Mexican trajectory and absolute levels of height diverged after the 1800s, as stature in France increased, stagnated in Northern Italy and Southern Spain, and declined in Mexico.[65] As measured by heights, living standards in Mexico kept pace with these and other countries over the eighteenth century, but declined in relative terms in the nineteenth century.

Population Growth, Climatic Disasters, Food Prices, and Heights

The similarities with the European experience in the eighteenth century remind us of Florescano's finding that cycles in corn prices resembled price cycles in Europe. Florescano proposed that global climatic processes explained the common pattern of prices and agricultural cycles in Mexico and Western Europe.[66] Komlos argued that climatic disturbances similarly shaped the trajectory in early-modern France. Population growth pressed on agricultural productivity ceilings and heightened vulnerability to climate changes.[67] A colder climatic cycle in the eighteenth century thus stressed food production and negatively affected nutritional status. Do changes in population, the climate, and real prices help explain the declining biological standards of living in Mexico?

Population. The lack of detailed population data allows only a general overview of this possible connection. Population was certainly growing fast in Mexico, at rates faster than 1% a year, except from 1810 to 1830. Population growth contrasts with the decline in height (see Figure 6). The stagnation in demographic growth from 1810 to 1830 was similarly accompanied by a flatter trend in heights. Yet the relationship between demographic growth and height decline is problematic when seen in more detail: In decades of fast demographic growth (1790s and 1800s), height declined as much as in decades of demographic stagnation (1810s and 1820s). Aggregate population growth suggests a fiercer competition for scarcer resources, but it is not enough to explain the overarching trend in height. More empirical study and a clearer theoretical model certainly are needed to advance in the direction of a Malthusian argument.

Figure 6.
Population and Heights in Central Mexico.

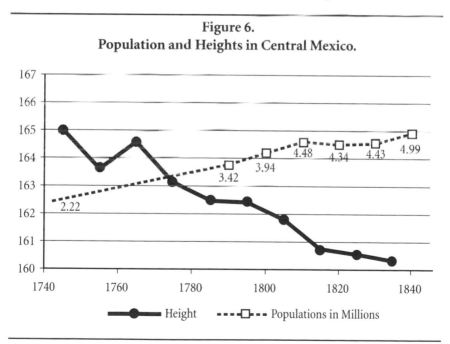

Source: McCaa, "The Peopling," 606, using the shares for the central and central-northern region for 1790–1840. For 1742 I used McCaa's estimation in Garner, "Economic History Data Desk," and interpolated the share of the region based on the 1790–1840 data.

Note: Population is represented in a logarithmic scale.

Climate. Repeated early frosts caused immense damage to crops in eighteenth-century Mexico (particularly to corn). This has prompted climate historians to propose that the final years of the Little Ice Age had a negative consequence on living standards and to problematize the relationship between climatic disasters and environmental adaptability.[68] The El Niño-Southern Oscillation phenomenon has also been proposed as a major climatic factor. El Niño changes rainfall regional and seasonal patterns and increases the risk of erosion due to torrential downpours; it is followed by a La Niña cold phase, which also disrupts the expected rainfall patterns, brings dry conditions in mid-summer, and reduces temperatures in the fall. Besides direct effects on aggregate food production, El Niño warm and cold phases likely raised fears of ensuing problems in the food supply.[69] Using a widely cited chronology of El Niño events and annual tree-ring growth series, I argued elsewhere that bad climatic conditions in the first years of life had a negative effect of half to one centimeter on a person's height, depending on the urban or rural origin of the soldier.[70] Here I use a more recently published chronology of El Niño events based on consistent archival resources from Trujillo, Northern Perú,[71] and relate it to annual variations in height to gauge its effect on it.

Figure 7 provides a visual examination of the relationship of El Niño and heights by plotting five-year moving averages of adult height against El Niño events.[72] The first noticeable fact is that the there is a higher concentration of events toward the end of the eighteenth century and in the early nineteenth century. In particular, a sequence of El Niño events (1785–1787, 1791–1794, 1800–1804, 1811–1814) coincided with sharp short-term declines in height.[73] This fact is consistent with previous research on agricultural crises stating that the accumulation of adverse agricultural conditions for two or more years caused the worst damage. There are important discrepancies, such as in the 1750s, characterized by the absence of El Niño events but a pronounced height decline. Finally, the stable trend in heights from 1780 to 1800 contrasts with more frequent El Niño events in these decades.

Food Prices. Grains, in particular corn, were the staple in Mexican diet and represent the single largest item in the consumer basket. The upward trend toward the end of the colonial period is well documented and was likely related to the growing pressure on resources. Moreover, as the population increasingly relied on the market to obtain food, food prices become more indicative of conditions of access to food. Figure 8 represents the five-year moving average of height against a five-year moving average of real grain

Figure 7.
El Niño Events and Annual Height.

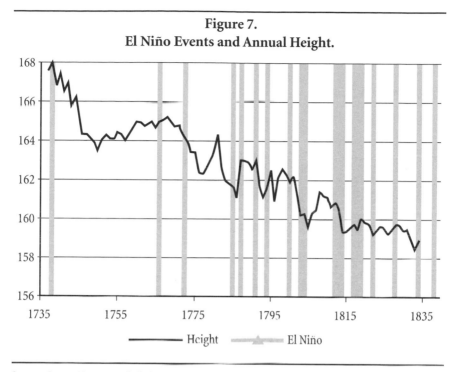

Source: García Herrera et al., "Chronology of El Niño Events."

Note: Each grey bar depicts a "possible" or "probable" El Niño event. The height series was constructed using the same independent variables as in Table 2, but with birth-year dummy variables. The resulting estimate was smoothed using a five-year moving average. The reference population is from the center region, age 23 or older, illiterate and dark-skinned.

prices (i.e., grain prices adjusted by earnings) in Mexico City.[74] The resulting series confirms the well-documented increase in corn and wheat prices from the 1780s to the end of the colonial period, but shows that the price increase outpaced wage gains and extended into the early national era. As prices increased, heights declined. As with population and climate, the relationship is not mechanical and there are short-term exceptions. For instance, the decline in real prices from the 1810s into the early 1830s coincided with a further decline in height, albeit at a slower pace than before. Still, in all, over the long run real prices increased, and heights declined.

Regression analysis helps move beyond the visual inspection and quantify the effect of El Niño and changes in prices on height. Table 4 reports the coefficients of the regression using the annual height estimation as the dependent variable, and annual real prices and the count of El Niño events within a five-year moving window.[75] In all of the specifications, both factors

Figure 8.
Heights and Real Grain Prices in Mexico City.

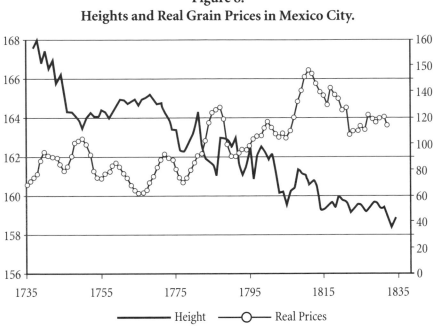

Source: Real grain prices from Challú, "Agricultural Crisis," 43–44.

Note: Real grain prices are in index format, where 100 is the average.

are statistically significant and have a large effect on height. Columns 1 and 2 are partial correlations, while column 3 includes the two variables in the same model and then estimates the effects of one variable holding the other constant (e.g., a price hike with no El Niño event, or vice versa). In this last specification, it becomes clear that real grain prices have a strong effect on height even in the presence of an El Niño event; conversely, climatic factors still explain height variations even in the absence of price changes. The effects are large. For instance, a price increase from 1 to 1.28 (one standard deviation) caused height to decline by almost one centimeter, while the presence of one El Niño event reduced height by 0.7 cm. The upward trend in real grain prices and the more frequent El Niño events had a strong negative effect that accounts for almost 25% of the decline in adult height.[76] Still, the effect is aggregate and does not differentiate the experiences of different social groups. To this analysis we move in the next section.

Table 4.
Effects of El Niño Events and Real Grain Prices on Average Height.

	(1) Coefficient	(2) Coefficient	(3) Coefficient	Mean and standard deviation
Real Grain Price Index	−4.66 **		−3.38 **	1 (0.28)
El Niño event (five-year moving average)	−1.57 **	−0.70 *	0.94	(0.96)
Constant	167.09 **	162.78 *	166.47 **	
R²	0.16	0.04	0.19	
N	98	98	98	

Source: See Figures 7 and 8.

Notes: All effects in centimeters. The annual height series was used. Durbin-Watson tests reject the hypothesis of autocorrelation of residuals. Two stars denote a p-value below 0.01; one star, on or below 0.05. The El Niño variable has a value of 1 when there was one event within the five-year win-dow centered in the birth year, 2 if there were two events, and so on.

Height Gaps, Inequality, and Post-Independence Decompression

The average heights of different social groups and their gaps serve as a meas ure of inequality in nutritional status and socioeconomic conditions expe-rienced at the time of physical growth. According to Table 2, indicators of better opportunities have a significant and positive association with height over the entire period. Soldiers who knew how to sign were 1.68 cm taller. Light-skinned soldiers were 1.98 cm taller. The insurgents captured in the 1810s, most of whom were Indian, were 1.19 cm shorter. These differences are not as pronounced as those found among the elites and popular sectors in Europe or late-nineteenth century Mexico, but they are significant within the working classes. More remarkably, height gaps changed over time, indi-cating a change in inequality. In this section I focus on height gaps by liter-acy and by rural or urban origin. The analysis, reported in Table 5, is based on truncated regressions that make the inequality variables interact with birth cohorts. The birth cohorts used in this analysis encompass relatively long periods in order to achieve higher frequencies.

The trajectories of height of literate and illiterate soldiers, as inferred by their ability to sign their recruitment form, are shown in Figure 9. The height decline was remarkably more pronounced among the illiterate sol-diers. Overall, the height of literate soldiers declined less than two cen-timeters throughout the period, and more than four centimeters for the

Table 5.
Heights by Birth Cohort and Socioeconomic Groups.

Variable	(1) Literacy Coefficient	(2) Complexion Coefficient
Birth cohort 1730–1750	2.77 **	2.31 **
Birth cohort 1751–1780	2.5 **	1.13
Birth cohort 1781–1810	Ref.	Ref.
Birth cohort 1811–1821	−1.29 *	−1.69 **
Birth cohort 1822–1840	−1.52 **	−1.93 **
Signature	1.8 *	1.67 **
X 1730–1750	−1.03	Ref.
X 1751–1780	−3.24 **	Ref.
X 1781–1810	Ref.	Ref.
X 1811–1821	0.77	Ref.
X 1822–1840	1.27	Ref.
White complexion	1.87 **	0.94
X 1730–1750	Ref.	−0.05
X 1751–1780	Ref.	0.25
X 1781–1810	Ref.	Ref.
X 1811–1821	Ref.	1.58
X 1822–1840	Ref.	1.79 *
Rural	−0.54	−0.47
Capitals	−0.56	−0.58
Villas (medium-sized towns)	0.2	0.19
Central region	Ref.	Ref.
Northwest region	0.86 **	0.87 **
South region	−0.56	−0.61
Manila regiment	−3.26 **	−3.1 **
Military census	−0.55	−0.18
Insurgents	−1.56	−2.02
National army	−0.41	−0.63
Mexican foot	−1.03 **	−0.98 **
Grenadiers	5.3 **	5.55 **
18	−2.25 **	−2.15 **
19	−1.87 **	−2.03 **
20	−1.81 **	−1.81 **
21	−0.54	−0.51
22	0.22	0.22
23+	Ref.	Ref.
Constant	162.71 **	163.2 **
Sigma	6.21 **	6.2
Observations	3516.0	3516.0

Source: Anthropometric dataset, see text.
Note: Obtained through a Maximum-Likelihood Truncated Regression. All units in centimeters. One star denotes p (statistical significance) $\leq$ 0.1; two stars, p $\leq$ 0.05.

**Figure 9.
Estimated Mean Height by Birth Cohort and Literacy.**

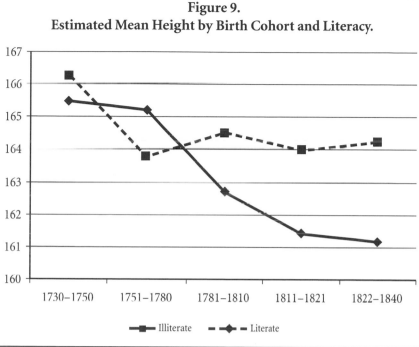

Note: Figure based on Table 5, column 1, setting the light skin, rural, capitals, villas, Northwest, South, age and army division dummy variables to zero.

illiterate. The gap became apparent from 1780 on, and expanded from two to three centimeters by the end of the period. White soldiers similarly gained height relative to the dark-skinned (Table 5, column 2). The difference increased from about one centimeter at the end of the eighteenth century to almost three centimeters by the end of the period.

The widening gap suggests that individuals who grew under more economic hardships (e.g., those unable to attain an education) were more vulnerable to the worsening of overall conditions and experienced a more pronounced loss of biological (and material) well-being. This pattern is consistent with studies of inequality in the late colonial period, aptly summarized by Van Young: "the rich get richer and the poor get skewed."[77] More surprising is the fact that the height differential was still high and even increased after 1810. This evidence defies the idea that there were improvements in the distribution of wealth, although certainly this is only one component in the overall inequality of opportunities experienced by different groups.

Figure 10.
Estimated Mean Height by Birth Cohort and Rural Origin.

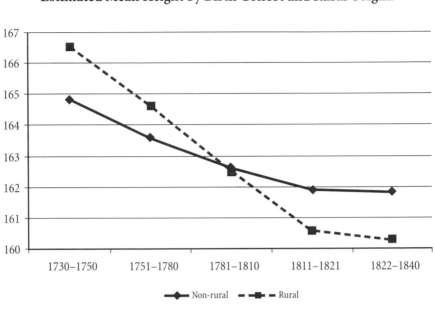

Note: Figure based on Table 6, col. 1, setting the signature, light skin, capitals, villas, Northwest, South, age, and army division dummy variables to zero

   The breakdown of height trends by rural and urban populations provides another look at the changes in the relative positions of large social sectors in Mexican society; the regression analysis of birth cohort and rural-urban origin interactions is reported in Table 6. The urban or rural origin of an individual was, and still is, an important differentiator in Mexican society. While in recent times cities have enjoyed advantages, it is unclear how these sectors fared before the large investments in urban infrastructure and a development that concentrated public resources in the urban economy. I rely on two forms of identification of the urban and rural sectors. The first, represented in Figure 10, identifies soldiers as having a rural background if they either declared an hacienda as their place of origin, or have a rural occupation. The height trend by rural or non-rural origin shows a steep, six-centimeter decline in rural heights and a moderate decline among the rest. The diverging trends are remarkably gradual and consistent: the rural population was 1.7 cm taller before 1780, had no height advantage by the turn of the century, and was 1.6 cm shorter after independence; this decline is statistically significant (see Table 6, column 1).

Table 6.
Heights by Birth Cohort and Rural–Urban Origin.

	(1)	(2)
Birth cohort 1730–1750	2.21 **	1.73
Birth cohort 1751–1780	0.95	1.41
Birth cohort 1781–1810	Ref.	Ref.
Birth cohort 1811–1821	-0.71	-1.7 **
Birth cohort 1822–1840	-0.8	-1.93 **
Signature	1.67 **	1.69 **
White complexion	1.87 **	1.88 **
Rural	-0.10	-0.49
X 1730 1750	1.80	
X 1751–1780	1.14	
X 1781–1810	Ref.	
X 1811–1821	-1.24	
X 1822–1840	-1.47	
Capitals	-0.57	-2.08 **
X 1730–1750		1.65
X 1751–1780		-0.44
X 1781–1810		Ref.
X 1811–1821		2.65 **
X 1822–1840		2.54 **
Villas (medium-sized towns)	0.24	0.49
X 1730–1750		-0.64
X 1751–1780		-0.41
X 1781–1810		Ref.
X 1811–1821		-0.42
X 1822–1840		-0.28
Central region	Ref.	Ref.
Northwest region	0.78 **	0.86 **
South region	-0.48	-0.49
Manila regiment	-2.89 **	-2.61 **
Military census	-0.47	-0.61
Insurgents	-2.05	-2.32
National army	-0.47	-0.86
Mexican foot	-1.05 **	-1.01 **
Grenadiers	5.43 **	5.39 **
18	-2.13 **	-2.18 **
19	-1.85 **	-1.89 **
20	-1.79 **	-1.8 **
21	-0.55	-0.59
22	0.24	0.18
23+	Ref.	Ref.
Constant	162.63 **	163.4 **
Sigma	6.23 **	6.23 **
Number of observations	3516.0	3516 **

Source: Anthropometric dataset, see text.
Note: Obtained through a Maximum-Likelihood Truncated Regression. All units in centimeters. Two stars denote p (statistical significance) ≤ 0.05.

Figure 11.
Estimated Mean Height by Birth Cohort and Urban Origin.

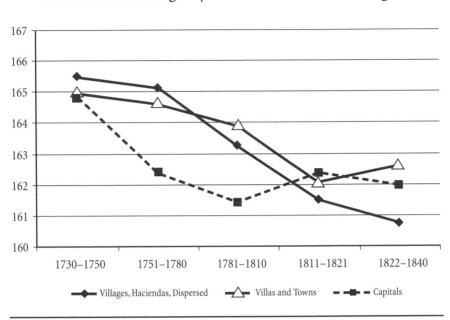

Note: Figure based on Table B.2, col. 2, setting the variables signature, light skin, rural, Northwest, South, age, and measurement correction to zero.

A second approach identifies the population with an urban origin using the declared place of origin (see the second column of Table 6, and Figure 11). Place of origin is classified in three categories: metropolis and provincial capitals; towns (*villas*); and the remainder (villages and haciendas). It is likely that in some cases the city or town declared as the place of origin was the closest urban locality or the *cabecera* (center of the jurisdiction), particularly when the actual location was close to that center.[78] While the problem should not be exaggerated, as the *filiaciones* do distinguish between locality and *cabeceras*, the trends can be more accurately interpreted as related to the effects associated with proximity to urban centers. The resulting trends, shown in Figure 10, are consistent with the identification of the rural population attempted above. The height of the non-urban population (e.g., those coming from villages and haciendas) slid over the generations more than it did in the urban categories. Before 1780, villages and haciendas were at the top of the chart; in 1781–1810 the towns took the lead. The soldiers born in capital cities were the shortest before 1810 but converged with the rest after 1810. While some of the gaps are not statistically significant, the pattern is clear that the population in urban centers suffered less height decline than the rural population and subsequently urban and rural heights converged.

In agreement with recent studies in the anthropometric literature, the evolution of the urban-rural height gap defies the notion of an "urban penalty."[79] It suggests that the improvement in biological well-being in urban areas is not just associated with the creation of the modern public health infrastructure and advances in food conservation, but is also related to the capacity of the cities to secure their food supply from the countryside. The explanation of this emerging gap has little to do with improvements in the disease environment, particularly because the public works initiatives of the late eighteenth century were concentrated in the largest cities and were largely ineffective.[80] The smallpox vaccination campaign was perhaps the most successful public health initiative of this era, and this is reflected in a reduction of the disease among soldiers. One out of five soldiers born in the nineteenth century had smallpox marks, down from one in every three in the eighteenth century. Yet the reduction was well distributed in the urban and rural population, and smallpox marks had no measurable effect on adult height, ruling out the control of smallpox as a factor explaining the convergence of urban and rural heights.

The shifts in the urban-rural gap are more likely related to the mounting difficulties of the rural population to secure its food supplies in a context of increasing commercialization of the agricultural sector and growing power of the urban centers in procuring its food supplies. As the city population and the mining sector grew, so did the demand for marketed food. This growing demand enlarged the city supply areas, integrated local markets in central Mexico, and pushed up the prices in rural districts.[81] While this favored landowners, for a large sector of the rural population access to land had become more precarious over the second half of the eighteenth century and, as a result, peasants did not benefit from increasing prices. Even more, the tragedy of the famines likely resulted in the decapitalization and increasing destitution of the rural poor.[82] The mass influx of rural dwellers to the cities in 1785–86 and 1809 supports the idea of widespread destitution in rural areas caused by famine.[83]

I hypothesize that the long-run decline of rural height that extended after the insurrection in the 1810s can be accounted for by the persistence both of the large demand for marketed food and of landed elite power, even despite the climate of popular mobilization. The urban sector maintained its relative importance. In some regions, the urban population did lose relative importance, as in Puebla and Veracruz. Elsewhere, the population of cities increased at rates comparable to, or higher than, overall population growth. Overall, from the end of the eighteenth century to the 1830s or 1850s, the available evidence shows comparable growth rates in cities and the entire population.[84] The vitality of the urban sector is also evidenced by the capacity of its manufacturing sector to withstand the strong pressures brought by the industrial revolution.[85] The output of the mining industry declined, but important centers such as Zacatecas maintained their silver production levels, and mines such as La Valenciana partially recovered production by the 1830s.[86] That is, the sector employed in non-food production was still a sizable share in the Mexican economy and fueled a continuing demand for marketed food.

More importantly, there is a disjuncture between changes in political power and the distribution of income. It is established that the landed elites moved to strategies aimed at defending their wealth in light of popular mobilization.[87] Yet in the core area of the hacienda economy, the Bajío, the diminished position of the hacendados did not translate into a loss of wealth and perhaps other forms of political and economic power. Land values remained very high after independence and outpaced the growth in nominal unskilled wages and even grain prices.[88] Haciendas were sold to rancheros in the Bajío, Jalisco, and Michoacán, pointing to some redistribution of wealth, but as Chowning's work on Michoacán shows, upward mobility was beneficial to select members of the middle classes, not to the poor majority.[89] A report on Querétaro's economy and population in 1845, for instance, shows that hacienda and rancho owners (1.2% of the state population) earned 15 to 38 times more income than rural workers (who represented 61%, if not more, of the state's workforce). Rancho tenants (*arrendatarios de ranchos*), the emerging new group of rural entrepreneurs and likely the beneficiaries of the hacendados' problems, represented 6% of the population and earned 8 times less than the hacendados.[90] In short, important signs point to the fact that the decompression of rural tensions was not accompanied by a more equal distribution of income or a loss of power by the landed elites.[91]

Conclusions

The estimation of trends in average height allows the social and economic historian to assess changes in human welfare of large segments of the population. In addition, data on climatic events and the cost of major food staples now make it clear that Mexicans experienced an impressive decline in their economic welfare in the eighteenth and the early nineteenth centuries. The trend in height shows the second half of the eighteenth century as a critical moment of steep decline in living standards. The timing closely resembles Brading and Wu's thesis, stated more than thirty years ago, of a century-long stagnation that began in the 1760s and extended into the 1860s. The measure of the decline is that only by the 1930s did the average height of soldiers surpass the average of the mid-eighteenth century.[92]

From an international perspective, Mexicans' height in the mid-eighteenth century was "not too short" (as Dobado and García recently put it). The declining trend over the second half of the eighteenth century was nothing exceptional in international perspective either. The early nineteenth century, however, was a watershed as the trends diverged: height recovered or stagnated in France, Spain, and other countries, but it continued to decline in Mexico: by the 1830s, Mexicans had finally become "too short." In comparative terms, then, low living standards in Mexico started not early in the colonial period, but in its last decades and in the nineteenth century. From a historiographic perspective, this conclusion gives new support to Coatsworth's classic argument that placed the roots of Mexican underdevelopment in the nineteenth century, while it contradicts the optimist view that inequality and living standards improved in the early national era.[93] I have proposed that population growth, more frequent El Niño events, and real grain prices reduced the availability of food and had a likely detrimental effect on living standards. Population growth has been frequently pointed out as the ultimate culprit of declining living standards and rising inequality in eighteenth-century Mexico and elsewhere.[94] Population certainly increased as heights declined, augmenting demand for food and pushing the agricultural frontier to less fertile lands, hence increasing the vulnerability to adverse climate conditions and increasing agricultural prices, but we need more fine grained data to fully develop an explanatory model. I estimated the effect of El Niño and real grain prices and found it significant, yet moderate. Changes in the two variables explain about a quarter of the overall decline in height from the 1740s to the 1830s.

More important than aggregate factors (food availability, price levels, population growth) are the differential effects of these pressures in different social groups. I ultimately propose that a fundamental shift in entitlements took place, whereby a larger fraction of the population came to depend on the market to satisfy its food needs.[95] The demand for marketed food increased as the economy became more specialized and complex. In the countryside, the response to these structural changes was the increasing commercialization of agriculture and greater leverage of the *hacendados*, throwing peasants into the commercial economy. As more people depended on their wage income to secure their access to food, and as food prices increased, living standards declined, particularly among those of a lower socioeconomic status.

Notes

* I appreciate comments and suggestions by John Coatsworth, Alejandra Irigoin, John Komlos, Emilio Kouri, John Murray, Amy Robinson, Ricardo Salvatore, Richard Steckel, John Womack Jr., and the anonymous reviewers. Any omission or error is my exclusive responsibility.

1. Tutino, *From Insurrection to Revolution*, 75. An insightful account of the impact of the famine in another northern area is Rojas, *Gobierno y élite local*, 121.
2. On the decadal cycle, see Florescano, *Precios del maíz*.
3. On epidemics, see Malvido, "Factores de despoblación"; Cooper, *Epidemic Disease*; Thomson, *Puebla*, chap. 4; Márquez Morfín, *La desigualdad ante la muerte*. The incidence rate of smallpox is based on the military data presented later in this chapter.
4. For Mexico City see Márquez Morfín, *La desigualdad ante la muerte*, 293; McCaa, "The Peopling," 617–619. The median age of death in San Luis Potosí is based on burial reports in Archivo Histórico del Estado de San Luis Potosí, Intendencias, vol. "1820 (5)," exp. 9; vol. "1821 (4)," exp. 2; vol. "1821 (12)"; Secretaría General de Gobierno, "1827 (40)," exp. 6 (Dec. 1827).
5. Brading and Wu, "Population Growth and Crisis," 26. In San Luis Potosí, deaths below age 6 represented 24%; see previous footnote for sources.
6. Márquez Morfín, "Unequal in Death"; Márquez Morfín, *La desigualdad ante la muerte*.
7. Brading and Wu, "Population Growth and Crisis," 34–35.
8. For example, Calderón de la Barca, *Life in Mexico*, 76, 110, 171, and 476–76; 110, 171, and 477. On diet, see Super and Vargas, "Mexico"; Pilcher, *Que vivan los tamales*. On a more urban perspective, see Haslip-Viera, *Crime and Punishment*, 32.
9. Besides the already mentioned demographic history studies, see Calvo, "Démographie historique"; Morin, "Population et épidémies"; Lugo Olín, "Población de Cuautitlán."
10. Florescano, *Precios del maíz*, 189; Garner, "Price Trends"; García Acosta, *Los precios del trigo*. On agricultural crises see Ouweneel, *Ciclos*; Van Young, "The Age of Paradox."
11. See, for example, Knight, *Mexico: The Colonial Era*, 226.
12. Van Young, "Conflict and Solidarity"; Van Young, "The Age of Paradox"; Tutino, *From Insurrection to Revolution*, 61–82.
13. Endfield and O'Hara, "Degradation, Drought, and Dissent"; Endfield and O'Hara, "Conflicts Over Water in 'The Little Drought Age' in Central Mexico"; Fernández Tejedo, Endfield, and O'Hara, "Estrategias."
14. Ponzio, "Globalisation and Economic Growth in the Third World"; Dobado and Marrero, "Mining-Led Growth."
15. Dobado Gonzáles and García, "Neither So Low"; Dobado Gonzáles, "Precios y salarios en la Nueva España borbónica."
16. McCaa, "The Peopling," 288.

17. Tutino, *From Insurrection to Revolution*, 228–242; Tutino, "The Revolution in Mexican Independence."

18. Brading and Wu, "Population Growth and Crisis." For another case and similar conclusions, see Lugo Olín, "Población de Cuautitlán."

19 On the 1833 Cholera epidemic, see Malvido, "Cólera morbus"; Márquez Morfín, *La desigualdad ante la muerte*; Oliver, "La pandemia"; Velasco, "La epidemia."

20. Coatsworth, "Obstacles."

21. Salvucci, "Mexican National Income."

22. Chowning, *Wealth and Power*, 160–175.

23. The consulted collections are the following: Archivo Histórico de Hacienda, vols. 38, 539, 543, 587, 603, 739, 903, 2289, 2524; Filipinas, vols. 8, 11, 13, 54, 61; Indiferente de Guerra: 14B, 20A, 27B, 29, 40B, 49B, 52A, 59B, 76, 82B, 84, 91, 92, 99C, 74, 92, 120, 207, 104A, 105A, 107A, 110, 110A, 114A, 116A, 119A, 120A, 123B, 149, 167, 207, 208, 213B, 248A, 248B, 304B, 306B, 340A, 410A, 421A, 505A; Indiferente Virreinal: 1003, 1693, 1884, 1899, 2400, 2944, 3805; Padrones, 5, 6, 8, 11, 13, 16, 18, 19, 20, 21, 23, 24, 29, 38, 43, 109, 113; Guerra, 94, 317; Guerra y Marina, 1er Regimiento de Infantería, 1er Regimiento de Infantería Activo de México, 1er Regimiento de Infantería Permanente, 3er Regimiento de Infantería, 4to Regimiento de Infantería, 4to Regimiento Permanente, 7mo Regimiento de Infantería, Batallón Activo de Celaya, Regimiento de Infantería Activo de Puebla, Regimiento de Infantería del Rey Fixo de Manila, Regimiento de Infantería Expedicionario de Murcia, Regimiento de Infantería Permanente Activo de Guanajuato, Regimiento de Infantería Provincial de Toluca, Regimiento Permanente de Guerrero, Regimiento Permanente de Iguala, Regimiento Permanente de Veracruz, Regimiento Permanente del Palmar, Regimiento Permanente Húsares–Guardia; Operaciones de Guerra: 127, 52, 666, 68. 80 cases were collected in other archives: the Archivo Histórico del Estado de San Luis Potosí, Secretaría de Gobernación, 1826 (1), 1826 (8), 1827 (2); 26 cases from the Nettie Lee Benson Latin American Collection (University of Texas at Austin), O'Gorman, Z1.

24. Individuals younger than 18 were eliminated due to fast rates of height gain.

25. The term *filiación* stands for identification document; the strict sense of the word is genealogical lineage, and in fact the parents' names and place of origin were the main way of identification in the earliest enrollment documents available for consultation.

26. Some other records, such as the *media filiación* and the census and militia rolls, report less information and do not require the soldier's signature. They typically provide information on place of origin or residence, age, height, and often times occupation, physical traits, and racial classification.

27. For a similar problem, see Salvatore and Baten, "A Most Difficult Case."

28. This was the case of the 1791–2 military census records. Because there was a special category for short stature, the 60-inch measurement did not show the abnormal concentration of cases observed in other units.

29. Point of truncation stands for the value below which there are fewer cases than the prediction of the normal distribution. In the statistical analysis, all cases below this point are truncated (i.e., removed) from the analysis. The distribution of cases then follows the truncated normal distribution. The analysis of specific distributions by army units and recruitment cohorts, which is presented succinctly here, is based on Komlos' criticism of Floud in Komlos, *Stature, Living Standards*.

30. Cámara Hueso, "Fuentes antropométricas," 113–114; Lucuze, *Disertación sobre las medidas militares.*

31. See Archer, *The Army in Bourbon Mexico*, 231–233.

32. The 1791 military census, the Regimiento de la Corona de la Nueva España, and the Ejército del Norte, however, show a frequency of cases with five feet that is consistent with a truncation point at 60 inches.

33. "Medidas"; Ministerio de Justicia y Fomento, *Sistema Métrico*, 16. The measures vary slightly (a tenth of a milimeter) depending on the source and may reflect the deterioration of the standards. On the Burgos foot, see Carrera Stampa, "Evolution of Weights," 3. The metric equivalence of the Mexican inch according to dictionaries of weights and measures was from 2.316 to 2.328 cm.

34. See *Ley de Sorteo*, 13 June 1838, in Centro de Estudios de Historia de México [Condumex], 355.08.72 V.A. Art. 14 refers to the "pulgadas mexicanas."

35. In addition to the 1838 *Ley de Sorteo*, see Arrillaga, *Recopilación*, 107–108, 145–146, 249–250; Ministerio de Guerra y Marina, *Reglas*, art. 14; and AGN, Colección de Historia de México, vol. 8, 184. I thank Linda Arnold for pointing out most of these sources.

36. The Shapiro-Wilk test of normality has a probability of 0.957.

37. Cope, *The Limits*; Guardino, *The Time of Liberty*.

38. I understand race here as a social construct rather than biological difference. It is unlikely that these traits can effectively distinguish different genetic pools, given the high degree of miscegenation for more than two hundred years and the convergence in lifestyles.

39. In one of every six cases, skin color was missing. It was imputed using other physical traits, racial descriptions, or family name patterns. On imputing missing data, see King, "Analyzing Incomplete Political Science Data." The imputation procedures used in this study do not affect the overall proportions of the imputed variable and do not affect in significant ways the results of the analysis of heights. The primary gain is in retaining a higher number of cases, which permits a more refined analysis of height trends. On the importance of large datasets in anthropometric analysis, see Komlos, "How to (and How Not to)."

40. On phenotype, patterns in family names, ethnicity, and race see Cope, *The Limits*, 55–67.

41. Vaughan, "Primary Education," 37, based on Lira's work.

42. This assessment is also backed in the association of signature with don status and patterns in family names (family names common among *castas* had a lower signature rate).

43. Signature was missing in 23% of the cases. The missing attribute was imputed using occupation and "age heaping," both variables that have a very high degree of correlation with signature. Age heaping stands for the abnormal proportion of cases in ages that are multiple of five (e.g., 20, 25, and so on), and it is an indicator of quantitative literacy, closely associated to other forms of human capital. Soldiers with a rounded age were 10% less likely to sign their forms than other soldiers. On quantitative literacy, see A'Hearn, Baten and Crayen, "Quantifying Quantitative Literacy: Age Heaping and the History of Human Capital."

44. Occupation was available for a large number of cases, but it was not used in the analysis of heights because literacy and skin color captured most of the variation of height and were more consistent categories over the entire time period.

45. Cook, "The Population of Mexico in 1793," table 8. Commercial-professional includes Cook's groups II and III and students (originally in group I). Group VI (tribute contributors) was removed from calculations. I included cases with no reported occupation in the military records in the unskilled group. The statistical report on Querétaro in del Raso, "Notas estadísticas," 214; the proportions (following Cook's classification) were 4% commercial and professional, 14% skilled and semi-skilled, and 82% unskilled.

46. The *labradores* were 21% of the sample, compared to 23% in the 1793 census; dependent workers (*gañanes, jornaleros, and mineros*) were 38% and 60%, respectively. The proportions hold when cases not meeting the height requirement are reported, suggesting these differences are related to recruiting.

47. The colonial army excluded Indians and preferred Spaniards over other categories, although the practice of recruitment widely varied with the official instructions (see Archer, *The Army in Bourbon Mexico*, 235; Vinson, *Bearing Arms*). After independence, recruitment was not officially based on race, but the national army faced strong opposition from Indians to enroll and eventually desisted from this attempt in 1853 (see DePalo, *The Mexican National Army*; Guardino, *The Time of Liberty*, 253–254).

48. Most of the soldiers were both native and resident from the same place. The comparison between places of residence and of origin shows that migration was common but intraregional; a similar conclusion is in the literature: Haslip-Viera, "The Underclass"; Garavaglia and Grosso, *Puebla*; Moreno Toscano and Aguirre Anaya, "Migrations."

49. This regional characterization is based on Miño Grijalva, *El mundo novohispano*, 119–269; McCaa, "The Peopling," 608; Tutino, *From Insurrection to Revolution*. On the north-south gradient, see Kelly, *Physical Anthropology*; López-Alonso, "Height."

50. The regional proportions *ca.* 1800 were taken from Tutino, *From Insurrection to Revolution*, 392.

51. With the exception of Querétaro, these were also seats of intendancies (1786–1824).

52. The list of villas was extracted from Humboldt, "Tablas geográficas políticas."

53. The percent of the population in capitals and *villas* was derived from Humboldt, and *Estadísticas Históricas de México*, Cuadros 1.3. On the urbanization rate, see Miño Grijalva, *El mundo novohispano*, 37.

54. Cook, "The Population of Mexico in 1793."

55. A'Hearn, "A Restricted"; A'Hearn, "Anthropometric Evidence"; Komlos, "An Anthropometric History"; Komlos, "How to (and How Not to)."

56. In interpreting the significance I pay more attention to magnitudes and the logical importance of the relationships; see Ziliak and McCloskey, *The Cult of Statistical Significance*. On sample sizes and anthropometric analysis, see Komlos, "How to (and How Not to)."

57. See López-Alonso, chap. 3 in this collection, and Kelly, *Physical Anthropology*.

58. In this approach to account for potential measurement and recruitment differences, I follow A'Hearn, "Anthropometric Evidence."

59. The official conversion tables, for instance, diverged: in 1857 one Mexican inch was equal to 2.328 cm, later corrected to 2.325861; see *Guía para el conocimiento*; Ministerio de Justicia y Fomento, *Sistema Métrico*. The conversion factor given by a dictionary from 1825 was 2.3196 cm per Mexican inch. Similarly, the customary Paris-to-Burgos ratios given in the contemporary literature (31:36 inches and 6:7 feet) imply slight differences as well. In short, the conversion between measurement units has some uncertainty that is accounted for in the dummy variable.

60. Estimated height gain by age is consistent with López-Alonso, "Growth with Inequality," 100, and Komlos, "An Anthropometric History," 184.

61. Given how consistently the sigma is estimated across the specifications in tables 2–4, I did not constrain the dispersion of the truncated regression. On the discussion of this issue, see A'Hearn, "A Restricted"; Komlos, "How to (and How Not to)."

62. For instance, Wald tests on the differences between the coefficient for the 1760s and the 1810s (and afterward) reject the hypothesis that the difference was zero at the 0.05 threshold; Wald tests on the difference between the 1740s and the 1780s and afterwards return similar results. The comparison between the 1790s and later cohorts can be directly obtained by looking up the third column in Table 2.

63. The 3-cm increase in heights can partially be accounted for by differences in the sample: the Federal army was a volunteer force, while the national army in the early and mid nineteenth century relied extensively on the levy and lottery. I have not reported results for Mexican inmates in nineteenth-century prisons of the Southwest United States, in Carson, "Biological Standard," 415, because the underlying demographic is too different from the other figures reported here.

64. Komlos, "An Anthropometric History," 183–185; A'Hearn, "Anthropometric Evidence," 371–373. In Argentina heights also declined from 1785 to 1805, see Salvatore, "Heights and Welfare," 107.

65. Besides the cases cited by A'Hearn and Komlos, the United States, Argentina, and Great Britain through the 1830s also conform to the pattern of improvement or stagnation; see Costa and Steckel, "Long-term Trends," 51, for data on the United States.

66. Florescano, *Precios del maíz*, 127.

67. Komlos, "An Anthropometric History"; A'Hearn, "Anthropometric Evidence," 377.

68. Swan, "Mexico in the Little Ice Age"; Ouweneel, *Shadows over Anáhuac*, 72–100; Endfield, "Climate and Crisis in Eighteenth Century Mexico."

69. See Florescano and Swan, *Breve historia de la sequía en México*, 18–20, and 119–149; Magaña et al., "Impact of El Niño"; Tiscareño López et al., "Modeling."

70. Challú, "Agricultural Crisis," 31.

71. García-Herrera et al., "Chronology of El Niño Events."

72. The annual height series was estimated with the same variables as the decadal model. Birth years with fewer than four cases were removed from the analysis; of the remaining 98 years, the median number of cases is 27. Given the lower frequencies, the annual series loses precision but still captures the overarching trend.

73. The only exception is the 1817–1819 event, which was accompanied by a decline in height. However, this event was deemed as "possible" in García-Herrera's series; the other sequences of events were deemed as "probable."

74. On this index see Challú, "Agricultural Crisis," 28–30. The price index includes corn, wheat, and *frijol* beans, with weights set at 50%, 30% and 20% respectively. For the wage component I used unskilled construction workers' wages. There is a high correlation of food prices and these wages in Mexico's major cities in the late colonial period.

75. The five-year moving window is intended to reflect that El Niño events are frequently preceded or followed by La Niña events, which also have disturbing effects on agricultural production. The use of the annual indicator mitigates the effects but not the interpretation presented here.

76. This was estimated by calculating the sum of the effects of the variables using the average values for the 1740s and 1830s, and estimating the total effect relative to the measured change in height.

77. Van Young, "The Rich Get Richer."

78. The *filiaciones* frequently distinguish between the locality and the jurisdiction, and that the *cabecera* name is then used as the jurisdiction.

79. Martínez-Carrión and Moreno-Lázaro, "Was there an Urban Height Penalty"; Reis, "Urban Premium."

80. On public works see, for instance, Cruz Velázquez, "Política sanitaria"; Diaz-Trechuelo Espinosa, Pajarón Parody and Rubio Gil, "El virrey Don Juan Vicente," 109–113; Riley, "Public Works"; León Mesa, "Servicios públicos." In the two decades after the outbreak of insurgency, public provisioning declined, at least in Mexico City; see Miño Grijalva, "Población y abasto," 26–31.

81. Challú, "Grain Markets," 162–289.
82. See De Waal, *Famine That Kills.* De Waal proposes that famine should be primarily seen as a threat to a way of life, rather than as massive death due to starvation. Peasants' responses primarily attempt to counter the risk of becoming destitute and losing land and capital.
83. On migration to cities motivated by shortages, see Miño Grijalva, "Población y abasto," 27.
84. *Estadísticas históricas de México*, table 1.3.
85. Dobado González, Gómez Galvarriato and Williamson, "Globalization."
86. Brading, *Haciendas and Ranchos*, 201–204.
87. Miller, "The Mexican Hacienda."
88. Brading, *Haciendas and Ranchos*, 82–85.
89. Chowning, *Wealth and Power*, 160–175. Similarly, Garavaglia and Grosso, *Puebla*, shows a recovery of hacienda agriculture in the Puebla region by the 1830s.
90. del Raso, "Notas estadísticas," 214.
91. Considered from a political economic perspective, this can be understood as a problem of persistence of elite power in a context of profound political change; see Acemoglu and Robinson, "Persistence of Power, Elites, and Institutions."
92. Compare with Moramay López-Alonso's chapter in this book (Table 3).
93. McCaa, "The Peopling"; Tutino, *From Insurrection to Revolution*; Tutino, "The Revolution in Mexican Independence." For a similar argument, that inequality declined (albeit briefly) after independence, see Williamson, "Five Centuries."
94. Hoffman et al., "Real Inequality," 351.
95. This idea is based on Tilly, "Food Entitlement, Famine, and Conflict" and Tilly, "Food Supply."

References

A'Hearn, B., J. Baten, and D. Crayen. "Quantifying Quantitative Literacy: Age Heaping and the History of Human Capital." *Universitat Pompeu Fabra Economics Working Paper* 996 (2006).
A'Hearn, Brian. "A Restricted Maximum Likelihood Estimator for Truncated Height Samples." *Economics and Human Biology* 2 (2004): 5–19.
———. "Anthropometric Evidence on Living Standards in Northern Italy, 1730–1830." *Journal of Economic History* 63, no. 2 (2003): 351–381.
Acemoglu, Daron, and James A. Robinson. "Persistence of Power, Elites, and Institutions." *American Economic Review* 98, no. 1 (2006): 267–293.
Archer, Christon I. *The Army in Bourbon Mexico, 1760–1810.* Albuquerque: University of New Mexico Press, 1977.
Arrillaga, Basilio José. *Recopilación de leyes, decretos, bandos, reglamentos, circularos y providencias de los supremos poderes y otras autoridades de la República Mexicana.* Mexico: Impr. de A. Boix, 1861.
Blázquez Domínguez, Carmen, Carlos Contreras Cruz, and Sonia Pérez Toledo, eds. *Población y estructura urbana en México, siglos XVIII y XIX.* Xalapa: Universidad Veracruzana, 1996.

Bogin, Barry, and Ryan Keep. "Eight Thousand Years of Economic and Political History in Latin America Revealed by Anthropometry." *Annals of Human Biology* 26, no. 4 (1999): 333–351.

Brading, David, and Celia Wu. "Population Growth and Crisis: Leon, 1720–1860." *Journal of Latin American Studies* 5, no. 1 (1973): 1–36.

Brading, David A. *Haciendas and Ranchos in the Mexican Bajío. León 1760–1860.* Cambridge: Cambridge University Press, 1978.

Calderón de la Barca, Frances. *Life in Mexico.* Berkeley: University of California Press, 1982.

Calvo, Thomas. "Démographie historique d'une paroisse mexicaine: Acatzingo (1606–1810)." *Cahiers des Amériques Latines* 6 (1972): 7–42.

Cámara Hueso, Antonio D. "Fuentes antropométricas en España: problemas metodológicos para los siglos XVIII y XIX." *Historia Agraria* 38 (2006): 105–118.

Cámara, Antonio D. "Long-Term Trends in Height in Rural Eastern Andalucia." *Historia Agraria* 47 (2009): 45–67.

Carrera Stampa, Manuel. "The Evolution of Weights and Measures in New Spain." *Hispanic American Historical Review* 29, no. 1 (1949): 2–24.

Carson, Scott Alan. "The Biological Standard of Living in 19th century Mexico and in the American West." *Economics and Human Biology* 3, no. 3 (2005): 405–419.

Challú, Amílcar. "Grain Markets, Food Supply Policies and Living Standards in Late Colonial Mexico." Ph.D. Dissertation, Harvard University, 2007.

———. "Agricultural Crisis and Biological Well-Being in Mexico, 1730–1835." *Historia Agraria* 47 (2009): 21–44.

Chowning, Margaret. *Wealth and Power in Provincial Mexico: Michoacán from the Late Colony to the Revolution.* Stanford: Stanford University Press, 1999.

Coatsworth, John H. "Obstacles to Economic Growth in Nineteenth-Century Mexico." *American Historical Review* 83, no. 1 (1978): 80–100.

Commons, Aurea. *Las Intendencias de la Nueva España.* Mexico City: Universidad Nacional Autónoma de México, 1993.

Cook, Sherburne F. "The Population of Mexico in 1793." *Human Biology* 14 (1942): 499–515.

Cooper, Donald B. *Epidemic Disease in Mexico City, 1761–1813.* Austin: Texas University Press, 1965.

Cope, R. Douglas. *The Limits of Racial Domination: Plebeian Society in Colonial Mexico City, 1660–1720.* Madison: The University of Wisconsin Press, 1994.

Costa, Dora L., and Richard H. Steckel. "Long-term Trends in Health, Welfare, and Economic Growth in the United States." In *Health and Welfare during Industrialization*, ed. Richard H. Steckel and Roderick Floud, 47–89. Chicago: University of Chicago Press, 1997.

Cruz Velázquez, Romeo. "La política sanitaria en Veracruz de 1790 a 1820." In *Población y estructura urbana en México, siglos XVIII y XIX*, ed. Carmen Blázquez Domínguez, Carlos Contreras Cruz, and Sonia Pérez Toledo, 187–198. Xalapa: Universidad Veracruzana, 1996.

DePalo, Jr., William A. *The Mexican National Army, 1822–1852.* College Station: Texas A&M University Press, 1997.

De Waal, Alexander. *Famine That Kills: Darfur, Sudan.* New York: Oxford University Press, 2005.

del Raso, José Antonio. "Notas estadísticas del departamento de Querétaro, formadas por la asamblea constitucional del mismo, y remitidas al supremo gobierno, en cumplimiento de la parte primera del artículo 135 de las Bases Orgánicas." *Boletín de la Sociedad Mexicana de Geografía y Estadística* Tomo III (1852): 171–223.

Díaz-Trechuelo Espinosa, María Lourdes, Concepción Pajarón Parody, and Adolfo Rubio Gil. "El virrey Don Juan Vicente de Güemes Pacheco, Segundo Conde de Revillagigedo." In *Los Virreyes de Nueva España en el reinado de Carlos III*, ed. José Antonio Calderón Quijano, 85–366. Sevilla: Escuela Gráfica Salesiana, 1967.

Dobado Gonzáles, Rafael. "Precios y salarios en la Nueva España borbónica en perspectiva internacional comparada." Paper presented at the Tercer Congreso Internacional de Historia Económica de la AMHE, Cuernavaca, 2007.

Dobado Gonzáles, Rafael, and Héctor García. "Neither So Low Nor So Short! Wages and Heights in Eighteenth and Early Nineteenth Centuries Colonial Latin America." Paper presented at A Comparative Approach to Inequality and Development: Latin America and Europe, Madrid, 2009.

Dobado González, Rafael, Aurora Gómez Galvarriato, and Jeffrey Williamson. "Mexican Exceptionalism: Globalization and De-Industrialization, 1750–1877." *The Journal of Economic History* 68, no. 3 (2008): 758–811.

Dobado, Rafael, and Gustavo A. Marrero. "The 'Mining-Led Growth' in Bourbon Mexico, the Role of the State and the Economic Cost of Independence." Boston Area Latin American History Workshop, Harvard University, 2006.

Endfield, Georgina H. "Climate and Crisis in Eighteenth Century Mexico." *The Medieval History Journal* 10, no. 1–2 (2007): 99–125.

Endfield, Georgina H., and Sarah L. O'Hara. "Degradation, Drought, and Dissent: An Environmental History of Colonial Michoacan, West Central Mexico." *Annals of the Association of American Geographers* 89, no. 3 (1999): 402–419.

———."Conflicts over Water in 'The Little Drought Age' in Central Mexico." *Environment and History* 3 (1997): 255–272.

Estadísticas históricas de México. 3rd ed. Aguascalientes: Instituto Nacional de Estadística, Geografía e Informática, 1994.

Falcón, Ignacio. *Plana Mayor del Exército. Noticia Histórica.* 1845.

Fernández Tejedo, Isabel, Georgina Endfield, and Sarah O'Hara. "Estrategias para el control del agua en Oaxaca colonial." *Estudios de Historia Novohispana* 31 (2004): 137–198.

Florescano, Enrique. *Precios del maíz y crisis agrícolas en México (1708–1810).* Mexico City: El Colegio de México, 1969.

Florescano, Enrique, and Susan Swan. *Breve historia de la sequía en México.* Xalapa: Universidad Veracruzana, 1995.

Fogel, Robert. "Economic Growth, Population Theory and Physiology." *American Economic Review* 84 (1994): 369–395.

García Acosta, Virginia. *Los precios del trigo en la historia colonial de México*. Mexico City: Ediciones de la Casa Chata, 1988.

García-Herrera, Ricardo, Henry F. Díaz, Rolando R. García, María del Rosario Prieto, David Barriopedro, Rodolfo Moyano, and Emiliano Hernández. "A Chronology of El Niño Events from Primary Documentary Sources in Northern Perú." *Journal of Climate* 21, no. 9 (2008): 1948–1962.

Garner, Richard. "Price Trends in Eighteenth-Century Mexico." *Hispanic American Historical Review* 65, no. 2 (1985): 279–326.

———. "Economic History Data Desk," Economic History Data Desk.

Gerhard, Peter. *A Guide to the Historical Geography of New Spain*, rev. ed. Norman: University of Oklahoma Press, 1993.

Guardino, Peter F. *The Time of Liberty: Popular Political Culture in Oaxaca, 1750–1850*. Durham: Duke University Press, 2005.

Guía para el conocimiento de monedas y medidas de los principales mercados de Europa, en las operaciones del comercio, con una noticia de las dimensiones de las medidas de áridos y agrarias que se usan en los Estados Unidos Mexicanos. Mexico City: Oficina de Ontiveros, 1825.

Haslip-Viera, Gabriel. "The Underclass." In *Cities and Society in Colonial Latin America*, ed. Louisa Schell Hoberman and Susan Migden Socolow. Albuquerque: University of New Mexico Press, 1986.

———. *Crime and Punishment in Late Colonial Mexico City, 1692–1810*. Albuquerque: University of New Mexico Press, 1999.

Hoffman, Philip T., David S. Jacks, Patricia A. Levin, and Peter Lindert. "Real Inequality in Europe since 1500." *Journal of Economic History* 62, no. 2 (2002): 322–355.

Humboldt, Alexander von. "Tablas geográficas políticas del Reyno de Nueva España que manifiestan la superficie, población, agricultura, fábricas, comercio, minas, renta y fuerza militar," 1803, in http://bibliotecadigital.ilcc.edu.mx/sites/humb/humboldt/index.html.

Kelly, Arthur Randolph. *Physical Anthropology of a Mexican Population in Texas: A Study in Race-Mixture*. New Orleans: Middle American Research Institute, Tulane University of Louisiana, 1947.

King, Gary. "Analyzing Incomplete Political Science Data: An Alternative Algorithm for Multiple Imputation." *American Political Science Review* 95, no. 01 (2002): 49–69.

Knight, Alan. *Mexico: The Colonial Era*. Cambridge: Cambridge University Press, 2003.

Komlos, John, ed. *Stature, Living Standards, and Economic Development: Essays in Anthropometric History*. Chicago: The University of Chicago Press, 1994.

Komlos, John. "How to (and How Not to) Analyze Deficient Height Samples." *Historical Methods* 37, no. 1 (2004): 160–173.

————. "An Anthropometric History of Early-Modern France." *Economic History Review* 7, no. 2 (2003): 159–189.

León Mesa, C. René de. "Servicios públicos y conflictos jurisdiccionales entre las autoridades de México y Guadalajara." In *Núcleos urbanos mexicanos, Siglos XVIII y XIX: Mercado, perfiles sociodemográficos y conflictos de autoridad*, 373–400. Mexico City: El Colegio de México, Centro de Estudios Históricos, 2006.

López-Alonso, Moramay. "Height, Health, Nutrition and Wealth: A History of Living Standards in Mexico, 1870–1950." Ph.D. Dissertation, Stanford University, 2000.

————. "The Ups and Downs of Mexican Economic Growth: the Biological Standard of Living and Inequality, 1870–1950." *Economics and Human Biology* 1, no. 2 (2003): 169–186.

————. "Growth with Inequality: Living Standards in Mexico, 1850–1950." *Journal of Latin American Studies* 39, no. 1 (2007): 81–105.

Lucuze, Pedro de. *Disertación sobre las medidas militares que contiene la razón de preferir el uso de las nacionales al de las forasteras*. Madrid: Francisco Furiá y Burgada, 1773.

Lugo Olín, María Concepción. "La población de Cuautitlán durante el siglo XIX." In *Demografía histórica de México: siglos XVI-XIX*, ed. Elsa Malvido, and Miguel Angel Cuenya, 123–137. Mexico City: Instituto Mora, 1993.

Magaña, Victor, Jorge L. Vázquez, José L. Pérez, and Joel B. Pérez. "Impact of El Niño on Precipitation in Mexico." *Geofísica Internacional* 42, no. 3 (2003): 313–330.

Malvido, Elsa. "El cólera morbus de 1833: un cambio en el sistema patológico nacional. Estudio de caso: la ciudad de Puebla." Paper presented at the IV Encuentro de la ADHILAC, Tlaxcala, 1991.

————. "Factores de despoblación y de reposición de la población de Cholula en la época colonial (1641–1810)." In *Demografía histórica de México: siglos XVI-XIX*, ed. Elsa Malvido, and Miguel Angel Cuenya, 63–111. Mexico City: Instituto Mora, 1993.

Malvido, Elsa, and Miguel Angel Cuenya, eds. *Demografía histórica de México: siglos XVI-XIX*. Mexico City: Instituto Mora, 1993.

Márquez Morfín, Lourdes. *La desigualdad ante la muerte en la ciudad de México. El tifo y el cólera*. Mexico City: Siglo XXI, 1994.

————. "Unequal in Death as in Life: A Sociopolitical Analysis of the 1813 Mexico City Typhus Epidemic." In *Building a New Biocultural Synthesis. Political-Economic Perspectives on Human Biology*, ed. Alan H. Goodman and Thomas L. Leatherman, 229–242. Ann Arbor: The University of Michigan Press, 1998.

Martínez-Carrión, José Miguel, and J. Moreno-Lázaro. "Was there an Urban Height Penalty in Spain 1840–1913?" *Economics and Human Biology* 5 (2007): 144–164.

McCaa, Robert. "The Peopling of Nineteenth-Century Mexico: Critical Scrutiny of a Censured Century." *Statistical Abstract of Latin America* 30, no. 1 (1993): 602–633.

————. "The Peopling of Mexico from the Origins to Revolution." In *A Population History of North America*, ed. Michael R. Haines and Richard H. Steckel, 241–304. Cambridge: Cambridge University Press, 2000.

"Medidas y pesos en la República Mexicana." In *Diccionario Universal de Historia y Geografía*. Mexico City: 1854.

Meisel, Adolfo, and Margarita Vega. "The Biological Standard of Living (and Its Convergence) in Colombia, 1870–2003." *Economics and Human Biology* 5, no. 1 (2007): 100–122.

Miller, Simon. "The Mexican Hacienda between the Insurgency and the Revolution: Maize Production and Commercial Triumph on the Temporal." *Journal of Latin American Studies* 16 (1984): 309–336.

Ministerio de Guerra y Marina. *Reglas que deberán observarse para el sorteo del ejército permanente y activo*. Mexico City: 1853.

Ministerio de Justicia y Fomento. *Sistema Métrico-Decimal*. Mexico City: Imprenta de Vicente García Torres, 1862.

Miño Grijalva, Manuel. *El mundo novohispano: Población, ciudades y economía, siglos XVII y XVIII*. Mexico City: El Colegio de México and Fondo de Cultura Económica, 2001.

———. "Población y abasto de alimentos en la ciudad de México, 1730–1838." In *Núcleos urbanos mexicanos, Siglos XVIII y XIX: Mercado, perfiles sociodemográficos y conflictos de autoridad*, 19–70. Mexico City: El Colegio de México, Centro de Estudios Históricos, 2006.

Moreno Toscano, Alejandra, and Carlos Aguirre Anaya. "Migrations to Mexico City in the Nineteenth Century: Research Approaches." *Journal of Interamerican Studies and World Affairs* 17, no. 1 (1975): 27–42.

Morin, Claude. "Population et épidémies dans une paroisse mexicaine: Santa Inés Zacatelco (XVIIe–XIXe siécles)." *Cahiers des Amériques Latines* 6 (1972): 43–74.

Oliver, Lilia. "La pandemia del cólera morbus. El caso de Guadalajara, Jal., en 1833." In *Ensayos sobre la historia de las epidemias en México*, ed. Enrique Florescano, and Elsa Malvido, 565–581. Mexico City: IMSS, 1982.

Osmani, S.R., ed. *Nutrition and Poverty*. Oxford: Oxford University Press, 1992.

Ouweneel, Arij. *Shadows over Anáhuac: An Ecological Interpretation of Crisis and Development in Central Mexico, 1730–1800*. Albuquerque: University of New Mexico Press, 1996.

———. *Ciclos Interrumpidos*. Mexico City: El Colegio Mexiquense, 1998.

Pilcher, Jeffrey M. *Que vivan los tamales! Food and the Making of Mexican Identity*. Albuquerque: University of New Mexico Press, 1998.

Ponzio, Carlos. "Globalisation and Economic Growth in the Third World: Some Evidence from Eighteenth-Century Mexico." *Journal of Latin American Studies* 37, no. 3 (2005): 437–467.

Reis, Jaime. "'Urban Premium' or 'Urban Penalty'? The Case of Lisbon, 1840–1912." *Historia Agraria* 47 (2009): 69–94.

Riley, James D. "Public Works and Local Elites: The Politics of Taxation in Tlaxcala, 1780–1810." *The Americas* 58, no. 3 (2002): 355–393.

Rojas, Beatriz. *Las instituciones de gobierno y la élite local: Aguascalientes del siglo XVII hasta la independencia*. Zamora, Mich.: El Colegio de Michoacán and Instituto Mora, 1998.

Salvatore, Ricardo. "Heights and Welfare in Late-Colonial and Post-Independence Argentina." In *The Biological Standard of Living in Comparative Perspective*, ed. John Komlos and Joerg Baten, 97–121. Stuttgart: Franz Steiner Verlag, 1998.

Salvatore, Ricardo, and Joerg Baten. "A Most Difficult Case of Estimation: Argentinian Heights, 1770–1840." In *The Biological Standard of Living in Comparative Perspective*, ed. John Komlos and Joerg Baten, 90–96. Stuttgart: Franz Steiner Verlag, 1998.

Salvucci, Richard. "Mexican National Income in the Era of Independence, 1800–1840." In *How Latin America Fell Behind: Essays on the Economic Histories of Brazil and Mexico, 1800–1914*, ed. Stephen Haber, 216–242. Stanford: Stanford University Press, 1997.

Secretaría de Guerra y Marina. *Memoria de la Secretaría de Estado y del Despacho de la Guerra y Marina, Leída por el Escmo. Sr. General D. José María Cornel en la Cámara de Diputados el día 7 de enero de 1839 y en la de senadores el 8 del mismo.* Mexico City: 1839.

Steckel, Richard H. "Stature and the Standard of Living." *Journal of Economic Literature* 33, no. 4 (1995): 1903–1940.

———. "Strategic Ideas in the Rise of the New Anthropometric History and Their Implications for Interdisciplinary Research." *Journal of Economic History* 58, no. 3 (1998): 803–821.

———. "Heights and Human Welfare: Recent Developments and New Directions." *Explorations in Economic History* 46, no. 1 (2009): 1–23.

Super, John C., and Luis Alberto Vargas. "Mexico and Highland Central America." In *The Cambridge World History of Food*, ed. Kenneth F. Kiple and Kriemhild Coneé Ornelas, 1248–1254. Cambridge: Cambridge University Press, 2000.

Swan, Susan L. "Mexico in the Little Ice Age." *Journal of Interdisciplinary History* 11, no. 4 (1981): 633–648.

Thomson, Guy P. C. *Puebla de los Angeles: Industria y sociedad de una ciudad mexicana, 1700–1850.* Puebla: Benemérita Universidad Autónoma de Puebla, 2002.

Tilly, Charles. "Food Supply and Public Order in Modern Europe." In *The Formation of National States in Western Europe*, ed. Charles Tilly, 380–455. Princeton: Princeton University Press, 1975.

Tilly, Louise A. "Food Entitlement, Famine, and Conflict." *Journal of Interdisciplinary History* 14, no. 2 (1983): 333–349.

Tiscareño López, Mario, César Izaurralde, Norman Rosenberg, Alma Delia Báez González, and Jaime Salinas García. "Modeling El Niño Southern Oscillation Climate Impact on Mexican Agriculture." *Geofísica Internacional* 42, no. 3 (2003): 331–339.

Tutino, John. *From Insurrection to Revolution in Mexico: Social Bases of Agrarian Violence, 1750–1940.* Princeton: Princeton University Press, 1986.

———. "The Revolution in Mexican Independence: Insurgency and the Renegotiation of Property, Production, and Patriarchy in the Bajío, 1800–1855." *Hispanic American Historical Review* 78, no. 3 (1998): 367–418.

Van Young, Eric. "Conflict and Solidarity in Indian Village Life: The Guadalajara Region in the Late Colonial Period." *Hispanic American Historical Review* 64, no. 1 (1984): 55–79.

———. "The Age of Paradox: Mexican Agriculture at the End of the Colonial Period, 1750–1810." In *The Economies of Mexico and Peru during the Late Colonial Period, 1760–1810*, ed. N. Jacobsen and H.-J. Puhle, 64–90. Berlin: Colloquium Verlag, 1986.

———. "The Rich Get Richer and the Poor Get Skewed: Real Wages and Popular Living Standards in Late Colonial Mexico." Paper presented at the All-UC Economic History Conference, 1987.

Vaughan, Mary Kay. "Primary Education and Literacy in Nineteenth-Century Mexico: Research Trends, 1968–1988." *Latin American Research Review* 25, no. 1 (1990): 31–66.

Velasco, María del Pilar. "La epidemia del cólera de 1833 y la mortalidad en la Ciudad de México." *Estudios Demográficos y Urbanos* 7, no. 1 (1992).

Vinson, Ben. *Bearing Arms for His Majesty: The Free-Coloured Militia in Colonial Mexico*. Stanford: Stanford University Press, 2001.

Weir, David. "Economic Welfare and Physical Well-Being in France, 1750–1990." In *Health and Welfare during Industrialization*, ed. Richard H. Steckel and Roderick Floud, 161–200. Chicago: University of Chicago Press, 1997.

Williamson, Jeffrey. "Five Centuries of Latin American Inequality." NBER Working Paper Series no. 15305, National Bureau of Economic Research, August 2009.

Ziliak, Stephen Thomas, and Deirdre N. McCloskey. *The Cult of Statistical Significance: How the Standard Error Costs Us Jobs, Justice, and Lives*. Ann Arbor: University of Michigan Press, 2008.

3

Living Standards of the Mexican Laboring Classes, 1850–1950: An Anthropometric Approach

Moramay López-Alonso

Mexican historiography is prolific in the study of the emergence of the industrial working classes between 1850 and 1950, but it fails to address the issue of living standards explicitly. There is also an extensive historiography on the peasantry, and it has the same shortcomings. Interestingly, the decline in living standards is frequently mentioned as a cause of the social and political tensions that developed during this period. At the same time, economists interested in development, growth, and convergence issues in Latin America have stressed the need to study the evolution of living standards in a long-term perspective. Yet most such studies cover only the period since 1950; one study has noted that the data series available do not go back further in time and those that do are not reliable.[1] This is correct. There have been recent attempts to calculate estimations for the Latin American region covering a longer period of time, but these studies often fail to give an accurate picture of each country because certain measures, such as inequality, are not captured in data series constructed to draw multinational comparisons.[2]

There are many ways to conceptualize and measure living standards.[3] The most common methods use material indicators such as GDP per capita, real wages, life expectancy, and literacy. Using such indicators for Mexico presents several difficulties because, prior to 1940, the information available on GDP per capita, mortality, demographic data, real wages, and prices is scattered and/or unreliable.

This chapter seeks to fill this void in the literature by using anthropometric measures to assess the evolution of living standards of the Mexican population from a long-term perspective, as has been done for other countries in the world.[4] It concentrates on physical stature as a measure of an aspect of the quality of life, the biological standard of living. More specifically, it focuses on adult stature, which is a reflection of the quality of health and nutrition during childhood.

Richard Steckel suggests that in analyzing stature and living standards, one should take into consideration three equally important elements: 1) the timing of industrialization relative to the recognition of the germ theory of disease and public health; 2) the extent of urbanization; and 3) diet.[5] I will incorporate these elements in the sections below to show that in Mexico industrialization, recognition of the germ theory of disease, and understanding of the importance of public health systems took place at basically the same time. Urbanization was rather incipient until the 1920s. Traditional diet prevailed in most of the country for the whole period; cities, however, had a wider variety of foodstuffs, and in the north and the Bajío region meat intake was higher.

I use databases of heights of the recruits to the cavalry corps and federal army, all of them members of the laboring classes. By laboring classes I mean all the people at work in the various sectors of the economy, both formal and informal; this definition does not include people belonging to the upper strata of the population or indigents.

The period 1850–1950 is relevant to study the evolution of the biological standards of living in Mexico for three basic reasons. First, during this period Mexico underwent deep social, political, and economic transformations when its leaders recognized the need to improve the standards of living of the population by creating social welfare institutions, even if different leaders were moved by different political reasons.[6] Second, it was a time when Mexico experienced at least two waves of industrialization and economic growth.[7] Moreover, following the trajectory of developed Western countries, many technological innovations were adopted, some of which helped to improve the quality of public health in the growing cities.[8] Thus, the Mexican nation was not only experiencing economic recovery for most of this time period; governments also undertook construction of public works and launched health-care programs that resulted in the improvement of biological standards of living of those who had access to these services.[9] The third reason concerns the Revolution of 1910 in which the popular classes were deeply involved, generally with the common goal of improving their living conditions by either improving their working conditions and raising their wages in the case of the expanding industrial proletariat, or in the case of the peasantry, by recovering lands that had been seized from them in the previous half century as a result of the Reform Laws of the 1850s or as a result of the survey of public lands during the last quarter of the nineteenth century.[10]

During these hundred years, I argue, Mexico underwent some positive transformations that were accompanied by periods of sustained economic growth. Under those circumstances, living standards could have improved significantly, yet this does not appear to have been the case for the laboring classes. The benefits of economic growth and public health were too unevenly distributed to have a positive impact on the living standards of the whole population as they did not reach a substantial portion of the lower-income groups. Failure to benefit more of the population during Porfirio Díaz's regime (1876–1910) had to do with the motivations to undertake investments for this purpose in the first place. Public health and public works programs during the Díaz regime were the initiative of members of Díaz's cabinet who wished to emulate what the Western world was doing in order to gain the endorsement of the international community and thus become part of the group of "modern nations." These public health initiatives did not seek to close the gap in the quality of life across social classes. This explains why most public works were concentrated in the main cities, especially Mexico City, at a time when the great majority of the population lived in the countryside.[11]

The administrations that followed the Díaz regime took over the programs started by the Porfirian policy makers, but labeled the benefits as part of the revolutionary project. As early as 1916, Venustiano Carranza stated that one of the goals of the revolution was securing the nation's social welfare.[12] Reforms proposed in Article 123 of the 1917 Constitution were written to improve the working conditions and legal rights of the industrial proletariat. The purpose of Article 27 was to ameliorate the peasantry's economic and social conditions through an agrarian reform that would redistribute land among those who actually worked it. It is not clear, however, that policy makers were serious about improving living standards beyond the mere amendment of the constitution, whether by enforcing fully such legal changes, or by trying to assess their results. In fact, had government officials actually enforced such changes, the improvements in living standards would have been spectacular, as we will be able to show later when we contrast the results with those of other countries. Although investments continued to be made in social programs in the decades that followed the end of the revolution as much as federal budget and political conditions allowed, public intellectuals directly proceeded to assume, on the basis of stated inputs, that living standards of the population had improved, without making an assessment based on outputs or results.[13]

The remainder of this chapter is divided into four sections. The one below presents an overview of Mexican history to provide the reader with a notion of the social, political, economic, and demographic circumstances that prevailed during this period. The next section describes the sources of data and presents some descriptive statistics. The third section analyzes the trends in height, the compositional effects, and it makes a comparison with other countries. Finally, I draw the main points together into a conclusion.

Historical Overview

After nearly ten years of war, Mexico gained its independence from Spain in 1821. A decade of war left the new-born nation in economic distress. The decades that followed continued to set challenges to the new nation both internally and externally. In the domestic sphere the problems were economic, political, and social. The new government inherited unhealthy public finances; during the last years of colonial rule, the Spanish crown had extracted all the rents it could from silver production to finance its wars. The independent government derived much of its revenue from taxes on trade, but trade had been severely prejudiced by the numerous years of warfare.[14] Although the new government was able to draw resources from the expropriation and sale of the property of the Catholic Church, these resources were poorly allocated for the most part. Agricultural output could fulfill the demand of the population provided there were no droughts, heavy rains, or frosts. Years of bad crops produced handsome gains for speculators while they placed a financial burden on governments that sought to avoid a subsistence crisis. Moreover, lack of political stability made road travel dangerous, thereby increasing the cost of bringing grains into cities. There were constant quarrels between conservatives and liberals over the best way to govern the nation. Such quarrels led to civil warfare.

Further, there were constant threats of foreign invasion as well as threats of secession by frontier provinces. The threats of foreign invasion were the result of Mexico's inability to meet its financial obligations with foreign creditors, as well as the expansionist projects of other nations.[15] Fighting these domestic and international threats was costly to a government already impoverished and lacking credibility in the international markets.

The Mexican nation failed to meet many of its initial challenges. In the early 1820s, much of today's Central America declared its independence from Mexico. In the 1830s, Texas seceded. In the 1840s, the United States annexed nearly half of Mexico's territory. During the 1860s, France invaded and occupied Mexico. Conservatives largely supported the French project, while liberals, led by Benito Juárez, struggled against the French in a guerrilla war.

Meanwhile, public finances were in constant distress for at least four reasons. First, the recurrent internal armed uprisings of liberal or conservative factions and the resulting continuous changes in executive and legislative power added to federal budget expenses. Second, the numerous threats of foreign invasion increased military expenses that also added to the federal bill. Third, in the absence of an income tax, the only source of revenues for the federal government were tariffs on imports and exports, which were hard to collect given the constant state of chaos in the country. Last, default on foreign debt service payments resulted in the loss of financial credibility in the international community, which closed the possibility of loans from abroad. It was no surprise that the government was broke most of the time and that improving the living conditions of the lower classes was not its priority.

Porfirio Diaz seized power in 1876 with the slogan of "order and progress." In order to achieve these goals he had to negotiate with the regional political bosses to restore peace; he also had to signal to both foreign and national investors that he would respect their property rights to attract investments and promote much needed economic growth. He paid dearly for political loyalty, and gave away numerous privileges and entitlements to businessmen to convince them to invest in Mexico. Peace was gradually attained but required continuous surveillance and a more effective and mobile army.[16] Díaz recognized the need for an army that was disciplined and well trained. Within the limitations of the federal budget, he was able to professionalize the federal army.[17] He also reinforced the cavalry in order to minimize the possibility of being overthrown by a military coup; the *Rurales* force, directly loyal to him, was meant to create a counterbalance to the federal army.

Slowly but surely Díaz was able to balance the fiscal budget and regain credibility with the international financial community. In the 1880s, Mexico recognized the foreign debt of former administrations and resumed payments. In 1896 the fiscal budget was balanced for the first time. Economic growth and limited industrialization occurred through export-led growth and by granting tax and tariff exemptions to national and foreign entrepreneurs.[18] Under this development strategy, the main beneficiaries of economic growth and industrialization were the elites with political connections as well as foreign investors. Certainly more jobs were created in commercial agriculture, mining, industry, and transport as new economic activities multiplied and export-led growth took off. With the opening of railway lines it was easier to learn about job opportunities in other areas and to move there without causing a radical separation of people.[19] The increase in labor demand meant that more people would be employed, although this did not automatically translate into better living conditions. If we were to judge by the examples of the first nations to industrialize, we would expect that living standards of the industrial proletariat decreased at first and then improved gradually.[20] However, we should note that in these countries industrialization preceded by several decades the advent of massive construction of public works and the implementation of public health programs. Thus, in Great Britain, France, and the United States, there was industrialization first, and second—nearly a century later—comprehensive public works and public health programs. In Mexico, by contrast, they were coterminous.

The thirty-four-year regime of Porfirio Díaz came to an abrupt end in 1910. Growing discontent among people who failed to benefit from the economic advance led to a political revolution, which submerged the country in a series of popular revolts and political intrigues that lasted for nearly two decades. Interestingly, while this was a period of political instability, it was not one of economic stagnation.[21] Therefore we may suppose that during the revolution and the decades that followed there were no potential stressors that could depress the living standards of the population; at least the damages of the revolution were not as severe as periods of economic stagnation. Moreover, the Mexican industrial proletariat's expectations of better working and living conditions rose as workers from various regions associated in unions. The immediate consequences of revolution for the living standards of the peasantry (the overwhelming majority of the population) are more complex to evaluate, given the degree to which peasants were involved in the fight, the continuation of conflict during the Cristero rebellion, and the targeted improvements in land distribution before Cárdenas' big push for land reform. The decades that followed were devoted to reconstruction and reorganization. In the 1920s, the well-being of the people became one of the major points in the political agenda and one of the leitmotifs of the revolutionary government.

Following the 1910 Revolution, improving social welfare became a priority of all presidential administrations. Unfortunately, at many points in time, this priority did not go beyond the announcement of good intentions. For example, during the 1920s, policies were often implemented in such a way that they could not produce any tangible results, as was the case of land redistribution in many parts of Mexico. It also happened that institutional changes were implemented but results were meager, as was the case of the 1931 Federal Labor Law. The impact of the 1929 world economic crisis and its aftermath were not to blame for the paucity of actions conducive to better social welfare in Mexico, because by 1934 an era of economic prosperity had begun.[22]

Public Health Policies, Demography, and Living Standards

Much has been written on the history of diseases, epidemics, and health practices in Mexico from pre-Columbian to present times.[23] Most of the literature examines specific regions, the history of a particular disease, or a particular epidemic outbreak. The few censuses that were undertaken during the colonial and the early national periods did document this kind of information. But these studies are seldom based on a systematic analysis of data. Yet there is a demographic history of Mexico that is indeed based on a systematic analysis of data and that has reasonably estimated the evolution of population growth, given the quality of data. Since the late 1940s there have been rigorous attempts by demographic historians to calculate the population of the Valley of Mexico on the eve of the Spanish arrival and to gauge the devastating effects of the biological encounter between the new and old worlds. Most of these estimates are the result of joint efforts among demographers, archaeologists, and historians. For subsequent periods, the Spanish Crown continued to gather population data for tribute and tax collection purposes. Unfortunately, during the early years of the independence period (post 1821), the quality of data produced by government agencies declined, in contrast to the colonial period, for lack of funds.

The extant literature thus allows us to assert that at the beginning of its existence as an independent nation, Mexico was a rural society with the demographic characteristics of the Old Regime, namely high fertility and mortality rates.[24] Mexican cities were relatively small and were unhealthy places to live, like most cities in the more developed world. During the nineteenth century there were epidemic outbreaks of cholera, measles, and typhoid in most of the main cities. These epidemics were similar in their symptoms and effects on morbidity and mortality to epidemics in other pre-industrial or industrial societies of the same time period.[25] This similarity is not surprising, given that medical and scientific research was still in its infancy everywhere in the world.[26]

In Mexico, significant institutional changes in health and the provision of social care occurred during the nineteenth century. In the early years of the national period the care of the sick and the poor was still carried out by the Catholic Church. The clergy ran most hospitals, poor houses, and orphanages. Gradually, and as part of the redefinition of the duties of the new nation state, it was decided that all forms of welfare provision should no longer depend entirely on the Catholic Church but rather should be undertaken by the government. In 1841 a council on health matters was created (Consejo Superior de Salubridad) to advise the government on sanitation concerns and regulate the practice of medicine.[27] The state of public finances made this decision difficult to implement, but private lay charities managed by wealthy philanthropists began to take over health initiatives. The decreasing power and wealth of the Church allowed this transition to take place without much struggle. However, the scope of the initiatives of private welfare institutions was rather limited for most of the nineteenth century. The best example of this type of institution is the Mexico City Poor House.[28]

Some studies of the intellectual history of public health policies during the Porfirian era speculate on the beliefs of policy makers on health and welfare matters.[29] From this literature we get a grasp of the intellectual origins of the public health initiatives of the Díaz administration in the 1880s. Mexican scientists were up to date with scientific knowledge and technological advances taking place in the developed world to an extent rarely matched at any other point in the history of Mexico.[30] The adoption of new techniques of measurement became relevant to define the Mexican nation.[31] This was possible due to the conjunction of two favorable facts: first, the country was recovering economically and second, among the *científicos* there was a critical mass of professionals in the medical sciences who were keeping up with scientific research and innovations in Europe and with the debates over public hygiene. Positivist ideology influenced prominent members of the president's cabinet, who sought to transform Mexico into a modern nation. Improving hygiene in accordance with international standards was their starting point. For this it was necessary to organize public health institutions that would be in charge of policy design.

As early as 1879, a public health council was created with a federal budget and a federal consultative group. In the agenda of policy makers, hygiene was considered "as part of the politico-cultural transformation called modernization. . . . Scientific hygiene that emerged in Mexico was of major importance for the betterment of the sanitary conditions of the nation, and it was also indispensable to achieving a modern urban culture."[32] Scientists of that time had to convince policy makers of the importance of their ideas on public hygiene to get them adopted as policy initiatives. The 1889 Sanitary Code was a result of these efforts. Likewise, construction of drainage and sewage systems in Mexico City was undertaken from the late 1880s until 1905. At the same time, there were efforts to provide "hygienic education" to the urban population, with the aim of cleaning the cities, preventing disease, and educating people to clean their homes.[33] These policies were intended in part to improve Mexico's image abroad to attract foreign investments and European migration. Of these two objectives, only the first one was successfully achieved.

At the end of the Porfiriato, public health initiatives had reached only the main cities in Mexico and most of the efforts had been centered on Mexico City.[34] The revolutionary governments were interested in extending the coverage of Porfirian public health policies across the nation as a whole.

One change that transformed the implementation of some public health policies concerned the training orientation of new physicians. During the nineteenth century, most doctors who led the health institutions and policy design were trained in France.[35] In contrast, during the first decades of the twentieth century, as medical research in the United States began to gain importance, a growing number of Mexican medical students began to study there. These doctors returned to Mexico with new ideas on public health.[36] As early as 1920, the Rockefeller Foundation, through its international health division, began a partnership with the Mexican department of public health to introduce health services in rural areas of Mexico. The partnership involved U.S. personnel working for the foundation and Mexican doctors and nurses who had had some training at The Johns Hopkins School of Public Health.[37] The international division of the Rockefeller Foundation launched its programs in places that had some strategic importance for the development of export businesses. It was in their best interest to improve the health conditions of the local population, as healthier people would make better potential workers.[38] And despite the Mexican government's desire to assert its independence vis-à-vis any other nation, it was badly in need of resources to undertake all its programs, so it agreed to receive this help for three decades.[39]

The Rockefeller Foundation programs, however, did not reach all rural regions in need, and the lag in applying public welfare measures in rural areas after the revolution was most probably exacerbated because of the rural exodus and distressed public finances. The rural exodus in the first half of the twentieth century forced government authorities to continue to concentrate their efforts within the cities, yet even so they were not able to keep up with the rapid growth in population. In the cities the divide was between the rich who lived in the central parts of the city with all the comforts of a modern metropolis, and the poor who settled in the periphery in living conditions similar to the pre-industrial city.

In addition to public health policies, it is necessary to take into account population growth. Towards the end of the nineteenth century some changes occurred, bringing Mexico out of its Old Regime pattern. Even if at a slow pace, urbanization was proceeding, along with migration and emigration. There was a slight decline in mortality and fertility rates. This assertion regarding mortality is based on the growth rates that can be inferred from the estimates of total population, changes in the mix of causes of death, and some scattered information on life expectancy for various times and places. Fertility rates declined slightly due to an increase in the age of marriage in contrast to that of the colonial period. Still, the age of first marriage was low and the percentage of women who married was high in comparison to European standards of that time period.[40]

Recent studies reveal a more precise account of the demographic costs of the revolution. There is now little dispute about its being a demographic disaster, although there has been little agreement on the magnitude or on the components of the disaster. The total population declined by approximately a million people between the 1910 and the 1921 censuses. Historians have generally attributed this loss to emigration to the United States, lost births, and war deaths. New calculations have shown that war casualties accounted for most of the loss, making the Mexican Revolution as costly as the Spanish Civil War.[41] It is then surprising that although Mexico suffered the greatest demographic catastrophe of the twentieth century in the Americas, by the 1960s it was already confronting a problematic demographic explosion.

How did this demographic pattern affect the evolution of the biological living standards of Mexico's population? Few studies in Mexican historiography address this question directly. The general view of mid-twentieth-century economic historians is that living standards of the working classes deteriorated during the last decade of the Díaz administration and improved after the revolution.[42] These classic studies are based on two traditional indicators of living standards, namely price and wage series. The disadvantage of these studies is that the data series on which they are based are incomplete. This type of study tends to cover only a specific portion of the population at a specific time period, which provides only a part of the history.

One recent study revisits this topic for the years 1900–1920 and is based on new series constructed for this purpose, which are reliable and provide a more detailed argument on the evolution of living standards. The findings of this study suggest that the living standards of the industrial working classes did not start to deteriorate until the last four years of the Porfiriato, and that during the years of the revolution the armed conflict did not necessarily affect these workers' employment. The revolution favored the strengthening of the labor movement, but from 1914 the rise in prices due to monetary anarchy took a toll on workers' purchasing power; hence their living standards deteriorated.[43]

Sources of Data and Statistics

The primary sources are the recruitment files of inducted soldiers from the military archives of the ministry of defense (Secretaría de la Defensa Nacional, SDN) and the recruitment files of the *Rurales* corps, from the national archives (Archivo General de la Nación, AGN). Both samples contain information such as height, occupation prior to recruitment, literacy, place of birth, age, place and date of recruitment.

The Federales

The data about the federal military (popularly referred to as the *Federales*) are drawn from the Archivo de la Secretaría de la Defensa Nacional. It contains the files of soldiers who are still alive (Sección de Personal Activo) as well as the Sección de Cancelados, which includes the files of deserters and dismissed personnel, and the Sección de Personal Extinto, which has the files of the deceased.[44] It should be noted that this is an army of volunteers, as there was no conscription during the period of study.

To enter the military a man had to: (a) be between the ages of 18 and 45; (b) be a Mexican citizen; (c) be at least 1.60 m tall; (d) have no chronic or contagious diseases, handicap, deafness, or idiocy; (e) have no physical defect "or monstrous or ridiculous appearance"; and (f) understand the Castilian language (Spanish). However, these criteria were not strictly enforced. Height and health were the least enforced requirements, followed to a lesser extent by age and Spanish comprehension. Age and place of birth were self-reported, because birth certificates were not widely issued in Mexico until the 1930s, and parishes did not issue copies of baptismal records. Heights were measured in metric units and rounded to the nearest centimeter at the time of recruitment. The place of recruitment allows us to examine if recruitment was done in places where social unrest was occurring, in regions where density of population was high, or in regions with a strategic importance. Nonetheless, these data are insufficient for inferring migration patterns or drawing comparisons between rural and urban dwellers. For the military it was important to know how many people had enlisted in each of the recruitment centers; the place of origin provided a general idea of who the volunteers were, but there was no further motivation to collect more detailed information about soldiers. Soldiers who were younger than age 18 or older than age 50 are excluded from this analysis.[45] Occupation before joining the army is used to infer the social class of the soldiers.

Rurales

President Benito Juárez formed the rural police in the 1860s for two basic purposes: first, to have an armed force that would report directly to the president;[46] second, to show the public that in the midst of political turmoil and economic stagnation, the government was truly attempting to improve public security. At this time the country was ridden by bandit gangs who robbed and kidnapped on country roads as well as in the cities.[47] The government was under financial stress and it could not afford a large army; as an alternative, Juárez decided to form a mounted rural police force. There was no conscription for this force because it was conceived as a corps of volunteers who would be loyal to the president. They were paid a higher wage than regular soldiers. Recruits, however, had to pay for their weapons, horses, and uniforms, with the cost of these items being deducted from their wages. Hence their higher pay did not mean they earned more than their federal army counterparts. This explains why among the *Rurales* rates of desertion were as high as among federal recruits.

Porfirio Díaz continued to support and make use of the rural police force in the same spirit as his predecessors, resorting to the police to promote political centralization.[48] He gave monetary rewards and political privileges to rural policemen who proved their loyalty to him, devoting a good part of the federal budget to this purpose.[49] With the end of the Díaz administration, the rural police corps broke down; many of its members eventually joined the different factions of revolutionary armies or went back to banditry.

The data for rural soldiers are drawn from the *Legajos de Gobernación* of the 1821–1910 Public Administration section of the AGN. The sample used here covers all recruits between the age of 23 and 50 who served in the rural militia and for whom there is a recorded numeric stature.[50] The data set has 6820 soldiers. The recruits of this corps came mainly from the Bajío, fewer from the center; very few from the north. Half of them came from rural areas and the rest from small towns and cities.[51] More than half of the recruits were landless peasants or mine workers, a third were artisans. The average age of recruitment was 30 years. Half of them were illiterate. Although this corps was a cavalry division, it did not draw people of higher social standing who would be expected to have horses. *Rurales* could join the force and not own a horse, since one could be provided upon recruitment.[52]

Given the number and type of complaints presented by the civil population against the *Rurales*, it is doubtful that members of this corps actually worked to maintain public security. Corruption was the rule in the management of this army, and disciplinary problems were constant and numerous. Reports are frequent about soldiers stealing weapons and other equipment to resell. It seems from the reports that these men joined the rural force to extract rents while they found something better to do. They often abused their authority in towns where they were stationed. Sometimes they would ally with the local prefect and then become a threat to the population.

Rurales who tired of their position deserted and were able to profit from selling their equipment. In a sense they were cashing in their initial investment required to join the force. It is then not surprising to find that desertion rates were high in spite of the severe punishments for deserters.[53] Tracking down deserters was so expensive that superiors preferred to recruit new soldiers to replace those who left the service. This explains the high number of recruitment records compared to the relatively small size of the corps.[54]

Figure 1.
Four Regions of Mexico.

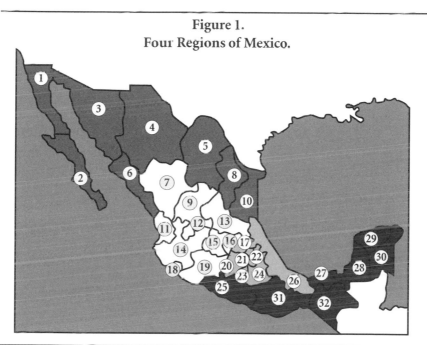

Status	Regional Dummies
Baja California Norte (1), Baja California (2), Sonora (3), Chihuahua (4), Coahuila (5), Sinaloa (6), Nuevo León (8), Tamaulipas (10)	North
Durango (7), Zacatecas (9), Nayarit (11), Aguascalientes (12), San Luis Potosí (13), Jalisco (14), Colima (18), Michoacán (19)	Bajío
Guanajuato (15), Querétaro (16), Hidalgo (17), Estado de México (20), Distrito Federal (21), Tlaxcala (22), Morelos (23), Puebla (24), Veracruz (26)	Center
Guerrero (25), Tabasco (27), Campeche (28), Yucatán (29), Quintana Roo (30), Oaxaca (31), Chiapas (32)	South

Table 1.
Number of Observations by Set of Records and Birth Cohort.

Decade of birth	1840–49	1850–59	1860–69	1870–79	1880–89	1890–99	1900–09	1910–19	1920–29	1930–39	1940–49	Total
Rurales total	345	1232	2097	1432	1194	520						6820
Rurales (>159 cm)	319	1169	1994	1358	1155	463						6458
Rurales (>160 cm)	313	1147	1965	1338	1137	453						6353
Rurales (23 yrs & older)	341	1159	1631	1022	888	7						5048
Federales total				146	525	1687	2350	574	468	287	199	6236
Federales (>159 cm)				131	445	1371	1957	510	364	223	175	5176
Federales (>160 cm)				131	430	1311	1902	492	334	213	163	4976
Federales (23 yrs & older)				118	436	1271	1330	287	290	79	54	3865

Note: Only soldiers older than 18 years are included.
Sources: See text.

Characteristics of the Samples

Sample sizes are reported in Table 1. The recruits of both samples came mostly from the center and the Bajío (center/north) regions (Fig. 1). Men were generally recruited between the ages of 18 and 30. Most of the draftees were working-class males, mainly unskilled workers. Both of these samples contain a very small number of records of recruits who belonged to the better-off classes. Thus my research concentrates mainly on the evolution of standards of living of the laboring classes.[55] I define working classes as unskilled and skilled manual workers who lived in rural and urban areas. Table 2 shows the social-occupational classification I have specified.

It is difficult to define the recruit's social class in this sample according to his occupation prior to recruitment. Historians rightly argue that

Table 2.
Socio-occupational Classification.

Occupational Groups	Occupational Dummies
Labrador (farm worker/farmer)	Unskilled
Campesino (peasant)	Unskilled
Jornalero (laborer)	Unskilled
Obrero (worker)	Unskilled
Minero (miner)	Unskilled
Albañil (construction worker)	Unskilled
Zapatero (shoemaker)	Skilled manual laborer
Talabartero (saddler)	Skilled manual laborer
Tejedor (weaver)	Skilled manual laborer
Sastre (tailor)	Skilled manual laborer
Operario (machine operator)	Skilled manual laborer
Herrero (blacksmith)	Skilled manual laborer
Carpintero (carpenter)	Skilled manual laborer
Curtidor (tanner)	Skilled manual laborer
Comerciante (merchant)	Skilled manual laborer
Panadero (baker)	Skilled manual laborer
Chofer (chauffeur)	Skilled manual laborer
Filarmónico (musician)	Skilled white-collar
Mecanógrafo (typist)	Skilled white-collar
Profesor de instrucción primaria (school teacher)	Skilled white-collar
Tenedor de libros (bookkeeper)	Skilled white-collar
Empleado federal (federal employee)	Skilled white-collar
Propietario (landowner)	Elite
Médico (physician)	Elite
Abogado (lawyer)	Elite
Ingeniero (engineer)	Elite
Estudiante (student)	Students were assigned to their father's occupational category.

Sources: See text.

although occupational analysis is important, potentially it can be misleading because of regional variations in working conditions and compensation. For instance, in order to have a detailed picture of industrial workers' quality of life in this period, what mattered most was where the individual with a particular occupation worked in the productive process. This is one disadvantage of macroeconomic long-term studies vis-à-vis regional, sector-specific studies covering a brief time period.

In the case of the military samples, the army life of the recruits started when they enlisted. Background was not as important as what happened during service. The information recorded at the time of recruitment was gathered to have a general idea of who the individual was in case of desertion. For instance, a typical recruitment record only states that an individual was, say, 25 years of age, born in Silao in the state of Guanajuato, and that the occupation prior to recruitment was *albañil* (construction worker), in addition to his stature of 162 cm. If the soldier served his three-year service or even less time, then one could find a detailed account of how many times he had been arrested and the account of his transgressions, which commonly included spending the night outside of the quarters, being found drunk, smoking marijuana, gambling, being disrespectful to superiors, or showing up at roll call with an untidy uniform. Occasionally, and at best, one finds some information on diseases contracted during service and, if the recruit died, maybe his cause of death. Cases of desertion contain extensive narratives on the different witnesses' accounts of the event.

It is important to point out that heights were not recorded in a strict way, and thus many recruitment files have no record of height. Earlier measurements were recorded in feet, inches, and lines; and it is not uncommon to find height described as small, medium, tall (*bajo, mediano, alto*).[56] The metric system was not officially adopted until 1884, and it was not until years later that its use became widespread. Files lacking a height record were not included in the sample. Only 60% of the files examined had heights, and approximately 60% of the files that did have heights also had complete information on the rest of the variables.[57] In addition, rates of desertion were high in both samples, so it is hard to have a long-term follow-up of these soldiers.

Scholars studying other parts of the world would find it odd that race has not been discussed, especially given the fact that Mexico was a former colony of Spain with a large indigenous population and that during the colonial period slaves were brought from Africa. The classic question is whether there were any racial differences in height. However, race in Mexico during this time period cannot be treated in the same way as in the United States, for instance, for two basic reasons: one biological, the other legal. Miscegenation was common in Mexico since the Conquest among the indigenous peoples, Africans, and Europeans; this was especially true for the popular classes. Although there were classifications for each degree of mixing known as the *castas* system, in practice they were more relevant as elite ideologies to justify their social standing than to map an individual's position in society. Indeed, social historical studies on racial classifications made during the colonial period show that individuals were commonly able to change their racial identity according to their needs.[58] Therefore, from the biological point of view, detailed race differentiation is hard to do on the basis of mere observation. Moreover, soon after the struggles for independence began, the *castas* system was abolished and racial classifications were dropped. By the second half of nineteenth century it was not possible to find a racial category in a military recruitment record since, from the legal point of view, such information was irrelevant.

Analysis of Heights and Compositional Effects

Because of the minimum height requirements in military samples we expect to find a shortfall on the left side of the distribution. Figures 2 and 3 show the histograms of the data bases. In Figure 4 I plot average height by decade of birth using the Komlos and Kim averages on truncated height distributions. This method provides an accurate estimate of the trend, but not of the levels (which are upwardly biased).

The Komlos and Kim method of calculating the trend does not standardize the estimates for the correlates. Therefore is not possible to account for compositional effects. In order to account for these it is necessary to do a regression analysis adapted to truncated samples, using maximum likeli hood methods to estimate the effect of independent variables on height. Truncated regressions provide consistent unbiased estimates of the coefficients of the independent variables, as well as their standard errors, thereby allowing for further statistical inference, such as the calculation of the *t*-values of the estimates.[59] The independent dummy variables include occupation, decade of birth, age, and region of birth (Table 3). Moreover, regressions were run on the adult part of the sample and on the whole sample, including youths (ages 18 to 22). Before examining the trends and their implications, it is important to clarify that Figure 6 corresponds to the sample that only included adults. Moreover, in these specifications the number of *Rurales* born during the 1890s and of the *Federales* born in the 1940s is too small to consider the coefficient reliable. Thus there will be no attempt to explain such observations.

According to the estimated trends, there is an increase in heights for the generation born during the 1840s and 1850s. Interestingly, this finding is consistent with an assessment of the performance of the national economy in the mid-nineteenth century, which asserts that in the 1840s agricultural

Figure 2.
Height Distribution by Recruitment Year: Adult Male *Federales.*

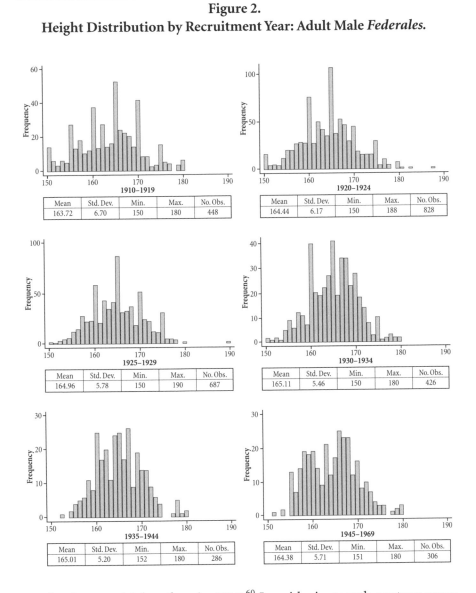

Mean	Std. Dev.	Min.	Max.	No. Obs.
163.72	6.70	150	180	448

1910–1919

Mean	Std. Dev.	Min.	Max.	No. Obs.
164.44	6.17	150	188	828

1920–1924

Mean	Std. Dev.	Min.	Max.	No. Obs.
164.96	5.78	150	190	687

1925–1929

Mean	Std. Dev.	Min.	Max.	No. Obs.
165.11	5.46	150	180	426

1930–1934

Mean	Std. Dev.	Min.	Max.	No. Obs.
165.01	5.20	152	180	286

1935–1944

Mean	Std. Dev.	Min.	Max.	No. Obs.
164.38	5.71	151	180	306

1945–1969

production was higher than in 1810.[60] In mid-nineteenth century more food may have been available, which would explain why soldiers from a rural, laboring-class background were getting taller. In contrast, there is a decline in heights for the generations born in the 1860s and 1870s. This implies that children growing up and attaining their adult height in the 1880s and 1890s were eating less than the previous cohorts. Mexico was still an agricultural nation. The frequently repeated claim that the privatization

Figure 3.
Height Distribution by Recruitment Year: Adult Male *Rurales.*

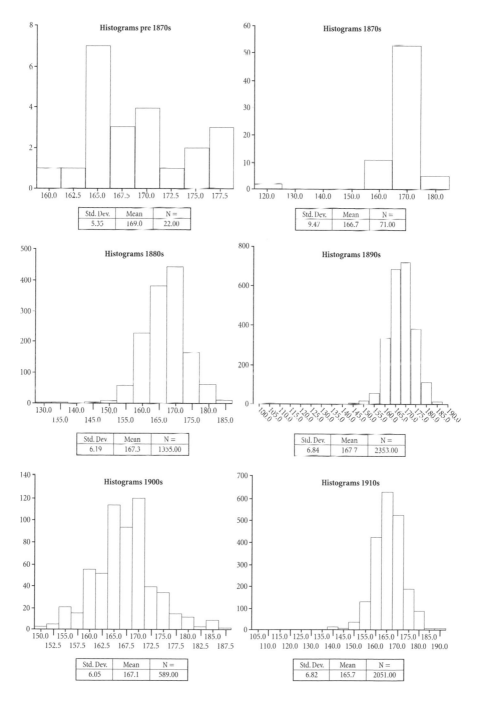

Figure 4.
Mean Heights Using the Komlos and Kim Method.

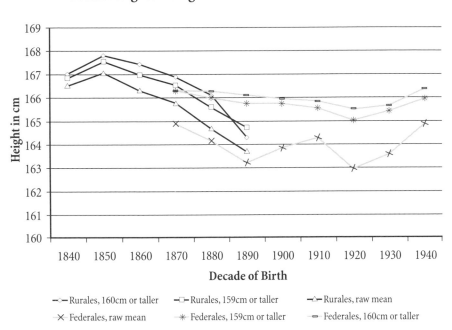

—◇—Rurales, 160cm or taller   —□—Rurales, 159cm or taller   —△—Rurales, raw mean

✕ Federales, raw mean   * Federales, 159cm or taller   — Federales, 160cm or taller

of communal peasant lands as a result of the Lerdo Law and the survey of public lands had a negative effect in the quantity of food available to children and adolescents from peasant families may be valid.

The generations born in the 1880s, 1890s, and 1900s experienced a slight recovery, which indicates that individuals attaining adulthood from 1900 to 1920 were getting more food than those who were born in the two preceding decades. This result indicates that the economic policies launched during the Porfiriato and their by-products, namely export-led growth, incipient industrialization, the development and increase in the means of transportation and the resulting integration of markets, provided some level of relief to the conditions of the popular classes. Yet, if we are to judge by the evolution of stature, their biological standard of living did not return to mid-nineteenth century levels, which implies that any improvement was rather limited.

There is a substantial decline in height for the generation born in the 1910s, that is, children and adolescents who grew up during the armed rebellion and its aftermath in the first years of the post-revolutionary era (1920s). According to the literature applying the New Institutional Eco-

Table 3.
Regression Model: Dependent Variable (height cm).

Independent variables	1. *Federales*		2. *Rurales*	
	160cm (a)	160cm (b)	160cm (a)	160 cm (b)
Constant	167.1*	167.6	169.85*	167.68*
Occupation				
Unskilled	Ref.	Ref.	−1.24	−0.57
Skilled manual workers	0.7**	0.5	Ref.	Ref.
Skilled white collar workers	0.9	0.8		
Provenance				
North	Ref.	Ref.	Ref.	Ref.
Bajío	−1.2*	−1.4*	−0.5	−0.47
Center	−3.4*	−3.5*	−1.42	−1.40
South	−4.1*	−3.6*	−0.29	−2.91
Age (years)				
18	−2.3*		−2.47	
19	−2.4*		−1.14	
20	−2.1*		−2.74	
21	−0.8*		−2.29	
22	−0.6		−1.75	
23 or more	Ref.		Ref.	
Birth decade				
1840s			Ref.	Ref.
1850s			1.52	1.53
1860s			0.81	0.82
1870s	Ref.	Ref.	0.24	0.24
1880s	0.2	0.0	−0.96	−0.93
1890s	0.2	0.0	−1.71	−1.70
1900s	0.2	0.2		
1910s	0.0	−0.7		
1920s	−0.2	−0.3		
1930s	1.8**	−0.3		
1940s	2.1**	1.8		
Deserters	−0.4	−0.5	N.A.	N.A.
χ^2	265.3	142.5	91.67	87.32
N	4976	3194	6027	4412

Note: The regressions were estimated with STATA'S trunk. reg. routine.

For the *Federales* the constants refer to adult, unskilled workers, non-deserters from Northern Mexico born in the 1870 and 1879.

For the *Rurales* the constant refers to adult, skilled manual workers from North of Mexico born between 1840 and 1849.

Sources: See text.

*Significant at 1% level.

**Significant at 5% level: a) pertains to the whole population, and b) pertains to adults only.

Figure 5.
Mean Heights of *Rurales* by Region.

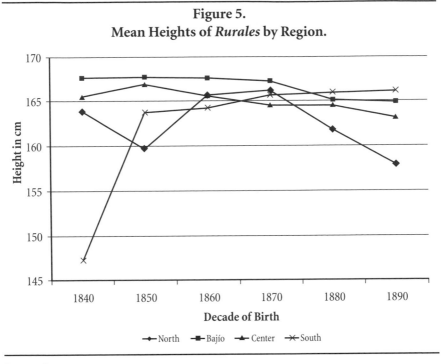

Sources: See text.

Figure 6.
Estimated Mean Heights Using Truncated Regression.

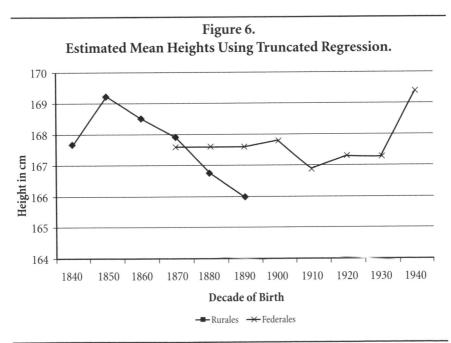

Sources: Table 3, models 1.b and 2.b.

nomics approach to Mexico, this period was not one of economic disruption but of continuing industrialization. This same period showed an increase in the size of the industrial proletariat and a significant rural exodus.[61] Knowing these two facts, the deterioration in biological standards of living of this generation suggests two solid explanations. First, food shortages are normally associated with war; the Mexican Revolution is no exception to this phenomenon. As a result of the armed conflict between 1911–20, there was less food available. The second explanation involves the deleterious impact of the early stages of industrialization on the health of the urban proletariat. In this sense Mexico was experiencing what the United States and some Western European countries experienced in the previous century.

The subsequent, incipient improvement of the generations born in the following two decades, the 1920s and the 1930s, is what differentiates Mexico from other Western countries. These generations of popular classes grew up under better economic conditions, at the beginning of the "Mexican miracle" and, at the very least, the onset of more options for work, especially later in the 1930s. Working conditions of the industrial proletariat improved. The peasantry received some support, albeit not in a systematic manner, and those who did not find opportunities in the countryside could search for new opportunities in the cities or in the United States. In addition, public health initiatives that covered a substantial portion of the population began to be implemented. In this regard Mexico resembled countries in the developed world. The sharp drop in infant mortality and the rise in the life expectancy of generations born in these decades is solid evidence of this. According to human biology, a rapid and sharper gain in height was thus possible. The increase in height is much too small to reflect economic change, however; as mentioned before, the 1940s results are based on too few observations to allow us to draw any conclusion.

In general there was a decline in the average height of laborers born during the 1860s and 1870s; heights then stagnated until the late 1930s. The recovery in average heights coincides with the launching of welfare policies aimed at improving income distribution and public health.[62] The timing of industrialization, the adoption of the germ theory of disease, and public health policies in Mexico were coterminous, but the last two had a limited impact on raising the biological standards of the laboring classes. For one thing, the growth of the industrial proletariat was modest compared to the size of the working population, and industrialization was not the main engine of economic growth at the time.[63] In addition, the investments in public health infrastructure undertaken during the post-revolutionary period were limited, hence their effects were also insufficient. Moreover, the quality of diet of the laboring classes barely improved during this period. All these facts contrast with the performance of the economy, thus reinforcing the notion that the Mexican economy was growing and modernizing, but the wealth created did not reach the laboring classes.[64]

What can we make of these results if we analyze them in comparative perspective? Comparing these findings with those of countries with similar features and backgrounds would show us Mexico's relative standing in the world. Table 4 presents a comparison of both European and Latin American countries that share some common features, in particular the onset of industrialization and economic spurt at similar times. Judging from these measurements, Mexico does not exhibit a substantial discrepancy in the mid-nineteenth century; nonetheless, it falls behind by the end of the nineteenth century and does not catch up thereafter. The lack of increase in stature in the first decades of the twentieth century is also notable in light of the evolution of stature in Western Europe, and in other late industrializing Latin American countries.

Table 4.
International Comparison of Adult Males.

Year	Spain[1]	Italy[2]	Argentina[3]	Colombia[4]	Mexico[5]
1840					166.5
1850	161.9				167.0
1860	162.1				166.3
1870	162.3			167.8	165.8
1880	163.0	162.7		168.8	164.7
1890	163.4	163.1		168.5	163.4
1900	164.2	163.8	168.48	168.5	163.8
1910	165.1	164.1	168.17	168.4	164.3
1920	164.4	164.7	169.44		163.0
1930	165.5		170.32		163.5

Sources and notes:
1. Dolores and Carrión, "The Relationship," 9.
2. Drukker and Tassenaar, in Steckel and Floud, eds., *Health and Welfare*, 357–59.
3. Salvatore, "Stature Decline," 244. Standardized mean height of conscripts, skilled workers.
4. Meisel and Vega, table 1 of chapter 4 in this collection (elite passport applicants). Note that average heights for all Colombian males rose from 163.5 (1910–14) to 165.2 (1930–34).
5. Raw means from *Federales* and *Rurales* corps. 1840s–1860s: *Rurales*; 1870s–1890s: *Federales* and *Rurales*; 1900s–1930s, *Federales*.

In Mexico, regional differences are not absent from the results of this study, nor are differences among the popular classes. In both of these samples the coefficients of regression results show that men from the north were taller than their counterparts from the center and south. As mentioned in earlier studies, this difference could be caused by two basic factors: people lived in lower densities of population and had less exposure to epidemic diseases, and their diet had a higher protein content.[65] Skilled manual workers are taller than unskilled manual workers. Indeed, soldiers who had a trade were approximately a centimeter taller than those who were unskilled. As mentioned above, even within trades there were differences in lifestyle depending on where the worker came from and his specific productive activity.

Conclusions

The findings of this study provide the reader with a long-term perspective of the evolution of the quality of life of the Mexican popular and working classes and explain how this evolution relates to the economic performance and development of the nation. As noted, there is a decline for cohorts born during the first decades of this study; then heights stagnate until the late 1930s. The evolution of stature during the first years covered here suggests that the economic depression of the mid-nineteenth century did not have a negative effect on the biological standard of living. Conversely, the changes in land tenure policy undertaken in the 1870s and throughout the first decades of the Díaz administration appear to have had an adverse effect on the living standards of the popular classes, still mostly rural. The economic growth and development attained during the heyday of the Porfiriato seem to have alleviated at least partially the negative implications of land tenure, since heights made a slight recovery. The growth of an industrial proletariat and the 1910 Revolution took a toll on the well-being of the popular classes as heights declined again, and substantially.

Surprisingly, the implementation of public health initiatives, changes in labor law, agrarian reform, and the onset of the Mexican miracle seem to have done little to improve the biological standard of living of the laboring classes. The generations who grew up during this period of policy initiatives and social change did not manage to reach the levels of stature of their counterparts who lived nearly a century earlier. Biologically, such an increase in heights was feasible. Other nations of Latin America appear to have done better, even without a revolution and its resulting institutional changes that ostensibly aimed to benefit the working classes.[66]

By examining some demographic variables we can assert that there were some improvements from all the changes: life expectancy rose and infant mortality declined. But why were working-class Mexicans not growing taller? The answer to this question may be explained by the nature of formal and informal institutions.

The post-revolutionary governments undertook substantial institutional reforms relating to public welfare. These reforms, however, had a limited reach because they were insufficient to keep up with the needs of the rapidly growing population. In the late 1940s, Daniel Cosío Villegas pointed to the paradox of substantial amounts of government spending on welfare programs coupled with the rising number of people living in poverty.[67]

Cultural values, which can be deemed informal institutions that define the norms of social behavior, also contributed to hinder growth in stature. As mortality declined, fertility rates continued to be as high as they had been historically. Voluntary birth control did not expand in Mexico as it did in Western European populations or in the United States. Motherhood continued to be a sacred value in society at all socio-economic levels; thus it is not surprising that Mexico was able to recuperate its demographic losses during the revolution and then expand its population dramatically. Population growth remained a major concern in future decades.[68] Nonetheless, the government did not see a need actually to design and implement a policy that would address the increasingly obvious and worrisome problem of demographic explosion. The Mexican demographic pattern resulted in an increase in the number of members per household and, in working class families, it certainly had an impact on the quantity and quality of nutrients allocated to each member, even if wages increased or the number of working hours declined. This suggests that more people survived, but not necessarily under better circumstances.

Notes

1. "An important challenge in analyzing the evolution of poverty and inequality in Latin America is data quality and availability." Székely and Montes, "Poverty and Inequality," 587.
2. See Astorga, Berges and Fitzgerald, "The Standard of Living in Latin America"; Székely and Montes, "Poverty and Inequality."
3. "The history of welfare, of change over time in physical and spiritual well-being, encompasses most of the research and teaching that historians do." Coatsworth, "Welfare."
4. There are studies on evolution of living standards using anthropometric measures for the history of England, Ireland, the United States, France, Italy, Germany, Spain, Australia, Scandinavian, as well as Asian and African countries. In Latin America there are studies on Argentina and Colombia.
5. Steckel, "Stature, and the Standard of Living," 1915.

6. Even though the nature of discourse changed over time before and after the 1910 Revolution, the need for social improvement was present. For instance, in 1902 the important intellectual Justo Sierra argued that "There exists . . . such a thing as Mexican social evolution . . . This evolution, no doubt is just beginning. When we look back at our conditions previous to the final third of the past century we see what a long way we have come. . . . It is not insignificant." Sierra, *The Political Evolution*, 367–8. In 1913, prior to assuming power, Venustiano Carranza asserted: "The country has been living in illusion starved and luckless, with a handful of laws that are of no help to it; we have to plough it all up, drain it and then truly construct," quoted in Krauze, *Biography of Power*, 343.

7. "[. . .] commercial expansion, economic growth, and early industrialization came to Mexico after the 1860s . . . This economic transition from stagnation to growth came in two stages. In the first, economic growth began slowly in the late 1860s based primarily on investments in railroads and mining and thus accompanied by rising foreign trade . . . In the second stage, growth continued for two decades after 1890, still concentrated in the export sector and foreign trade, but with an increasing tendency toward diversification." Beatty, *Institutions and Investment*, 23–24.

8. "Whatever contribution the technological and scientific advances of the eighteenth and nineteenth centuries may have made ultimately to this breakthrough, escape from hunger and high mortality did not become a reality for most ordinary people until the twentieth century." Fogel, *Escape from Hunger*, 8.

9. The first initiatives to construct public works and to provide health-care services were in the major cities. See Agostoni, "Discurso médico"; Blum, "Conspicuous Benevolence"; Tenorio-Trillo, *Mexico at the World's Fairs*.

10. See Holden, *Mexico, and the Survey of Public Lands*, chapter 1; Friedrich, *Agrarian Revolt in a Mexican Village*, chapter 3; Womack. *Zapata and the Mexican Revolution*, epilogue; Vanderwood, *God, and the Power of Guns*, chapter 4. Although Holden argues against the generalized seizing of lands as a result of the survey of public lands, his study focuses on regions of Mexico that had a low density of population and where there were no serious disputes over land between peasant communities and large landholders.

11. "It must be conceded that Porfirian hygienists produced the proper scientific image of Mexico for both national and international consumption. The actual sanitary transformation was, of course, most visible in places like Mexico City, but the vast territory and the general indigence of most of the population made the Porfirian achievements look insignificant to a close observer"; Tenorio-Trillo, *Mexico at the World's Fairs*, 156.

12. "The present Revolution aspires first and foremost, aside from its pursuit of social welfare, to preserve above all the integrity of the nation and its independence." Quoted in Krauze, *Biography of Power*, 355.

13. According to Wilkie, "The Revolution's program of state directed integration of Mexican social and economic life has always been justified on the basis that it

has given the poor classes a better standard of living." *The Mexican Revolution,* 20. For a thorough review on the traditional historiography of the revolution, see Womack, "The Mexican Economy during the Revolution, 1910–1920."

14. "Mexico imposed high tariffs on most of its imports because it was not very import dependent and relied heavily on customs revenue to meet the fiscal requirements of the state." Kuntz Ficker, "Institutional Change," 165.

15. "The Mexican government's suspension of payments in 1828 on its early British loans (issued in 1824 and 1825) led to a traumatic six decades of conflict with foreign creditors." Marichal, "The Construction of Credibility," 93.

16. "Díaz weakened the influence of the army by establishing other para-military forces which were frequently of better caliber than the army." Katz, "Liberal Republic and the Porfiriato," 85.

17. "Díaz augmented the military budget (in absolute though not in relative terms)." Ibid.

18. "Porfirian Mexico's tariff, patent, and tax exemption policies altered the economic environment of those who sought to invest in Mexico. When foreign and Mexican entrepreneurs invested in domestic industry, they not only banked on the opportunities they perceived in the Mexican marketplace but they also responded to the particular incentives created by the federal policy." Beatty, *Institutions and Investment,* 46.

19. Coatsworth, "Indispensable Railroads," 952.

20. "Differences in average height by social class or occupation are a useful indicator of inequality in the biological standard of living. Before the twentieth century, occupational or class differences in stature were usually several centimeters larger in Europe compared with the United States. In eighteenth century Germany, for example, children of aristocrats were 8 to 10 centimeters taller than children of the lower classes, an advantage that closed somewhat as adults. The advantage of the upper classes was even larger in nineteenth-century England, where 14-year-old Sandhurst boys, who attained approximately the 15th centile of modern NCHS height standards, exceeded the stature of those from the slums of London (taken in by the Marine Society) by 10 to 15 centimeters. . . . The large differences in stature by social class within Europe before the end of the nineteenth century indicate that the European climb to modern height standards involved very large gains for the lower and middle classes." Steckel, "Stature and the Standard of Living," 1922–3, 1925.

21. See Haber, Razo, and Maurer, *Politics of Property Rights,* 15.

22. "It is clearer that popular militancy, following the familiar pattern, became more marked as the economy revived, which it did with some rapidity, thanks in part to the inflationary Keynesian policies pursued by Alberto Pani as Secretary of the Treasury (1932–3). . . . By 1934, GDP was back to 1929 levels, the peso was stabilized, and the economic outlook was encouraging." Knight, "The Rise and Fall of Cardenismo," 247.

23. Among the many scholars who contributed to this field we can mention Alfred Crosby, Elsa Malvido, Lourdes Márquez Morfin, and América Molina del Villar,

to cite a few. Malvido and Molina Del Villar have created a working group on the history of health and disease from the pre-Columbian period to the present.

24. Livi Bacci, *Population in Europe,* chapter 5.

25. "Life expectancy at birth in old-regime societies was low, usually between 25 and 35 years. Only in those rare periods free of economic difficulties, social unrest, or disease did it reach 40. In England, where the chances of survival were greater than on the continent, during an almost 300-year span from 1541 to 1826 there were only three brief five-year intervals (two during the fortunate Elizabethan era) in which life expectancy reached 40. The more advanced European countries only achieved a life expectancy of 40 in the early nineteenth century, while the peripheral regions of Europe had to wait until the next century. The life expectancy of the old-regime populations was therefore strictly limited." Ibid., 61–2.

26. "It is then the microbe that emerges as the primary factor of demographic constraint in old-regime societies, as the cause of disease and the majority of the deaths. . . . Knowledge of this type (transmission of diseases) remained rudimentary at best until the nineteenth century." Ibid., 63.

27. Tenorio Trillo, *Mexico at the World's Fairs,* 147.

28. For a thorough study on the history of this institution see Arrom, *Containing the Poor.*

29. For a thorough explanation on the intellectual origins of the public health initiatives during the Díaz administration see Tenorio Trillo, *Mexico at the World's Fairs,* chapter 9; Agostoni, "Discurso médico," provides a clear and extensive explanation of the efforts made by government agencies to disseminate public health information in Porfirian Mexico City.

30. Tenorio Trillo, *Mexico at the World's Fairs,* 157.

31. Cházaro García, "Medir y valorar," 5.

32. Ibid., 147.

33. Agostoni, "Discurso médico," 12.

34. Blum, "Conspicuous Benevolence," 7.

35. Birn, *Marriage of Convenience,* 45.

36. Ibid., 47.

37. Ibid., 1.

38. Ibid., 269.

39. Ibid., 261.

40. "In late colonial Mexico, marriage was nearly universal. A church census of the archbishophric of Mexico covering more than one million people reveals that in 1779, 89% of females of marriageable age were married or widowed. A century and a half later, according to the 1930 census it had fallen twenty points to 69% (compared with the 73% in the United States in the same year)." McCaa, "Peopling of Mexico," 292. Compare with Livi-Bacci, *Population of Europe,* chapters 5 and 6.

41. "Of a total demographic cost of 2.1 million, excess deaths accounted for two-thirds, lost births one fourth, and emigration considerably less than one-tenth of the total." McCaa, "The Missing Millions," 396.

42. The classic studies mentioned are those of Rosenzweig, *El Desarrollo Económico,* and El Colegio de México, *Estadísticas Históricas del Porfiriato.*

43. Gómez-Galvarriato, "Evolution of Prices," 345–6; 365.

44. The archive of the Secretaría does not allow researchers to consult any of the files of soldiers or retired soldiers who are still alive.

45. Following the findings of human biologists, we only consider the age ranges when people have reached adult height and when they start shrinking. For historical populations adult height is attained by all individuals by age 23. Also for historical populations shrinking generally starts at age 50.

46. "[. . .] the plan called for the creation of four corps of rural policemen, each with its commander, paymaster, 18 officers and 255 enlisted men." Vanderwood, *Disorder and Progress,* 49.

47. "[. . .] kidnappings were [not] in any way limited to the countryside. The bandits also braved Mexico City." Ibid., 48.

48. "Díaz invested 55 percent of Mexico's revenue in military and police services, and another 30 percent to maintain a contented bureaucracy . . . Díaz made them loyal to him by setting very strict examples of political discipline." Ibid., 68.

49. As we mentioned earlier, peace was not instantly restored. Díaz invested years and good sums of money to attain social and political stability in the whole national territory.

50. In order to build this sample all boxes that contained the recruitment files and muster rolls were reviewed. There were recruitment files in approximately 60 percent of the boxes; 70 percent of the recruitment files corresponded to soldiers 23 years and older. Most of the recruits were born between 1860 and 1890.

51. These are rough estimates because this data set suffers from the same deficiencies as that for the *Federales.*

52. Vanderwood, *Disorder and Progress,* chapter 4.

53. "Captured deserters ended up with an army battalion in the hellholes of Veracruz and Yucatán but most who deserted were never captured or even pursued." Ibid., 109.

54. "By 1880 he (the President) had expanded the force by 90 percent to 1,767 men." Ibid., 70.

55. For further discussion on the differences in heights across social classes see López-Alonso, "Short in Cash," and López-Alonso and Porras Condey, "The Ups and Downs."

56. Only records with metric unit measurements were included in this sample.

57. In the regression results it becomes evident that not all files have full information on all the variables we are taking into account.

58. Cope, *The Limits of Racial Domination,* chapter 3.

59. Komlos, "How to (and How Not to)." In addition, it estimates the sigma of the height distribution (provided that the truncation point is to the left of the mean).

60. "By 1842, L. Alamán had been appointed Director of the Dirección General de Agricultura e Industria. In his first 'Memoria sobre el estado de la agricultura e

industria de la República' in 1843, Alamán addressed national income directly. "Everything [induces] me to believe that the whole of agricultural production, considered in toto, is greater today than in the epoch that preceded 1810." Here Alamán explicitly compares agricultural production in 1842 to production before 1810. Mexico was an agricultural nation; if production in 1842 was larger than in 1810, national income must have been as large in 1842 as it had been earlier." Salvucci, "Mexican National Income," 223.

61. Bortz and Haber, *Mexican Economy,* chapter 8; Haber, Razo and Maurer, *Politics of Property Rights,* chapter 1.

62. López-Alonso, "Growth with Inequality ," 104.

63. Hernández Chávez, *Mexico,* 260.

64. López-Alonso, "Growth with Inequality," 102.

65. For a thorough discussion on the quality of diet across regions see López-Alonso, "Height, Health, Nutrition and Wealth," chapter 6.

66. See Meisel and Vega's chapter in this book.

67. "Wherefore the bloody paradox in which the government, while waving the revindicatory flag of an impoverished people by prevarication and theft and embezzlement, created a new high and low middle class which in the end dragged the Revolution and the country itself once more to the brink of social and economic inequality." Cosío Villegas, "Mexico's Crisis," 480.

68. For instance, Octavio Paz, in *The Labyrinth of Solitude,* commented: "Only in an atmosphere of freedom and openness to criticism can true problems of Mexico be defined and discussed, some of them are immense — for instance, the population explosion—but the government has not even attempted to discuss them" (261).

Primary Sources

Archivo General de la Nación, Archivos de Guerra y Marina, Legajos de Gobernación, 1821–1920.

Secretaría de la Defensa Nacional, Dirección General de Archivo e Historia, Sección de Cancelados y Sección de Personal Extinto.

References

Agostoni, Claudia. "Discurso médico, cultura higiénica y la mujer en la ciudad de México al cambio del siglo (XIX–XX)." *Mexican Studies/Estudios Mexicanos* 18, no.1 (2002): 1–22.

Arrom, Silvia Marina. *Containing the Poor: The Mexico City Poor House, 1774–1871.* Durham: Duke University Press, 2000.

Astorga, Pablo, Ame R. Berges, and Valpy Fitzgerald. "The Standard of Living in Latin America during the Twentieth Century." *Economic History Review* 58, no. 4 (2005): 765–796.

Beatty, Edward. *Institutions and Investment: The Political Basis of Industrialization in Mexico before 1911.* Stanford: Stanford University Press, 2001.

Bethell, Leslie. *The Cambridge History of Latin America.* 5 vols. Cambridge: Cambridge University Press, 1986.

Birn, Anne-Emmanuelle. *Marriage of Convenience: Rockefeller International Health and Revolutionary Mexico.* Rochester: University of Rochester Press, 2006.

Blum, Anne. "Conspicuous Benevolence: Liberalism, Public Welfare, and Private Charity in Porfirian Mexico City." *The Americas* 58, no. 4 (2001): 7–38.

Bortz, Jeffrey L., and Stephen Haber. *The Mexican Economy, 1870–1930: Essays on the Economic History of Institutions, Revolution, and Growth.* Stanford: Stanford University Press, 2002.

Bulmer-Thomas, Victor, John H. Coatsworth, and Roberto Cortés Conde. *The Cambridge Economic History of Latin America: The Long Twentieth Century.* 2 vols. Cambridge: Cambridge University Press, 2006.

Cházaro García, Laura, "Medir y Valorar los Cuerpos de una Nación: Un Ensayo sobre la Estadística Médica del Siglo XIX en México." Unpublished Ph.D. dissertation. UNAM 2000.

Cherry, Steven. *Medical Services and the Hospitals in Britain, 1860–1939.* Cambridge: Cambridge University Press, 1996.

Coatsworth, John H. "Indispensable Railroads in a Backward Economy: The Case of Mexico." *Journal of Economic History* 39, no. 4 (1979): 939–960.

———. *Los Orígenes del Atraso.* Mexico: Editorial Alianza, 1991.

———. "Welfare." *American Historical Review* 101, no. 1 (1996): 1–12.

Coatsworth, John H. and Alan M. Taylor, eds. *Latin America and the World Economy since 1800.* Cambridge MA: DRCLAS/Harvard University Press, 1998.

Cope, R. Douglas. *The Limits of Racial Domination: Plebeian Society in Colonial Mexico City 1660–1720.* Madison: University of Wisconsin Press, 1994.

Cosio Villegas, Daniel. "Mexico's Crisis." In *The Mexico Reader: History, Culture, Politics,* ed. Gilbert M. Joseph and Timothy J. Henderson, 470–481. Durham: Duke University Press, 2002.

Dolores, Ramón María, and José Miguel Martínez Carrión, "The Relationship between Height and Economic Development in Spain, A Historical Perspective." Documento de Trabajo no. 912, Asociación Española de Historia Económica, December 2009.

El Colegio de México. *Estadísticas Históricas del Porfiriato.* Mexico City: El Colegio de México, 1969.

Fogel, Robert William. *The Escape from Hunger and Premature Death, 1700–2100: Europe, America and the Third World.* Cambridge: Cambridge University Press, 2004.

Friedrich, Paul. *Agrarian Revolt in a Mexican Village.* Chicago: University of Chicago Press, 1977.

Gómez-Galvarriato, Aurora. "The Evolution of Prices and Real Wages in Mexico from the Porfiriato." In *Latin America and the World Economy since 1800,* ed. John H. Coatsworth and Alan M. Taylor, 347–378. Cambridge MA: Harvard University, 1998.

Haber, Stephen. *How Latin America Fell Behind: Essays In the Economic Histories of Brazil and Mexico, 1800–1914.* Stanford: Stanford University Press, 1997.

Haber, Stephen. "The Commitment Problem and Mexican Economic History." In *The Mexican Economy, 1870–1930: Essays on the Economic History of Institutions, Revolution, and Growth*, ed. Jeffrey Bortz and Stephen Haber, 324–336. Stanford: Stanford University Press, 2002.

Haber, Stephen, Armundo Razo, and Noel Maurer. *The Politics of Property Rights: Political Instability, Credible Commitments and Economic Growth in Mexico, 1876–1925*. Cambridge: Cambridge University Press, 2003.

Haines, Michael R., and Richard H. Steckel. *A Population History of North America*. Cambridge: Cambridge University Press, 2000.

Hernández Chávez, Alicia. *Mexico: A Brief History*, trans. Andy Klatt. Los Angeles: University of California Press, 2006.

Holden, Robert H. *Mexico and the Survey of Public Lands: The Management of Modernization, 1876–1911*. DeKalb: Northern Illinois University Press, 1994.

Katz, Friedrich. "The Liberal Republic and the Porfiriato, 1867–1910." In *Mexico since Independence*, ed. Leslie Bethell, 49–124. Cambridge: Cambridge University Press, 1991.

Knight, Alan. "The Rise and Fall of Cardenismo c.1930–c.1946," In *Mexico since Independence*, ed. Leslie Bethell, 241–320. Cambridge: Cambridge University Press, 1991.

Komlos, John. "Stature and Nutrition in the Habsburg Monarchy: The Standard of Living and Economic Development." *American Historical Review* 90 (1985): 1149–1161.

———."How to (and How Not to) Analyze Deficient Height Samples: An Introduction." *Historical Methods* 37 (2004): 160–173.

Komlos, John, and Joo Han Kim. "Estimating Trends in Historical Heights." *Historical Methods* 23 (1990): 116–120.

Krauze, Enrique. *Mexico: Biography of Power: A History of Modern Mexico, 1810–1996*, trans. Hank Heifetz. New York: Harper Collins, 1997.

Kuntz Ficker, Sandra. "Institutional Change and Foreign Trade in Mexico, 1870–1911." In *The Mexican Economy, 1870–1930: Essays on the Economic History of Institutions, Revolution, and Growth*, ed. Jeffrey Bortz and Stephen Haber, 161–204. Stanford: Stanford University Press, 2002.

Livi-Bacci, Massimo. *The Population of Europe: A History*, trans. Cynthia De Nardi and Carl Ipsen. Oxford: Blackwell Publishers, 2000.

López-Alonso, Moramay. "Short in Cash, Short in Stature: The Contrasts in Physical and Capital Formation in Mexico, 1890–1930." Mimeo, 2003.

———. "Growth with Inequality: Living Standards in Mexico, 1850–1950." *Journal of Latin American Studies* 39, part 1 (2007): 81–105.

López-Alonso, Moramay, and Raul Porras Condey. "The Ups and Downs of Mexican Economic Growth: The Biological Standard of Living and Inequality, 1870–1950." *Economics and Human Biology* 1 (2003): 169–186.

Marichal, Carlos. "The Construction of Credibility: Financial Market Reform and the Renegotiation of Mexico's External Debt in the 1880s." In *The Mexican*

Economy, 1870–1930: Essays on the Economic History of Institutions, Revolution, and Growth, ed. Jeffrey Bortz and Stephen Haber, 93–119. Stanford: Stanford University Press, 2002.

McCaa, Robert. "The Peopling of Mexico from Origins to Revolution." In *A Population History of North America*, ed. Michael R. Haines and Richard H. Steckel, 241–304. Cambridge: Cambridge University Press, 2000.

———. "Missing Millions: The Demographic Costs of the Mexican Revolution." *Mexican Studies, Estudios Mexicanos* 19, no. 2 (2003): 367–400.

———. *La Calidad de Vida Biológica en Colombia: Antropometría Histórica, 1870–2003*. Cartagena: Centro de Estudios Económicos Regionales, Banco de la República, 2007.

Paz, Octavio. *The Labyrinth of Solitude: The Other Mexico, Return to the Labyrinth of Solitude, and The United States, the Philanthropic Ogre*, trans. Lysander Kemp, Yara Milos, and Rachel Phillips Belach. New York: Grove Press, 1985.

Rosenzweig Hernández, Fernando, *El Desarrollo Económico de México 1800–1910*. México: Colegio Mexiquense A.C.-ITAM, 1989.

Salvatore, Ricardo D. "Stature Decline and Recovery in a Food-Rich Export Economy: Argentina 1900–1934." *Explorations in Economic History* 41 (2004): 233–255.

Salvucci, Richard J. "Mexican National Income in the Era of Independence, 1800–40." In *How Latin America Fell behind: Essays in the Economic Histories of Brazil and Mexico, 1800–1914*, ed. Stephen Haber, 216–242. Stanford: Stanford University Press, 1997.

Sandberg, Lars G., and Richard H. Steckel, "Was Industrialization Hazardous to Your Health? Not in Sweden!" In *Health and Welfare during Industrialization*, ed. Richard H. Steckel and Roderick Floud, 127–160. Chicago: University of Chicago Press, 1997.

Sierra, Justo. *The Political Evolution of the Mexican People*, trans. Edmundo O'Gorman. Austin: University of Texas Press, 1969.

Steckel, Richard H. "Stature and the Standard of Living." *Journal of Economic Literature* 33, no. 4 (1995): 1903–1940.

Steckel, Richard H., and Roderick Floud, eds. *Health and Welfare during Industrialization*. Chicago: University of Chicago Press, 1997.

Székely, Miguel, and Andrés Montes. "Poverty and Inequality." In *The Cambridge Economic History of Latin America*. 2 vols., ed. Victor Bulmer-Thomas, Roberto Cortés Conde, and John H. Coatsworth, vol. 2, 585–645. Cambridge: Cambridge University Press, 2006.

Tenorio-Trillo, Mauricio. *Mexico at the World's Fairs: Crafting a Modern Nation*. Berkeley: University of California Press, 1996.

Vanderwood, Paul J. *Disorder and Progress: Bandits, Police and Mexican Development*. Lincoln: University of Nebraska Press, 1981.

———. *The Power of God against the Guns of Government, Religious Upheaval in Mexico at the Turn of the Nineteenth Century*. Stanford: Stanford University Press, 1998.

Wilkie, James W. *The Mexican Revolution: Federal Expenditure and Social Change since 1910.* Berkeley: University of California Press, 1967.

Womack, John Jr. *Zapata and the Mexican Revolution.* New York: Vintage Books, 1970.

———. "The Mexican Economy during the Revolution, 1910–1920: Historiography and Analysis." *Marxist Perspectives* 1, no. 4 (1978): 80–123.

———. "The Mexican Revolution, 1910–1920." In *The Cambridge History of Latin America: Bibliographical Essays,* 11 vols., ed. Leslie Bethell, 385–405. Cambridge: Cambridge University Press, 1995.

4

Stature of the Colombian Elite before the Onset of Industrialization, 1870–1919

Adolfo Meisel and Margarita Vega

Introduction

The nineteenth century was a period of economic decline and civil wars in many Latin American countries. Colombia experienced both: economic decline until around 1850, and numerous civil wars, of which the War of the Thousand Days (1899–1902), with an estimated 100,000 casualties, was the bloodiest.[1] The study of the standard of living during this time of turmoil is very important, for it can help us understand the impact of economic and political events on people's lives.

The problem with determining the standard of living in this period is that the relevant information is often not available. For the period before 1905 there are almost no estimates for Colombia's GDP per capita, and the available records for wages and salaries are very fragmentary. Additionally, there are no reliable price indexes for the nineteenth century, so that it is quite difficult to gauge the evolution in the purchasing power of various groups. For this reason the advances in anthropometric history in the last 30 years are very helpful for a better understanding of the behavior in the material standard of living, at least during a sub-period of the nineteenth century.

Since the pioneering work of Robert W. Fogel and his associates in the late 1970s on anthropometric history, economic historians have increasingly resorted to height as a measure of the biological standard of living, as adult stature reflects both the net nutritional status during the years of growth (0–18 years old) and the genetic potential.[2]

The anthropometric information found in passports issued in Colombia to people born from 1870 to 1919 thus becomes an important source for tracing the evolution in the biological standard of living.

In this chapter we study the heights of more than 16,000 Colombians, mostly from the elite, born between 1870 and 1919. The quality of the information is very good, especially because it is available for a relatively long time period, covers both men and women, and contains additional data, such as destination, reason for traveling, and place where the passport was issued.

The database, and the results obtained in this paper, complement a previous study done by the authors for the period 1905–1985 using a larger sample from national ID cards.[3] The advantage of using the passport records for the period under study is that it allows us to know something of what was happening with the standard of living for one group of Colombians born in the last thirty years of the nineteenth century and the first two decades of the twentieth.

The Data

Colombia began to issue passports in 1824, when the recently created republic issued a law authorizing the granting of passports to Colombians who found themselves abroad.[4] The information on heights was obtained from the passport records of the Colombian Ministry of Foreign Relations and the national archive.[5] This information has never yet been used by social scientists, although it is in excellent condition. These records are valuable not only for anthropometric history but also for social history.

For citizens born between 1870 and 1919, we obtained a total of 15,911 observations from the passport archives (see Table 1). The number of cases per year of birth steadily increased until 1906, when 420 records for men and 219 for women were found. Then the number of observations drops to 83 per year, for both men and women. All passports that reported the exact height were included, while those with no height or only a general description such as tall, average, or short, were discarded. In most of our analysis we have used information only for those Colombians who obtained their passports when they were between the ages of 18 and 60. The reason for using this range is that adult height is achieved by about 18 years of age and at more advanced ages, such as the 60s, height may decrease. The passport data also contain 924 observations for those who were under 18 years old when they obtained that document, which were removed from the analysis.

The information in these passports included name, city where it was issued, date of issue, age, height, color of eyes and hair, destination, reasons for trip abroad, and occupation. It also included a photograph. The place of birth was not reported. All the above information is available in the database we have constructed, except the eye and hair color, which we did not consider useful for our purposes.

Table 1.
Average Heights Obtained from Passport Records, 1870–1919.

Date of Birth	Average Male Height	Average Female Height	Increase in Height for Men (%)	Increase in Height for Women (%)	Number of Observations (Men)	Number of Observations (Women)	Total Observations	Standard Deviation (Men)	Standard Deviation (Women)	Coefficient of Variation (Men)	Coefficient of Variation (Women)	Centimeters Increased (Men)	Centimeters Increased (Women)
1870–1874	167.4	158.1			195	120	315	8.44	6.20	0.0497	0.0393		
1875–1879	168.2	157.5	0.5%	-0.4%	393	197	590	7.01	6.21	0.0415	0.0395	0.79	-0.62
1880–1884	168.7	158.2	0.3%	0.5%	594	331	925	6.90	7.64	0.0407	0.0483	0.51	0.73
1885–1889	168.8	158.9	0.1%	0.4%	881	390	1,271	7.23	7.72	0.0428	0.0486	0.18	0.68
1890–1894	168.5	158.7	-0.2%	-0.1%	1,229	512	1,714	7.29	7.56	0.0432	0.0477	-0.31	-0.22
1895–1899	168.5	158.3	0.0%	-0.3%	1,591	688	2,279	7.13	7.72	0.0423	0.0488	-0.01	-0.42
1900–1904	168.3	158.2	-0.01%	0.0%	1,739	887	2,626	6.71	7.46	0.0398	0.0472	-0.24	-0.06
1905–1909	168.7	158.1	0.3%	-0.1%	1,871	1,006	2,877	6.77	7.01	0.0401	0.0444	0.44	-0.09
1910–1914	168.3	158.6	-0.3%	0.3%	1,246	835	2,081	7014	6.86	0.0424	0.0433	-0.43	0.46
1915–1919	168.6	158.7	0.2	0.1	651	555	1,206	6.89	6.58	0.0407	0.04715	0.33	0.14
TOTAL	168.39	158.33	0.7%	0.4%	10,390	5,521	15,911					.24	0.59

Source: Archivo General de la Nación and archives of the Foreign Ministry (hereafter: AGN_FM), and calculations by the authors.

Note: Includes only persons whose age was between 18 and 60 years.

Consulted passport documents contain information on the name of the person, date of birth, anthropometric characteristics, occupation, reason for traveling, the year of application and country of destination. These data serve multiple purposes beyond anthropometric analysis. For our particular analysis we can assert that the majority of passport holders was a relatively homogenous group of the better-off groups of the population: skilled and clerical workers, and well-known members of the elite.

The quality of the height data was tested by applying the Lilliefors and Jarque-Bera normality tests to the observations of each year. In both tests, and for almost every year, at the 3% level of significance the null hypothesis of normality was accepted. Figure 1 shows the frequency distribution for this sample for both men and women, using the data for the period as a whole.

Figure 1.
Frequency Distribution of Height.

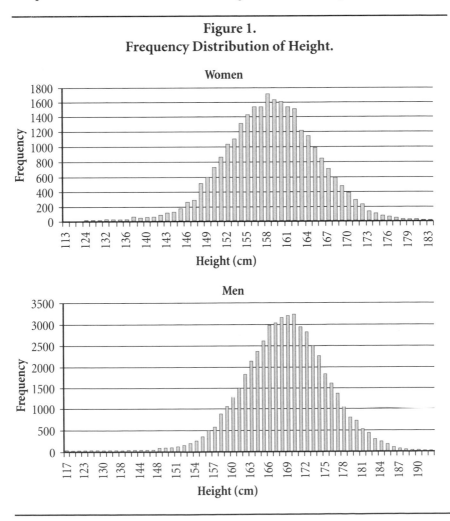

Source: Calculations by the authors.

Map 1.
Colombian Cities Where Passports Were Issued.

In a previous study we had obtained information for the height of Colombians from national ID cards beginning in 1905. Yet it is important to have some knowledge about the evolution of height before 1905, especially since after 1905 the growth of coffee exports allowed Colombia to make the transition from a stagnant to a rapidly growing economy. The data on height obtained from passports was extended until 1919, so that we could compare the results obtained from this source with those from the ID cards. When the heights from these two sources are compared (see Figure 2), it is evident that the average height obtained from passports is above that obtained from the ID cards: about 8 cm for women and about 5 cm for men.

Figure 2.
Average Height from Passports and ID Cards, 1909–1919.

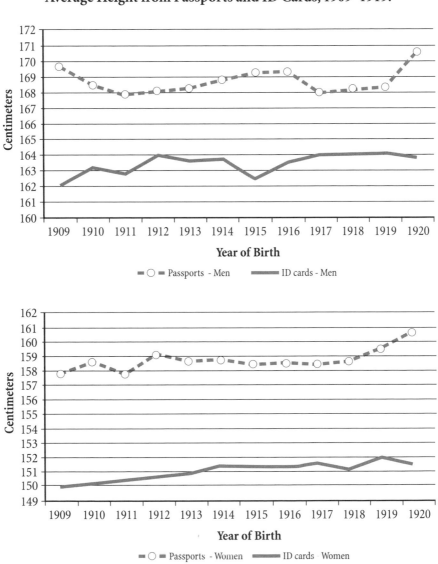

Sources: AGN_FM for passport data; for ID cards, Registraduría Nacional del Estado Civil (hereafter: RNEC) and calculations by the authors.

The reason for the difference in average height between passport and ID card holders is that the ID sample represents the Colombian population as a whole, whereas the passport holders represent a small segment of the population that belongs to the social, economic, and cultural elite.

In a study of Mexico, López-Alonso used information from passports issued between 1910 and 1935, with people born from the 1870s to the 1910s (3,970 observations). She found that the height of males from the passport sample, composed mainly of skilled manual workers, white-collar workers, and members of the elite and their servants, remained fairly stable up to the last three decades of the nineteenth century. She also found a recovery for the cohorts which grew up during the years of the Mexican Revolution (1910–1917). Her results show that, for males, the tallest category of the elite was 4.4 cm taller than the unskilled workers. For the twentieth century there was no sign of an upward trend in average height until the 1940s.[6]

For the United States, Marco Sunder used a database with 19,722 observations for males born in the period 1800–1900, and 5,992 for females born in the period 1820–1900, constructed from passport applications. There too passport applications reflect the height of the wealthier segments of the population.[7] Sunder shows that for the first half of the nineteenth century the height of passport applicants remained fairly stable, unlike that of the majority of the population, which experienced a significant fall in average height during the half century before the U.S. Civil War: the so-called Antebellum Puzzle. Additionally, beginning about the middle of the century the height of passport applicants increased rapidly, and by 1900 they had an average height that was reached by the rest of the population only four decades later.[8]

The Colombian Economy

During the first decades after independence, the territory of what is now Colombia, like most of Latin America, experienced a drop in its per capita GDP.[9] Between 1802–1804 and 1846–1850, per capita exports in real terms fell by 42%.[10] However, exports recovered in the following two decades as a result of a short-lived boom in tobacco exports. After 1880, and until 1910, export growth again stagnated, although experiencing short-term fluctuations.[11] As a result, in 1913, among the Latin American countries, only Haiti and Honduras had fewer exports per capita than Colombia (see Table 2).[12]

Table 2.
Latin American Exports and Foreign Investment, 1913
(Latin America=100).

Country	Per Capita Exports	Per Capita Foreign Investment
Argentina	343	306
Cuba	337	188
Uruguay	287	225
Chile	192	104
Costa Rica	130	121
Bolivia	90	16
Nicaragua	73	20
Brazil	65	78
Panama	60	13
Republica Dominicana	53	4
Venezuela	51	20
Paraguay	48	33
Mexico	47	131
Guatemala	46	48
Peru	46	37
Ecuador	44	15
El Salvador	40	15
Colombia	**34**	**8**
Haiti	31	14
Honduras	27	34

Source: Ocampo, *Colombia y la economía*, 53.

The fall in exports in the final decades of the nineteenth century and first decade of the twentieth seems to have led to a reduction in real wages. According to William P. McGreevey, real salaries in coffee production areas were falling from the early 1880s to the first decade of the last century.[13]

However, McGreevey argues that sometime between 1905 and 1915 there occurred a transition from a period of virtual stagnation or decline to one of rapid economic growth.[14] That spurt does not seem to have increased real salaries or the standard of living for the majority of the population, at least not until the 1910s. Thus it is important to emphasize that the standard of living in Colombia in the period 1870–1905 seems to have been basically stagnant. As we shall see, the anthropometric evidence that we have gathered using passports corroborates this.

Trends in Average Height
For the period 1870–1919, the records for Colombian passports include the heights of 10,390 men and 5,521 women 18 to 60 years old. As shown in Table 1 and Figure 3, the increase in height for men between 1870–1874 and 1915–1919 was only 1.24 cm, less than 0.25 cm per decade. In the case of women the rate of increase was even lower, 0.12 cm per decade. Furthermore, the trend for the heights of men and women in the period 1870–1919 is not statistically significant.[15]

Figure 3.
Average Height of Men and Women Born between 1870–1919.

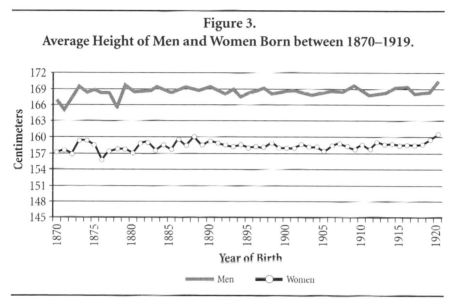

Source: AGN_FM and calculations by the authors.

The dispersion in the heights of Colombians who obtained passports in the period 1918–1940, as measured by the coefficient of variation, was relatively constant, with a coefficient for the trend that is not statistically significant. The coefficient of variation is an important indicator of interpersonal inequality in height.

The coefficient of variation of height fluctuated around 0.04, for both men and women (see Figure 4). Thus the dispersion is less than what was observed in the period 1910–1919 with the heights obtained from the national ID card, which was around 0.044 for men and 0.050 for women. Only towards 1980 does the dispersion of height obtained from the ID card data approach a level similar to that observed for passports in the period 1870–1919. Thus it can be concluded that the group in the passport sample was relatively homogeneous in social and economic terms.

Figure 4.
Coefficient of Variation of Average Height, 1870–1919.

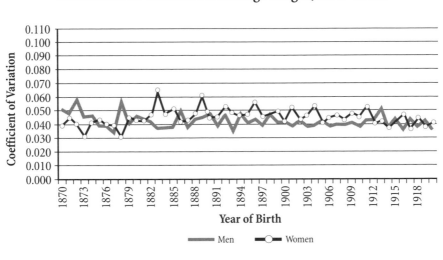

Source: AGN_FM and calculations by the authors.

The difference between the height of men and women born in the period 1870–1919 remained almost unchanged, with men's height exceeding that of women by about 10 cm. This is a much smaller gap than was observed for the height difference between men and women in the period 1910–1985 using the ID card information. In this latter case the difference was above 11 cm, and was as high as 13 cm in some sub-periods. Because we do not have detailed information on nutrition levels by gender and social class, it is only possible to infer that girls of growing age in lower-income households suffered greater discrimination in the allocation of food than their male siblings. Although the height of Colombians who obtained passports in the period 1918–1940 was stagnant, international comparisons show that this group was tall relative to citizens of other countries. Table 3 shows the height of men for a group of countries *circa* 1900. Colombian men were taller than men from Great Britain, France, Italy, and Indonesia. Only the citizens of the United States, Sweden, Norway, and Holland were taller than the Colombian elite men in our sample. However, it is important to keep in mind that the information on height for most countries included in Table 3 is based on the height of military recruits except for Mexico from a database of the elite, and for Colombia, from passport records—a database which at the time included mostly people from the elite and some skilled workers.

Table 3.
International Comparisons of Adult Male Heights, *circa* 1900.

Country	cm
Sweden[a]	172.5
United States [a]	171.0
Norway[a]	171.0
Mexico[b]	170.1
Netherlands[c]	169.0
Colombia[d]	**168.5**
Great Britain[a]	167.0
France[e]	165.5
Italy[f]	164.5
Spain[g]	163.6
Indonesia[h]	160.8

Sources:
a. Steckel, "Stature and the Standard," 1919.
b. Lopez-Alonso and Porras, "The Ups and Downs," 182.
c, e. Drukker and Van Meerten, "Beyond Villermé," 46.
d. AGN_FM and calculations by the authors.
f. Federico, "Heights, Calories," 291.
g. Martínez-Carrión, "Estatura, salud," 32–41.
h. Height for 1901. Van der Eng, "An Inventory," 177.

Possible Biases in the Sample

That the sample obtained from passports is not representative of the total Colombian population is evident when comparing the average height obtained from passports and ID cards. Table 4 shows that in the period 1910–1914 the height of women obtained from passports was 7.8 cm above the height obtained from ID cards. In the case of men the gap is smaller but significant: 4.8 cm in 1910–1914 and 5.0 cm in 1915–1919.

Table 4.
Differences in Height between Passports and ID Cards.

Period	Men Passports	Men ID card	Difference Men	Women Passports	Women ID card	Difference Women
1905–1909	168.7	162.0	6.7	158.1	150.0	8.1
1910–1914	168.3	163.5	4.8	158.6	150.8	7.8
1915–1919	168.6	163.6	5.0	158.7	151.5	7.2

Source: RNEC, AGN_FM and calculations by the authors.

Another important difference between the heights observed in the passport records and those of the ID cards is that in the former the long-term trend is constant, while in the latter there is a clear positive trend in height, as can be seen in Figure 5.

Figure 5.
Average Height of Men and Women by Passports and ID Cards,
1870–1985.

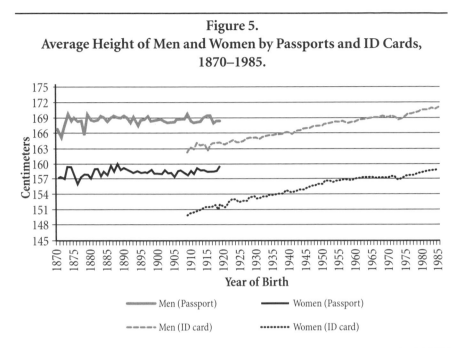

Source: AGN_FM and calculations by the authors.

By 1960–1964, Colombian men holding ID cards attained the height obtained from passports in 1919; women attained such height around 1980–1984. Yet, present-day studies still show large differences in the average height of Colombians according to their socio-economic stratification, which suggests that the contemporary elite must have a stature that is above the current average for the overall population. For example, in the sample obtained by Ordoñez, Polania, and Ramirez for the early 1990s, the height of men from the highest socio-economic strata was 9.5 cm. above that of those from the lowest strata.[16] This implies that at some point between 1919 and the 1980s the average height of the elite must have increased relative to that of the average population.

Furthermore, these results indicate that in the early twentieth century the Colombian elite was not achieving its potential height. Even if at that level of development its purchasing power allowed it to have proper nutrition,

perhaps because of health reasons it was not achieving its genetically determined maximum height.

The research of the epidemiologist Thomas McKeown suggests that the
reason why the members of the Colombian elite were not achieving their
potential height, even if they had a good diet and adequate personal hygiene,
was because the medical advances that improved life expectancy and height
were available only in the late 1920s and 1930s, at the earliest.[17] Until the
mid-1950s, the remarkable improvements in health and the decline in mortality observed in the developed countries since the eighteenth century were
mostly attributed to advances in medical technology. However, McKeown
challenged that consensus, showing that until the late 1920s, at the earliest,
the effect of the advances in medical technology on overall mortality was
minimal, even in the developed countries. In his view the main reason for
the almost continuous decline in mortality, which began in the early eighteenth century in countries like England, was better nutrition, owing to the
rise in agricultural productivity, advances in transportation, and expansion
of international trade. Better nutrition had such a large impact on mortality because there is a synergy between nutrition and the ability to resist
infectious disease: when a person is well fed, the possibility of surviving certain infectious diseases, such as tuberculosis, increases.[18]

After the 1870s, advances in public health observed in the more developed countries, such as England, also contributed to the drop in mortality.
Public health improved mainly as the result of the construction of modern
water supply and sewage systems. According to McKeown, it was probably
not until 1935, with the introduction of sulphamids, that changes in medical technology significantly contributed to the reduction in mortality.[19]

In Colombia, until the beginning of the twentieth century, there were
almost no advances in public health, so that any fall in mortality was probably the result of gains in nutrition. The only major changes in this period
were in the distribution of water in Bogotá, Colombia's capital and largest
city.

Until 1888, the distribution of water in Bogotá was similar to what it had
been during the colonial period. Water was conducted through clay pipes to
public fountains spread out through the city. There it was poured into clay
pots, which were sold from house to house by women who carried the pots
on their heads or on the backs of burros—the so called *aguateras,* who were
an important part of urban life until the late nineteenth century. In 1888,
the first aqueduct was inaugurated in Bogotá, but the water it carried was
not treated at all. It was not until 1921 that water was chlorinated. As a
result, there was a significant drop in the incidence of typhoid fever.[20]

In Medellín, Colombia's second city, the situation was not much different from that of Bogotá with respect to public health. During the colonial period and throughout the nineteenth century, the main source of drinking water was a creek which traversed the city, Santa Elena, and there were many complaints about its contamination. For that reason, city officials forbade the washing of clothes, donkeys, and mules before 8:00 a.m., in order to allow the inhabitants to get the drinking water they needed for the day, before the water was affected by those activities.[21]

Probably the situation in the rest of Colombia with respect to public health was even worse than in the two main cities, the richest in the country. Bogotá is located in the most fertile valley in Colombia and lies at an altitude of 2600 meters. At the beginning of the twentieth century, Medellín was the main city of the prosperous coffee region of Colombia and the major industrial center of the country. Additionally, the altitude of these cities makes for better health than the tropical low lands. Thus, it is not until the 1920s that the average height of the Colombian elite can be expected to show an upward trend that would allow it to maintain a height above the rest of the population.

The trend in the average height of the employees of the Colombian Central Bank over the 20th century supports the hypothesis that only after the 1920s the privileged in Colombia experienced gains in height (see Figure 6).[22] Central Bank employees resemble the passport sample in that they were urban dwellers with formal education. In the 1910s (when the two series overlap) the height of these two groups is comparable. Over most of the twentieth century, Central Bank employees were consistently about 4 cm taller than the national average. Thus, the average stature of men from the elite moved upward from 168.6 cm in 1915–19 to 172 cm in 1984, as represented by men of the Central Bank. The height of Central Bank female employees similarly increased from 158.7 cm in 1915–19 to 163 cm in 1984.

Destinations and Reasons for Traveling
The analysis of height according to where people traveled reveals interesting patterns. People who traveled to the United States, Canada, and Europe were the tallest. In contrast, those who went to Central America and the islands of the Caribbean were 1.5 cm shorter than the men and women from the former group (see Figure 7). Obviously, those who traveled farthest tended to be from more privileged backgrounds and thus tended to be taller, as there is a correlation between social class and height, especially in the first stages of economic growth.

Figure 6.
Average Height by Passports, ID Cards, and
Central Bank Employee Records.

Sources: RNEC, AGN_FM, Colombian Central Bank and calculations by the authors.

There also seems to be a correlation between the reason for traveling abroad and height. Some people went to foreign countries for medical reasons. Since health treatments in Europe or the United States—the places most often chosen for such care—were costly, only the richest (and tallest) Colombians could afford this type of travel. The largest gap observed in height according to the motive for traveling is found for women. For example, those who went abroad as emigrants were 3.0 cm. shorter than those who did it for health reasons (Figure 8).

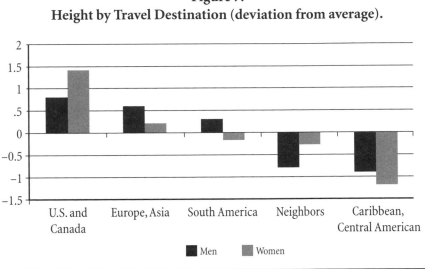

Figure 7.
Height by Travel Destination (deviation from average).

Source: AGN_FM and calculations by the authors. Neighbors = Ecuador, Panamá and Venezuela.

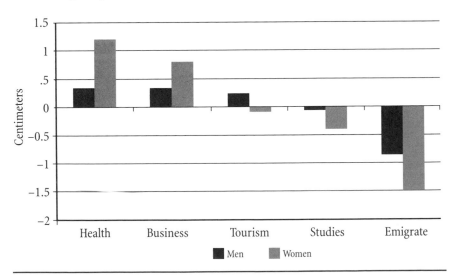

Figure 8.
Height by Reason Given for Travel (deviation from average).

Source: AGN_FM and calculations by the authors.

Regional Aspects

The passport records for the period under discussion do not include information on the place of birth, only the city where the passport was issued. Passports could be obtained by Colombian citizens at the time in 12 cities, mostly departmental capitals. More than half were issued in Bogotá (4,820 for men and 2,546 for women). It is sensible to assume a close relation of the city of birth to the city of issue and its hinterland.

Information about the place in which the passport was obtained shows an interesting correspondence with average height. The shortest persons were issued passports in the cities close to the frontier (Pasto, Popayán, Cúcuta) or in seaports (Santa Marta, Cartagena). A reason for this pattern could be that to travel abroad from a city in the interior, like Bogotá or Medellín, was much more costly than to depart from a city close to the border. Thus people from interior cities who traveled to foreign countries were probably better off than those who left from the seaports and frontier cities. Workers who were not especially prosperous could afford foreign travel from the latter cities because distances, at least to neighboring countries such as Ecuador, Venezuela, and Panama, were relatively short.

Figure 9.
Regional Deviation from Average Height.

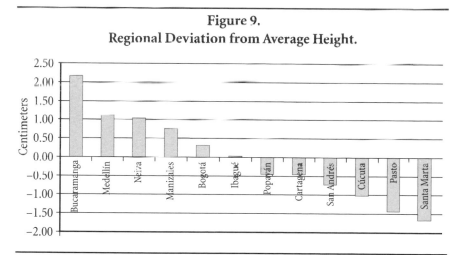

Note: Deviations were calculated as coefficients in a regression that controlled for year of birth and gender.
Source: AGN_FM and calculations by the authors.

Regional differences using a restricted least-squares regression with regional dummies show differences between −1.6 cm and 2 cm from the mean of height for all the cities (see Figure 9). Although we do not have information on the levels of GDP per capita for the Colombian regions until the second half of the twentieth century, there is some knowledge, derived from indirect sources such as tax revenues per capita, on the relative regional levels of prosperity for the period discussed in this chapter. That prosperity was closely associated with the production of coffee, the main export of Colombia since the end of the nineteenth century. In 1898, the region of Santander had a participation of 44.3% in the total production of coffee, while Antioquia's was 11.5%.[23] It is perhaps not a coincidence that the tallest group, according to the cities where the passports were issued, corresponded to Bucaramanga and Medellin, the capitals of Santander and Antioquia, respectively. In the other extreme, we find the lowest average height for the cities of Santa Marta, Pasto, and Cúcuta. All three are located away from the prosperous regions of the country. Santa Marta is a seaport in the Caribbean, which was in a situation of economic stagnation, as were Cúcuta, on the border with Venezuela, and Pasto, in the south of the country, near the border with Ecuador.

Conclusions

This study has examined the evolution of stature in Colombia, using a database with more than 16,835 observations from the passport records for persons born in the period 1870–1919, who are primarily representative of the elites.

The main conclusion drawn from the above analysis is that height was stagnant throughout this period for elite Colombians born during this span. The fact that per capita GDP was also probably stagnant at the time is perhaps not the main reason for this result, which we tentatively attribute to poor health conditions. Since the majority of those included in this sample belonged to the elite, it is likely that they were relatively well fed and had less to worry about confined spaces and similar problems that adversely affected the health of the lower classes in Colombia and elsewhere. As a result, these Colombians were taller than French and British workers of the time.

A second conclusion is that they were significantly taller than Colombians who did not belong to the elite (by almost 5 cm).

The third conclusion, which is somewhat surprising, is that by present Colombian standards this group was short. While the average height for men in this group in 1900 was 168.2 cm, Colombians born in 1985 grew to an average height of 170.6 cm. Even if the Colombian elite was well fed at the beginning of the twentieth century, the health conditions under which it lived were probably holding back its physical growth. Only in the late 1920s, when the international advances in modern medical technology would have been felt, could the health impediments for advances in height have begun to be eliminated. Additionally, not until the 1930s were there modern water supply systems in the main cities, a situation that severely hindered the possibility of eliminating water-borne infectious diseases, such as typhoid fever and cholera.

Notes

* The authors acknowledge the collaboration of Margarita Vanegas, Director of the Archives of the Ministry of Foreign Relations, Mauricio Tovar and his staff at the Archivo General de la Nación, and the assistance of Jesica Salamanca and Katherine Gaviria for the construction of the database, as well as comments by Haroldo Calvo, Julio Romero, Richard Steckel and the editors. For comments please contact ameisero@banrep.gov.co, or mmvegaa@yahoo.com.

1. The best introduction to the history of Colombia in the 19th century is Palacios and Safford, *Colombia: Fragmented*.
2. For an introduction to the field of anthropometric history see Steckel, "Stature and the Standard."
3. Meisel and Vega, "La estatura."
4. Salamanca, *Manual para el servicio*, 208–222.
5. Sunder, "On the Biological."
6. López-Alonso and Porras, "The Ups and Downs."
7. Sunder, "On the Biological."
8. Ibid., 9. Coatsworth, "Economic and Institutional."
9. Coatsworth, "Economic and Institutional."
10. Ocampo, *Colombia y la economía*, 87.
11. Ibid., 89.
12. Ibid., 53.
13. McGreevey, "The Transition," 45.
14. Ibid., 44.
15. The coefficients of the annual trend of average height are 0.013 cm per year for both men and women, and are not statistically significant at the 5% confidence level. The result is consistent with variable frequency weights by years, and a control for the place of issuance.
16. Ordoñez, Polania and Ramirez, "La estatura," Table 4.
17. McKeown, *The Origins*.
18. Fogel, "Nutrition and the Decline," 440, 481.
19. McKeown, *An Introduction*.
20. EAAB, *Historia del agua*, 59–67.
21. EEPPM, *Una mirada*, 8.
22. The Central Bank sample was constructed by the authors with 16,909 observations from the archives of the Colombian Central Bank (Banco de la República).
23. Melo, "El despegue," p. 178.

Primary Sources

Archivo General de la Nación, "Registro de Pasaportes." Cities of Bogotá, Medellín, y Manizales, 1918–1940.

Archivo del Ministerio de Relaciones Exteriores, "Registro de Pasaportes." Cities of Bucaramanga, Cartagena, Cúcuta, Ibagué, Neiva, Pasto, Popayán, San Andrés, y Santa Marta, 1918–1940.

Archivos del Departamento de Recursos Humanos, Banco de la República, Colombia, 1923–2004.

References

Coatsworth, John H. "Economic and Institutional Trajectories in Nineteenth-Century Latin America." In *Latin America and the World Economy since 1800,* ed. John H. Coatsworth and Alan M. Taylor. Cambridge: DRCLAS/Harvard University Press, 1998.

Drukker, Jan W., and Michiel A. Van Meerten. "Beyond Villermé and Quetelet: The Quantitative Relation between Sex and Age-specific Height and Real Per Capita Income." In *The Biological Standard of Living in Three Continents, Further Explorations in Anthropometric History,* ed. John Komlos, 25–58. Boulder: Westview Press, 1995.

EAAB [Empresa de Acueducto y Alcantarillado de Bogotá]. *Historia del agua en Bogotá, de la colonia al año 2000.* Bogotá: 1968.

EEPPM [Empresas Públicas de Medellín]. *Una mirada al pasado, una visión del futuro.* Medellín: 2000.

Federico, Giovanni. "Heights, Calories and Welfare: A New Perspective on Italian Industrialization, 1854–1913." *Economics and Human Biology* no. 1 (2003): 289–308.

Fogel, Robert W. "Nutrition and the Decline in Mortality since 1700: Some Preliminary Findings." In *Long-Term Factors in American Economic Growth,* ed. Stanley L. Engerman and Robert E. Gallman. Chicago: University of Chicago Press, 1986.

López-Alonso, Moramay, and Raúl Porras, "The Ups and Downs of Mexican Economic Growth: The Biological Standard of Living and Inequality, 1870–1950." *Economics and Human Biology* 1, no. 2 (2003).

Martínez-Carrión, José. "Estatura, salud y bienestar en las primeras etapas del crecimiento económico español. Una perspectiva comparada de los niveles de vida." Documentos de trabajo de la AHE, no. 0102 (2001).

McGreevey, William P. "The Transition to Economic Growth in Colombia," in Roberto Cortés Conde and Shane Hunt, ed., *The Latin American Economies, Growth and the Export Sector, 1880–1930.* Teaneck: Holmes and Meir, 1985.

McKeown, Thomas. *The Origins of Human Disease.* Oxford: Basil Blackwell, 1988.

———, *An Introduction to Social Medicine.* Oxford: Basil Blackwell, 1974.

Meisel, Adolfo and Margarita Vega. "La estatura de los colombianos: un ensayo de antropometría histórica, 1910–2003." *Revista del Banco de la República*, Bogotá, 77 no. 922 (August 2004).

Ocampo, José A. *Colombia y la economía mundial 1830–1910*. Bogotá: Tercer Mundo Editores, Colciencias-Fedesarrollo, 1998.

Ordoñez, Antonio, Doris Polania, and Gustavo Ramírez. "La estatura como indicador de desarrollo económico y social en Colombia." Informe Final. Bogotá: Fedesarrollo, 1992.

Palacios, Marco and Frank Safford. *Colombia: Fragmented Land, Divided Society*. New York: Oxford University Press, 2002.

Salamanca, Luis Humberto. *Manual para el servicio exterior de Colombia*. Bogotá: Ministerio de Relaciones Exteriores, 1959.

Steckel, Richard, "Stature and the Standard of Living." *Journal of Economic Literature* 33, no. 4 (1995): 1903–1940.

Sunder, Marco. "On the Biological Standard of Living of the Wealthy in 19th Century America." Paper presented at the World Cliometric Congress, Venice, Italy, July 9, 2004.

Van der Eng, Pierre. "An Inventory of Secular Changes in Human Growth in Indonesia." In *The Biological Standard of Living on Three Continents, Further Explorations in Anthropometric History*, ed. John Komlos. Boulder: Westview Press, 1995.

5

Better-off in the Thirties: Welfare Indices for Argentina, 1900–1940

Ricardo D. Salvatore

Ever since A. C. Pigou distinguished between "economic welfare"—the welfare derived from income and expenditure—and "quality of life"—the welfare derived from other sources and situations—economists, statisticians, and historians have been concerned with devising more comprehensive measures of welfare.[1] The acknowledgment of severe limitations in the use of income or consumption as measures of social welfare has led some scholars to devise ways of adjusting the existing estimates of GDP for income distribution, gender bias, environmental deterioration, and changes in the preference for leisure.[2] Others had tried to develop new indexes. Among them the most popular have been the Physical Quality of Life Index, the poverty rate, and the Human Development Index (HDI).[3] In the last twenty years, anthropometric historians have added mean stature to the list of indicators used for measuring welfare. Being a robust indicator of net nutrition, mean stature provides an individualized and direct measure of "biological welfare."[4] The gain in stature has been acknowledged as a key component of the improvement in the quality of life, as important as the increase in life expectancy, the fall in infant mortality, or the decline in fertility.[5]

Historians have applied some of these indexes, in particular the HDI, to evaluate the long-run evolution of welfare. For European economies, for example, Crafts has estimated a variant of the HDI with interesting results. In Latin America the use of these indexes for historical analysis has been more restricted, but economists have utilized them in order to compare the social development of the region with that of Europe.[6] The evaluation of Argentine economic development and welfare, just as the historical study of Latin American economies, has depended almost exclusively upon measurements of income and consumption. New work on heights has underscored the distinction between economic growth and biological welfare and called attention to the importance of stature for evaluating regional development.[7] Old characterizations of economic growth based upon traditional income measures still dominate the way we look at the Argentine past. The problem is that these measures (per capita GDP and real wages) present contradictory views of welfare—at least for the period 1900–1940, when Argentina evolved from an agrarian-export economy to an industrial economy.

This chapter aims to re-assess the question of Argentine well-being (economic, social, biological) during the first four decades of the twentieth century using new, composite, ordinal indices of welfare. First, I review some contrasting views about economic growth and welfare in modern Argentina. Second, I examine how a robust indicator of biological welfare (mean stature) contradicts the reading of the past given by income, export, and consumption indicators. Evidence about heights points to the existence of nutritional stress in the early 1900s, not accounted for in other economic indicators, and shows a more robust and sustained increase in nutrition and health status for the 1920s and 1930s. In the third section, I integrate these findings about stature and well-being into general or composite indexes of welfare. These indices had two salient characteristics: they are ordinal, hence able to overcome the aggregation problems associated with other indices (including the HDI); and they include stature and caloric consumption as key indicators of welfare, a missing dimension among other measurements of welfare.

The results of these estimates reinforce the need to revise the traditional characterization of Argentine economic development during this period ("golden age" versus "retardation of growth"). In terms of welfare, the 1920s and 1930s seem preferable—in terms of the "average Argentine"—to the early decades of the century. The analysis provides some tentative explanations about the factors that might have influenced net nutrition in the long-run. Its aim is double: to highlight the importance of mean stature as an indicator of the "biological standard of living," and to present a way of integrating this indicator with more traditional measurements of consumer welfare and economic capabilities.

Contrasting Views of Argentine Economic Development

During the period 1880 to 1914, the Argentine economy has been portrayed as a case of successful export-led growth. Rapid growth in agricultural exports, primarily cereals and beef, translated into relatively high rates of growth in income per capita. The country's remarkable economic performance during this period was attributed to its relative high levels of agricultural

productivity, to the rapid expansion of basic resources (land, labor, and capital), and to wise economic policies. Markets functioned almost without regulation and, since 1899, the currency was tied to the international gold
standard.[8] Typically, this was the case of an "open-space" economy that, with
abundant land resources and the attraction of labor and capital from abroad,
was able to grow in a rapid and sustained fashion. In this success story (the
"golden age") two actors, Spanish and Italian immigrants and British capital, were crucial in peopling the Pampas, constructing modern productive
units and basic infrastructure, and generating a specialized economy well
integrated into international goods, labor, and financial markets.

The interwar period, on the other hand, has been characterized as one of
declining growth, loss of international competitiveness, and growing state
regulation of markets. In 1967 Di Tella and Zymelman suggested that the
period 1914–1933 be considered as a "great delay" to industrialization.[9] The
period witnessed a deceleration of economic growth, neglect of basic infrastructure, and the exhaustion of the main abundant resource, land. The
First World War had dramatically reduced the inflows of capital and labor
and this, combined with the closing of the frontier, translated into reduced
rates of growth. Contemporary critics blamed the over-specialization in
agricultural exports for much of the country's ills, among them: the economy's small capacity to absorb new technologies, an excessively urbanized
population given to consumption of imported goods, immigrants who concentrated in the Littoral region and thus did not contribute to national economic integration, and politicians who disregarded the internal market.[10]
Other historians, while acknowledging the grave economic consequences
of the First World War, considered the 1920s as prosperous years in which
the Argentine economy grew faster than those of the United States, Canada,
and Australia.[11]

ECLA economists and nationalists likewise argued that the agrarian-
export economy generated a type of growth that was too dependent upon
external factors and not conducive to the development of the domestic
market or to a more egalitarian distribution of income.[12] To them, the crisis of the 1930s was the great divide that stimulated industrialization,
strengthened the domestic market, and redistributed income toward wage-
earners. Recently, A. Taylor has refurbished the thesis of the "great delay,"
suggesting that, in comparison with other economies of the period,
Argentina experienced a "retardation" of growth during the interwar years.
At the root of this unsatisfactory economic performance was a perverse
population/savings dynamic. A rapid growth in dependency rates had
"eaten up" the savings capacity of the country, making it even more

dependent upon external financing at a time when capital markets were closing up on Latin America.[13] The idea that in the interwar years Argentina broke away from the world economy and, as a consequence, reduced its rate of growth has been suggested by Williamson-Taylor, della Paolera-Taylor, and Gerchunoff-Llach.[14]

The crisis of the 1930s has been considered as a period of opportunity for Latin America in spite of the shock suffered by the external sector. Deprived of its crucial imports by the sharp fall in exports and the shortage of foreign exchange, countries had to supply the domestic market with their own industries. In Argentina in particular, the Great Depression was a phenomenon of short duration: by 1934 the economy was already in full recovery.[15] Stimulated by the sudden change in relative prices (via exchange controls and tariff increases), industrialization proceeded at a rapid pace in the mid-1930s, creating an impressive industrial capacity by 1943.[16] Those who stressed political liberties and workers' rights recalled the "thirties" as a time of electoral fraud, police repression, and a decline in labor organization and power. Commentators dubbed it "the infamous decade."[17] Sociologist Gino Germani considered the 1930s as the prelude to Peronism: a decade characterized by poverty and mass internal migrations that created urban masses dissatisfied with progress, the future clientele of Juan D. Perón.[18]

These evaluations of Argentine long-term development do not take into account three important dimensions of welfare. First, they overlook the existence of important regional differences in the levels of economic performance and do not integrate into the analysis any measure of inequality in the distribution of income. Second, they fail to incorporate the increasing capabilities of the population in terms of educational attainment and improvements in health and nutrition. Furthermore, these evaluations, based solely on economic performance, make it difficult to integrate the perceptions and experience of the main social actors about the process of economic development. The questions of inequality, political corruption, and police repression figured prominently in the discourse of anarchists, socialists, syndicalists, and middle-class *radicales*. Important moments of social protest disrupted the tranquility of the conservative republic (most notably, the strikes of 1902 and 1904, the urban tenant riots of 1907, and the 1912 uprising of tenant farmers). Later, during the Unión Cívica Radical administrations, as distributional struggles rose, widespread strikes paralyzed the country (especially in 1917–19). After the "Tragic Week" of 1919, a steep increase in police repression, aided by nationalist armed bands, seriously weakened the labor movement.

Income and Socioeconomic Well-being

Available evidence on per capita GNP supports the idea of a rapidly growing economy during the periods 1902–1913 and 1921–1929. In the long
run, this growth did not translate into impressive welfare gains owing to
the devastating effect of two external shocks: WWI and the Great Depression. The impact of the war was such that the per capita income of Argentines in 1917 was similar to that of 1900. In the postwar period, recovery was
strong. Still, only in 1924 did per capita income exceed the previous peak of
1912. In the years 1927–29 per capita incomes reached absolute peaks. But
then the Great Depression brought income down to the levels of the early
1900s. The income of 1932 was lower than that achieved in 1906–1908. After
the recovery of 1933–34, the economy continued to grow until the end of
the decade. The gains in economic welfare, however, were quite poor: there
was no change in per capita income between 1925 and 1935; and the income
of 1940 was smaller than that attained in 1929.

Real wages show a different evolution. The combined effect of rising food
prices and stagnating nominal wages (in large part due to the pressure of
mass immigration) made real wages fall during the years 1905–1909. After
a timid recovery in 1910–12, real wages continued to fall until 1918. During the period 1915–18, war-induced inflation was the main factor behind
the fall of real wages. The post-WWI recovery was strong (unions traded off
wage increases for a decline in strike activity), as real wages reached a peak
in 1928. In fact, the "twenties" appear as good years for workers. Real wages
were higher in 1922–1928 than in any year from 1900 to 1920. The "thirties,"
by contrast, appear as a lost decade: a period in which real wages failed to
grow. The decline in real wages resulting from WWI was more dramatic
than the one generated by the Great Depression. For the whole period we
can distinguish two situations: one characterized by declining real wages
when income was growing (1906–1912); the other characterized by both
income and real wage growth (1921–1929).[19]

Clearly, to evaluate workers' welfare we need also an estimate of unemployment. This information is unavailable before 1917, and after that
period, available only for the city of Buenos Aires. For the period we have
data on real "family income" (1913–1929), the information provides more
pessimistic outcomes than the series of real wages. Between 1913 and 1919,
workers lost 42 percent of their family income, mostly due to inflation.
Recovery in the 1920s was strong, but not sufficient. By 1928, workers' families had an almost identical real income as in 1914. Towards the late 1920s
the reduction in family size brought about a very small improvement in
workers' welfare.[20]

Figure 1.
Per Capita GNP and Real Wages.

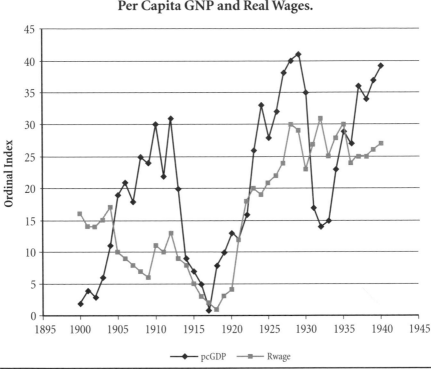

Source: See Appendix, at the end of the chapter.

Other stylized facts need to be integrated into this picture. First, this was a period in which a vociferous and influential minority (elite members with positivist and conservative leanings) devoted great efforts to the national assimilation of immigrants, chiefly through the school system.[21] Cultural nationalists gave new impulse to the efforts of late-nineteenth-century liberals to attain high levels of literacy, under the principles of non-confessional, compulsory, free elementary education. Hence, starting from the early years of the century, the numbers of schools, teachers, and pupils grew faster than the population.[22] Not surprisingly, Argentina achieved great progress in terms of school attendance and literacy as a result of this policy. The percentage of children ages 6 to 14 attending schools increased from 48 percent in 1900 to 84 percent in 1940. During the same period, the rate of literacy, as measured by the basic reading skills of 18-year-old recruits, went from 67 percent to 88 percent.[23] Newland estimates that the rate of literacy (population over 10) rose from 52 percent in 1900 to 73 percent in 1925 to

Figure 2.
Literacy and Schooling.

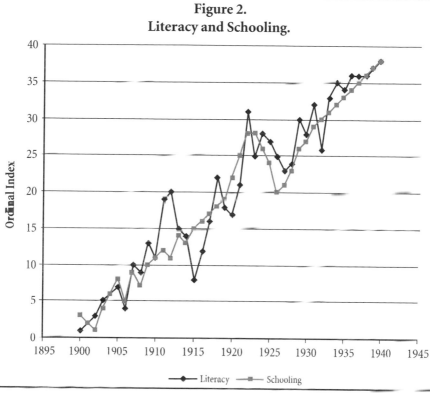

Source: See Appendix.

88 percent in 1950.[24] Thus, the capabilities of Argentines were greatly improved by public investments in human capital. The progress in schooling was only mildly affected by the two great external shocks to the economy (WWI and the Great Depression), while the figures of literacy seem unaffected by WWI.[25]

This was also a period when the Hygienists—with sympathies among the socialist movement—were able to influence public policy in the wide range of health-related areas. After the panic of the yellow fever epidemic (1871), this expert community produced a model of sanitary reform that included proper sewage and water drainage facilities, medical control of immigrants, regulated prostitution, compulsory vaccination, and the control of food production and distribution.[26] During 1900–1940 a significant expansion in medical attention and services, provided in part by ethnic-based mutual-aid organizations, emerged from the labor movement.[27] At first, the results of this sanitary improvement were most noticeable in the

Figure 3.
Life Expectancy and Infant Mortality.

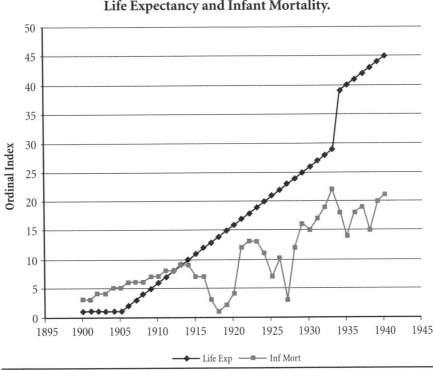

Source: See Appendix.

city of Buenos Aires, but over time other cities in the interior benefited as well. Consequently, indicators of health and longevity showed significant improvements. During the period 1900 to 1940, life expectancy increased from 40 to 58 years, infant mortality fell from 128 to 90 per 1000,[28] and gross mortality declined from 23 to 10 per 1000.[29] Infant mortality figures indicate clearly how difficult it was at first to control infectious diseases— there were important regressions in sanitary improvement in the period of WWI and in 1924–27.

The programs of national education and public health reform certainly had an impact on the welfare of the average Argentine, something which does not emerge so clearly in national income figures.[30] Also, the story of Argentine development would be incomplete if we did not mention that the period was marked by great changes in the levels of social conflict. Since the beginning of the century (1902–1904), an anarchist and syndicalist leadership managed to build a powerful labor movement (the famous FORA)

Figure 4.
Social Order and Export Performance.

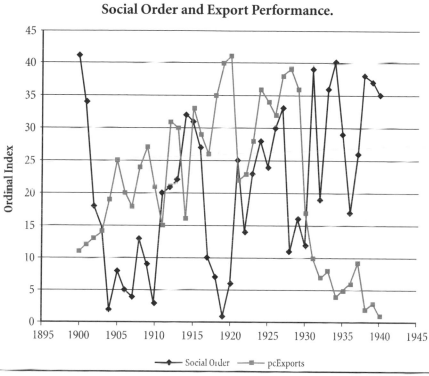

Source: See Appendix.

using a confrontational approach to industrial relations. Social protest thrived in the first two decades of the century, the number of strikes peaking in the years 1917–1919. Afterwards, greater state repression and the internal divisions within the labor movement (the ascendance of the socialists and other bread-and-butter unionists) brought pacification to the field of industrial relations.

The rise in labor militancy in 1917–19 (taken here as low points of "social order") was associated with the uncertainty of wartime inflation and to the perception that Argentina—unlike what the official propaganda stated—was a country of great social inequalities. Whether this perception was accurate or not, the level of social conflict that it generated caused a great deal of anxiety and insecurity to the rest of the population. To many, the Tragic Week of 1919 was a watershed in Argentine history.[31] In this episode the state, assisted by squads of nationalists from the Patriotic League, organized a major repression against immigrant workers and their organizations.

This event (which confirmed the fear of social chaos anticipated by the Tenant Strike of 1907 and the rural uprising of 1912) spelled for many elite politicians the end of an era of permissiveness and internationalism.[32] From then on, many shifted to more nationalistic positions, and began to argue for selective immigration, more social control, better distribution of income, and greater doses of patriotic education.

Stature and Biological Well-being

Statistics about per capita GDP and real wages are not as comprehensive as we would like them to be. GDP estimates overlook a series of important economic activities and calculate consumption as a residual element. The real wage series, particularly for the period 1900–1913, cannot be taken as representative of a vast spectrum of work categories. For this reason, neither per capita income nor real wages are absolutely reliable as indicators of the Argentine standard of living. Therefore we have to resort to other indicators. The availability of nutrients constitutes an important element of families' welfare function. To evaluate the evolution of this indicator, we have estimated the caloric intake generated by a basket of nine basic foodstuffs and expressed it in per capita terms. Results are summarized in Figure 5.

Figure 5.
Daily Caloric Intake Per Capita (nine basic foodstuffs).

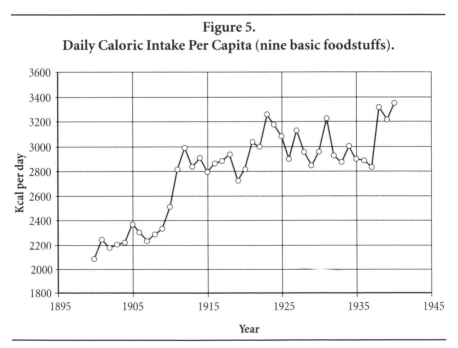

Source: See Appendix.

Estimates of caloric availability tend to reinforce the traditional story. Argentina was a food-rich country, with per capita calories ranging between 2,800 and 3,200 during the period 1913–1935. Considering that people had other sources of nutrients than these nine basic foodstuffs, actual average caloric intake must have been higher. The expansion of agricultural exports also generated a domestic abundance of foodstuffs (at international prices). Domestic per-capita consumption of calories seemed to have followed closely the evolution of exports. The "cereal boom" of 1902–1912 augmented by 40 percent the amount of calories available for each Argentine. Food supply was maintained during the war years (except for a minor fall in 1919), increasing in the immediate postwar period. The 1920s produced ups and downs in per capita caloric consumption, around an average of 3,000 calories.

The fall in real wages and per capita GDP during the period 1913–18 is not reflected in the figures of caloric availability and consumption. Our estimates do not contemplate the waste of calories in the production and distribution process. Nor have they been corrected for changes in the composition of families and in the relative prices of foodstuffs. Hence, our estimates of "caloric intake" are only valid inasmuch as they confirm our suspicion that Argentina was a food-rich economy and that caloric consumption was growing on the average. But averages do not tell the whole story. To assess the evolution of welfare, we need to find out how these calories were distributed among social classes, income groups, occupations, and regions.

By contrast, the average stature of recruits presents a clear situation of deterioration of biological welfare between 1901 and 1910, then recovery until the early 1920s, and then continued growth until 1940.[33] On the basis of this evidence, the extent of the "nutrition stress" could be extended to the whole period 1903 to 1918. All recruits born during this period (except for those born in 1906) experienced poorer nutritional and health conditions during their childhood than those born before and after. Between 1900 and 1940 the stature of Argentine recruits increased 3.4 centimeters (from 168.1 cm to 171.5 cm). The period 1900–1910 witnessed an absolute decline of 0.9 centimeters; during 1910–1920 stature augmented by 1 cm; in the period 1920–30 recruits gained 1.2 cm; and 2.1 cm in the 1930s.

There were clearly two phases in the evolution of stature: a declining phase, from 1901 to 1910; and a rising phase, from 1910 to 1929. During this second phase, much of the growth (from 1910 to 1918) was just recovery of the nutritional-health status attained in 1902–1903. This allows us to formulate the existence of an interesting "double puzzle" in the evolution of nutritional or biological welfare.

Figure 6.
Average Stature of Recruits ("crude means").

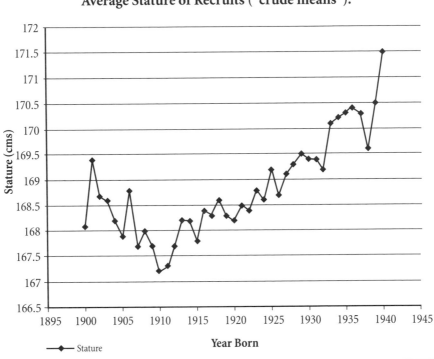

Source: See Appendix.

The first puzzle refers to the existence of nutritional stress in an economy rich in food, during a period in which Argentina's production and exports of wheat, corn, and other grains grew at remarkable rates. The growth of beef exports was delayed with regard to the "grain boom," but equally remarkable in performance. How can we account for this decline in net nutritional status during the cereal boom?

One possible answer is that mass immigration depressed the real wage so rapidly that families could not adjust their food basket to protect themselves from nutritional deterioration. Under this perspective, the high wage flexibility of this international labor market would account for the nutritional stress. We may call this the "labor market glut" hypothesis. A second possible answer lies in the accumulation strategies of immigrants, who for the sake of saving depressed the food intake of their families or, more likely, used their children to complement the family income. We may call this the "immigrant frugality" hypothesis. A third possible explanation is that proprietors of real estate in urban and rural areas charged exorbitant prices for rent, forcing the newcomers to allocate less money to basic necessities, in particular, underfeeding their children. We may call this the "landlord cruelty" hypothesis.

The second puzzle refers to the fact that major external shocks to the economy (the First World War and the Great Depression) caused only minor declines in average stature. How to explain this apparent anomaly? One possible answer relates to family strategies that privileged nutrition and children's well-being. Maintaining the level of family nutrients might have involved a combination of the following strategies: a) reducing non-food expenses, b) substituting cheaper foodstuffs (potatoes instead of beef, for example), or c) maintaining the consumption of "growth-enhancing" items, such as milk and cheese. Another possible explanation relates to state social policies. Growing state enforcement of regulations against child labor (through the Department of Labor) made it less feasible for families to send children to work at times of economic crises. It is also possible that the diffusion of information about child care, nutrition, and disease prevention produced a positive effect in the population at large. Why did these policies become effective only after WWI? Further research is needed to answer this question.

What seems clear is that between the first (1900–1918) and the second phase (1919–1940), families learned to cushion the impact of shocks to income and employment. The early decade of the century was a period of absolute deterioration of health and nutritional status, while the 1930s show the greatest gains in net nutrition. While improvements in sanitary conditions were certainly a factor, the closing of the economy lowered the relative price of the export commodity (food) vis-a-vis domestic manufactures. Quite likely, the reduction of child labor played also a role. The 1920s were prodigal in legislation protective of labor rights, including the limitation of working hours and of female and child labor. A bread-and-butter unionism accomplished, in the context of renewed economic growth, what the conflictive years of WWI had not: a doubling of real wages between 1918 and 1929.[34]

Composite Indexes of Welfare

As we have seen, per capita GNP, exports, and real wages figures tell quite different stories about Argentine welfare. Moreover, these indicators do not correlate well with measurements of human capital, health, and nutrition. To overcome this apparent contradiction, we need a more comprehensive measure of welfare, one that would include, in addition to income, at least the improvements in education, health, nutrition, and social order. Ideally, our comprehensive welfare measure should describe the whole range of improvements of capabilities and satisfactions of average Argentines. In practice, there are some important technical difficulties in formulating them.

Since people's dimensions of welfare are multiple, in principle a cardinal index seems appropriate to capture this diversity of needs (or welfare functions). But cardinal indexes have two main problems. If multiple indicators are used, we run the risk of minimizing the influence of some important component of welfare. In addition, cardinal indexes leave the weighting problem unresolved. What is the contribution of each attribute (indicator) to aggregate or social welfare? By necessity, we need to solve the question of aggregation and weights by resorting to ordinal preferences. And, rather than choosing a particular index, we shall work with a group of indexes, representing different combinations of four components of welfare.[35] Part of the exercise consists in evaluating how effective and sympathetic are these indexes in ordering preferences about past (historical) situations.

Methodology

Drawing on Crafts's work for industrialized economies, I have produced composite indices of welfare using the Dasgupta and Weal method of aggregation.[36] Dasgupta-Weal indexes are simple aggregations of the ranking orders of distinct indicators. The summation itself is later transformed into a ranking order using the Borda rule.[37] This method has two chief advantages. First, errors in measurement of particular indicators do not greatly affect the results. Secondly, the weighting problem is avoided. The method compares ranks, not absolute magnitudes. Its main disadvantage is that we can only compare different states of well-being. We can affirm that, according to a given index, 1930 was better than 1910. But we cannot evaluate the magnitude of the improvement or decline.

Though this indexing method has been used mainly for comparisons across countries, I have used it to make intertemporal comparisons of welfare. The justification for this is the following. Social actors can look back at a certain period of time and rank their relative welfare according to multiple characteristics: income, longevity, infant mortality, nutrition, etc. The Borda rule assures that this ranking is independent from the chosen initial point (the base year). While in principle it is possible to take any number of indicators or attributes, I have chosen to take four at a time. This narrows the spectrum of possibilities, but at the same time it makes it easier to evaluate the effect produced by the attributes chosen. The attributes had to comply with an additional restriction. There always had to be one indicator of each of the following domains: income, nutrition, health, and education.[38]

To interpret the results correctly, the nature of ordinal indexes and the way they are built need to be understood.[39] On the one hand, the Borda rule tends to "flatten" the index, attributing a single change in rank to a given increase in the sum of individual attributes. On the other hand, if all other attributes are equal, a small change in one of the attributes elevates the rank by one position. This "inflation" of the index could be compensated by establishing a strict rule of ordering: that is, attributing a higher rank only when at least two components of the index have increased (in whatever magnitude).

The Indicators Used

To estimate composite indices of welfare we used ten basic indicators: per capita income (GNP), real wages, per capita exports, per capita caloric intake, adult stature, literacy rate, schooling rate, infant mortality rate, life expectancy, and number of strikes. Details about the reliability and source of these data are provided in the Appendix. While it could be argued that strikes and per capita exports are short-run indicators that do not measure well the long-term evolution of living standards, we wanted to include these two indicators to see what information they could add to measurements of capabilities, income, and health. The former was taken as an indicator of social conflict (workers' unhappiness with their current income and work conditions); the latter as an indicator of the health of the export economy, that is, reflecting the welfare of merchants, landowners and tenants, agricultural workers, and, in general, the towns of the Pampa region.

This choice of indicators and their aggregation necessarily has some shortcomings. It could be argued that I am putting indicators of long-run performance (such as income and longevity) together with indicators of income cycles (per capita exports) and workers' short-term dissatisfaction (strikes). It could also be argued that a certain degree of double-counting is implicit in adding longevity and income. Part of the gain in life expectancy, G. Williamson argues, has to be attributed to income and consumption and is, consequently, endogenous. The rest of the gains in longevity are associated to societal changes in sanitation and, to that extent, can be considered exogenous.[40] The same criticism applies to the correlation between nutrition and longevity: increases in income lead to better nutrition which in turn facilitates better health in adult life. While it would be preferable to measure only the net gains in longevity (that is, the exogenous part) and to separate the gains in nutrition that are not attributable to income (for example, those due to increased information about diets and child care), at this point, this type of statistical refinement is not possible.

Another shortcoming of these indices—and this is also due to the lack of sources—is the absence of measures of income inequality. At a given level of income, the social utility will be lower if the distribution of income is more unequal than in the opposite case. The risk of overstating the welfare derived from an income level is always present when working with average indices. However, it could be argued that heights and infant mortality are indirect indicators of inequality; that they are highly correlated with measures of poverty. In the end, we are faced with a dilemma: whether to follow the road of adjusting real income for income distribution, urban "disamenities," gender inequality, and other factors—a road that is still quite dependent on the absolute magnitude of the indicators—or try to use a group of ordinal indices aggregating the various dimensions of human welfare. It is precisely this possibility of aggregating short-term improvements in income, health, nutrition, and education that compensates for the shortcomings of composite indices.

Co-variation

Most of the indicators show remarkably low co-variation. This might indicate either that each of them provides additional information of a particular dimension of well-being, or that there are significant errors of measurement associated with some of these indicators. Table 1 presents the Spearman rank-correlation coefficients for the ten indicators chosen. Only in four pairs (amongst the 45 reported in the table) the correlation coefficient is 0.80 or higher. All these exceptionally high co-variations are reasonable: schooling and literacy; infant mortality and literacy; and life expectancy with both infant mortality and schooling. In 27 pairs (out of 45) the coefficient is under 0.60.

Per capita GDP seems to behave very differently from heights ($r = 0.37$), caloric consumption ($r = 0.48$), infant mortality ($r = 0.54$), and schooling ($r = 0.51$). The best predictor of per capita GDP is literacy, with an $r = 0.62$, a clear indication of the importance of human capital in growth of Argentine income. The three indicators of income correlate very poorly amongst themselves. Per capita GDP is unrelated to per capita exports. The correlation between per capita GDP and real wages is only 0.58. Income growth seems to have generated negative or regressive income redistribution. The correlation between real wages and per capita exports has a negative sign. Whenever there was an export bonanza, based on food exports (meat and grain), workers had to pay higher prices for necessities. This is to be expected in export economies that do not protect workers' budgets from external price increases.

Table 1.
Spearman Correlation Coefficients.

Indicador	Per capita GDP	Life expectancy	Infant mortality	Literacy	Schooling	Stature	Real wages	Caloric consump.	Strikes	Per capit exports
Per capita GDP	1	0.57	0.54	0.62	0.51	0.37	0.58	0.48	0.03	0.07
Life expectancy	0.57	1	0.77	0.96	0.97	0.76	0.68	0.75	0.42	-0.22
Infant mortality	0.54	0.77	1	0.80	0.79	0.58	0.72	0.56	0.42	-0.46
Literacy	0.62	0.96	0.80	1	0.96	0.70	0.67	0.78	0.37	-0.24
Schooling	0.51	0.97	0.79	0.96	1	0.70	0.64	0.77	0.38	-0.24
Stature	0.37	0.76	0.58	0.70	0.70	1	0.76	0.47	0.45	-0.42
Real wages	0.58	0.68	0.72	0.67	0.64	0.76	1	0.47	0.46	-0.44
Caloric consump.	0.48	0.75	0.56	0.78	0.77	0.47	0.47	1	0.44	0.02
Strikes	0.08	0.42	0.42	0.37	0.38	0.45	0.46	0.44	1	-0.41
Per capita exports	0.07	-0.22	-0.46	-0.24	-0.24	-0.42	-0.44	0.02	-0.41	1

Human capital indicators correlate better with indicators of health than with those of income. Infant mortality is closely associated with literacy and schooling, and presents a somewhat different evolution than life expectancy. Schooling and literacy are close substitutes (r = 0.96) because they measure the same phenomenon from different angles ("process" versus "product"). A good correlation between indicators of educational attainment and mortality (infant and general) is also expected. The success of campaigns against infectious and endemic diseases crucially depended upon the dissemination of information about hygiene. Schools were the vehicle for these campaigns.

Indicators of nutrition (stature and caloric consumption) present us with a different "reality" than that expressed by the traditional measure of income (pc GDP). At the time of rapid income growth and export bonanza (first decade of the century), workers suffered nutritional stress. Conversely, during the external shocks of WWI and the Great Depression, stature continued to grow, almost uninterrupted. For this reason, per capita exports cannot even qualify as an indicator of workers' welfare. Its highest levels coincide with the lowest levels of real wages as well as with moderate income levels (the closed economy of the 1930s generated better levels of per capita GDP).[41] Stature and caloric consumption themselves are poorly correlated (r = 0.47). This could be due to the difference between "gross" and "net" nutrition, as well as to errors in measurement. Labor strikes, a measure of social dissatisfaction, are not closely associated with any of the remaining indicators.

In short, except for a group of four indicators that are very closely related (life expectancy, infant mortality, literacy, and schooling), the rest of the variables present different information to contribute to our composite index. Though there is a problem of double-counting in aggregating these indices, few of them are near substitutes of the others.

Analysis of Results

The Ordinal Quality of Life indexes are presented in Table 2. Figures 7–12 illustrate these results. The numbers in the y-axis represent rankings rather than absolute magnitudes. All indexes show important, long-run improvements in welfare between 1900 and 1940. They also reveal critical periods in the evolution of Argentine welfare. This is particularly true during the period of most rapid economic growth: 1900–1915. Considering the twelve indexes, in half of them the average person cannot be said to be better off in 1915 than in 1906. Compared to this early period, the post-WWI era seems remarkably better. A similar exercise would show that in twelve out of twelve cases, the average Argentine was better off in 1925 than in 1917. And the same is true with regard to the comparison between 1938 and 1925 (1938 > 1925).

Table 2.
Composite Welfare Indexes.

Year	OrQL1*	OrQL2*	OrQL3*	OrQL4*	OrQL5*	OrQL6*	OrQL7*	OrQL8*	OrQL9*	OrQL10*	OrQL11*	OrQL12*
1900	1	1	2	3	5	1	1	2	1	1	14	13
1901	4	4	11	8	18	2	2	3	9	2	16	11
1902	2	2	9	4	9	1	3	1	7	2	7	6
1903	4	3	10	7	13	3	4	3	6	3	6	5
1904	6	5	10	7	16	4	6	6	3	5	3	2
1905	8	6	2	2	3	7	5	7	1	6	6	3
1906	14	9	8	5	7	6	4	4	9	5	10	2
1907	9	6	2	1	1	5	6	5	2	6	5	1
1908	15	9	3	2	2	8	5	5	5	7	12	4
1909	16	9	4	2	4	10	10	8	4	8	9	3
1910	17	11	5	4	7	14	10	9	3	12	8	4
1911	18	10	12	6	11	12	12	10	6	11	13	10
1912	21	14	14	8	21	18	9	18	8	13	18	15
1913	19	12	13	10	6	15	11	12	11	9	16	12
1914	11	8	12	9	14	13	15	15	12	4	15	16
1915	3	7	1	8	17	9	8	11	9	2	11	14
1916	7	10	6	11	10	11	14	13	14	2	11	14
1917	5	8	5	11	8	11	16	14	10	1	2	8
1918	13	13	10	12	15	17	8	17	12	4	4	9
1919	10	14	7	13	10	13	7	13	11	4	1	4
1920	12	15	8	14	12	16	13	16	13	5	5	7
1921	20	16	15	15	19	19	17	19	15	10	17	18
1922	22	17	19	16	23	20	21	21	16	14	14	17
1923	24	18	19	18	24	25	21	27	20	15	21	24
1924	27	21	17	17	27	27	23	24	17	18	23	25
1925	24	20	18	19	23	23	18	23	18	16	20	23
1926	26	18	17	17	31	22	22	20	19	17	24	22
1927	25	23	16	20	25	28	28	25	16	19	26	29
1928	29	24	20	21	28	27	30	26	21	23	22	21
1929	34	26	23	22	30	24	19	22	23	26	28	19
1930	30	25	21	21	29	28	26	26	22	20	22	20
1931	27	21	23	23	28	25	22	30	24	16	27	31
1932	23	19	22	24	20	22	20	28	25	15	19	26
1933	28	22	25	25	22	21	25	26	26	16	29	28
1934	31	27	27	26	31	31	26	32	29	20	31	32
1935	32	28	25	30	32	30	27	31	27	22	30	30
1936	33	29	26	27	26	29	29	30	30	21	25	26
1937	35	31	28	29	30	32	24	29	31	25	32	27
1938	33	30	24	28	27	33	31	33	28	24	33	34
1939	36	32	29	31	33	34	32	33	32	26	34	33
1940	37	33	30	32	34	35	33	34	33	27	35	35

In many of these indexes the effect of the Great Depression appears relatively modest compared with the decline of welfare in the period 1907–1915. Postwar recovery was remarkably rapid, and the "thirties" continued and intensified the improvement attained in the prior decade. The stability of real wages and the great improvements in educational attainment more than compensated for the short-term variations in infant mortality and in caloric intake. The years 1938 to 1940 marked absolute peaks, in many cases overshadowing the welfare attained in the late 1920s. In all indexes, the last three years of the 1930s rank higher than 1929, the best year of the export-led growth.[42]

The first two indexes (OrQL1* and OrQL2*) shown in Fig.7 share the same indicators for income (per capita GDP) and nutrition (stature), differing only in the indicators for education (literacy vs. years of schooling) and public health (infant mortality vs. life expectancy). The general picture that both indexes convey is the same. Almost every combination of welfare in the 1930s (except for 1932 using OrQL1* and 1933 using OrQL2*) is

Figure 7.
Indexes OrQL1* and OrQL2.*

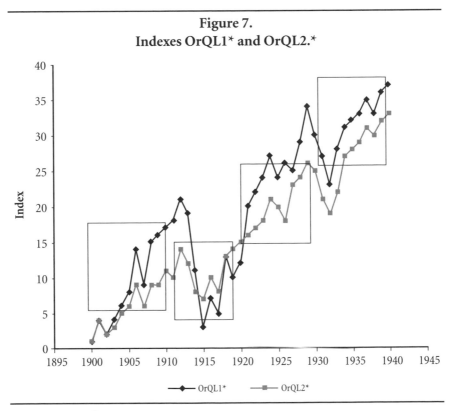

Source: See Appendix.

Notes: OrQL1* (infant mortality; stature; literacy; per capita GDP); OrQL2* (life expectancy; stature; schooling; per capita GDP).

Figure 8.
Indexes OrQL3* and OrQL4.*

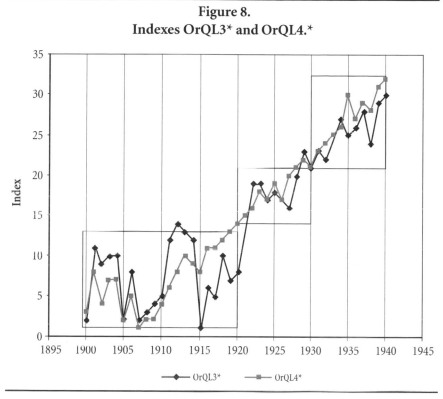

Source. See Appendix.

Notes: OrQL3* (infant mortality; stature; literacy; real wages); OrQL4* (life expectancy; stature; schooling; real wages).

better than the level of welfare attained in the 1900s and in the 1910s. The same could be said in comparison with the 1920s, with the exception of the years 1924, 1928, and 1929. When one compares the level of welfare in the 1920s with that of the period 1900–1919, the situation is more ambiguous. The 1920s are better than the 1910s (with the exception of 1911, 1912, and 1913 in OrQL1*), but it is not true that all or most situations of welfare in the 1920s are better than those in the 1900s.

Both indexes show absolute declines in welfare in the periods 1912–1915 and 1929–1932. Whereas the second period coincides with the Great Depression, the former decline seems surprising. Generally, scholars admit that the beginning of WWI brought about a recession in the external trade, finances, and economic well-being of Argentines, but few would admit that the deterioration of standards of living started a year earlier (1913). The recovery from the war years—a period of clear deterioration of welfare— becomes clear only after 1921.

Indexes OrQL3* and OrQL4* use real wages instead of per capita GDP as income indicator (see Figure 8). Here again the 1930s are better than the 1920s, and the twenties better than the period 1900–1919. For the first decade of the century, both indexes confirm the deterioration of welfare between 1901 and 1907–09 and show little or no gains in welfare between 1903–04 and 1916–17. According to these indexes, the impact of the Great Depression was almost negligible. The outbreak of WWI appears as a dramatic event only when using index OrQL3*. Index OrQL4* (life expectancy, stature, schooling, and real wages) permits a narrative of Argentine welfare completely different from the traditional views. It shows an absolute decline of welfare between 1901 and 1908–09 (both indexes do) and, starting in 1910, a sustained increase, only interrupted by minor setbacks in 1914–15, 1926–27, and 1936.

The indexes illustrated in Figure 9 use caloric consumption as indicator of nutrition. In all other components, they are similar to OrQL1* and

Figure 9.
Indexes OrQL5* and OrQL6.*

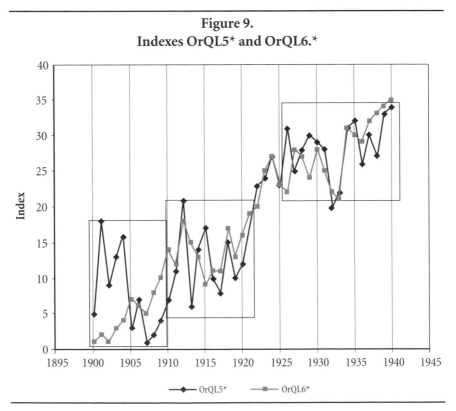

Source: See Appendix.

Notes: OrQL5* (infant mortality; caloric consumption; literacy; pc GDP); OrQL6* (life expectancy; caloric consumption; schooling; pc GDP).

OrQL2*. In terms of comparative welfare, we can assert, on the basis of these indicators, that any year in the period 1925–1940 was better than any year in the period 1900–1910. With certain exceptions, the period 1925–1940 also looks better than the period 1910–1921. These indexes (OrQL5* in particular) show greater cyclical variation than other indexes, and present a less optimistic evaluation of the 1910s and of the 1930s.

Indexes OrQL7* and OrQL8* reflect the combined influence of caloric consumption and real wages (see Figure 10). The trend here is definitely upward, beginning with the first years of the century. One of these indexes (OrQL7*) shows important setbacks in 1915, 1918–19, 1925, 1929, 1932–33, and 1937. The other (OrQL8*) is more stable over time, showing declines in welfare in 1913, 1915, 1919, 1924–26, 1932–33, and 1935–37. What appears unusual about these indexes is the "bad" score attributed to years considered generally of good economic and social performance: 1929, 1924–26, 1936–37. In other regards, these indexes (together with OrQL4* and

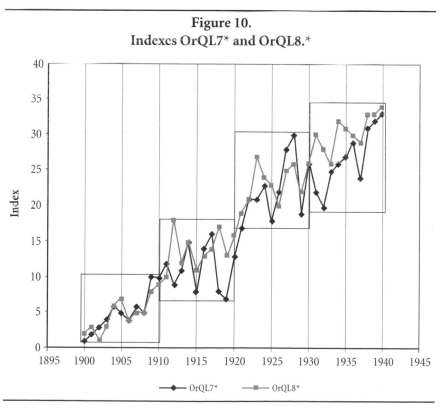

Figure 10.
Indexes OrQL7* and OrQL8.*

Source: See Appendix.

Notes: OrQL7* (infant mortality; caloric consumption; literacy; real wages); OrQL8* (life expectancy; caloric consumption; schooling; real wages).

OrQL9*) are among the most optimistic about the long-run evolution of Argentine welfare.

A divergent pattern emerges when socioeconomic indicators are compared with biological indicators, as in Figure 11. The curve representing "biological welfare" (OrQL9*) shows fewer short-run fluctuations and more sustained growth than the one representing socioeconomic welfare (OrQL10*). This result might seem obvious. Longevity, children's health, and nutrition respond less to short-term fluctuations in income than to long-term efforts to improve sanitation, maternal care, and food habits. GDP and real wages are, conversely, more directly affected by short-run cyclical fluctuations. The index representing "socioeconomic welfare" magnifies the negative shocks of 1912–1917 and 1929–1932, both shocks being apparently powerful and long-lasting.[43] If we look at biological indicators (including heights), a completely different scoring emerges. There is nutritional and health stagnation until 1910–12, then slight improvement into

Figure 11.
Indexes OrQL9* and OrQL10.*

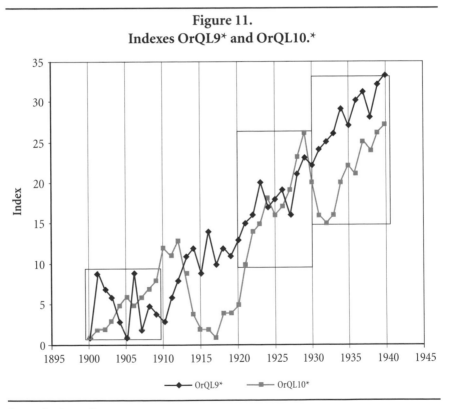

Source: See Appendix.

Notes: OrQL9* (infant mortality; stature; life expectancy); OrQL10* (pc GDP; real wages; literacy).

the WWI years, and strong growth after 1919. The improvement in "biological welfare" was sustained between 1920 and 1940, with minor setbacks in 1924, 1926, 1930, and 1936.

Another interesting result ensued when an indicator of workers' dissatisfaction or social unrest (labor strikes) was used in lieu of measures of educational achievement. Compare Figure 12 with Figure 7. Still, the period 1920–1940 is better than the first two decades of the century. But other types of comparisons are difficult to sustain. Social unrest produces a deterioration of well-being in the first decade of the twentieth century, which coincides with the period of nutritional stress captured by the height data (which no composite index so clearly shows). These indexes (OrQL1* and OrQL11*) also present the years 1912–1915 as a time of deteriorating well-being, but prolong this situation into the years 1919–20.[11] The inclusion of labor strikes makes the welfare index more erratic in the twenties and the improvement of welfare in the thirties less impressive. Workers' perception that after 1919–21 the institutionalization of the labor movement and the

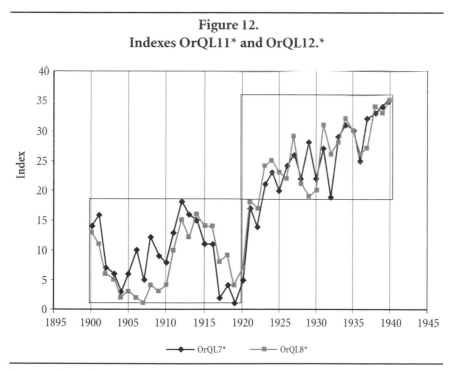

Figure 12.
Indexes OrQL11* and OrQL12.*

Source: see Appendix.

Notes: OrQL11* (pc GDP; stature; infant mortality; strikes); OrQL12* (real wage; caloric consumption; life expectancy; strikes).

"pacification" that followed (when the anarchist and anarcho-syndicalist influence waned) were a mixed blessing are confirmed by these indexes.

Conclusions

When we compare all eight indexes, the results are unequivocal. As Figure 13 indicates, all situations in the 1930s (except for two "outliers") are better than all situations in the period 1900–1914 (except for one "outlier"), traditionally considered the best part of the Golden Age. The sustained progress in education, nutrition, and health was so important that it overshadowed temporary setbacks in income in the long run. Regardless of the choice of indicator of composite welfare, we can safely say that Argentines were better off in the thirties.

This result calls for a reconsideration of the welfare effects of economic growth in Argentina. During the period of the so-called Golden Age, welfare improved according to certain indicators and deteriorated according to others. Though the general trend was upward, important setbacks in infant mortality, nutrition, and real wages complicated the scoring of composite

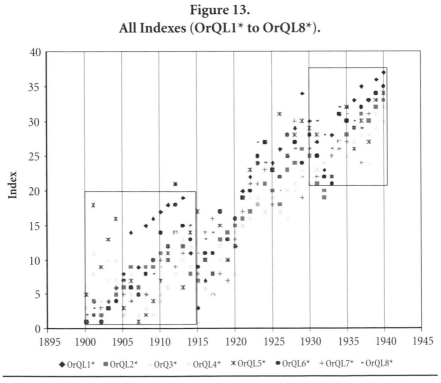

Figure 13.
All Indexes (OrQL1* to OrQL8*).

♦ OrQL1*   ■ OrQL2*   OrQ3*   OrQL4*   ✳ OrQL5*   ● OrQL6*   + OrQL7*   - OrQL8*

Source: see Appendix.

welfare, rendering contradictory results. For the periods 1914–1929 and 1929–1939 there is no ambiguity: the progress of welfare is evident, regardless of the composite index used. The so-called Great Delay was, from the perspective of human welfare, a period of unequivocal improvement.

If a worker would evaluate past situations of welfare using indexes 1 to 12, he/she would reach the following conclusions:

a) he/she would be unable to say that 1914 was better than 1901 in four out of twelve cases;

b) he/she would be certain that (under all combination of indexes) 1929 was better than 1914 and that, except for one index, 1939 was better than 1929;

c) he/she would have to admit that 1939 was in all cases better than 1901; the same is true for the comparison 1929 > 1901.

Table 3.
Comparative Welfare.
(> means "better than" in the strict criterion)

Welfare Index	1914 > 1901	1929 > 1914	1939 > 1929	1939 > 1901
OrQL1*	true	true	true	true
OrQL2*	true	truc	true	true
OrQL3*	**false**	true	true	true
OrQL4*	**false**	true	true	true
OrQL5*	**false**	true	true	true
OrQL6*	true	true	true	true
OrQL7*	true	true	true	true
OrQL8*	true	true	true	true
OrQL9*	true	true	true	true
OrQL10*	true	true	**false**	true
OrQL11*	**false**	true	true	true
OrQL12*	true	true	true	true

How efficient are these ordinal indexes in capturing variations in human welfare? Are the variations among indexes so important that the welfare narrative is completely altered by the choice of indicator? As expected, the Spearman coefficients indicate that all indexes are highly correlated among themselves.[45] This means that in the long run (when trying to evaluate if an average Argentine was better off in 1939 than in 1901) the choice of indicator does not really matter. But in the short run this is not the case.

The choice of indicator is crucial for the period 1900–1920, when results appear more dispersed. It is less so for the period 1920–1940, in which the indexes tend to group along the trend. Still, the dispersion among indexes in this period is such that they render completely different valuations of crucial years.

As expected, indices with longevity and schooling tend to smooth out the description of national well-being. These indices present a more optimistic outlook than those that include infant mortality and stature. The first group of indices seems to measure better the long-term performance of growth (as it affects human capabilities and health), while the latter group appears more sensitive to short-term setbacks in government revenues and policy emphasis. "Better off in the thirties" is the appropriate summary of the conclusions reached by aggregating welfare indicators into ordinal indices. But the reader should keep in mind that, by construction, these indices do not say much about other key dimensions of human welfare: democratic liberties, security of property and life, and social equality. Stature, a robust measure of net nutrition, behaved in the Argentine case as a poor predictor of income. After the nutritional stress of the first decade of the twentieth century, net nutrition continues to growth almost uninterrupted—similar to the development of other indicators of increased capabilities and welfare (longevity and schooling).

Appendix

Statistical Sources

The *GNP Estimate* comes from CEPAL. It does not include economic activities usually included in the national accounts of other countries. As recognized by the Argentine Central Bank, the 1947 estimations (for the period 1935–1945) failed to include housing costs and actual rents produced by real estate property. In agriculture, activities such as raising horses and goats, cultivating fruits, vegetables, and forage crops, raising fowl (except chickens), and hunting and fishing were not included. When in 1955 officials of the Secretary of Economic Affairs revised the estimates for the period 1935–54, they noticed that neither they nor their predecessors had attributed any production figure to the enormous number of independent artisans revealed by the 1914 census. In 1958 CEPAL only replicated the methodology used by Economic Affairs for the period 1900–1955, "with much more reduced and perhaps less reliable statistical sources" (in the words of the Banco Central experts). Looking at the tables published by CEPAL it is clear that they estimated private consumption by difference. The main effort was devoted to the estimation of gross production, physical capital, and investment. No attempt was made to calculate apparent consumption and to crosscheck these estimates against the rich budget surveys of the 1920s. **Sources:** Banco Central de la República Argentina, *Series históricas de cuentas nacionales de la Argentina,* vol. 3 (Buenos Aires: BCRA, 1976); H. Dieguez: "Crecimiento e inestabilidad del valor y el volumen físico de las exportaciones argentinas en el período 1864–1963," *Desarrollo Económico* 12: 46 (1972); and Vicente Vázquez Presedo, *Estadísticas históricas argentinas (comparadas).* Buenos Aires: Editorial Macchi, 1976.

Real Wage Data result from the linkage of quite good data on urban wages for the period after 1914 with very poor data for the period 1900–1914. Nominal wages for this latter period consist on the simple average between two categories of workers: workers of a cookie factory and wages of policemen. The same could be said about the price index: the cost of living for the period 1914–1940 comes from very good (though partial, urban) budget surveys of urban industrial workers. To the best of my knowledge, this series does not include wages for workers in the interior provinces. **Sources for wages:** Roberto Cortés Conde, *El progreso argentino, 1880–1914* (Buenos Aires: Sudamericana, 1979). **For cost of living:** Jeffrey G. Williamson and

Alan M. Taylor, "Convergence in the Age of Mass Migration," National Bureau of Economic Research, NBER Working Paper (1994).

Export Data are quite reliable. In fact, there are long-term, standardized series of quantum, prices, and values for the whole period 1864–1940. Per capita exports are perhaps a good indicator of the purchasing power of people whose work and property depended upon the export economy. But, unfortunately, it is a very partial and imperfect indicator of overall economic performance. **Source:** Same as for Income.

Caloric Intake. These are aggregates of series of per capita consumption (in kg or liters) of nine basic items: flour, rice, sugar, cooking oil, potatoes, beef, milk, butter, and cheese, then transformed into calories. They were estimated through the method of "apparent consumption." There are still problems with these estimates, particularly the presence of cycles, for we have not successfully isolated the variation in inventories. Also, the data for the period 1910–1940 are more reliable than that corresponding to the period 1900–1910. **Source:** Own estimate, in collaboration with Damián Antúnez.

Literacy and Schooling. The series of "literacy" refers to the reading and writing skills of 18-year-old males enlisted for military service. (Women in Argentina had consistently higher educational attainment.) The figures are too optimistic, showing perhaps a very basic level of literacy. Data on school attendance are quite accurate and are, in fact, closely correlated with the "literacy" rate. Information of average years of schooling is difficult to obtain. So, this set of data has not been corrected by years of schooling. Moreover, series of literacy and school attendance cannot tell us anything about the "skilling" or "de-skilling" of the labor force during a process of export-led growth, simply because they do not measure labor skills. **Source for literacy:** E. Nelson, *El analfabetismo en la República Argentina* (Santa Fe: Universidad Nacional del Litoral, 1939); and Consejo Nacional de Educación, *El analfabetismo en la República Argentina* (Buenos Aires: Consejo Nacional de Educación, 1963). **For schooling:** Consejo Nacional de Educación, *Informe presentado al Ministerio de Justicia e Instrucción Pública* (Buenos Aires: Imprenta Oficial, 1936); and Ministerio de Educación, Departamento de Estadística Educativa, *La enseñanza primaria en la República Argentina: 1913–1963* (Buenos Aires: Imprenta Oficial, 1964).

Infant Mortality information is quite reliable for the period 1910–1940. It is a national average that probably has a strong urban bias. Only for the city of Buenos Aires do we have continuous series of infant mortality since 1870. **Source:** Carlos García Mata, "La mortalidad infantil en la República Argentina," *Economía Argentina*, 28:164 (1932); and "Resúmenes estadísticos y su expresión gráfica: Mortalidad infantil," *Economía Argentina*, 40: 277 (1941).

Life Expectancy. There are excellent continuous data for the city of Buenos Aires, but for the national average, we only have estimates at a few benchmarks: 1883, 1905, 1914, and 1947. **Source:** Jorge L. Somoza, "La mortalidad en la Argentina entre 1869 y 1960," Cuadernos Sociología y Ciencia Política no. 3, Buenos Aires, Instituto Torcuato Di Tella, 1971.

Strikes. The number of strikes is a quite reliable estimator, taken by the National Department of Labor. Other alternative indicators of social unrest could have been chosen, such as number of strikers or number of days lost. But the number of strikes seems to capture well enough the social dynamic. **Source:** Roberto Korzeniewicz, "Historical Sociology of the Labor Movement in the Semi-periphery: Argentina, 1887–1973," Ph.D. dissertation, SUNY at Binghamton, 1988; Departamento Nacional del Trabajo, División de Estadísticas, *Estadística de las huelgas* (Buenos Aires: Imprenta Oficial, 1940); and "Resúmenes estadísticos y su expresión gráfica: Estadísticas Sociales--Ocupación," *Economía Argentina*, 40: 281 (1941).

Table A1.
Value of Individual Indicators.

Year	Income per capita	Life expectancy	Infant mortality	Literacy	Schooling	Heights	Real wages	Calorie consumption	Strikes	Exports per capita
1900	2075	40.0	128	66.93	48.6	168.1	100	2086	41	33.5
1901	2187	40.0	128	68.44	48.1	169.4	94	2242	57	36.0
1902	2084	40.0	127	69.45	48.0	168.7	94	2177	106	37.7
1903	2325	40.0	127	70.75	49.0	168.6	95	2203	114	41.7
1904	2514	40.0	126	71.30	50.3	168.2	101	2220	322	51.4
1905	2762	40.0	126	72.49	50.9	167.9	89	2368	147	61.0
1906	2788	41.0	125	69.82	50.2	168.8	87	2297	217	52.3
1907	2713	41.9	125	73.00	51.0	167.7	85	2233	231	51.0
1908	2855	42.9	125	72.85	50.6	168	84	2281	118	60.5
1909	2820	43.8	124	74.25	53.2	167.7	83	2329	138	62.8
1910	2876	44.7	124	73.27	54.4	167.2	90	2508	298	56.5
1911	2788	45.7	123	78.47	55.0	167.3	89	2810	102	47.5
1912	2882	46.6	123	78.49	54.4	167.7	92	2985	99	67.6
1913	2766	47.6	122	75.07	56.3	168.2	87	2833	95	65.3
1914	2406	48.5	122	74.51	55.6	168.2	85	2903	64	48.5
1915	2363	48.9	124	72.70	57.1	167.8	76	2794	65	68.5
1916	2252	49.3	124	73.39	58.6	168.4	71	2858	80	64.7
1917	2033	49.6	128	76.52	61.2	168.3	61	2874	138	62.6
1918	2365	50.0	138	79.39	61.6	168.6	52	2929	196	77.5
1919	2498	50.4	134	78.25	63.2	168.3	71	2720	367	107.7
1920	2529	50.8	127	77.84	66.3	168.2	73	2810	206	108.1
1921	2527	51.2	116	78.82	67.1	168.5	91	3027	86	58.4
1922	2649	51.5	112	83.40	69.2	168.4	104	2990	116	58.8
1923	2838	51.9	112	79.96	69.2	168.8	107	3245	93	63.4
1924	2954	52.3	117	82.55	68.0	168.6	106	3172	77	77.8

Table A1.
Value of Individual Indicators. (continued)

Year	Income per capita	Life expectancy	Infant mortality	Literacy	Schooling	Heights	Real wages	Calorie consumption	Strikes	Exports per capita
1925	2855	52.7	124	81.62	66.8	169.2	111	3079	89	73.3
1926	2910	53.1	120	80.02	65.7	168.7	112	2894	67	67.7
1927	3028	53.5	128	79.49	66.0	167.1	118	3123	58	90.0
1928	3125	53.8	116	79.65	66.5	169.3	126	2948	135	92.3
1929	3182	54.2	103	82.83	68.0	169.5	124	2841	113	78.7
1930	2972	54.6	106	82.53	68.5	169.4	113	2949	125	50.7
1931	2704	55.0	101	83.68	71.3	169.4	122	3217	43	30.9
1932	2565	55.4	95	81.55	71.4	169.2	129	2924	105	24.8
1933	2639	55.7	86	85.73	72.2	170.1	119	2866	52	25.4
1934	2800	56.1	97	86.47	74.2	170.2	123	2997	42	20.4
1935	2875	56.5	107	86.41	75.9	170.3	126	2891	69	21.2
1936	2852	56.9	97	87.06	76.7	170.4	118	2878	109	22.7
1937	3006	57.3	95	87.14	80.5	170.3	119	2823	82	30.9
1938	2964	57.6	106	87.74	81.9	169.6	119	3308	44	18.0
1939	3028	58.0	91	88.27	83.9	170.5	121	3205	49	19.2
1940	3029	58.4	90	88.8	84.4	171.5	122	3342	53	15.9

Notes

1. Pigou, *Wealth and Welfare* and *The Economics of Welfare*. See also Steckel, "Stature and the Standard of Living."
2. Horrell and Humphries, "Old Questions, New Data."
3. Atkinson, "Measurement of Poverty"; Morris, *Measuring the Condition*; Ravaillon, "Measuring Social Welfare"; and United Nations, *Human Development*.
4. Komlos, "Shrinking in a Growing Economy?" and *Biological Standard of Living*; Steckel, "Stature and the Standard of Living."
5. For the importance of the public health revolution in increasing the standard of living of developing nations, see Fogel, "Economic Growth, Population Theory, and Physiology," and Easterlin, "Looking Backward."
6. Crafts, "The Human Development Index" and "Dimensions of the Quality of Life"; and Albala-Bertrand, "Aggregate Welfare in Latin America."
7. See Salvatore, "Stature Decline and Recovery," "Stature, Nutrition and Regional Convergence," "Regional Dimensions of Economic Development," and "Heights and Welfare in Late-Colonial."
8. Adelman, *Frontier Development*; Díaz Alejandro, *Essays on the Economic History*; Cortés Conde, *El progreso argentino*; Vázquez Presedo, *El caso argentino*, among others.
9. Di Tella and Zymelman, *Etapas del desarrollo económico argentino*. For a counter-argument, see Díaz Alejandro, *Essays on the Economic History*, 61–65.
10. Bunge, *Problemas económicos*; Llach, *La Argentina que no fue*.
11. Gerchunoff and Llach, *Ciclo de la ilusión y el desencanto*, 61–106.
12. See Ferrer, *Economía argentina;* and Prebisch, *Capitalismo periférico*.
13. Taylor, "External Dependence."
14. Gerchunoff and Llach, *Ciclo de la ilusión y el desencanto*; della Paolera and Taylor, *Straining at the Anchor;* Williamson and Taylor, "Age of Mass Migrations."
15. Díaz Alejandro, "Stages of Industrialization," and Thorp, *Latin America in the 1930s*.
16. Barbero and Rocchi, "Industry"; Chu, "Great Depression and Industrialization"; and Villanueva, "Origen de la industrialización argentina."
17. See Ciria, *Década infame*. On the condition of the labor movement see Munk, *From Anarchism to Peronism*, and Tamarin, *Argentine Labor Movement*. New evidence on strike activity and the emergence of industrial unions show that labor turned more militant in the second half of the 1930s. See Korzeniewicz, "Labor Unrest."
18. Germani, *Política y sociedad*.
19. It is tempting to characterize the first growth spurt as "impoverishing growth" and the second growth spurt as "growth with distribution."
20. See Salvatore, "Stature Decline and Recovery," 14.
21. Escudé, *Fracaso del proyecto argentino*.
22. Tedesco, *Educación y sociedad*. A more pessimistic assessment of early progress in literacy can be found in Spalding, "Education in Argentina."

23. Census figures are slightly different. They show the rate of illiteracy falling from 54 percent in 1895 to 35 percent in 1914, 38 percent including the semi-literate. Thus, the literate population was 62 percent in 1914. Spalding, "Education in Argentina," 45.
24. Newland, "The Estado Docente," 452.
25. This would imply that somehow Argentina's political system (its federalist structure, in particular) served to maintain levels of state investment in education even in periods of economic recession. Perhaps the decline in federal fiscal revenues during external shocks affected the secondary school system (under federal responsibility) more than the elementary school system (jointly financed by the nation and the provinces).
26. On the influence of *Higienismo* on industrial regulations see Barrancos, *Escena iluminada*, 177–207, and Recalde, *Salud de los trabajadores.*
27. See Belmartino, *La atención médica argentina,* chapters 1–2.
28. In the capital city the decline was more impressive, from 123 to 50.
29. Compared with other contemporary developed countries, Argentina's infant mortality rates were still too high in 1940, but its standards of education were in the upper range of the international scale.
30. Valued at the cost of the service, health and education appeared undervalued in terms of the capabilities they contributed to the population at large.
31. McGee, "Liga Patriótica Argentina," and Munk, "Cycles of Class Struggle."
32. Baer, "Tenant Mobilization," and Suriano, "Huelga de inquilinos."
33. This section is based on Salvatore, "Stature Decline and Recovery."
34. Gerchunoff and Llach, *Ciclo de la ilusión y el desencanto,* 79–81.
35. In my view, the Human Development Index is a particular variant of Dasgupta-Weale indexes, which evaluate social development relative to other countries. My estimates evaluate welfare in an inter-temporal comparison. They are not prescriptive: no argument is made about the preference of a combination of attributes to another.
36. Crafts, "Dimensions of the Quality of Life."
37. Dasgupta and Weale, "Measuring the Quality of Life."
38. In the last group of estimates (indices OrQL9* to OrQL12*) this restriction was relaxed. In order to separate "social-economic" from "biological" welfare, I worked with indexes that had three components. And, in order to introduce an indicator of social unrest, one key ingredient of the index (human capital) had to be dropped.
39. In an earlier version of this chapter, I tried a cardinal or absolute aggregation of welfare, working with changes in both attributes and weights (again, taking four attributes at a time). The general effect noted is that the choice of indicator could be determinant, much more than the weights.
40. Williamson, "British Mortality."
41. If consistency should be the rule, then per capita exports might be a good indicator of "bad-being."

42. Using the per capita GDP, the conclusion would have been different: in 1940 the country had not yet recovered to the level of income per capita achieved in 1929.

43. According to OrQL10*, only in 1922 did Argentines recover the level of socioeconomic well-being attained in 1912. It took exactly ten years. The same could be said about the Great Depression: in 1939 Argentines were enjoying comparable levels of welfare as in 1929.

    The Great Depression also brought about an important decline in "socioeconomic welfare."

44. This coincides with the reading that real wages would give us: that the situation continued to deteriorate in the immediate postwar period; but no composite index containing real wages shows this.

45. For lack of space, we do not report these coefficients among indices.

References

Adelman, Jeremy. *Frontier Development. Land, Labour and Capital on the Wheatlands of Argentina and Canada, 1890–1914.* Oxford: Clarendon Press, 1994.

Albala-Bertrand, José Miguel. "Evolution of Aggregate Welfare and Development Indicators in Latin America and the OECD, 1950–85." In *Welfare, Poverty, and Development in Latin America,* ed. Christopher Abel and Collin Lewis, 33–48. Houndsmill: Macmillan, 1993.

Altimir, Oscar and Juan Sourrouille. "Measuring Levels of Living in Latin America. An Overview of Main Problems." World Bank, LSMS Working Paper no. 3. Washington, D.C.: 1980.

Atkinson, A.B. "On the Measurement of Poverty," *Econometrica* 55, no. 4 (1987): 749–764.

Baer, James A. "Tenant Mobilization and the 1907 Rent Strike in Buenos Aires," *The Americas* 43, no. 9 (1993): 343–368.

Baily, Samuel L. *Immigrants in the Lands of Promise. Italians in Buenos Aires and New York City, 1870–1914.* Ithaca: Cornell University Press, 1999.

Barbero, María Inés, and Fernando Rocchi, "Industry." In *A New Economic History of Argentina,* ed. Gerardo della Paolera and Alan M. Taylor, 261–294. Cambridge: Cambridge University Press, 2003.

Barrancos, Dora. *La escena iluminada. Ciencias para trabajadores, 1890–1930.* Buenos Aires: Plus Ultra, 1996.

Belmartino, Susana. *La atención médica argentina en el siglo XX. Instituciones y procesos.* Buenos Aires: Siglo XXI Editores, 2005.

Bergson, Abram, "Pareto on Social Welfare." *Journal of Economic Literature* 21, no. 1 (1983): 40–46.

Bunge, Alejandro E. *Problemas económicos del presente.* Buenos Aires: REA, 1920.

Chu, David S. "The Great Depression and Industrialization in Latin America: Response to Relative Price Incentives in Argentina and Colombia 1930–1945." Ph.D. dissertation, Yale University, 1972.

Ciria, Alberto et al. *La década infame*. Buenos Aires: C. Pérez, 1969.

Cortés Conde, Roberto. *El progreso argentino, 1880–1914*. Buenos Aires: Sudamericana, 1979.

Crafts, N. F. R. "The Human Development Index: Some Historical Comparisons." Department of Economic History, London School of Economics, Working Paper no. 33, July 1996.

———. "Some Dimensions of the 'Quality of Life' during the British Industrial Revolution," *Economic History Review* 50, no. 4 (1997): 617–639.

Dasgupta, Partha, and Martin Weale, "On Measuring the Quality of Life." *World Development* 20, no. 1 (1992): 119–131.

Deaton, Angus. "The Measurement of Welfare. Theory and Practical Guidelines." World Bank, LSMS Working Paper no. 7, Washington, D.C.: 1980.

Della Paolera, Gerardo, and Alan M. Taylor. *Straining at the Anchor: The Argentine Currency Board and the Search for Macroeconomic Stability, 1880–1935*. Chicago: University of Chicago Press, 2001.

Díaz Alejandro, Carlos F. "Stages in the Industrialization of Argentina." Buenos Aires: Instituto Torcuato Di Tella, 1966.

Díaz Alejandro, Carlos F. *Essays on the Economic History of the Argentine Republic*. New Haven: Yale University Press, 1970.

Di Tella, Guido, and Manuel Zymelman. *Las etapas del desarrollo económico argentino*. Buenos Aires: Eudeba, 1967.

Easterlin, Richard A. "Looking Backward at Economics and the Economy. The Worldwide Standard of Living since 1800," *Journal of Economic Perspectives* 14, no. 1 (2000): 7–26.

Escudé, Carlos. *El fracaso del proyecto argentino: Educación e ideología*. Buenos Aires: Instituto Torcuato Di Tella / Editorial Tesis, 1980.

Ferrer, Aldo. *La economía argentina: las etapas de su desarrollo y problemas actuales*, 2nd. ed. Buenos Aires: Fondo de Cultura Económica, 1965.

Fogel, Robert W. "Economic Growth, Population Theory, and Physiology: The Bearing of Long-Term Processes on the Making of Economic Policy," *The American Economic Review* 84, no. 3 (1994): 369–395.

Gerchunoff, Pablo, and Lucas Llach. *El ciclo de la ilusión y el desencanto. Un siglo de políticas económicas argentinas*. 2nd. ed. Buenos Aires: Ariel, 2005.

Germani, Gino. *Política y sociedad en una época de transición*. Buenos Aires: Paidós, 1962.

Ho, Teresa H. "Measuring Health as a Component of Living Standards," World Bank, LSMS Working Paper no. 15, Washington, D.C.: 1982.

Horrell, Sara, and Jane Humphries. "Old Questions, New Data and Alternative Perspectives: Family's Living Standards in the Industrial Revolution," *Journal of Economic History* 52, no. 4 (1992): 849–880.

Jenkins, Stephen, Arie Kapteyn, and Bernard Van Praag, eds. *The Distribution of Welfare and Household Production*. Cambridge: Cambridge University Press, 1998.

Jorgenson, Dale W. "Aggregate Consumer Behavior and the Measurement of Social Welfare." *Econometrica* 58, no. 5 (1990): 1007–1040.

Komlos, John. "Shrinking in a Growing Economy? The Mystery of Physical Stature during the Industrial Revolution." *The Journal of Economic History* 58, no. 3 (1998): 779–802.

Komlos, John, ed. *The Biological Standard of Living in Three Continents: Further Explorations in Anthropometric History.* Boulder: Westview Press, 1995.

Korzeniewicz, Roberto P. "Labor Unrest in Argentina, 1930–1943," *Latin American Research Review* 28, no. 1 (1993): 7–40.

Llach, Juan José. *La Argentina que no fué. Las fragilidades de la Argentina agro-exportadora (1918–1930).* Buenos Aires: IDES, 1985.

McGee, Sandra F. "The Visible and Invisible Liga Patriótica Argentina, 1919–28: Gender Roles and the Right Wing," *The Hispanic American Historical Review* 64, no. 2 (1984): 233–258.

Morris, Morris D. *Measuring the Condition of the World's Poor. The Physical Quality of Life Index.* New York: Pergamon Press, 1979.

Moya, José C. *Cousins and Strangers. Spanish Immigrants in Buenos Aires, 1850–1930.* Berkeley: University of California Press, 1998.

Munk, Ronaldo. *Argentina: From Anarchism to Peronism. Workers, Unions and Politics, 1855–1985.* London: Zed Books, 1987.

———. "Cycles of Class Struggle and the Making of the Working Class in Argentina, 1890–1920." *Journal of Latin American Studies* 19, no. 1. (1987):19–39.

Newland, Carlos. "The Estado Docente and Its Expansion: Spanish American Elementary Education, 1900–1950." *Journal of Latin American Studies,* 26, no. 2 (1994): 449–467.

Othick, John, "Development Indicators and the Historical Study of Human Welfare: Towards a New Perspective," *Journal of Economic History* 43, no. 1 (1983): 63–70.

Pigou, Arthur Cecil. *Wealth and Welfare.* London: Macmillan, 1912.

———. *The Economics of Welfare.* London: Macmillan, 1932.

Prebisch, Raúl. *Capitalismo periférico: crisis y transformación.* México: Fondo de Cultura Económica, 1981.

Ravallion, Martin, "Measuring Social Welfare with and without Poverty Lines." *American Economic Review* 84, no. 2 (1994): 359–364.

Recalde, Héctor. *La salud de los trabajadores en Buenos Aires (1870–1910) a través de las fuentes médicas.* Buenos Aires: Grupo Editor Universitario, 1997.

Salvatore, Ricardo D. "Heights and Welfare in Late-Colonial and Post-Independence Argentina." In *The Biological Standard of Living in Comparative Perspective,* ed. John Komlos and Joerg Baten. Stuttgart: Steiner Verlag, 1998.

———. "Stature Decline and Recovery in a Food-Rich Export Economy: Argentina 1900–1934." *Explorations in Economic History* 41, no. 3 (2004): 233–255.

———. "Stature, Nutrition and Regional Convergence. The Argentine Northwest in the First Half of the 20th Century." *Social Science History* 28, no. 2 (2004): 297–324.

Spalding, Hobart A. "Education in Argentina, 1890–1914: The Limits of Oligarchical Reform," *Journal of Interdisciplinary History* 3, no. 1 (1972): 31–61.

Steckel, Richard H. "Strategic Ideas in the Rise of the New Anthropometric History and Their Implications for Interdisciplinary Research." *Journal of Economic History* 58, no. 3 (1998): 803–821.

———. "Stature and the Standard of Living." *Journal of Economic Literature* 33, no. 4 (1995): 1903–1940.

Sturmey, S. G. *Income and Economic Welfare.* London: Longmans, 1959.

Suriano, Juan. *Movimientos sociales: La huelga de inquilinos de 1907.* Buenos Aires: Centro Editor de América Latina, 1983.

Tamarin, David. *The Argentine Labor Movement, 1930–1945: A Study in the Origins of Peronism.* Albuquerque: University of New Mexico Press, 1985.

Taylor, Alan M. "External Dependence, Demographic Burdens, and Argentine Economic Decline after the Belle Epoque." *Journal of Economic History* 52, no. 4 (1992): 907–936.

Tedesco, Juan Carlos. *Educación y sociedad en la Argentina (1880–1945).* Buenos Aires: Ediciones Solar, 1986.

Thorp, Rosemary, ed. *Latin America in the 1930s: The Role of the Periphery in World Crisis.* New York: San Martin's Press, 1984.

United Nations. *Human Development Report 1991.* New York: Oxford University Press, 1991.

Vázquez Presedo, Vicente. *El caso argentino. Migración de factores, comercio exterior y desarrollo 1874–1914.* Buenos Aires: Eudeba, 1979.

Villanueva, Javier, "El origen de la industrialización argentina." *Desarrollo Económico* 12, no. 47 (1972): 451–476.

Williamson, Jeffrey G. and Alan M. Taylor, "Convergence in the Age of Mass Migration," National Bureau of Economic Research, NBER Working Paper (1994).

Williamson, Jeffrey G. "British Mortality and the Value of Life, 1781–1931." *Population Studies* 38, no. 1 (1984), 157–172.

———. "Globalization, Convergence and History." *Journal of Economic History* 56, no. 2 (1996): 277–306.

6
Growth and Inequalities of Height in Brazil, 1939–1981

Leonardo M. Monasterio, Luiz Paulo Ferreira Noguról, and Claudio D. Shikida

Introduction

Inequality within Brazilian society is present in various dimensions. Income is concentrated both regionally and individually. While part of the population enjoys living standards and patterns of consumption comparable to those of developed countries, many families live in poverty. About one third of the population lives below the poverty line, according to official data and criteria. The poorest 20% account for 1.5% of total national income, while the richest 20% account for 68%.[1] By comparing data from different states, we find that the difference in life expectancy between the richest states and the poorest ones is more than eight years. Per capita income in the poorest region is equal to one fourth of that observed in the Southeast, the richest region of the country.[2]

The recent publication of a survey including anthropometric data on the Brazilian population has generated a great deal of controversy in the media and in academic circles.[3] Some researchers have concluded that the *Pesquisa de Orçamentos Familiares 2002–2003* (the Family Budget Survey, henceforth POF) showed that obesity was a more serious problem than undernutrition.[4] In fact, the data do suggest that even among the population in the lower strata, excess weight or obesity is more common than weight deficit. In these strata, 24% of men were overweight or obese, while only 4.5% had a weight deficit. Some analysts therefore assumed that differences in nutrition among the various classes had disappeared in Brazil. However, some of those who were most involved in anti-hunger campaigns, including President Luís Inácio Lula da Silva, mistrusted the validity of the results presented by the IBGE (Instituto Brasileiro de Geografia e Estatística, the Brazilian Institute of Geography and Statistics).[5] We argue that the optimistic interpretation of excess weight is only one suggested by the POF data.

When we change the focus to the height of Brazilians, we can verify that in spite of the social improvements which took place during the twentieth century, there is a long way to go before the country reaches acceptable patterns of equality and well-being.[6]

In 1829, Villermé identified an empirical relationship between height and social class among the inhabitants of Paris and concluded: "The circumstances which accompany poverty delay the age at which complete stature is reached and stunt adult height."[7] Since then, scientific research has shown that when the objective is to evaluate the quality of nutrition and the living conditions of populations, both in a wide sense and in the long term, the average stature of individuals is an excellent summary index. It reflects not only the average income of society as a whole, but also the degree of access to food, together with the body's consumption of energy, expenditure of energy at work and other physical activities, plus the influence of diseases, especially during childhood.[8]

This chapter shows that six centimeters is the approximate difference of height between adults in the richest and the poorest quintiles of the Brazilian population. Contrary to common belief, the literature notes that genetic differences, despite their individual impact, are unimportant when we consider all individuals in terms of stature. In any given population, there are tall and short individuals, but their average height can be determined by external conditions. Genes and the environment influence the height of each individual, but living conditions are the most important factor for whole populations. Thus, in adulthood, height is bound up with both nutrition and health, aspects which would be difficult to identify through more common indicators of human welfare, such as monetary income.

Economic historians such as Richard Steckel, John Komlos, and Robert Fogel[9] collaborated in the creation of this research field. They have analyzed the heights of American Indians and slaves, eighteenth-century German aristocrats, and military personnel from a range of countries. These heights have varied at different periods and in different locations, in accordance with variations in living conditions.

This chapter uses the POF data to evaluate evolution and inequality in Brazil within this dimension. Considering that height reflects the conditions in which populations used to live, rather than current conditions, it would be ideal if there were data available about the childhood of the adults who were interviewed by the IBGE. As this information is not available, other analytical strategies have had to be implemented. On the basis of cross-section data, proxies have been used to estimate those aspects of living conditions which have had an influence on the average stature of the adult Brazilian population. Regression analysis has allowed us to estimate these effects.[10]

Our interpretation of the IBGE's POF data states that the height of most Brazilians is below its potential because existing living conditions are far from satisfactory. Even when we consider the progressive reduction in undernutrition, the existence of basic sanitation in most Brazilian urban areas, and the debate about the need for education on nutrition (which shows that part of the population does not have problems of undernutrition but problems relating to a low-quality diet), there are still significant inequalities in income as well as in the access to health and general sanitation services. All these factors are reflected in the differences of height among Brazilians, taking into account the different geographic regions and the disparities in income. We therefore reiterate the importance of using anthropometrics in evaluating the results of social and economic policies, rather than using just the traditional measures.

Height and Living Conditions: A Summary

The energy generated by the consumption of food can be divided into two categories: one is for the maintenance of vital functions, and the other is a reservoir of energy for physical activities, especially work. When nourishment is inadequate for these, there is also a "third demand" caused by diseases, which tend to reduce the body's ability to absorb the nutrients ingested. In this case, without an improvement in nourishment, the individual, besides being exposed to a life-threatening risk, becomes temporarily incapable of working, since there is no energy left over for corporeal activities except those necessary for baseline maintenance.[11]

Throughout history, human beings have had a wide range of dietary patterns. These patterns reflect not only "cultural preferences," but also the access of populations to food, which is conditioned by a constant interactive process between income and material civilization. A. Sen gives an example of this process when he writes about the Irish famines.[12] The English officials tended to blame the Irish themselves and their eating habits for the calamity they were experiencing. According to Sen, this reflected the lack of understanding and the cultural distance between the two countries.[13] In fact, the heavy consumption of potatoes in Ireland was more the result of poverty than of choice.

In Europe and the United States, the literature emphasized not only the process of the increase in the height of populations in the twentieth century, but also the occurrence of cycles. The average American in the mid-eighteenth century was taller than in the mid-nineteenth century, and both were shorter than in the twentieth century.[14] However, per capita income in the United States did not follow similar cycles. It increased continuously over the period in question, even though economic growth rates varied significantly. Thus, although there is a strong correlation between per capita income and height, there is no simple linear relationship. Likewise, from the eighteenth to the twentieth century there was a similar cycle in England, even though the average Englishman was shorter than the average American. The inhabitants of the United States, who were taller than all Europeans from the eighteenth century to the 1950s, were then overtaken by the average Dutchman and Scandinavian.

One of the interpretations for the height cycle phenomenon in several populations, according to which nineteenth-century men were shorter than eighteenth- and twentieth-century men, is that higher income levels under the Industrial Revolution did not compensate for urban living costs, the variation in the relative prices of foodstuffs, long journeys to and from the place of work (which also applied to women and children), and insalubrious living conditions in industrial centers—what Cuff called "hidden cost of development."[15] Fast urbanization overloaded the infrastructure and imposed a decrease in basic sanitary conditions. High demographic density, which marks urban zones, also made them more subject to the dissemination of diseases.[16] Other perverse effects of economic growth on stature are more subtle. Market integration, along with all its known benefits, put the populations that were once isolated inside commercial networks. Thus, the possibility of contact with new diseases became larger, imposing a new demand on the organisms and reducing the height of adult individuals. Cuff identified this effect in Pennsylvania during the first half of the nineteenth century. Given the due controls, areas that were more integrated and closer to navigable canals had shorter individuals. In the twentieth century, however, the relationship between income and height tended to be direct, since the "hidden cost of development" was reduced by means of social legislation, investments in health and education, basic sanitation, treatment of drinking water, and other improvements.

Few recent studies examine the anthropometric history of Latin America in the twentieth century. Meisel and Vega analyze a striking 8 million observations' database concerning the height of Colombians from 1910 to 2002.[17] Salvatore examines the evolution of stature in Argentina during the first half of the twentieth century.[18] Regardless of short periods of falling statures, both studies show an overall trend of increasing heights.

In support of the arguments relating to income and to the harsh living conditions faced by workers during the Industrial Revolution, Robert Fogel states that the difference in height between rich and poor English people was 12 centimeters in the nineteenth century.[19] The same situation pertained in Germany and France. As time went by, the increase in the overall level of income, relatively greater among the poor than among the rich, and the creation of social welfare institutions, led to a decrease in the difference in height between the two categories. In England today, the difference in height between people of higher and lower income is only 2.5 centimeters. This difference has disappeared completely in Sweden and in the Netherlands, where men are 1.81 meters tall on average.[20]

In the United States, the increase in income from 1875 to 1995, for example, led to a substantial relative decrease in expenditure on nutrition, clothing, and shelter. This indicates that people were able to purchase the essential goods for the satisfaction of these needs, which correlates strongly with the stature of the population. In the nineteenth century, expenditure relating to the three items mentioned above absorbed 74% of the budget of American families, but only 13% at the end of the twentieth century.[21]

If there are no nutritional restrictions, individuals likely experience intense physical growth in the early years and adolescence. Girls tend to conclude this process of growth before boys. After these two periods of maturation, the speed of growth tends to decrease until it stabilizes. When there is an event that seriously restricts good nutrition, the increase in height tends to cease during this period, but some recovery is likely to occur later, in a new phase of nutritional plenty.

As an example of this, the case of American slaves, as outlined by Steckel, is worthy of note. During childhood, the slaves suffered serious nutritional restrictions and were prey to diseases caused by the conditions of slavery and the lack of knowledge of simple hygiene. The maternity leave granted to slave women was too short to allow adequate breastfeeding, which apparently ended when the child was 3 months old. Moreover, the high density of children living in the same environment and using the same eating utensils greatly facilitated diarrhea, measles, and chickenpox. The effects of nutritional deficiencies on growth, given the short period of breastfeeding, and the lack of hygiene in childhood, show up as slave children's lowest centiles of height in contemporary growth charts. As adolescents, the American slaves were fed better and they recovered part of the growth deficit that had taken place in the early years of their lives.[22]

Abundant international evidence thus links the average height of populations to their past and present living conditions. It is clear that increases in per capita income, better income distribution, and positive social policies in general have beneficial effects on the height of individuals.

Empirical Evidence

Overview

Steckel argues that height can be an excellent index of quality of life and development, following the agenda proposed by Sen:

> Stature measures performance by health history rather than inputs to health, which has the advantage of incorporating the supply of inputs to health as well as demands on those inputs. [23]

Gilberto Freyre, the renowned Brazilian sociologist, in *Casa Grande & Senzala*, which is required reading for the study of slavery, tells that he was inspired to write the book when, upon travelling to the United States in the 1920s, he realized that Afro-Americans were visibly taller than Afro-Brazilians. [24] In his opinion, this difference was less due to climatic and racial factors (at that time considered essential in determining individual characteristics) than to the different social regimes to which populations with similar origins were subjected. [25]

The empirical evidence collected and put forward by anthropometric historians corroborates Freyre's view:

> In a review of studies covering populations in Europe, New Guinea, and México, L. A. Malcolm (1974) concludes that differences in average height between populations are almost entirely the product of the environment. Using data from well-nourished populations in several developed and developing countries, Martorell and Habicht (1986) report that children from Europe or Africa (or of European or African descent), and from India or the Middle East, have similar growth profiles. [26]

Steckel further elaborates on tropical environments:

> Although tropical climates have a bad reputation for diseases, Maurice King (1966) argues that poor health in developing countries is largely a consequence of poverty rather than climate. A group of diseases are spread by vectors that need a warm climate, but poverty is responsible for the lack of doctors, nurses, drugs, and equipment to combat these and other diseases. Poverty, via malnutrition, increases the susceptibility to disease. [27]

Over the course of the twentieth century, the height of different peoples tended to increase as a result of improvements in the environments where they lived.[28] These improvements went considerably beyond the attainment of higher income levels, which allow people to feed themselves better, and include social gains from public policies that mitigate people's exposure to infectious agents, such as adequate sanitary inspection of food, treatment of water, and efficient garbage and sewage collection.[29]

The recent stagnation of height and increase in weight in the United States relative to other developed economies illustrates the importance of public provisioning. The U.S. population, in the eighteenth and nineteenth centuries and for a great part of the twentieth century, was one of the tallest in the world. At present, besides being relatively tall, Americans, unlike continental Europeans, have a high incidence of obesity as measured in the American Body Mass Index (hereafter referred to as BMI). Komlos and Baur argue that the American BMI reflects the lack of social welfare mechanisms that exist in most Western European countries. Specifically, the lack of comprehensive health assistance and unemployment insurance exposes children to temporarily insufficient nutrition (thus compromising their growth) and to unsatisfactory medical care. As attested by the authors, the effect on Americans' health is evident: compared with Europeans, who have a lower per capita income, Americans have a lower life expectancy rate and a higher child mortality rate.[30]

Income distribution is also an important factor in average heights. The Gini coefficient is negatively related to average height in the populations analyzed; that is, the worse the income distribution in a particular country, the lower the average height.[31] Concentration of income reduces stature for two obvious reasons. First, low-income people constitute the majority of the population and they will have the greatest difficulty in accessing the necessary nutrients to satisfy their genetic potential. Second, health care also correlates positively with levels of income. Diseases are responsible for "nutrient waste," because a sick person tends to have more difficulty in absorbing nutrition. Thus, low income and high susceptibility to pathogenic factors combine to reduce the height of populations.

The POF Microdata

The POF 2002–2003 provides microdata on the profile of income, expense, and life conditions of the Brazilian population. The sampling criteria are intended to be representative of the population as a whole.[32] The anthropometric measures were taken by trained agents and all the interviewees were measured. For the adults, height was measured with rulers graduated in millimeters. The individuals were measured standing, barefoot, and with the help of a ruler in measuring the hair and pressing it down. Although the rulers were graduated in millimeters, the data were rounded off to centimeters. The Kolmogorov-Smirnov test applied to the entire POF sample and to individual cohorts does not reject the hypothesis of a normal distribution of the height values.[33] We found an abnormal number of height measurements ending in 0 and 5, but corroboration with common years in the *Pesquisa Nacional sobre Saúde e Nutrição* show no systematic bias that would affect the interpretation of rates of change over time.[34]

It is important to stress that this is a cross-sectional database and we do not have longitudinal anthropometric data. The research considered only POF microdata related to men who, at the time they were interviewed, were between 21 and 65 years of age. We have selected just the men in order to follow the historical anthropometric research tradition and make the data comparable.[35] After the usual cleaning of the data, just over 40,000 observations remained.

Aging and the Reconstruction of the Secular Trend of Height
A simple analysis of the POF cross-section data on height shows that people who were born in 1940 have an average height of 1.65 m, whereas it was almost 1.71 m for the 1980s cohorts. This represents an increase of almost 1.5 cm per decade, but though it is a substantial increase, even larger ones have been recorded.

However, this inverse relationship between height and age, in a cross-sectional study, must be cautiously analyzed. First, individuals tend to lose height from the age of 40 onwards. Although bones do not diminish in length, changes in vertebrae, intervertebrate discs, standing positions, and foot curvature tend to aggravate height loss. The degree of the loss depends on several factors; physical activity and nourishment seem to be the main determinants.[36]

Research by Niewenweg and colleagues,[37] based on data on the Dutch population in the twentieth century, suggest adding to the current height of an A-year-old individual ($A > 21$) the following expression: $0.042 \times (A - 21) + [0.0015 \times (A - 21)]^2$. But there seems to be no agreement about how to do this adjustment, despite its importance.[38] Sorkin and colleagues, in a literature review, assert that no study shows the necessary concerns about the problem of adjustment for shrinkage with age. Their conclusion is revealing:

> In all future studies, researchers should strive for greater epidemiologic rigor than has been the norm for studies of the rate of height change with age. As we noted above, the investigators should describe the methods used to standardize the measurement of height and to assure that methodologic drift did not occur over time.[39]

Moreover, basing his hypothesis on extensive literature, Fogel[40] asserts that shorter individuals tend to have lower life expectancy rates. The same factors which are responsible for rates of growth below their potential can cause more delicate conditions of health later in life. In the present case, this means that shorter individuals tend to be absent in the older age ranges of the sample.

It is impossible to guarantee that the height of the Brazilian population follows the trend identified by Niewenweg and co-authors,[41] and we do not have mortality rates by cohort and heights in order to correct the mortality bias. Therefore, another procedure was followed in order to evaluate the long-term trend in the stature of Brazilians: to merge the POF 2002–2003 data with those from the *Pesquisa Nacional de Saúde e Nutrição 1989* (hereafter PNSN) and with the *Estudo Nacional de Despesas Familiares 1974–1975* (henceforth ENDEF).[42] The three surveys, based on representative national samples, contain anthropometric data measured by governmental agents.[43]

In order to minimize shrinkage and mortality problems, in each survey we considered only the heights of individuals up to 40 years old. In the periods in which there was an overlap between POF and PNSN and between PNSN and ENDEF, the results were weighted according to the number of observations in each research sample. The results of this procedure are presented in Figure 1 below. The evidence shows that average height for the cohorts born between 1939 and 1982 increased by 3.2 centimeters.[44] This steady increase is remarkable and it shows that biological living conditions have improved, notwithstanding the severe and lingering inequality in Brazil.

Let us consider 0.8 cm per decade as the true value of the average increase of heights of Brazilian men. This is below the 1 cm per decade rate that Monteiro et al.[45] estimated when they compared the 1952 and the 1967 Brazilians cohorts and that Meisel and Vega observed for Colombia.[46] Moreover, the literature has already identified much higher growth rates. Van Wieringen[47] sustained that the stature of Dutch men grew 2.2 cm per decade in the beginning of the twentieth century and 2.7 in the postwar period.

It is important to note that Brazilians who were born in 1981 had, at the beginning of the twenty-first century, an average height (170.8 cm) similar to that of Americans and Norwegians (171 cm) at the beginning of the twentieth century, but below that of Swedes (172 cm), and above that of the British (167 cm), Dutch (169 cm), and French (165 cm). Even against other Latin American countries Brazil does not stand out in height measurements. For example, recruits born in Buenos Aires in the decade of 1930 were as tall as the male Brazilians in the 1981 cohort.[48]

Figure 1.
Secular Trend of Height in Brazil, 1940–1980 (in cm by year of birth).

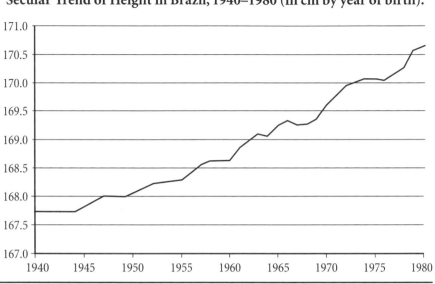

Sources: ENDEF, PNSN, POF.

Note: The annual series was smoothed using a three-year moving average.

Regional Differences and Their Evolution
The analysis of the evolution of aggregated data omits important regional and income differences. Figure 2 below represents the differences between regional and national average height in Brazil. People living in the South of the country, whatever the cohort, tend to be three or more centimeters taller than those from other regions. People living in the Central-Western and Southeastern regions tend to be similar in height, and are about two centimeters above the average. On the other hand, the stature of people living in the North and Northeastern regions tends to be two centimeters below the average. The most noticeable fact is that, despite the increase in Brazilian average height, people living in the North and Northeastern regions failed to catch up. This gap contrasts with the economic convergence between regions and states that has been identified in Brazil.[49] This suggests that persisting regional socioeconomic differences go beyond GDP per capita measurements which are reflected in the anthropometric data. Unfortunately, the data used here do not provide information about migration. We only have information about the individual's current place of residence, not the place where he grew up. At first, this would seem to be a serious distortion, because there were substantial internal migratory movements in

Figure 2.
Height Deviations from National Average by Region.

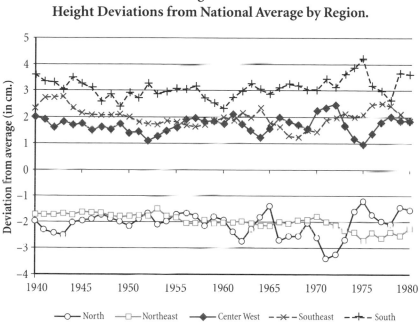

Sources: ENDEF, PNSN, POF.

the decades analyzed, especially from the Northeast to the Southeast. However, because migrants tend to move to richer locations, this distortion tends to inaccurately reduce—rather than increase—regional differences. In other words, height differences between Northern and Northeastern populations, in comparison with Southeastern, Southern, and Central-Western populations, are more significant than the available data can reveal.

Height, Income, and Regional Differences
The last row in Table 1 shows that 6 centimeters is the difference in height between the poorest and the richest quintiles.[50] If, as these data demonstrate, this difference has persisted since the 1930s, we can say that, contrary to the pattern in rich countries, in Brazil there was a process of economic growth which benefited the population as a whole (since the quintile average height increased), but unevenly, and not favorably to the poor. As height differences between rich and poor people did not diminish in all the regions of the country, or even among regions, it follows that policies to reduce regional inequalities were incapable of eliminating them. In fact, the current

average height of a 21-year-old Northern and Northeastern inhabitant is near the (adjusted) stature of Brazilians born in 1940.[51]

It is therefore evident that part of the regional difference in height is due to regional differences in living conditions. When individuals are divided into quintiles by region and their heights are examined, an interesting picture appears (Table 1). Differences in regional stature persist in each income quintile. Northern residents in the richest quintile, for example, are about 3.6 centimeters shorter than Southern residents in the same quintile. As for the poorest quintile, the difference is as much as 5 centimeters.

Table 1.
Average Heights by Macroregion and Per Capita Family Income Quintile.

Region	Poorest Quintile	2nd Poorest Quintile	Intermediate Quintile	2nd Richest Quintile	Richest Quintile	Total
North	165.15	165.95	167.06	168.15	170.28	167.06
Northeast	165.44	166.40	167.29	168.87	170.95	167.12
Center West	168.40	169.05	170.34	171.40	172.95	170.72
Southeast	168.71	169.09	170.15	171.02	172.91	170.95
South	170.04	169.84	170.67	172.21	173.82	171.96
Total	166.09	167.36	168.80	170.35	172.35	168.99

Source: Authors, based on POF.

We verified, in the POF data, that the statures of Brazilians vary significantly according to the region where they live. In richer and less unequal regions, with better educational and health services, individuals are taller.

The regional difference in height must be considered as an additional component of Brazilian regional differences. Nowadays, the country is divided into five regions, which have their own identities not only in geography but also in economic and social welfare.

The roots of this regional inequality were examined by several authors, such as Furtado, Leff, Denslow Jr, Buescu, and more recently Menezes Filho et al.[52] In general, their works locate the origins of such differentiation in the nineteenth century, especially for the Southeast and the Northeast. In fact, as a mosaic of agro-exports, principally of raw materials, each portion of the Brazilian territory experienced a different economic performance. Thus, while the sugar exports in the Northeast tended to stagnate 150 years ago, the coffee exports had their most expansive growth period in Southern Rio de Janeiro and São Paulo.

Brazilian industrialization occurred in a regionally centralized manner.[53] Although at the end of the nineteenth century industries developed in

almost every Brazilian state, in the twentieth century they tended to concentrate in Rio de Janeiro (the main industrial center in Brazil until the
1920s) and São Paulo. Despite the strong industrial concentration around
São Paulo, there was also considerable industrial growth in other states. Yet
the Southeast and the South have integrated industrial structures and are
the richest regions in Brazil. Those two regions have the best basic sanitary
conditions, hospital network coverage, education, and so on. The other
three regions, despite their industrial growth, are distinctly poorer and in
greater need of social welfare infrastructure.

We believe that the stature differences resulted from the interregional
development differences throughout the twentieth century, in which industrial development was strongly associated with the availability of resources
to improve material conditions of life.

Height, Color, and Income
In the POF data, the interviewees were classified in five "color" categories:
Branco, Preto, Amarelo, Pardo, and *Índio.*[54] Some of those labels, such as
Branco and *Preto,* are used in daily language by Brazilians. *Índios* are considered as such, in Brazil, when they keep aspects of the traditional indigenous culture; if they lose those aspects, they do not always keep their
identity. Nowadays the word *Pardo* is rarely used by Brazilians in daily language, although in past centuries it was often used. Finally, *Amarelo* is used
by governmental institutions to identify Brazilians of East Asian origin; in
colloquial language, however, Brazilians refer to them as "Japanese" or "Chi-
nese," no matter what Asiatic country their ancestors are from.

In Brazil, the relationships among colors, races, and ethnic groups
changed considerably throughout the twentieth century in comparison with
past centuries. We can say that other than the traditions of indigenous peoples, color does not indicate any particular lifestyle or even ethnicity that
distinguish specific groups from the rest of the Brazilian population.[55] European immigration after the 1930s diminished and did not keep alive ethnic
traditions that are associated with racial identities in other countries of the
continent. Besides diminished immigration, another factor strongly contributed to the suppression of ethnic identities in favor of the construction
of a national identity: the state. From the Revolution of 1930 to the end of
the military dictatorship in 1985, governments worked to create and enforce
national symbols to the detriment of ethnic identities. During the period
mentioned above, *samba* was elected the national music, even though its
origins can be related to Bahia, Rio de Janeiro, and partially São Paulo and
thus not to all of Brazil. *Futebol* (i.e., soccer), another symbol to which

Brazilians relate, was the object of specific policies throughout the referred period. It is noticeable that the ethnic identities to which the soccer clubs originally related were intentionally erased. Last, especially between 1930 and 1945, came the proclamation of the "Brazilian race," in which miscegenation virtues were exalted, opposing the racist beliefs that tended to disqualify it. It is thus possible to state that since the 1930s Brazil inclines towards the suppression of its former racial and ethnic identities.

And yet a certain color identity has persisted. This identity, built on a confused and subtle basis, still has significant effects; that is, the color of Brazilians tends to change from the darkest to the lightest as we move from the poorest to the richest people.[56] Thus, taking *Pretos* as an example, it is known that they are under-represented among the richer classes and among the people with high social prestige. At the same time, they are over-represented in poorer classes and in prisons. On the other hand, between *Brancos* and *Pretos*, and within the two mentioned groups, there is an enormous diversity of tones that IBGE showed in the *Pesquisa Nacional por Amostra Domiciliar* (National Household Sample Survey) of 1976: giving Brazilians the opportunity to identify their own color, 136 different definitions were counted, many of them with deep regional meaning.[57]

Is it possible to equate those 136 colors with the same number of ethnic groups and races? No, because miscegenation is constant, so children are often of different colors than their parents. Ethnic identities, usually fragile, also depend on lifestyles, not only on skin color, making it impossible to establish in Brazil an equivalence between ethnic groups and color. The results of the anthropometric analyses presented below adjust to what we affirmed: individuals belonging to the five color groups in which the Brazilians were classified in the POF data do not have significantly different statures, except for the *Índios*, who are formally identified as such when they maintain part of their own traditions and lifestyles. They are significantly shorter than average, thus confirming the claim that their inclusion in the Brazilian society has worked to their disadvantage.

While acknowledging that these five concepts and categories (*Amarelo*, *Branco*, *Preto*, *Pardo*, and *Índio*)[58] are problematic, we use them because we do not want to dismiss *a priori* either the possibility of differences in height related to color or race, or the aggregate of information made available in the database.

The data tabulated by income quintile and color also furnish interesting results. If we observe average heights only by reference to color, we could say that color is the main determining factor of height. *Branco* men are the tallest, followed by *Preto, Amarelo, Pardo,* and *Índio.* However, when the results are analyzed by quintile, we can see that:

- *Índios* are the shortest in the three lowest height strata;
- *Amarelos* are the shortest in the richer stratum;
- *Brancos* are the tallest in the two poorest quintiles and in the richest quintile;
- *Pretos* are the tallest in the intermediate and in the second richest quintiles.

These changes in order are due to a different distribution by color when we consider income quintiles. In the richest quintile, there are 29% *Branco,* but only 13.5% *Preto,* and 12.6% *Pardo.* Therefore, a significant part of the apparent height variation by color is in fact a result of the differences in income distribution *between* the colors, and not *within* the color groups themselves.[59]

Table 2.
Average Height by Color and Per Capita Family Income Quintile.

		Poorest Quintile	2nd Poorest Quintile	Intermediate Quintile	2nd Richest Quintile	Richest Quintile	Total
Amarelo	Average	164.33	164.56	169.03	168.37	168.57	167.75
	% of total color	11.39	11.39	14.56	22.15	40.51	100.00
Branco	Average	167.12	168.35	169.64	171.18	173.03	170.51
	% of total color	11.76	15.49	19.54	23.72	29.49	100.00
Índio	Average	162.96	160.79	165.69	170.06	170.86	164.80
	% of total color	33.12	24.84	16.56	11.46	14.01	100.00
Pardo	Average	165.69	166.76	167.97	169.28	171.05	167.69
	% of total color	26.57	23.39	20.40	17.06	12.58	100.00
Preto	Average	166.47	168.28	170.09	171.21	172.74	169.38
	% of total color	23.25	24.00	20.60	18.66	13.49	100.00
Total	Average	166.09	167.36	168.80	170.35	172.35	168.99
	% of total color	20.00	20.00	20.00	20.00	20.00	100.00

Source: Authors, based on POF.

The Model

If height is a good indicator of the quality of life, it is to be expected that this indicator will be affected by a range of socioeconomic, family, and environmental determinants. As mentioned above, it would be ideal if data on those determining factors during the individual process of physical maturation were available. In their absence, we have had to assume a correlation between present and past living conditions. We have also considered that individuals with a higher level of education, and higher per capita family income probably had better pre-adolescent living conditions. As such, height should be related to these variables. The database used also allows us to verify common assertions about regional or color differences which influence the quality of life.

In order to test our hypothesis, we started with the following equation:

$$Height = A + B[Y_1MY_2] + \Phi color\ dummies + \Omega color\ dummies *Y_2 \\ + \Theta other\ controls + \varepsilon \tag{1}$$

Y stands for a proxy of the household economic environment that affected the process of physical growth of the individual. It is measured on a logarithmic scale and is divided into Y_1 (variables related to family income), and Y_2 (variables related to individual human capital). The POF data only contains income by consumption unit, that is, by family, not per capita. In order to arrive at an estimate, we calculated per capita family income, i.e., the total income of the consumption units divided by the number of their members. Color dummies were created with *Preto* individuals as a basis for comparison. Other controls refer to regional dummies (*South, Northeast, Center-West* and *North*, with *Southeast* as a reference[60]), a rural dummy (as explained in the text, the history of Brazilian economic development is marked by an industrial and urban bias, so we would expect that rural populations were shorter than urban ones) and a control for age. Note that the results related to the rural/urban variable in Brazil must be cautiously interpreted. As Veiga[61] pointed out, the criterion currently used considers as urban the entire population resident in the main municipal district (the "urban zone" defined in the city planning policies), ignoring whether the area has the structural or functional characteristics of a city or not. This tends to overestimate the Brazilian urban population.

We acknowledge that there may be endogeneity in Y, so we postulated two alternative forms which are intended to verify the significance of subvectors Y_1 and Y_2 separately.

$$Height = A + BY_1 + \Phi color\ dummies + \Omega color\ dummies *Y_1 \\ + \Theta other\ controls + \varepsilon \tag{2}$$

$$Height = A + BY_2 + \Phi color\ dummies + \Omega color\ dummies *Y_2 \\ + \Theta other\ controls + \varepsilon \tag{3}$$

Finally, we had to consider the possibility that taller individuals have higher income. This causal relationship was emphasized by Schultz;[62] the hypothesis is that height is part of the health component of human capital[63] and would be an indicator of individual productivity. To control the possibility of reverse causality between height and income, a two-stage specification was estimated.

$$Height = A + BY_1 + \Phi color\ dummies + \Omega color\ dummies * Y_?$$
$$+ \Theta other\ controls + \varepsilon \qquad\qquad (4)$$
$$Y_1 = a + bY_2 + other\ instrument \quad s + u$$

Results

Table 3 reports the model using all the data at the individual level. Each column corresponds to a different specification of the equations discussed above, starting from the most general specification and then eliminating insignificant variables and possible endogeneity effects in the income and human capital variables. Specification (IV) uses a two-stage regression to address the latter issue. In specification (I), we noted that individuals who spent more years in school displayed higher stature. This effect is due to better nutritional conditions in their homes, given that in Brazil per capita family income in childhood is a determinant factor in people's education. In the color dummies, we note that only *Índio* is significant (*Preto* is the reference category). As for the interaction terms, there is significance only between color and human capital, and only for the color *Amarelo*. Even when we consider specifications (II) and (III), the results are similar. *Índio*, *South*, *North* and *Northeast* remain strongly significant in the three specifications. In (III), *Branco* is positive and significant. The interaction terms between human capital and color are significant only for *Amarelo* and *Índio* in specification (II).

In specification (IV), the endogeneity between income and human capital is considered. In this specification we verify that the relationship between height and income is non-linear (with increasing returns). This result gives weight to the thesis that, as regards regional influences (three of the four regional dummies are significant), income has a strong influence on the height of the individuals in the sample. Another regional influence is the urban-concentrated Brazilian economic development in the twentieth century. Specifications (III) and (IV) show that the rural population tends to be shorter than the urban one.

Overall, Table 3 demonstrates that inequalities of height among Brazilians are basically due to income, level of education, and region, and not due to color (except for *Índio*).[64] The results confirm what Table 2 had suggested: non-white people are shorter not because of their color as such; it is the lower socioeconomic condition of these groups that stunts their growth. Influences derived from the color of the individual appear only in *Índio* and

Table 3.
Econometric Analysis of Height Determinants at the Individual Level in Brazil, 1940–1980.

	I	II	III	IV
Constant	172.529	175.148	176.981	176.805
	(156.368) ***	(361.030) ***	(223.248) ***	(221.137) ***
LN(1+Years of education)	0.1224	−0.326		
	(0.509)	(−2.126) **		
(LN[1+Years of education])^2	0.467	0.881		
	(8.108)	(16.796) **		
LN (Age)	−2.277	−1.610	−3.416	−3.429
	(−18.504) **	(−13.434) **	(−30.001) ***	(−30.270) ***
LN(Family income per capita)	0.762		0.576	0.868
	(2.616) ***		(2.400) **	(3.597) ***
(LN[Family income per capita])^2	0.046		0.094	0.081
	(2.064) **		(4.483) ***	(3.855) ***
Preto	Ref.		Ref.	
Branco	0.472		0.828	
	(0.547)		(10.355) ***	
Pardo	0.273			
	(0.325)			
Amarelo	2.713	−2.169		
	(0.899)	(−4.015) ***		
Índio	−5.804	−5.542	−2.947	−4.019
	(−2.223) **	(−5.065) ***	(−4.399) ***	(−6.819) ***
*Branco**LN(Family income per capita)	−0.172			
	(−0.949)			
*Pardo**LN(Family income per capita)	−0.320			−0.230
	(−1.805)			(−7.997) ***
*Amarelo**LN(Family income per capita)	−0.412			−0.567
	(−0.690)			(−5.903) ***
*Índio**LN(Family income per capita)	0.063			
	(0.113)			
Southeast	Ref.	Ref.	Ref.	Ref.
Center	0.198			0.214
	(1.636)			(1.746)
South	0.806	0.708	0.746	0.829
	(6.102) ***	(5.921) ***	(6.210) ***	(6.180) ***
North	−2.836	−3.240	−2.933	−2.756
	(−22.102) ***	(−28.452) ***	(−25.638) ***	(−21.338) ***
Northeast	−2.341	−2.920	−2.497	−2.347
	(−21.765) ***	(−33.307) ***	(−27.898) ***	(−21.692) ***
*Branco**LN(1+Years of education)	0.009			
	(0.042)			
*Pardo**LN(1+ Years of education)	0.120			
	(0.582)			
*Amarelo**LN(1+ Years of education)	−1.964	−1.660		
	(−2.430) **	(−6.496) ***		
*Índio**LN(1+ Years of education)	1.145	1.213		
	(1.520)	(1.851)		

Table 3.
Econometric Analysis of Height Determinants at the Individual Level in Brazil, 1940–1980. (continued)

	I	II	III	IV
Rural	0.138		−0.339	−0.327
	(1.626)	(−4.057) ***	(−3.886) ***	
R^2	0.160	0.147	0.142	0.144
Observations	40,028	40,028	40,028	40,028
Standard error of regression	7.096	7.149	7.168	7.163
Sum of squared residuals	2,014,912	2,045,462	2,056,635	2,053,178
F–statistic	346.441	691.244	665.748	561.312

Source: POF 2002–3 microdata.

Notes: t-Statistic in parentheses. Least Squares in regressions I, II and III. In IV, Two–Stage Least Squares. Instruments: Constant, LN(1+Years of education), (LN[1+Years of education])2, LN(Age), (LN[Age])2, Índio, Pardo*LN(Family income per capita), South, North, Northeast.

** *significant at 5%.*

*** *significant at 1%.*

in the income interaction effect for *Pardo* and *Amarelo*, demonstrating that income increases for these groups of individuals have slightly less impact on their height. Thus, differences in height seem to be caused by inequalities of living conditions relating to the family (reflected in income and education level), and the wider environment where the individual lives (represented by the regional and the rural dummies).

Even when we consider the estimate made by using instrumental variables, we can argue that the individual's biological standard of living depends on factors such as income inequality or family income during childhood, and not at the time when their height was measured. It is expected that, *ceteris paribus*, higher state incomes have positive effects on average height because this is likely correlated with improved economic opportunities and a higher degree of state provisioning; conversely, states with higher income inequality would tend to have larger differences in height among the individuals in that state. In terms of individual height, however, it is not possible to forecast a clear effect. To explore these social effects at the individual level we include state-level variables in specifications (V), (VI) and (VII) reported in Table 4.[65]

In (V) and (VI), there is only a repetition of the procedure set out in the last table, in which we began with the more general specification and excluded the non-significant variables. Specification (VII) is similar to (IV) in that instrumental variables were used to make the estimate, again in an attempt to understand the relationship between human capital and income. Thus, for purposes of comparison, only (IV) and (VII) are to be considered.

The results of the two specifications are very similar. Nonetheless, it is worth emphasizing that *GDP per capita during childhood*, that is, the average state GDP per capita of each individual up to 15 years old, shows both positive and negative effects on stature.[66] The color dummies, in their turn, give a result which is similar to the first group of regressions: once again, only *Índio* is significant.

Estimate (VII) shows that height depends basically on economic conditions. Individuals who grew up in relatively richer states and families had more education and today have both higher income and stature. Again, the negative influence of the rural dummy on the heights found in the previous estimations is verified, which could be interpreted as a kind of historical inheritance of the initial health conditions, given the pattern of regional disparities in Brazil. Therefore, the results suggest that the "hidden cost of development"[67] was not sufficient to counterbalance the relatively better life conditions in the more developed areas of Brazil.

In Table 4, it is noticeable that the effect of state *GDP per capita during childhood* is particularly significant when compared to other variables. In specification (VII), a hypothetical increase of 1% in this variable brings about an increase of 0.14 cm in height. In the same specification, a strong impact of the rural dummy is noticeable. Despite the recommended caution in the interpretation of this variable, the results suggest that an individual in a rural zone would be approximately 0.38 cm shorter than one living in an urban zone.

Conclusions

Our study, using anthropometric data and econometric methods, provided further evidence that the severe inequalities at personal and regional levels affected the height of Brazilians. The result is in agreement with Baer and co-authors, who describe the indisputable health improvements in Brazil during the twentieth century, but conclude that the country

> still has an epidemiologic pattern where infectious and parasitic diseases (such as cholera, malaria, etc.), due to lack of adequate sanitary infrastructure, are still prevalent. This pattern is closely associated with Brazil's highly concentrated income distribution . . . Moreover, given Brazil's level of GDP per capita, the country's population should be enjoying a much better level of health status.[68]

Table 4.
Econometric Analysis of Height Determinants at the Individual and State Level in Brazil, 1940–1980.

	V	VI	VII
Constant	134.220	130.030	129.482
	(12.201) ***	(30.870) ***	(30.683) ***
LN(1+Years of education)	0.030		
	(0.116)		
(LN[1+Years of education])²	0.470		
	(7.723) ***		
LN (Age)	−0.100	−1.027	−0.891
	(−0.470)	(−5.033) ***	(−4.364) ***
LN(Family income per capita)	0.703	0.897	0.668
	(2.249) **	(3.505) ***	(2.610) ***
(LN[Family income per capita])²	0.039	0.070	0.089
	(1.623)	(3.150) ***	(3.985) ***
Preto	Ref.		
Branco	−0.204		
	(−0.224)		
Pardo	−0.391		
	(−0.440)		
Amarelo	2.300		
	(0.699)		
Indio	−8.395	−8.862	−8.344
	(−2.679) ***	(−2.916) ***	(−2.760) ***
Branco*LN(Family income per capita)	−0.082		
	(−0.423)		
Pardo*LN(Family income per capita)	−0.184	−0.163	
	(−0.969)	(−10.910) ***	
Amarelo*LN(Family income per capita)	−0.494	−0.501	
	(−0.772)	(−5.383) ***	
Índio*LN(Family income per capita)	0.832	1.159	1.147
	(1.216)	(2.139) **	(2.129) **
Southeast	Ref.	Ref.	Ref.
Center	0.620	0.681	0.625
	(4.364) ***	(5.082) ***	(4.661) ***
South	0.778	0.791	1.018
	(5.227) ***	(5.790) ***	(7.546) ***
North	−3.282	−3.067	−3.326
	(−15.490) ***	(−17.329) ***	(−18.896) ***
Northeast	−1.059	−0.935	−1.060
	(−6.820) ***	(−6.144) ***	(−6.978) ***
Branco*LN(1+Years of education)	0.132		
	(0.564)		
Pardo*LN(1+ Years of education)	0.151		
	(0.669)		
Amarelo*LN(1+ Years of education)	−1.395		
	(−1.621)		
Índio*LN(1+ Years of education)	0.679		
	(0.737)		

Table 4.
Econometric Analysis of Height Determinants at the Individual and State Level in Brazil, 1940–1980. (continued)

	V	VI	VII
Rural	0.066	−0.390	−0.375
	(0.732)	(−4.425) ***	(−4.244) ***
LN(State GDP during childhood)	6.980	8.049	8.063
	(4.304) ***	(8.880) ***	(8.778) ***
(LN[State GDP during childhood])^2	−0.386	−0.416	−0.412
	(−6.790) ***	(−7.448) ***	(−7.366) ***
State Gini Coefficient	−7.453		
	(−0.440)		
State Gini Coefficient*LN(State GDP during childhood)	0.884		
	(0.422)		
R^2	0.168	0.152	0.150
Observations	35712	35712	35712
Standard error of regression	7.066	7.130	7.143
Sum of squared residuals	1,781,584	1,814,740	1,821,863
F-statistic	277.926	460.303	523.319

Sources: POF 2002–3 microdata. State GDP from Azzoni, *Concentração Regional*, and IPEA GDP series.

Notes: t-Statistic in parentheses. Least Squares in regressions V and VI. In VII, Two-Stage Least Squares. Instruments: Constant, LN(1+Years of education), (LN[1+Years of education])^2, LN(Age), (LN[Family income per capita])2, *Índio, Pardo**LN(Family income per capita), *Amarelo**LN(Family income per capita), *Indio**LN(Family income per capita), Center, South, North, Northeast, Rural, LN(State GDP during childhood), (LN[State GDP during childhood])$.^2$

Nowadays, agreement is almost unanimous that GDP per capita is insufficient for measuring gains in welfare. More controversial is the discussion about how to supplement it. Part of the research is focused on the "capabilities" approach,[69] while another part tries to measure individuals' happiness directly.[70] This chapter has emphasized the importance of using stature as a means of evaluating the living conditions of different populations. This may lead to misunderstandings, but we do not suggest either that the height of individuals should be considered an aim in itself, or that there is any kind of superiority in taller people. We only suggest that in situations in which it is necessary to evaluate the economic and social needs of populations, height can be considered as a pertinent dimension.

Height differences between income strata in Brazilian society are persistent and relevant. According to Fogel,[71] shorter people have a higher risk of mortality and are more subject to certain diseases, even when they are in social conditions similar to tall people. Therefore, the unequal distribution of income and of sanitation and health services, which are responsible for the differences in height, generate an additional burden on the poorest populations, especially on those who have fewest resources to purchase medication and food, and to pay for health treatment.

The data on the evolution of the height of Brazilians from 1940 to 1980 confirm a well-known fact: despite the per capita increase in income over this period (3.2% a year), there was no equivalent improvement in the material conditions of life, and inequality remains a major problem.[72]

Notes

* The authors would like to thank the reviewers for comments and suggestions. Colin Lewis and María Alejandra Irigoin and the participants of the III Economics and Human Biology conference made perceptive comments on a previous version of the chapter. Martin D. Brauch provided excellent research assistance and comments. Leonardo Monasterio is grateful to the Brazilian Science Fund (CNPq) for financial support. The usual disclaimer applies.

1. Barros et al., "Desigualdade e pobreza," provides an analysis of inequality and poverty in Brazil. See Thorp, *Progress, Poverty and Exclusion* for an overview of 20th century Brazilian development experience.

2. PNUD, *Atlas do desenvolvimento humano.*

3. The controversy appeared in major Brazilian newspapers. See, for example, Peña, "Pesquisa."

4. See IBGE, *Pesquisa.*

5. Soares, "IBGE contesta," summarizes Lula's criticism and the reply from the IBGE.

6. See Baer et al., "Health in the Development Process," for an overview of the health improvements in Brazil.

7. Cited in Tanner, *A History of the Study,* 162.

8. Cuff, *Hidden Cost.*

9. Respectively: Steckel, "Height and Per Capita Income"; Komlos, *Nutrition;* and Fogel, *The Escape from Hunger.* See Steckel, "Heights and Human Welfare," for a recent survey of the research in anthropometric papers. The author shows that more than 20 papers per year on the subject were published between 1995 and 2008.

10. It is worth noting that the expression *regression analysis* comes from Francis Galton's research on the differences in height between generations (see Salsburg, *The Lady*).

11. "In France, during this era (1790) daily consumption was about 1,800 calories. A typical American male in his early thirties requires nearly 2,300 calories for baseline maintenance, and by implication the typical European of the late eighteenth century was much smaller and lighter. This evidence indicates that the diets in England and France near the end of the eighteenth century were so inadequate that approximately one-fifth of the labour force was incapable of

work or could do no more than three hours of light work daily" (Steckel, "Stature," 1925).

12. Sen, *Development as Freedom*, 204.

13. "Charles Edward Trevelyan, the head of the Treasury during the Irish famines, who saw not much wrong with British economic policy in Ireland (of which he was in charge), pointed to Irish habits as part of the explanation of the famines. Chief among the habitual failures was the tendency of the Irish poor to eat only potatoes, which made them dependent on one crop. Indeed, Trevelyan's view of the causation of the Irish famines permitted him to link them with his analysis of Irish cooking. 'There is scarcely a woman of the peasant class in the West of Ireland whose culinary art exceeds the boiling of a potato'. The remark is of interest not just because it is rather rare for an Englishman to find a suitable occasion for making international criticism of culinary art. Rather, the pointing of an accusing finger at the meagerness of the diet of the Irish poor well illustrates the tendency to blame the victim. The victims, in this view, had helped themselves to a disaster, despite the best efforts of the administration in London to prevent it" (ibid., 174–175).

   See Davis, *Late Victorian*, for an overview on the participation of bureaucrats and governors in famine epidemics in the world at the end of the nineteenth century.

14. See Komlos, *Nutrition*, and Fogel, *The Escape from Hunger*.

15. Cuff, *Hidden Cost*.

16. Before the development of modern conservation techniques, the supply of perishable foods for the cities was restricted. The distance between producing zones and consumers imposed a transportation cost and/or a decrease in the nutritional quality of food.

17. Meisel and Vega, "The Biological Standard."

18. Salvatore, "Stature Decline."

19. Cited in Fogel, *The Escape from Hunger*, 40.

20. Ibid., 41.

21. Ibid., 89.

22. Steckel, "Stature," 1924.

23. Ibid., 1906.

24. "I saw once, after three whole years away from Brazil, a group of Brazilian sailors—*mulatos* and *cafuzos*—disembarking I don't remember whether from the São Paulo or from the Minas on the soft snow of Brooklyn. They gave me the impression of being a caricature of men. . . . Miscegenation resulted in that. Nobody told me then, as Roquette Pinto told the aryanists in the Brazilian Congress of Eugenics in 1929, that those who I thought were Brazilians were not simply *mulatos* or *cafuzos*, but ill *mulatos* and *cafuzos*" (Freyre, *Casa Grande*, 77, authors' translation). *Mulatos* are usually described as descendants of *Branco* and *preto* people; *cafuzos* would have *Branco* and *Índio* ancestors.

25. "The serious diseases that have been undermining throughout generations the strength and the efficiency of the Brazilian population, whose unstable health conditions, uncertain labour ability, apathy and growth disturbances are attributed to miscegenation, are actually linked to large-scale monoculture plantations" (ibid., 79).
26. Steckel, "Stature," 1910.
27. Cited in ibid., 1911.
28. Respectively, Steckel, "Height," and Fogel, *The Escape from Hunger.*
29. Sen, *Development as Freedom.*
30. Komlos and Baur, "From the Tallest."
31. Steckel, "Stature," 1912–14.
32. IBGE, *Pesquisa.*
33. With the exception of the distribution of height in the 1944 and 1949 birth cohorts.
34. On the matter of rounding and heaping, see Komlos, "How to (and How Not to)."
35. Since the largest part of historical studies is based on military databases, the analyses are mostly about men.
36. Medline Plus.
37. Niewenweg et al., "Adult Height."
38. See, for example, Lera et al., "Predictive Equations," for an attempt to predict the height of the elderly for three samples in Latin America: São Paulo (Brazil), Santiago (Chile), and Mexico City (Mexico).
39. Sorkin, Muller, and Andres, "Longitudinal Change."
40. Fogel, *The Escape from Hunger,* 23.
41. Niewenweg et al., "Adult Height."
42. INAM, *Pesquisa;* IBGE, *Estudo.* The titles translate as National Survey of Health and Nutrition and National Study of Family Expenses, respectively.
43. We thank Amílcar Challú for the microdata referring to the PNSN. The other data in the PNSN are not comparable to those in POF and therefore cannot be combined in a unique econometric analysis. Unfortunately, the microdata referring to the ENDEF were not available, only the average height values and the number of observations by state and birth date interval.
44. Applying the adjustment suggested by Niewenweg et al., "Adult Height," to the POF data results in an increase of 3.8 cm in the height of Brazilians in the same period. One possible explanation for the 0.6 cm difference between the two procedures is that the shrinkage process was more intense among Brazilians than among the Dutch, as studied by those authors.
45. Monteiro, Benício, and Gouveia, "Evolução."
46. Meisel and Veiga, "The Biological Standard."
47. Cited in Monteiro, Benício, and Gouveia, "Evolução."
48. Salvatore, "Stature Decline."

49. Azzoni, "Concentração regional."
50. A comparison between the two extreme deciles increases the difference to more than seven centimeters.
51. In order to reduce regional inequalities, the Brazilian government created the Superintendency for the Development of the Northeast (SUDENE) in 1959 and the Superintendency for the Development of the Amazon (SUDAM) in 1966. However, they were not part of a consistent and stable public policy and their social and economic results are highly controversial. See Diniz, *A questão*, for an overview of regional development policies in Brazil and Pessôa, "Existe um problema," for a critical appraisal.
52. See, respectively, Furtado, *Formação*; Leff, *Subdesenvolvimento*; Denslow Jr., "As origens"; Buescu, *Brasil: disparidades*; and Menezes Filho et al., "Instituições."
53. Cano, *Desequilíbrios regionais*.
54. In English, *Branco* is "white," *Preto* is "black," *Amarelo* is "yellow," *Pardo* is "brown," and *Índio* is "native Brazilian" or "indigenous."
55. As the work of biologists show (for instance, Pena and Bortolini, "Pode a genética"), these racial classifications are not grounded in genetic differences and ancestors: Brazilians are predominantly *mestizos* descending from Africans, Europeans and American Natives, even those who consider themselves "pure" black or white.
56. Since the sixteenth century, identification by race in Brazil has been carried out in accordance with physical and social aspects, especially in terms of the categories *Branco*, *Preto*, *Índio* and *Pardo*. Consequently, it is possible that a *Pardo* or *Índio* person will be considered *Branco* if rich, and *Preto* if poor. In the same way, it is possible that a rich person who is categorized as *Branco* becomes poor, and from then on is considered *Pardo*. It is worth noticing that, if the criterion for African descent is 10% of African ancestry, which is reflected in certain genetic traits, more than 70% of the *Branco* Brazilian male population would be included in this category (Pena and Bortolini, "Pode a genética," 43).
57. Quoted by Schwarcz, "Nem preto," 47.
58. If such terms represented only colors, translating them would not be a problem. However, given the great tone variation accepted by each term, besides the social meaning that we intend to express, we understand that it is inadequate to translate the colors of Brazilians to English.
59. According to Steckel, "Stature," people from the Far East are possibly the only group in which genes seem to matter. Nevertheless, stature can be related to differences in diet. Even among the individuals of this ethnic group, per capita income and height are positively correlated.
60. The South comprises three Brazilian states: Rio Grande do Sul, Paraná, and Santa Catarina. The Northeast accounts for Bahia, Sergipe, Alagoas, Pernambuco, Paraíba, Rio Grande do Norte, Ceará, Piauí, and Maranhão. The Center-West has Goiás, Distrito Federal, Mato Grosso, and Mato Grosso do Sul. The North is composed by Rondônia, Acre, Amazonas, Pará, Roraima, and Amapá.

The Southeast region is the richest one in Brazil: São Paulo, Minas Gerais, Rio de Janeiro, and Espírito Santo.

61. Veiga, *Cidades Imaginárias*.
62. Schultz, "Wage Gains."
63. Kac, "Tendência," using a sample of Brazilian Navy recruits (1940–1965), found evidence that human capital is an important factor in anthropometric studies. Campino et al., "Health, Human Capital," find similar results with another sample, the "Pesquisa de Padrão de Vida (PPV)," of data collected between 1996 and 1997.
64. The *Branco* dummy showed significance in one of the regressions (III), but—as further explained   this significance disappeared in the better-specified regressions (IV and VII).
65. The sample was reduced by about 5,000 observations due to the lack of data on GDP or the Gini coefficient referring to several federative units (states) which were created after 1940.
66. The variable is a proxy for income during the growth period. In order to calculate it, we used data on the evolution of Brazilian GDP, as well as data on each state's population and participation in the GDP. For each 15-year-old individual in the sample, we calculated the GDP per capita in the state where he was interviewed for the POF. Considering that the place of the POF interview does not always coincide with the place where the individual grew up, it is a variable that tends to underestimate the effects of per capita income of the state of the 15-year-old individual, because the trend of migration was from poorer to richer states.
67. Cuff, *Hidden Cost*.
68. Baer et al., "Health in the Development Process," 421.
69. As defined by Sen, *Development as Freedom*.
70. Frey and Stutzer, "What Can Economists Learn."
71. Quoted by Fogel, *The Escape from Hunger*, 24.
72. Thorp, *Progress, Poverty and Exclusion*.

References

Azzoni, Carlos. "Concentração regional e dispersão das rendas per capita estaduais: análise a partir de séries históricas estaduais de PIB, 1939–1995." *Estudos Econômicos* 27, no. 2 (1997): 341–393.

Baer, Werner. *The Brazilian Economy: Growth and Development*. Westport: Praeger, 2001.

Baer, Werner, Antonio Campino, and Tiago Cavalcanti. "Health in the Development Process: The Case of Brazil." *Quarterly Review of Economics and Finance* 41 (2001): 405–425.

Barros, Ricardo Paes, Ricardo Henriques, and Rosane Mendonça. "Desigualdade e pobreza no Brasil: retrato de uma estabilidade inaceitável." *Revista Brasileira de Ciências Sociais* 15, no. 42 (2000): 123–142.

Buescu, Mircea. *Brasil: disparidades de renda no passado*. Rio de Janeiro: Saraiva, 1979.

Campino, Antônio, Carlos Augusto Monteiro, Wolney L. Conde, and Flávia M. S. Machado. "Health, Human Capital and Economic Growth in Brazil." Paper read at the 44th European Regional Science Conference, at Porto, Portugal, 2004.

Cano, Wilson. *Desequilíbrios regionais e concentração industrial no Brasil, 1930–1995*. Campinas: Universidade Estadual de Campinas, Instituto de Economia, 1998.

Cuff, Timothy. *The Hidden Cost of Economic Development: the Biological Standard of Living in Antebellum Pennsylvania*. Farnham: Ashgate Publishing, 2005.

Davis, Michael. *Late Victorian Holocausts: El Nino Famines and the Making of the Third World*. New York: Verso, 2001.

Denslow Jr., David. "As origens da desigualdade regional no Brasil." In *Formação Econômica do Brasil*, ed. F. Versiani and R. P. Barros. São Paulo: Saraiva, 1977.

Diniz, Clélio C. *A questão regional e as políticas governamentais no Brasil*. Belo Horizonte: CEDEPLAR, 2001.

Fogel, Robert W. *The Escape from Hunger and Premature Death, 1700–2100. Europe, America, and the Third World*. Cambridge: Cambridge University Press, 2004.

Frey, Bruno, and A. Stutzer. "What Can Economists Learn from Happiness Research?" *Journal of Economic Literature* 40 (2002): 402–435.

Freyre, Gilberto. *Casa Grande & Senzala, Obra Escolhida*. Rio de Janeiro: Nova Aguillar, 1977.

Furtado, Celso. *Formação Econômica do Brasil*. São Paulo: Editora Nacional, 1987 [1st. ed., 1959].

IBGE. *Estudo Nacional da Despesa Familiares 1974–1975*. Brasília: IBGE, 1975.

———. *Pesquisa de orçamentos familiares 2002–2003—Microdados* (2) [CD-Rom]. IBGE, 2005.

INAM. *Pesquisa Nacional sobre Saúde e Nutrição*. Brasília: INAM, 1990.

Kac, Gilberto. "Tendência secular em estatura em recrutas da Marinha do Brasil nascidos entre 1940 e 1965." *Cadernos de Saúde Pública* 14, no. 3 (1998): 565–573.

Komlos, John. "How to (and How Not to) Analyze Deficient Height Samples." *Historical Methods* 37, no. 4 (2004): 160–173.

———. *Nutrition and Economic Development in the Eighteenth-century Habsburg Monarchy: An Anthropometric History*. Princeton: Princeton University Press, 1989.

———. "Shrinking in a Growing Economy? The Mystery of Physical Stature during the Industrial Revolution." *Journal of Economic History* 58, no. 3 (1998): 779–802.

Komlos, John, and Marieluise Baur. "From the Tallest to (One of) the Fattest: The Enigmatic Fate of the American Population in the 20th Century." *Economics and Human Biology* 2, no. 1 (2004): 57–74.

Leff, Nathaniel H. *Subdesenvolvimento e desenvolvimento no Brasil*. Rio de Janeiro: Expressão e Cultura, 1991.

Lera, L. J., Luis Santos, C. García, P. Arroyo, and C. Albala. "Predictive Equations for Stature in the Elderly: A Study in Three Latin American Cities." *Annals of Human Biology* 32, no. 6 (2005): 773–781.

MedlinePlus. "Aging Changes in the Bones—Muscles—Joints." In MedlinePlus Medical Encyclopedia (2008). http://www.nlm.nih.gov/medlineplus/ency/article /004015.htm.

Meisel, Adolfo, and Margarita Vega. "The Biological Standard of Living (and Its Convergence) in Colombia 1870–2003. A Tropical Success History." *Economics and Human Biology* 5, no. 1 (2007): 100–122.

Menezes-Filho, Naércio, Renato Leite Marcondes, Elaine Toldo Pazello, and Luiz Guilherme Scorzafave. "Instituições e diferenças de renda entre os estados brasileiros: uma anállise histórica." Paper read at *XXXIV Encontro Nacional de Economia*, at Salvador, Bahia, 2006.

Monteiro, Carlos Augusto, Maria Helena D'Aquino Benício, and Nelson da Cruz Gouveia. "Evolução da altura dos brasileiros." In *Velhos e novos males da saúde no Brasil: a evolução do país e de suas doenças*, ed. C. Monteiro. São Paulo: HUCITEC/NUPENS-SUP, 1995.

Niewenweg, R., M. L. Smit, M. J. E. Walenkamp, and J. M. Wit. "Adult Height Corrected for Shrinking and Secular Trend." *Annals of Human Biology* 30, no. 5 (2003): 563–569.

Peña, Bernardo de la. "Pesquisa será desprezada." *O Globo*, 23 December 2004, section "O Pais," 3.

Pena, Sérgio D. J, and Maria Cátira Bortolini. "Pode a genética definir quem deve se beneficiar das cotas universitárias e demais ações afirmativas?" *Estudos Avançados* 18, no. 50 (2004): 1–20.

Pessôa, Samuel A. 2001. "Existe um Problema de Desigualdade Regional no Brasil?" Paper read at *XXIX Encontro Nacional de Economia*, at Salvador, Bahia, 2001. http://www.anpec.org.br/encontro2001/artigos/200105174.pdf.

PNUD. *Atlas do desenvolvimento humano* [CD-Rom]. IPEA/PNUD, 2003.

Salsburg, David S. *The Lady Tasting Tea: How Statistics Revolutionized Science in the Twentieth Century.* New York: W.H. Freeman, 2001.

Salvatore, Ricardo D. "Stature Decline and Recovery in a Food-Rich Export Economy: Argentina 1900–1934." *Explorations in Economic History* 41, no. 3 (2004): 233–255.

Schultz, T. Paul. "Wage Gains Associated with Height as a Form of Health Human Capital." *The American Economic Review* 92, no. 2 (2002): 349–353.

Schwarcz, L. M. "Nem preto nem branco, muito pelo contrário, cor e raça na intimidade." In *História da vida privada no Brasil: contrastes da intimidade contemporânea*, ed. L. M. Schwarcz and A. F. Novais, vol. 4, 175–243. São Paulo: Companhia das Letras, 1998.

Sen, Amartya. *Development as Freedom.* Oxford: Oxford University Press, 1999.

Soares, Pedro. "IBGE contesta declarações do presidente sobre a fome," 22 December 2004. http://www.al.rs.gov.br/Dep/site/materia_antiga.asp?txtID Materia=92779&txtIdDep=94

Sorkin, J. D., D. C. Muller, and R. Andres. "Longitudinal Change in the Heights of Men and Women: Consequential Effects on Body Mass Index." *Epidemiology Reviews* 21, no. 2 (1999): 247–60.

Steckel, Richard H. "Height and Per Capita Income." *Historical Methods* 16, no. 1 (1983): 1–7.

———. "Stature and the Standard of Living." *Journal of Economic Literature* 33, no. 4 (1995): 1903–40.

———. "Heights and Human Welfare: Recent Developments and New Directions." NBER Working Paper Series no. w14536 (2008). http://ssrn.com/abstract=1312629

Tanner, James M. *A History of the Study of Human Growth*. Cambridge: Cambridge University Press, 1981.

Thorp, Rosemary. *Progress, Poverty and Exclusion: An Economic History of Latin America in the 20th Century*. Washington, D.C.: Inter-American Development Bank, 1998.

Veiga, José Eli. *Cidades Imaginárias: o Brasil é menos urbano do que se calcula*. São Paulo: Autores Associados, 2002.

7

Human Development and Inequality in the Twentieth Century: The Mercosur Countries in a Comparative Perspective

Luis Bértola, María Camou, Silvana Maubrigades, and Natalia Melgar

Introduction

Since the United Nations introduced the concept of human development and started to work with the Human Development Index (HDI), a lively debate on measures and variables has been taking place. This debate has expanded recently to the field of economic history, where scholars strive to find an appropriate Historical Human Development Index. Our aim in this chapter is to analyze the performance, in terms of human development, of three Mercosur countries (Argentina, Brazil and Uruguay) as they compare with four core countries (France, Germany, the United Kingdom, and the United States) during the twentieth century. In the course of our discussion we examine the available series on human development and discuss some methodological aspects related to their construction, hoping to improve those we consider problematic or unconvincing.

As does the HDI, we will mainly rely on per capita income, education, and life expectancy series. Nevertheless, we will introduce several changes to the estimates. Per capita GDP will not be transformed into logarithms. With respect to education, we will include not only literacy rates, as historical estimates have done until now, but also school enrollment. In addition, we will explore changing the weight given to the different components of education to better capture countries' relative performance in different periods. With respect to life expectancy, we follow the conventional treatment.

Our main concern is to consider how the introduction of measures of inequality affects the Human Development Index. Assuming that overall welfare is higher if inequality is lower, we will estimate inequality in the distribution of income, longevity, and education, and construct a Historical

Human Development Index (HHDI) adjusted by inequality trends. In line with Hicks,[1] we call this index the Inequality-Adjusted Historical Human Development Index (IAHHDI). Because of data constraints, this attempt will only be done for Uruguay and the United States.

The results obtained are discussed later. The basic idea is that progress in human development is the result of innovations in the production of goods and services, in the preservation of life, and in educating the population. These achievements may be the result of various complementary forces: the capacity to produce knowledge, the capacity of learning by doing, and the capacity to exploit technological spillovers from more advances countries.

Our results are to a high degree preliminary and our discussion still is at an explorative level.

Background

Economic historians have been working hard on the reconstruction of historical GDP series, on the basis on which the pace of economic growth and its fluctuations could be discussed. If adequately adjusted for purchasing power, these series are also important for comparing levels of per capita income and examining their underlying determinants. The efforts made by hundreds of scholars have yielded important results, as shown by the impressive compendia published at short intervals by Angus Maddison,[2] estimates that remain exhaustive and disputable, but that significantly influenced our research.

Many criticisms have been directed towards the use of per capita GDP as a measure of welfare. Besides noting its technical shortcomings (the coverage of the informal sector, the lack of market prices for non-market production, the lack of consideration of the quality and welfare implications of the goods and services produced, and more), Amartya Sen criticizes especially the assumption of an equal distribution of income among people with different social backgrounds and needs. The doctrinal base for his theory is the concept of human capability: the ability of human beings to live lives they consider worthy and to enhance their substantive choices.[3]

Sen's approach demands, for empirical work, varied and seldom available information, especially on an historical dimension. Since 1990, the approach to measuring welfare has been recalibrated in the Human Development Index, in which per capita GDP, as a proxy for the standard of living, has been complemented by life expectancy and education as proxies for other aspects of the quality of life, probably not reflected by the per capita GDP. For the contemporary period, the HDI is complemented with the use of a wide variety of indicators that concern gender, knowledge, race, and age gaps. The varying quality and availability of these sources of information across countries raise difficulties for comparative long-run studies, like the one we aim to perform here.

In recent years, economic historical research has tried to extend the work on historical national accounts to the field of historical human development. For the Latin American countries, the first important contributions were those of Astorga and FitzGerald and the Oxford Latin America Data Base (OXLAD). First published as an appendix to Thorp's *Progress, Poverty and Exclusion*, this work was later upgraded in Astorga, Bergès and FitzGerald.[4] The index combines GDP, literacy rates, and life expectancy into a so-called Historical Living Standard Index for 6 Latin American countries during the twentieth century, and for 13 Latin American countries since the 1950s. The Index was also expressed in relation to the achievements of the United States. It looked as follows (1):

$$Hi = \frac{1}{3}\left[\left(\frac{(\log yi - \log 100)}{\log 40,000 - \log 100}\right) + \left(\frac{lifei - 25}{85 - 25}\right) + \left(\frac{liti - 0}{100 - 0}\right)\right] \qquad (1)$$

where yi is per capita income of country (i) expressed in 1970 international dollars; $lifei$ is life expectancy at birth in country (i); and $liti$ is the literacy rate in country (i).

The authors' two main conclusions were:[5]

1. "The main sub-period of development in Latin America during the twentieth century occurred between 1940 and 1980 when there was an unprecedented surge in economic growth and social improvement. That this coincided with the so-called 'import substitution' process is not surprising insofar as public investment and state-led basic education and health initiatives were associated with the rise in growth rates and the improvement in health, despite the inefficiencies and distortions generated by forced industrialisation ... It seems clear that this period saw the greatest structural change in the Latin American economy, and was marked by sustained and relatively stable growth and social improvement. In stark contrast, the periods from 1900 to 1940 and from 1980 to 2000 saw lower economic growth and far more instability."

2. "Social convergence occurred in the absence of economic convergence ... these patterns of growth and convergence raise some interesting questions regarding the relationship between economic growth and social progress, and suggest that the more simplistic endogenous growth models may need some rethinking."

Both conclusions are extremely important. The second one reinforces the idea that welfare cannot be approached by per capita GDP alone and that the evolution of the length and quality of life may have other determinants as well. The first one has great implications for the discussion of the Latin American performance in relation to policy-making. While the dominant approach during the 1970s–1990s pointed to import-substituting policies and state-led growth as the origin of Latin American relative backwardness, these results show a different picture, in which the later decades of the twentieth century, dominated by structural reforms and liberalization, appear as decades of relative stagnation.

Camou and Maubrigades[6] improved Astorga and FitzGerald[7] as they not only considered literacy rates in their approach to education, but also took into consideration school enrollment, following Bértola and Bertoni.[8] This attempt was limited to the case of Uruguay. It also incorporated updated per capita GDP and life expectancy estimates, as well as some changes in the parameters found in earlier versions of Prados.[9]

A recent and important contribution to Latin American historical human development, as yet unpublished, is the work of Leandro Prados.[10] He constructed a database for 1870–2000, including some Latin American countries and the OECD members. He mainly relied on the OXLAD database for Latin America (meaning, among other things, that education is solely approached through literacy rates) and on his own database and own purchasing-parity estimates for per capita GDP figures. Besides advancing a very interesting discussion of the state of the art, Prados developed several new technical aspects of the construction of the historical human development index:

- He used a convex achievement function to estimate the non-income variables, implying that an increase in the standard of living of a country at a higher level implies a greater achievement than if the increase had taken place at a lower level;

- The adjustment of the maximum and minimum values of life expectancy to more realistic levels: 80 and 20 years, respectively;

- The use of a geometric average: "a geometric average of the index's components has the advantage of reducing their substitutability significantly, somehow avoiding that an improvement in one attribute may offset a worsening in another, with a resulting neutral aggregate effect on the HDI."[11]

- It is remarkable that despite the convex achievement function for the non-income variables, a converse transformation is done in relation to income, so that a marginal welfare unit demands increasing growth in per capita income

Prados' index can be summarized in equation (2):

$$Hi = \sqrt[3]{\left[\left(\frac{\log yi - \log 100}{\log 40,000 - \log 100}\right) * \left(\frac{\log(80-20) - \log(80 - lifei)}{\log(80-20)}\right) * \left(\frac{\log 100 - \log liti}{\log 100}\right)\right]} \quad (2)$$

Prados' conclusions are to a large extent similar to those obtained by Astorga, Bergès and FitzGerald:

- "Income inequality (per capita GDP) between the OECD countries and Latin America increased especially in the last decades of the twentieth century (within-country inequality is not considered)."
- "The gap in human development between Latin America and the OECD countries shrank most during the central decades of the twentieth century. Even if the gap continued to decrease afterwards, it did so at a much slower rate, so that by 2000, it was still huge."[12]

In other words, Leandro Prados' results reinforce those obtained by Astorga, Bergès, and FitzGerald, as well as the comments already made in relation to them.

The Construction of an Inequality-Adjusted Historical Human Development Index (IAHHDI)

In constructing our index we will rely on the three basic components of the Human Development Index (life expectancy, education, and income), but introduce changes in the variables and in the weights of the components. Following Prados, we will use a geometric average of the components and introduce an adjustment for inequality.

Life Expectancy
For this component we will follow Prados in fixing the maximum and minimum values at 80 and 20, respectively, and in using a convex achievement function. The basic idea is that an increase in the standard of living of a country at a higher level implies a greater achievement than had it taken place at a lower level.

Education
The education component of the HDI is based on literacy rates (⅔) and school enrollment (⅓). These were also the criteria followed by Camou and Maubrigades.[13] Unlike Prados, we will not use a convex achievement

function here. As Prados worked with literacy rates alone, his aim was to counteract the fact that differences between countries tended to disappear as the 100% ceiling was approached. In the case of education, unlike for life expectancy, it is difficult to argue that marginal achievements are increasing at higher levels of coverage. Almost the opposite is true: once most of the population is literate, the existing infrastructure should make it easier to educate new generations.

Here we are facing a different problem: the variable itself (literacy) is not an adequate proxy for the level of education of the population. Once almost all the population is literate, it seems inconvenient that literacy rates represent two thirds of the education basket (if not 100% as in Prados). Our strategy will be to raise the ceiling itself, using a different education basket in which secondary and tertiary education weights are higher. We will compare the results obtained. Different baskets may be used to understand different periods and for the purpose of comparison at different levels of development.

The baskets to be used are as shown in Table 1.

Table 1.
The Education Index: Different Baskets.

	Model 1 %	Model 2 %	Model 3 %
Literacy	0.67	0.00	0.00
Enrollment	0.33	1.00	1.00
Coefficients for different education levels			
Primary	1.0	1.0	0.0
Secondary	1.4	1.4	1.0
Tertiary	2.0	2.0	1.4
TOT	4.4	4.4	2.4

Sources: Weights: Model 1, UN (2006); others, own assumptions.
Coefficients: Model 1, Goldin (1998); others, own assumptions maintaining the proportion between levels.

Per Capita GDP

The Human Development Index transforms per capita GDP into logarithms. As stated in the Human Development Report 2006: "In the HDI income serves as a surrogate for all the dimensions of human development not reflected in a long and healthy life and in knowledge. Income is adjusted because achieving a respectable level of human development does not require unlimited income."[14]

The concept "respectable level of human development" seems somewhat fuzzy and problematically close to the approach that focuses on the satisfaction of basic needs. To define a ceiling for "respectable level" is a difficult task: even more so when dealing with human development. However, the logarithm of the per capita GDP differs from the basic-needs approach, as the index continues to increase with rising income, even if decreasing marginally.

Nevertheless, the transformation into logarithms is somewhat arbitrary and has important implications. Astorga and FitzGerald didn't make this transformation in their 1998 paper, but they did so in a later work. The argument is not convincing: "The use of the marginal utility notion to scale per capita income cannot be anything other than arbitrary, although no more so than not scaling per capita income at all."[15]

A clearly controversial result is implied: the differences in the levels of per capita income between countries are reduced. Besides, and following Prados' point of view with reference to life expectancy, the paradox is that increasing human development should demand an increasing marginal effort, in terms of per capita GDP. Accordingly, it should lead us to a new transformation of the series, using a convex achievement function in order to capture this increasing marginal effort.

One argument not always present in the literature, but often mentioned by people working in the field, is that while per capita GDP may always continue to increase, life expectancy and literacy do have maximum levels. Our counter argument is: this is why the convex achievement function is used in the case of life expectancy, and why it is necessary to change the education basket. As it will be shown, the ceiling of the more ambitious education basket is far from being reached by any country. Per capita GDP has a ceiling too: 40.000 1990 PPP-dollars. In short, we decided not to transform the per capita GDP series into logarithms, but to work with the original series.

A Geometric Average
Following Prados[16] we will also estimate a geometric average, on the understanding that there is no perfect substitute for the different components of the index. The geometric average favors an even movement of all the components.

Our index is shown in equation (3).

$$Hi = \sqrt[3]{\left[\left(\frac{(yi - 100)}{40,000 - 100} \right) * \left(\frac{\log(80 - 20) - \log(80 - lifei)}{\log(80 - 20)} \right) * \left(\frac{edui - 0}{100 - 0} \right) \right]} \qquad (3)$$

Equity

Early in the history of the HDI some attempts were made to take inequality into consideration. The basic idea could be expressed in a marginalist way: with income unequally distributed, the above-average income of the rich should yield less welfare than the welfare loss of a below-average income of the poor. Other arguments can also be used to suggest that at a certain level of total GDP, welfare is higher if equally distributed than otherwise. Values, the existence of positive externalities, and the absence of negative externalities may be some of them.

The 1993 Human Development Report made an important attempt to include distributional, inter-individual inequalities into the index: y_i, as in equation (3), was transformed into $y_i^*(1 - G)$, where G stands for the Gini coefficient. The underlying assumption was that life expectancy and education were naturally much less unequally distributed than income.[17]

Hicks made a strong case for the existence of significant inter-individual inequality in life expectancy and education: "years of schooling [do] vary – from 0 to 20 . . . Life spans actually lived do indeed vary, from less than one year to over 100 years."[18] Accordingly, he made estimates of what he labeled the Inequality-Adjusted Human Development Index for some Third World countries with data from 1995, based on the U.N. HDI. However, unlike UNDP, he multiplied the whole numerator of each component of the index by 1 minus the specific Gini coefficient. His results showed that the Gini coefficients for education and age were above 30% in the clear majority of the cases, and even higher than income inequality in some countries (Bangladesh, Sri Lanka).[19]

We will adjust the HHDI by a geometric average of the Gini coefficients for income, life expectancy, and education, as in equation (4),

$$EHi = Hi * (1 - G) \qquad (4)$$

where EH_i stands for the Inequality-Adjusted Historical Human Development Index (IAHHDI), and G is for the geometric average of the three Gini coefficients. The same results are obtained if the whole numerator of each component of the Gini is multiplied by $1 - G$. In the case of life expectancy, similar Gini estimates were performed by Shkolnikov, Andreev and Begun.[20]

The Gini coefficients for income will be taken from various sources, while those for the distribution of age and education are our own estimates. In the case of education we construct a series of the stock of knowledge of different sectors of the population over 20 years of age, classified in 5 groups: illiterates, people who went to primary school, people who went to secondary school, people who studied at the university, and professionals. The coefficients applied to the population of these different levels of education were: 1.0, 2.0, 2.8, 4.0, and 5.4, respectively. These coefficients follow the same proportions as in Table 1, but take illiterates as the basic unit.

The total IAHHDI is as in equation (5).

$$EHi = \sqrt[3]{\left[\left(\frac{(yi - 100)}{40,000 - 100}\right)*\left(\frac{\log(80 - 20) - \log(80 - lifei)}{\log(80 - 20)}\right)*\left(\frac{liti - 0}{100 - 0}\right)\right]*}$$
$$\left(\sqrt[3]{(1 - Gyi)*(1 - Glifei)*(1 - Gedui)}\right)$$

(5)

The Data

Per Capita GDP
Per capita GDP figures had to be expressed in purchasing power parity, in order to make them comparable. The sources are Maddison[21] and Bértola and Porcile.[22]

Life Expectancy and Life Tables
The data on life expectancy are taken from OXLAD, and from Prados de la Escosura.[23] Life tables of Uruguay[24] and the United States[25] were used to estimate the distribution of life expectancy.

Education and Distribution of Education
The data on school enrollment are taken from Bértola and Bertoni[26] and updated with data from UNESCO.

The data on literacy rates are taken from the OXLAD (Latin America and the United States), and from Prados[27] (France, Germany, and United Kingdom).

The distribution of education was estimated on the basis of this data base.

Income Inequality
The Gini coefficient of Uruguay was taken from Bértola,[28] while that of the United States is based on Lindert[29] and the UNU/WIDER.[30]

Interpreting the Results

In this section we will present the relative performance of the three Latin American countries in relation to the four core countries in terms of the HHDI, stylize the main trends, and give a preliminary interpretation. We will also discuss the Uruguay-United States comparison with respect to the IAHHDI.

Although this chapter is primarily focused on the construction of the index and the evaluation of the results, thus taking a predominantly empirical character, we present a simplified theoretical framework which will help us to outline and discuss the outcome.

A Theoretical Framework

Bértola and Porcile[31] and Verspagen[32] discuss international differences in per capita GDP levels and growth. They attempt to characterize different convergence and divergence regimes between Argentina, Brazil, Uruguay, and the four core countries considered in the present chapter. These regimes are the result of the interaction between supply and demand forces and various policy measures, which in the end affect the income elasticity of demand for exports and imports and the degree of openness of the economies.

Here, we will attempt to expand the application of this theoretical framework to encompass the other components of the HHDI.

If we assume that per capita growth ultimately depends on technical change and innovation, we can identify the main sources for technical change as: (i) those arising from the country's science and technology efforts, proxied by the production of codified knowledge and expressed by the investment in R&D; (ii) those arising from "learning by doing" within production and by the technical change induced by demand, both proxied by changes of the productive structure in response to demand growth and technical change; (iii) technological spillovers from advanced to laggard countries, which in turn rely on the size of the gap and the domestic capabilities of the laggard countries.[33]

These forces may also be present at the levels of life expectancy and education. With respect to life expectancy: (i) research and development in the sciences of life and in health and nutrition technologies play a decisive role in the eradication of some mortality sources and the production of a healthy and long life; (ii) the existence of private or public enterprises and institutions linked to the "production" of health, proxied by the share of these branches in GDP and by health and social expenditures in total expenditures, may tell us about the "learning by doing" capacity of the population to improve life expectancy; (iii) the existence of a technological gap may stimulate improvements in life expectancy, given international or domestic institutions and organizations that are willing and able to assist in catching up.

Education can be approached in a similar way. Its achievements depend on the R&D activities related to educational issues, on the learning by doing by the educational institutions, and the international transfers of knowledge and education technologies developed elsewhere. Spillovers depend, in turn, on domestic capabilities. Different from life expectancy, which is a proxy for an output (years of life expected to live by the population), our education data are not able to catch any qualitative end result. In addition, our data do not include forms of education other than the formal primary, secondary, and tertiary. Learning while performing productive activities and learning in technical schools are out of reach. Likewise, the efficiency of the system is not considered. By that we mean the quality of the education and the time necessary to go through the system.

Inequality has been attracting increasing attention from scholars, both at the theoretical and the historical level. While various attempts have been made to connect income inequality and growth in Latin America from an institutional point of view (Acemouglu, Johnson and Robinson,[34] on wealth inequality and political power, and Engerman and Sokoloff,[35] on resource endowments) and from a neoclassical point of view (Jeffrey Williamson,[36] for example), not many connections have been established between inequality and technical change. Bértola[37] attempted to empirically approach income inequality in Uruguay and in other Southern settler societies, but the connection to the discussion on convergence and divergence regimes was still very timid. Willebald[38] made an attempt to connect recent theoretical links between growth, income distribution, and innovation with empirical research, with promising results. In a very broad sense, what may be important to elucidate is to what extent inequality trends are the result of pure market mechanisms, or of institutional arrangements.

Per Capita GDP[39]

The per capita GDP index (HGDP) is shown in Appendix Table 1. The general trends of relative per capita GDP growth reproduced in Figure 1 are very well known. An interpretation may be found in Bértola and Porcile.[40] The basic stylized facts are as follows:

> Argentina and Uruguay started the twentieth century at relatively high levels of per capita income. Around 1910–1930, the trend changed and a long-lasting divergence trend took place and deepened after the 1960s.
>
> Brazil, on the contrary, started at very low levels but showed recurrent catching-up cycles until 1980, when a new divergent trend started. Despite the catching-up trend in 1910–1980, Brazil remained a long distance from the core countries, but almost caught up with its Latin American neighbors.

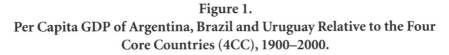

Figure 1.
Per Capita GDP of Argentina, Brazil and Uruguay Relative to the Four Core Countries (4CC), 1900–2000.

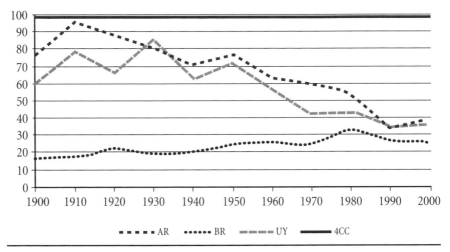

Source: Appendix Table 1.

Notes: 4CC is set to 100.

Argentina and Uruguay achieved high relative growth in 1870–1913, associated with a dynamic integration into the golden era of classic liberalism on the basis of inter-industry specialization in meat and temperate agricultural goods facing high-income elasticity of demand. Competitive advantages were classical, related to the relative abundance of factors of production. Argentina not only converged with but forged ahead of the European countries, following a path which, in its early phases, resembled (with less intensity) the successful experience of the United States. Uruguay achieved a short period of convergence on the basis of import substitution after World War II. However, this regime of convergence was inevitably short-lived as the international economy recovered and import substitution imposed increasingly higher costs. A change in the pattern of trade was therefore necessary to sustain convergence.

Brazil started a process of moderate convergence during a time when international trade collapsed because of major international crises (the Great Depression, World Wars I and II). Modest convergence was achieved in the 1930s by means of import-substituting industrialization. Brazil continued to converge moderately by means of new metal, machinery, and chemical industries established in the late 1950s. Structural transformation in the "developmentalist" period changed the growth trends of Brazil and gave rise to incremental, cumulative industrial learning. Although the domestic market remained as the principal outlet for industrial production, a slow but continuous process of export diversification occurred. By then, international trade grew at very high rates (1960–1973); later on (1973–78) international capital flows expanded, compensating for the loss of dynamism of international trade.

Argentina and Uruguay were not able to move from the first type of convergence regime to the second. Brazil had a wider gap to fill and adopted policies for structural change in a much more vigorous way than Argentina and Uruguay, and this is part of the explanation for the relative success of Brazil until 1980. Argentina and Uruguay suffered significantly from demand-side variables, related to changes in patterns of demand and to institutional arrangements in the international economy, which brought an end to the classical liberal era of British hegemony and redefined redefining the rules of the game in international trade. Supply-side variables were related to path dependency, and the failure of Argentina and Uruguay— and to a lesser extent Brazil—to build up an institutional framework conducive to rapid structural change and rapidly growing exports of manufactured goods. The experience of the decades following the debt crisis suggests that policies aimed at structural change in the region were too weak to allow the countries to catch up in the long run.

Owing to limited data availability, from now on we will only report inequality results for Uruguay and the United States (Table 2). **Income inequality** in the two cases shows a "U"-curve,[41] with bottom values in 1970. The increase in inequality does not seem to reach the figures of the early twentieth century. The reduction in inequality in 1910–1970 was probably more important in the United States than in Uruguay. The increase in inequality in Uruguay had a decisive turning point under the military dictatorship, which increased inequality to levels that later democratic regimes could not reverse.

The impact of inequality on per capita GDP growth is presented in Table 3. The United States received a 20% improvement in the GDP levels due to the reduction of inequality between 1910 and 1930, and a further 10% increase up to 1970. Afterwards, half of these gains were lost as inequality increased. In the case of Uruguay, the highest gain in inequality reduction was obtained in 1970 (20%) and again half of these gains had been lost by 2000. The comparative position of Uruguay in relation to the United States is somewhat worse in the case of the IAHGDP than in the case of the HGDP, because of higher average inequality figures.

Table 2.
Gini Coefficients of the Components of the HHDI,
Uruguay and the USA, 1910–2000.

	Income		Life Expectancy		Education		Total Geometric average	
	Uruguay	USA	Uruguay	USA	Uruguay	USA	Uruguay	USA
1910	0.472	0.490	0.305	0.291	0.154	0.055	0.323	0.301
1920	0.464	0.440	0.321	0.244	0.142	0.067	0.322	0.266
1930	0.465	0.390	0.287	0.199	0.126	0.096	0.307	0.239
1940	0.455	0.400	0.252	0.159	0.107	0.124	0.286	0.238
1950	0.438	0.360	0.187	0.125	0.096	0.142	0.255	0.217
1960	0.380	0.349	0.169	0.111	0.109	0.150	0.229	0.210
1970	0.363	0.341	0.167	0.108	0.118	0.166	0.224	0.211
1980	0.406	0.352	0.147	0.094	0.127	0.183	0.238	0.217
1990	0.416	0.378	0.125	0.089	0.147	0.197	0.242	0.231
2000	0.433	0.405	0.118	0.082	0.166	0.194	0.253	0.239

Sources: See text.

Notes: See Equation 5 for the calculation of the total.

Life Expectancy

Between 1900 and 2000, life expectancy in the core countries increased from 46 to 78 years, on average. While Argentina and Uruguay had slightly lower values at the beginning of the twentieth century, Brazil showed remarkably lower figures: 29. The life expectancy index (HLife$_i$) is in Appendix Table 2.

As shown in Figure 2, Brazil improved significantly until the 1970s, especially during the 1950s and 60s. Argentina and Uruguay showed some fluctuations around a similar relative level. After the 1980s, however, the three Latin American countries started a clearly divergent trend. By 2000, life expectancy in Argentina, Brazil, and Uruguay was 73, 68, and 75, respectively. The convex achievement function makes the differences with core countries appear to be even larger: Brazil, for example, shows values 45% of those of the core countries.

Relative life expectancy and per capita GDP performance show rather similar trends. Life expectancy was originally high in land- and resource-abundant Argentina and Uruguay. A large number of immigrants brought with them various kinds of knowledge which were combined with easy and relatively cheap access to basic foodstuffs. Even if inequality levels were higher than in Europe and the United States, real wages were relatively high in relation to those of the core countries (between 60 and 70%) and the most important cost was that of housing, while foodstuffs were much cheaper.[42] Thus, in terms of nutrition the living standards were similar.

Table 3.
Per Capita GDP Indices for Uruguay and the USA, 1910–2000 (1910=100).

	HGDP		IAHGDP		IAHGDP/HGDP		UY/USA	
	UY	USA	UY	USA	UY	USA	HGDP	IAHGDP
1910	100	100	100	100	100	100	62	65
1920	85	112	86	123	101	110	47	45
1930	138	126	140	150	101	120	69	60
1940	117	142	121	167	103	118	52	47
1950	150	195	160	244	107	125	48	42
1960	160	231	188	295	117	128	43	41
1970	167	307	202	397	121	129	34	33
1980	213	380	240	483	113	127	35	32
1990	210	475	232	579	111	122	28	26
2000	256	576	275	672	107	117	28	26

Source: See text.

A strong rise in life expectancy took place in the decades 1940–1980 in Argentina, in 1950–1990 in Brazil, and 1940–1960 in a more homogeneous Uruguay. In all cases, domestic efforts to develop social policies made it possible to learn how to handle risks and to make use of innovations introduced in the core countries, such as the use of antibiotics. The introduction of these innovations and the development of health systems allowed the Southern countries to reduce mortality rates, specially infant mortality, and to conditionally converge with core countries (Brazil) or maintain good relative positions (Argentina and Uruguay). However, in the long run, and when the most important factor explaining the increase in life expectancy became the extension of the life of the elderly, the Latin American countries diverged owing to their technological and systemic backwardness. Besides the changing demographic problems, political changes and economic performance weakened the welfare state. The results were noticed from the 1980s onwards (Argentina and Uruguay) and from the 1990s (in Brazil). In Becker and his co-authors' words:

> Finally, mortality data by cause of death are disaggregated to understand the determinants of the cross-country convergence in life expectancy observed between 1965 and 1995. Changes in mortality due to infectious, respiratory and digestive diseases, congenital and perinatal conditions, and "ill-defined" conditions are the most important factors producing the convergence in life expectancy, whereas

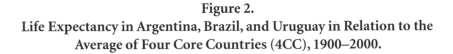

Figure 2.
Life Expectancy in Argentina, Brazil, and Uruguay in Relation to the Average of Four Core Countries (4CC), 1900–2000.

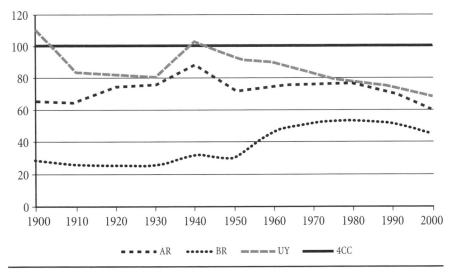

Source: Appendix Table 2.
Note: 4CC is set to 100.

changes in mortality due to nervous system, sensory organs, heart and circulatory diseases worked against convergence. This evidence suggests that the large changes in mortality observed in the developing world were due to the absorption of previously available technology and knowledge, while developed countries took advantage of recent advances on the frontier of medical technology.[43]

This seems to be a plausible explanation of the divergent trend we find in the late twentieth century. Likewise, it has to be stressed that our convex achievement function shows a divergent trend rather than stagnation of the Latin American countries' HLife.

Inequality in life expectancy follows a similar declining trend with time and with increasing life expectancy, as shown in Figure 3. For every period of time, "age inequality" (inequalities in life expectancy) was lower in the United States, and for every period of time, the life expectancy index (HLife$_i$) of the United States was higher than that of Uruguay. That means that the United States shows a structural lower inequality than Uruguay; i.e., for a similar life expectancy, the U.S. inequality levels are lower. In other

Figure 3.
Age Inequality (*Glife*ᵢ) and the Life Expectancy Index (*Hlife*ᵢ) in Uruguay and the United States.

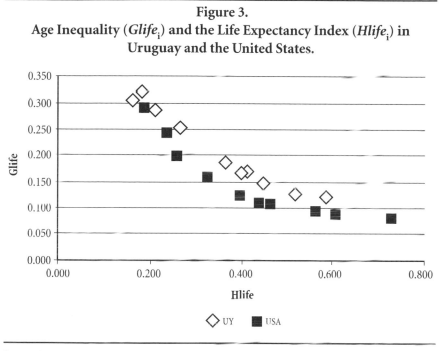

Source: See text.

words, when adjusted for inequality, the gap in life expectancy between the United States and Uruguay increases.

The United States showed a drastic fall in age inequality levels in 1910–1950; later on, the index diminished rather slowly. By contrast, the life expectancy index accelerated after the 1950s, without any spectacular reduction of inequality.

In the case of Uruguay the pattern is somewhat different, as inequality and the life expectancy index moved more smoothly, excepting for a sharp decline of GLife and a sharp increase in HLife between 1940 and 1950.

It is possible to link the phase of drastic reduction of age inequality in the United States and Uruguay to the phase in which life expectancy increased through the control of causes of mortality affecting a younger population, while the control of diseases affecting mainly the elderly didn't affect inequality so much.

The contribution of the reduction in inequality to the improvement of HLife was considerably higher in Uruguay than in the United States, as shown in Table 4. Especially important was the weight of the reduction of inequality in Uruguay in 1930–1950. However, the reduction of inequality

Table 4.
Life Expectancy Indices for Uruguay and the USA, 1910–2000
(1910=100).

	HLife		*IAHLife*		*IAHLife/HLife*		*UY/USA*	
	UY	USA	UY	USA	UY	USA	*Hlife*	*IAHLife*
1910	100	100	100	100	100	100	86	84
1920	102	121	110	134	108	111	77	69
1930	114	153	133	155	116	102	81	72
1940	132	167	177	206	134	123	82	72
1950	167	210	264	261	158	124	92	85
1960	230	256	305	295	133	115	94	87
1970	260	285	300	313	115	110	87	81
1980	255	302	341	386	134	128	79	75
1990	283	366	407	419	143	114	85	82
2000	329	395	467	509	142	129	81	77

Source: See text.

was at least as important in the United States as in Uruguay. The difference depends on the more important increase of U.S. life expectancy.

Education
We will report three different estimates using three different models of the education index as presented earlier. The results are shown in Appendix Table 3. Model 1 (Figure 4) uses the United Nations' weights for literacy rates and school enrollment. According to it, Argentina and Uruguay reached absolute convergence with the core countries in 1990. A strong process of convergence took place between 1910 and 1950, when the 90% level was already attained. Brazil, by contrast, had a much lower point of departure, and went through a strong catching-up process since the 1950s. By 2000 Brazil is still 20% below the core countries. This story is almost unbelievable: it strains credibility to find that Argentina and Uruguay have levels of education similar to the core countries. It is also hard to believe that Brazil is only 20% below the core countries. However, the result is not surprising when literacy rates answer for two thirds of total education.

Model 2 (Figure 4) shows a somewhat different and more credible picture. Leaving literacy rates aside, the index is only based on school enrollment at different levels. At first sight, it seems an error to neglect illiteracy. However, the index tries to take into account everything that pertains to education, and the maximum level is that of the total population with tertiary education. In fact, illiteracy is not neglected: it just appears as people who don't add to the index. The first important difference with Model 1 is that absolute convergence vanishes in the case of Brazil and even Uruguay. Brazil ceases to narrow the gap in the 1980s at a very low level. The spurt of the 1990s in Argentina and Uruguay vanishes; instead, we get an important increase in the 1980s, due mainly to the increased population with tertiary education, which to a large extent can be related to political democratization.

Model 3 (Figure 4) shows a quite different picture. When the index is constructed on the basis of secondary and tertiary education alone, Argentina and Uruguay remain at an important distance from the core countries, even if the trend is positive since the 1940s. Brazil, on the contrary, shows a cyclical movement, with convergence up to the 1950s, divergence afterwards, and recovery in the 1990s, without reaching the levels of 1950. The highly unequal and elitist Brazilian society remains 70% below the core countries.

Which index reflects reality in a better way? Ideally, we would like to construct a linked index, which could allow for structural change as average levels of education increase. Even if it were possible to construct such an index for every single country, it is difficult to construct one sole index for comparative purposes, as countries with different levels of development would have different internal structures.

The U.N. index may adequately reflect education attainment at early stages of development. However, in the second half of the century, as literacy rates approach the 100% level, this education basket seems badly suited to reflect real differences in human development. Besides, there is no need to combine literacy and school enrollment as if they were different things. If adequately used, school enrollment measures the level of education of a society. Model 3 looks especially adequate for the last decades of the twentieth century, as it helps to understand how wide the differences are with respect to higher education.

We think Model 2 is the best one to present the education picture in the long run, and we will use to construct our HHDI. The performance of the Latin American countries at the end of the twentieth century will probably be over-estimated.

Inequality in access to education increased steadily in the United States. However, the original inequality levels were extremely low, as illiteracy was almost non-existent but secondary and higher education was not yet generalized. The final inequality levels were still lower than those of the other components of the HDI and reflect a permanent increase of the access of new groups to higher education. In Uruguay, inequality in access to education went through trends similar to income inequality: a decreasing trend

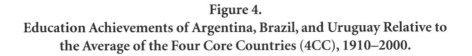

Figure 4.
Education Achievements of Argentina, Brazil, and Uruguay Relative to the Average of the Four Core Countries (4CC), 1910–2000.

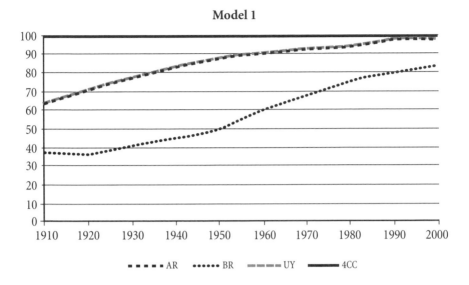

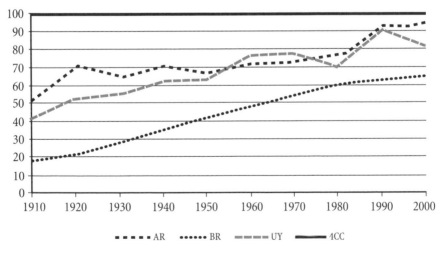

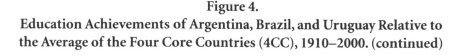

Figure 4.
**Education Achievements of Argentina, Brazil, and Uruguay Relative to
the Average of the Four Core Countries (4CC), 1910–2000. (continued)**

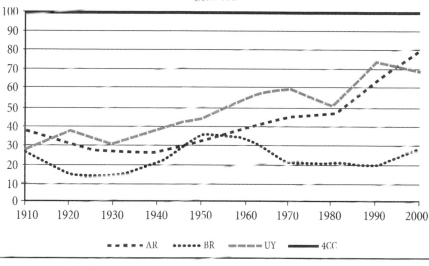

Source: Appendix Table 3.
Note: 4CC is set to 100.

until 1950, and increasing inequality afterwards to levels close to those of the starting point. While the egalitarian trend may be interpreted as the result of the strong reduction of illiteracy and the generalization of primary school enrollment, the second trend may be seen as the result of the expansion of secondary and tertiary education, long limited to select groups of the population. This latter trend is similar to the trend of the United States during the whole century. As shown in Table 5, the impact of inequality trends on the IAHEdu is not as important in the other indices: the result is a relatively better performance of Uruguay. Nevertheless, we have many doubts about this almost absolute convergence.

The Historical Human Development Index (HHDI)

Figure 5 shows the performance of Argentina, Brazil, and Uruguay in terms of Human Development and in relation to the four core countries. The index is constructed using Model 2 for education and a geometric average of the components.

Table 5.
Education Indices for Uruguay and the USA, 1910–2000 (1910=100).

	HEdu		IAHEdu		IAHEdu/Hedu		UY/USA	
	UY	USA	UY	USA	UY	USA	HEdu	IAHEdu
1910	100.0	100.0	100.0	100.0	100	100	37	33
1920	120.3	112.5	122.1	111.1	101	99	40	37
1930	142.8	136.8	147.6	130.9	103	96	39	38
1940	177.4	152.8	187.3	141.7	106	93	43	44
1950	213.8	167.7	228.6	152.2	107	91	48	50
1960	289.0	181.1	304.5	162.9	105	90	60	62
1970	345.0	223.8	359.7	197.4	104	88	57	61
1980	335.3	238.8	346.2	206.5	103	86	52	56
1990	438.0	204.4	441.8	173.8	101	85	80	85
2000	489.2	202.2	482.8	172.5	99	85	90	93

Source: See text.

Argentina reproduces a well-known story: its performance was very successful in the first decades of the twentieth century, converging with core countries, followed by a long-run divergence. The steep fall of per capita GDP was partly counterbalanced by improvements in life expectancy (education remaining stable). Divergence increased slightly until the 1980s, when the well-known "lost decade" left important scars. The relative improvement of education couldn't match the negative trend in GDP and life expectancy.

The Uruguayan case is very similar to the Argentine, with some nuances: starting from a lower level, its convergence with core countries advanced up to the 1950s, as a result of an acceptable GDP performance and improved life expectancy and education figures. The divergent trend started with a steep fall in the 1960s, when GDP stagnated, and was followed by relatively falling life expectancy and stagnating education figures. Since the 1980s, only education could resist the downward trend.

Brazil, on the contrary, started at very low levels, catching up steadily until 1980. All variables contributed to that movement: education rose steadily; per capita GDP had growth spurts in the 1940s and 1970s; and life expectancy increased especially in the 1950s. During the lost decade, however, Brazil not only started to diverge from core countries, but it also lost ground in relation to its Southern neighbors. Only in education was its performance acceptable.

If we think in terms of an input-output relation—in terms of how much life expectancy and education were helped by per capita GDP, i.e., what kind

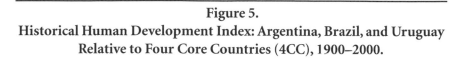

Figure 5.
Historical Human Development Index: Argentina, Brazil, and Uruguay
Relative to Four Core Countries (4CC), 1900–2000.

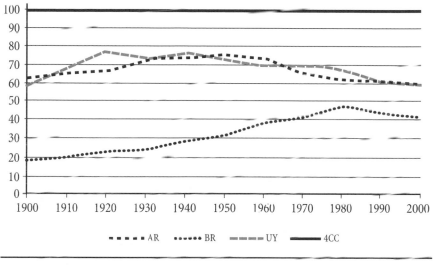

Source: Appendix Table 4.
Note: 4CC is set to 100.

ol lives we produce with the income we have at our disposal—the Latin American countries show an apparently better relation: best is Brazil and worst is the United States (see Figure 6). An alternative way to think about input-output is to assign an important role to technology transfers: technical change and GDP growth in the core countries are not able to increase human development dramatically, but the transfer of knowledge, technology, and innovation to laggard countries has a bigger impact there than what was possible to achieve on the basis of domestic GDP growth. To be sure, the capacity of laggard countries to make an intelligent and effective use of the technological gap directly depends on the domestic capabilities and efforts to develop educational and wealth systems.

Finally, we should mention that our results diverge from those obtained by Astorga and FitzGerald,[44] Astorga, Bergès, and FitzGerald,[45] and Prados.[46] What we obtain is a divergent trend in human development of Southern Cone countries, which started early in the twentieth century in Argentina, in the middle of the century in Uruguay, and in the 1980s in Brazil. In contrast, our colleagues found convergence in the central decades of the century and a relatively stable situation afterwards.

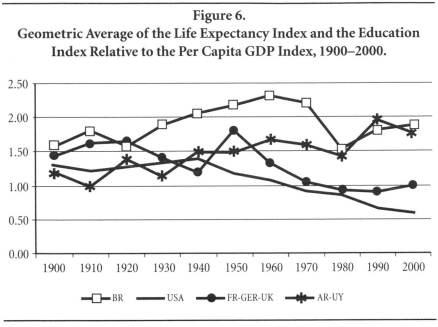

Figure 6.
Geometric Average of the Life Expectancy Index and the Education
Index Relative to the Per Capita GDP Index, 1900–2000.

Source: Appendix Table 4.

The differences may partly arise from the group of countries considered. It is well known that Argentina and Uruguay were among the most successful Latin American countries during the first globalization. The Brazilian timing (not the growth rates) is more representative of the average of the Latin American countries. However, the way in which our index is constructed surely explains much of the difference.

The Inequality-Adjusted Historical Human Development Index (IAHHDI) of Uruguay and the United States

This section is devoted to the discussion of the impact of inequality on human development. The basic idea is that human development is greater when it is evenly distributed. To test this proposition, the procedure, according to equation (5), is to adjust human development by an inequality index. The geometric inequality index was presented in Table 2. Inequality levels in Uruguay and the United States do not differ significantly (somewhat higher in Uruguay) and show a similar trend: decreasing inequality between 1910 and the 1960s; increasing inequality afterward. Both the downward and the upward trends were slightly more pronounced in Uruguay than in the United States. Thus, the way in which inequality affects human development is rather similar in both countries: increasing economic growth up to the 1960s and reducing it afterwards. This is a somewhat undesired result of this paper, as the inequality adjustment should be more important if the two countries showed different inequality levels and trends.

Appendix Table 5 summarizes the results. As the maximum level of the IAHHDI is achieved when all the components of the HHDI reach the maximum values **and** all of them are equally distributed (Gini=0), the levels of the index are significantly reduced. The best record in the United States, for example, was 0.377, in 2000.

In order to avoid the differences in levels of the HGDP, the HHDI, and the IAHHDP, we show the three in Figure 7 with a similar starting point in 1910. The figure may be read as an approach to several growth models under different combinations of the indices.

In the case of Uruguay it is noticeable that the HGDP index shows a clearly lower performance than the other two. The HHDI grows much more, and growth is even greater when distribution is considered. It is also interesting to notice that the gap among the indexes widened in 1930–1960, when policies promoting education and wealth distribution were especially strong and when inequality diminished after the 1940s. The gap widened again in the 1980s, when the country moved to democracy after a decade of dictatorship.

In the case of the United States, the picture is quite different. Both the HHDI and the IAHHDI grew faster than the HGDP until 1940. By then, infant mortality was eradicated and primary schooling generalized. Life expectancy and inequality decreased significantly. The second part of the century featured very fast per capita GDP growth with increasing inequality. HEdu was the weakest component of the HHDI of the USA and helped to widen the gap with HGDP, together with the inequality trends.

Conclusions

This paper presented a twentieth-century Historical Human Development Index (HHDI) for three Latin American countries (Argentina, Brazil, and Uruguay) and four core countries (France, Germany, United Kingdom and United States), and an Inequality-Adjusted Historical Human Development Index (IAHHDI) for Uruguay and the United States, based on the supposition that human development is higher if inequality is lower.

The **HHDI** has certain features which, considered together, make it different from previous attempts: the per capita GDP series were not log-transformed; life expectancy adopted a convex achievement function with maximum and minimum values 80 and 20 years, respectively; the education series was estimated with data on school enrollment alone, neglecting literacy rates. A geometric average of the indices was estimated. The **IAHHDI**

Figure 7.
Per Capita GDP, HHDI and IAHHDI, 1910–2000 (1910=100).

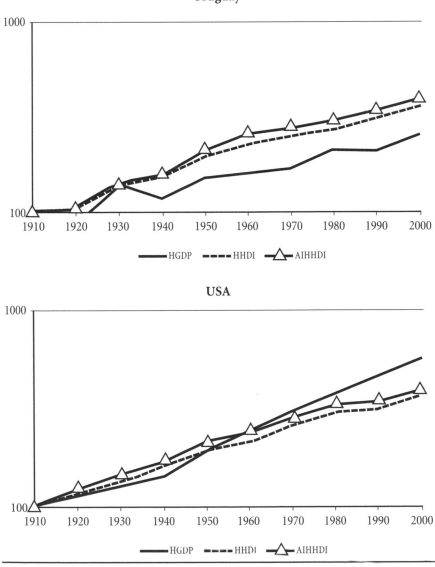

Source: Appendix Table 6.

is based on available inequality series for income distribution and our own estimates of inequality series for education and life expectancy of Uruguay and the United States.

The results were discussed and presented in comparative terms.

Relative **per capita GDP** growth is a well-known story. This paper doesn't add to Bértola and Porcile[47] in that respect: Argentina and Uruguay show a divergent trend since the early twentieth century while Brazil converges up to 1980, diverging later on. When adjusted for **inequality,** U.S. per capita GDP increased by 20% between 1910 and 1930, and a further 10% up to 1970. Afterwards, half of these gains were lost as inequality increased. In the case of Uruguay the increase amounted to 20% in 1970, while half of it was lost by 2000.

In terms of **life expectancy,** Brazil caught up significantly from very low levels until the 1970s. Argentina and Uruguay showed some fluctuations around similar levels. After the 1980s, however, the three Latin American countries entered a clearly divergent trend to levels below 75% of the core countries. The strong rise in life expectancy (1940–1980 in Argentina, 1950–1990 in Brazil, 1940–1960 in Uruguay) was mainly due to social investment that made it possible to take advantage of technological spillovers from the core countries and reduce mortality rates, especially infant mortality. As further increases in life expectancy became more related to the extension of the life of the elderly, and as social investment and economic growth weakened from the 1970s on, life expectancy was relatively reduced. **Inequality in life expectancy** follows a similar declining trend with time and with increasing life expectancy. The phase of drastic reduction of age inequality in the United States and Uruguay is related to the phase in which life expectancy increased through the control of mortality causes affecting the younger population. By contrast, the control of diseases among the elderly didn't affect inequality so much. When adjusted for inequality, the gap in life expectancy between the United States and Uruguay increases.

Our **education index** is more credible than the one used by the United Nations, as it takes into account the education of different segments of the population. The results themselves look more reliable. Argentina shows a stable position relative to the core countries in 1920–1980. During the 1980s some convergence is achieved owing to increasing population in secondary and tertiary education and to democratization. Brazil caught up significantly in 1910–1980, but could not surpass the 60% level. Uruguay caught up until 1960 and remained fluctuating around similar levels afterwards. We suspect that the Latin American countries' indices are overvalued at the end of the period.

Inequality in access to education started at very low levels and increased steadily in the United States. In Uruguay, inequality in access to education went through trends similar to those for income inequality: a decreasing trend until 1950, and increasing inequality afterwards to similar levels of those of the starting point.

When we combine the three components into the **HHDI** geometrically, we find that Argentina started to diverge at early stages of the twentieth century, Uruguay diverged at the mid-century, and Brazil continued to tighten the gap up to 1980. They all diverged after these dates. Our results diverge from those obtained by Astorga and FitzGerald,[48] Astorga, Bergès, and FitzGerald,[49] and Prados.[50] They all found convergence in the central decades of the century and a relatively stable situation afterwards.

If we think in terms of an input-output relation between per capita GDP as input and education and life expectancy as outputs, the Latin American countries appear in a better position: best is Brazil, and worst is the United States. Whereas technical change and GDP growth in the core countries are not able dramatically to increase human development at home, technological spillovers to laggard countries do have a stronger impact there. Laggard countries' ability to make an intelligent and effective use of the technological gap directly depends on the domestic capabilities and efforts to develop educational and wealth systems.

Total inequality in Uruguay and the United States decreased until the 1950s and increased afterwards to similar levels. While inequality affects human development within both countries, it doesn't help to understand the differences between them, owing to similarity of the Gini coefficients. In both cases different models may be noticed. Up to the mid-century point increasing inequality made the IAHHDI grow faster than the HHDI. The reverse is valid for the second part of the century.

Appendix

Appendix Table 1.
Per Capita GDP Index, *HGDP*, 1900–2000.

	AR	BR	UY	FR	GER	UK	USA
1900	0.067	0.014	0.053	0.070	0.072	0.110	0.100
1910	0.093	0.017	0.076	0.072	0.081	0.113	0.122
1920	0.085	0.022	0.065	0.078	0.068	0.111	0.137
1930	0.100	0.024	0.105	0.111	0.097	0.134	0.153
1940	0.102	0.029	0.089	0.099	0.133	0.169	0.173
1950	0.122	0.039	0.114	0.130	0.095	0.171	0.237
1960	0.137	0.056	0.122	0.187	0.191	0.214	0.281
1970	0.181	0.074	0.127	0.290	0.269	0.267	0.374
1980	0.203	0.128	0.162	0.376	0.351	0.322	0.463
1990	0.159	0.121	0.160	0.451	0.397	0.409	0.579
2000	0.212	0.137	0.194	0.519	0.464	0.494	0.702

Source: See text.

Note: HGDPi=(yi-100)/(40000–100), where y is per capita income.

Appendix Table 2.
Life Expectancy Index, *Hlife*$_i$, 1900–2000.

	AR	BR	UY	FR	GER	UK	USA
1900	0.093	0.040	0.157	0.132	0.142	0.141	0.154
1910	0.125	0.049	0.160	0.181	0.190	0.204	0.186
1920	0.161	0.055	0.180	0.183	0.216	0.230	0.234
1930	0.195	0.065	0.208	0.233	0.258	0.286	0.256
1940	0.224	0.081	0.263	0.165	0.255	0.276	0.323
1950	0.281	0.118	0.361	0.364	0.392	0.419	0.393
1960	0.339	0.214	0.409	0.463	0.453	0.458	0.438
1970	0.374	0.256	0.401	0.505	0.487	0.492	0.463
1980	0.438	0.308	0.446	0.593	0.572	0.562	0.562
1990	0.492	0.355	0.518	0.776	0.690	0.687	0.607
2000	0.525	0.393	0.590	1.000	0.863	0.856	0.732

Source: See text.

Note: $Hlife_i = (\log(80-20)-(\log80-life_i))/\log(80-20)$

Appendix Table 3.
Education Index, Hedu_i, 1900–2000.

MODEL 1.	Literacy	Enrollment (enr)	Primary (p)	Secondary (s)	Tertiary (t)
weights	α	β			
	0.67	0.33			
coefficients		ε	π	σ	τ
		4.4	1	1.4	2

	Argentina	Brazil	Uruguay	France	Germany	UK	USA
1900	0.35	0.24	0.35	0.59	0.67	0.65	0.63
1910	0.42	0.24	0.41	0.62	0.68	0.65	0.65
1920	0.48	0.24	0.47	0.63	0.68	0.67	0.67
1930	0.52	0.28	0.52	0.66	0.69	0.68	0.69
1940	0.58	0.31	0.57	0.68	0.70	0.69	0.70
1950	0.62	0.35	0.62	0.69	0.70	0.71	0.71
1960	0.65	0.43	0.64	0.71	0.70	0.71	0.72
1970	0.67	0.49	0.67	0.72	0.71	0.72	0.75
1980	0.68	0.55	0.68	0.72	0.72	0.73	0.76
1990	0.71	0.58	0.71	0.73	0.73	0.72	0.75
2000	0.73	0.62	0.72	0.74	0.76	0.74	0.74

MODEL 2.	Literacy	Enrollment	Primary	Secondary	Tertiary
weights	α	β			
	0.00	1.00			
coefficients		ε	π	σ	τ
		4.4	1	1.4	2

	Argentina	Brazil	Uruguay	France	Germany	UK	USA
1900	0.04	0.01	0.04	0.10	0.09	0.11	0.11
1910	0.05	0.02	0.04	0.10	0.10	0.09	0.12
1920	0.07	0.02	0.05	0.07	0.10	0.10	0.13
1930	0.07	0.03	0.06	0.10	0.10	0.10	0.16
1940	0.09	0.04	0.08	0.11	0.11	0.11	0.18
1950	0.10	0.06	0.09	0.12	0.12	0.15	0.20
1960	0.12	0.08	0.13	0.15	0.11	0.18	0.21
1970	0.14	0.10	0.15	0.17	0.16	0.19	0.26
1980	0.15	0.12	0.15	0.17	0.17	0.21	0.28
1990	0.20	0.13	0.19	0.21	0.21	0.18	0.24
2000	0.24	0.17	0.21	0.25	0.31	0.25	0.24

Appendix Table 3.
Education Index, H*edu*$_i$, 1900–2000. (continued)

MODEL 3.		Literacy	Enrollment	Primary	Secondary		Tertiary
weights		α	β				
		0	1				
coefficients			ε	π	σ		τ
			2.4	0	1		1.4
	Argentina	Brazil	Uruguay	France	Germany	UK	USA
1900	0.00	0.00	0.00	0.00	0.00	0.00	0.00
1910	0.00	0.00	0.00	0.01	0.02	0.01	0.02
1920	0.01	0.00	0.01	0.01	0.02	0.01	0.03
1930	0.01	0.00	0.01	0.02	0.03	0.02	0.06
1940	0.01	0.01	0.02	0.02	0.03	0.03	0.10
1950	0.03	0.03	0.03	0.05	0.04	0.10	0.12
1960	0.04	0.03	0.05	0.07	0.05	0.14	0.13
1970	0.07	0.03	0.09	0.13	0.09	0.14	0.22
1980	0.08	0.04	0.09	0.14	0.14	0.18	0.25
1990	0.13	0.04	0.15	0.20	0.22	0.16	0.22
2000	0.20	0.07	0.18	0.24	0.34	0.23	0.22

Source: See text.

Note: $Hedu_i = lit_i{}^*\alpha + ((p_i{}^*\pi + s_i{}^*\sigma + t_i{}^*\tau)/\varepsilon)^*\beta$

Appendix Table 4.
The Geometric Historical Human Development Indexes, 1900–2000.

	AR	BR	UY	FR	GER	UK	USA
Model G1							
1900	0.086	0.032	0.094	0.122	0.128	0.150	0.149
1910	0.114	0.037	0.112	0.139	0.150	0.168	0.172
1920	0.127	0.042	0.116	0.138	0.147	0.175	0.197
1930	0.147	0.050	0.150	0.176	0.176	0.201	0.218
1940	0.161	0.061	0.160	0.153	0.196	0.218	0.251
1950	0.191	0.082	0.201	0.223	0.206	0.267	0.303
1960	0.218	0.121	0.225	0.283	0.271	0.305	0.338
1970	0.254	0.151	0.235	0.343	0.327	0.339	0.396
1980	0.284	0.202	0.263	0.397	0.383	0.383	0.460
1990	0.285	0.212	0.290	0.480	0.441	0.433	0.492
2000	0.335	0.240	0.331	0.563	0.543	0.526	0.557
Model G2							
1900	0.064	0.020	0.068	0.096	0.098	0.119	0.119
1910	0.086	0.025	0.081	0.111	0.117	0.130	0.139
1920	0.099	0.029	0.085	0.100	0.114	0.135	0.162
1930	0.113	0.036	0.111	0.137	0.136	0.155	0.185
1940	0.126	0.047	0.122	0.121	0.153	0.171	0.216
1950	0.150	0.066	0.157	0.180	0.165	0.223	0.264
1960	0.176	0.098	0.185	0.236	0.215	0.263	0.297
1970	0.212	0.126	0.198	0.290	0.274	0.292	0.357
1980	0.240	0.170	0.220	0.338	0.326	0.335	0.418
1990	0.248	0.179	0.251	0.422	0.386	0.372	0.438
2000	0.300	0.208	0.291	0.504	0.500	0.470	0.496
Model G3							
1900	0.017	0.000	0.016	0.023	0.023	0.026	0.041
1910	0.037	0.014	0.035	0.043	0.065	0.053	0.073
1920	0.043	0.015	0.044	0.048	0.070	0.070	0.103
1930	0.054	0.019	0.059	0.076	0.088	0.088	0.136
1940	0.066	0.028	0.075	0.072	0.098	0.114	0.179
1950	0.095	0.050	0.111	0.131	0.112	0.193	0.225
1960	0.122	0.074	0.139	0.185	0.165	0.240	0.249
1970	0.164	0.082	0.165	0.263	0.231	0.266	0.335
1980	0.192	0.114	0.187	0.313	0.306	0.321	0.402
1990	0.215	0.117	0.231	0.414	0.392	0.359	0.426
2000	0.283	0.156	0.272	0.502	0.517	0.458	0.480

Source. Appendix Tables 1–3.

Appendix Table 5.
The Inequality-Adjusted Historical Human Development Index (AIHHDI) of Uruguay and USA, 1910–2000.

	UY			USA			UY/USA		
	HGDP	IIIIDI	AIHHDI	HGDP	HHDI	AIHHDI	HGDP	HHDI	AIHHDI
1910	0.076	0.081	0.055	0.122	0.139	0.097	62.4	58.5	56.6
1920	0.065	0.085	0.058	0.137	0.162	0.119	47.2	52.5	48.5
1930	0.105	0.111	0.077	0.153	0.185	0.141	68.7	60.1	54.7
1940	0.089	0.122	0.087	0.173	0.216	0.164	51.5	56.7	53.1
1950	0.114	0.157	0.117	0.237	0.264	0.206	48.2	59.5	56.6
1960	0.122	0.185	0.142	0.281	0.297	0.234	43.3	62.2	60.8
1970	0.127	0.198	0.153	0.374	0.357	0.282	34.1	55.4	54.5
1980	0.162	0.220	0.167	0.463	0.418	0.327	35.1	52.6	51.2
1990	0.160	0.251	0.190	0.579	0.438	0.337	27.6	57.3	56.5
2000	0.194	0.291	0.217	0.702	0.496	0.377	27.7	58.6	57.6

Source: Table 2 and Appendix Tables 1–3.

Notes

1. Hicks, "The Inequality-Adjusted."
2. Maddison, *L'economie mondiale.*
3. Sen, "Capacidad y biencstar."
4. Astorga, "The Standard of Living."
5. Ibid, 24.
6. Camou et al., "La calidad de vida."
7. Astorga, "The Standard of Living."
8. Bértola et al., "Educación y Aprendizaje."
9. Prados de la Escosura, "Improving the Human Development."
10. Ibid.
11. Ibid.
12. Ibid.
13. Camou et al., "La calidad de vida."
14. UNDP. *Human Development Report.*
15. Astorga, "The Standard of Living."
16. Prados de la Escosura, "Improving the Human Development."
17. UNDP, *Human Development Report*, 1993, 101.
18. Hicks, "The Inequality-Adjusted Human."
19. Ibid., Table 1, 1290.
20. Shkolnikov, "Gini Coefficient."
21. Maddison, *The World Economy: Historical Statistics.*
22. Bértola et al., "Convergence."
23. Prados de la Escosura, "Improving the Human Development."
24. Migliónico, *República oriental del Uruguay.*
25. National Vital Statistics Reports 2006.

26. Bértola et al., "Educación y Aprendizaje."
27. Prados de la Escosura, "Improving the Human Development."
28. Bértola, "A 50 años de la Curva de Kuznets."
29. Lindert, "Three Centuries of Inequality."
30. United Nations University WIDER, *World Income Inequality Database.*
31. Bértola et al, "Convergence."
32. Verspagen, *Uneven Growth.*
33. Ibid.
34. Acemoglu et al., "The Colonial" and "Institutions."
35. Engerman and Sokoloff, "Factor Endowments" and "The Evolution of Suffrage."
36. Williamson, "Globalization," "Growth," and "Real Wages."
37. Bértola, "A 50 años de la Curva de Kuznets."
38. Willebald, "Desigualdad y especialización."
39. This section draws extensively from Bértola et al., "Convergence."
40. Ibid. For other recent contributions on convergence and divergence between Latin America and the rest and within Latin America, see Edwards, "Crises and Growth," and Sanz, "Human Capital."
41. Notice that it is not an inverted "U"-curve as in Kuznets; see Bértola, "A 50 años."
42. Bértola et al., "Comparación Internacional."
43. Becker, "The Quantity and Quality," 27.
44. Astorga, "The Standard of Living."
45. Ibid.
46. Prados de la Escosura, "Improving the Human Development."
47. Bértola et al., "Convergence."
48. Astorga et al., "The Standard of Living."
49. Ibid.
50. Prados de la Escosura, "Improving the Human Development."

References

Acemoglu, Daron, Simon Johnson, and James Robinson. "The Colonial Origins of Comparative Development: An Empirical Investigation." *American Economic Review* (December 2001): 1369–401.

———. "Institutions as the Fundamental Cause of Long-Run Growth." In Philip Aghion and Steven Durlauf, *Handbook of Economic Growth*, 385–472. Amsterdam: Elsevier, 2006.

Ahuja, Vinod, and Deon Filmer. "Educational Attainment in Developing Countries: New Estimates and Projections Disaggregated by Gender." *Journal of Educational Planning and Administration* 10, no. 3 (July 1996): 229–254.

Astorga, Pablo, and Valpy FitzGerald. "The Standard of Living in Latin America during the Twentieth Century." Development Studies Working Paper no. 117, University of Oxford, May 1998.

Astorga, Pablo, Ame R. Bergés, and Valpy FitzGerald. "The Standard of Living in Latin America during the Twentieth Century." *Economic History Review* 48, no. 4 (November 2005): 765–796.

Becker, Gary S., Tomas Philipson, and Rodrigo R. Soares. "The Quantity and Quality of Life and the Evolution of World Inequality." Working Paper 9765, National Bureau of Economic Research, June 2003.

Bértola, Luis, and Reto Bertoni. "Educación y Aprendizaje: su contribución a la definición de Escenarios de Convergencia y Divergencia." Documento de Trabajo 46, Unidad Multidisciplinaria, Facultad de Ciencias Sociales, Montevideo, 1999.

Bértola, Luis, María Camou, and Gabriel Porcile: "Comparación Internacional del Poder Adquisitivo de los Salarios Reales de los Países del Cono Sur, 1870–1945." *Segundas Jornadas de Historia Económica*, Montevideo, July 1999.

Bértola, Luis. *Ensayos de Historia Económica: Uruguay en la región y el mundo.* Montevideo: Trilce, 2000.

————. "A 50 años de la Curva de Kuznets: Crecimiento y distribución del ingreso en Uruguay y otras economías de nuevo asentamiento desde 1870." *Investigaciones en Historia Económica* 3 (2005): 135–176.

Bértola, Luis, and Gabriel Porcile. "Convergence, Trade and Industrial Policy: Argentina, Brazil and Uruguay in the International Economy, 1900–1980." *Revista de Historia Económica. Journal of Iberian and Latin American Economic History* 1 (2006): 37–67.

Camou, María, and Silvana Maubrigades. "La calidad de vida bajo la lupa: 100 años de evolución de los principales indicadores." *Boletín de Historia Económica* 4 (2005): 51–63.

Edwards, Sebastián. "Crises and Growth: A Latin American Perspective." *Revista de Historia Económica – Journal of Iberian and Latin American Economic History* 25, no. 1 (2007): 19–51.

Engerman, Stanley, and Kenneth Sokoloff. "Factor Endowments, Institutions and Differential Paths of Growth. A View from Economic Historians from the United States." In S. Haber, *How Latin America Fell Behind: Essays on the Economic Histories of Brazil and Mexico, 1800–1914.* Stanford: Stanford University Press, 1997.

————. "The Evolution of Suffrage in the New World." *Journal of Economic History* 65, no. 4 (2005): 891–921.

Goldin, Claudia. "America's Graduation from High School: The Evolution and Spread of Secondary Schooling in the Twentieth Century." *Journal of Economic History* 58, no. 2 (June 1998): 345–74.

Hicks, Douglas A. "The Inequality-Adjusted Human Development Index: A Constructive Proposal." *World Development* 25 no. 8 (1997): 1283–98.

Lindert, Peter H. "Three Centuries of Inequality in Britain and America." In *Handbook of Income Distribution*, edited by A.B. Atkinson and F. Bourguignon, 167–215. Amsterdam: Elsevier, 2000.

Maddison, Angus. *L'economie mondiale 1820–1992.* Paris: OECD, 1995.

————. *The World Economy: Historical Statistics.* Paris: OECD, 2003.

Migliónico, Américo. *República oriental del Uruguay. Tablas Abreviadas de Mortalidad por Sexo y Edad, 1908–1999.* Montevideo: Ministerio de Salud Pública, 2001.

"National Vital Statistics Reports." United States, Center for Disease Control, 2006. http://www.cdc.gov/nchs/data/nvsr/nvsr53/nvsr53_15.pdf.

Offer, Avner. "Economic Welfare Measurements and Human Well-Being." Oxford University Discussion Papers in Economic and Social History no. 34, 2000.

———. "Introduction." In *Pursuit of the Quality of Life,* edited by Avner Offer. New York: Oxford University Press, 1996.

Prados de la Escosura, Leandro. "When Did Latin America Fall behind? Evidence from Long-run International Inequality." Paper presented at the Inter-American Seminar on Economics, NBER, México, December 2004.

———. "Long-Run International Differences in Real Income and Human Development: Evidence from Europe and the New World." Paper presented at the International Economic History Association Congress, Helsinki, August 2006.

———. "Improving the Human Development Index: A New Data Set for the Western World, 1850–2000" (mimeo), 2007.

Sanz, Isabel. "Human Capital and Convergence in Latin-America: 1950–2000." *Revista de Historia Económica/Journal of Iberian and Latin American Economic History* 1 (Jan. 2007): 87–122.

Sen, Amartya. "Capacidad y bienestar." In *La calidad de vida,* ed. Martha C. Nussebaum and Amartya Sen. Mexico: Fondo de Cultura Económica, 1993.

Shkolnikov, Vladimir M., Evgueni. E. Andreev and Alexander Z. Begun. "Gini Coefficient as a Life Table Function: Computation from Discrete Data, Decomposition of Differences and Empirical Examples." *Demographic Research* 8 (2003): 305–358.

Thorp, Rosemary. *Progress, Poverty, and Exclusion: An Economic History of Latin America in the 20th Century.* Baltimore: Inter-American Development Bank, 1998.

United Nations Development Program, 1990–2006. *Human Development Report.*

"World Income Inequality Database V 2.0b." WIDER, United Nations University, http://www.wider.unu.edu/wiid/wiid.htm, May 2007.

Verspagen, Bart. *Uneven Growth between Interdependent Economies. An Evolutionary View on Technology Gaps, Trade and Growth.* Aldershot: Avebury, *1993.*

Willebald, Henry. "Desigualdad y especialización en el crecimiento de las economías templadas de nuevo asentamiento, 1870–1940." *Revista de Historia Económica/ Journal of Iberian and Latin American Economic History* 25, no. 2 (Jan. 2007): 293–347.

Williamson, Jeffrey G. "Globalization and Inequality, Past and Present." *World Bank Research Observer* 12 (April 1997): 117–35.

———. "Growth, Distribution and Demography: Some Lessons from History." *Explorations in Economic History* 35 (July 1998): 241–71.

———. "Real Wages, Inequality, and Globalization in Latin America before 1940." *Revista de Historia Económica* 17 (special no.1999): 101–42.

8

Politics, Policy, and Mortality Decline in Chile, 1960–1995

James W. McGuire

Despite Chile's long history of competitive politics and its status as one of Latin America's most extensive welfare states, in 1960 its citizens had an average life expectancy at birth of only 57 years and an infant mortality rate of 120 per 1000, which was even higher than the rate of 115 per 1000 in much poorer Brazil.[1] One goal of this chapter is to explain why Chile in 1960, with its fairly high level of overall affluence, highly developed welfare state, strong and militant labor movement, and thirty years of political stability and competitive politics, had such high rates of early death.

Chile from 1960 to 1995 raised life expectancy and reduced infant mortality more steeply than any other country in Latin America.[2] By 1995 its infant mortality rate was second lowest (to Cuba's), and was not much higher than the rate in the United States (11 vs. 8 per 1000).[3] From 1960 to 1995 Chile's infant mortality rate went from being twice as high as Argentina's to twice as low, and from being the same as Brazil's to four times as low.[4] A second goal of the chapter is to explain why Chile did so well at reducing infant mortality from 1960 to 1995, and why it had such a low rate of infant mortality in 1995. Special attention is paid to assessing the extent to which Chile's rapid post-1960 mortality decline can be traced to the overall modernization of the country, in accordance with the "wealthier is healthier" conjecture,[5] and the extent to which it can be traced to specific government policies in health care and other areas.

Rapid mortality decline took place not only during eras of competitive politics (1960–1973; 1990–1995), but also during the military regime of General Augusto Pinochet (1973–1990). The steepest infant mortality decline occurred from 1973 to 1984, during the most repressive years of military rule, when the rate fell from 66 to 20 per 1000. Making this plunge even more remarkable, GDP per capita shrank during those twelve years, while income inequality and income poverty soared. The sharp drop of infant mortality from 1973 to 1984 raises questions: did policies of the military government contribute to the plunge? If so, which policies contributed, and why did the government enact them? What does Chile's experience tell us about how political democracy affects social welfare policies, and about how social welfare policies affect mortality decline?

The Quality of Mortality Data and the Evolution of Mortality Rates

Most experts express confidence in Chilean vital registration statistics from 1960 onward.[6] Chilean vital registries may omit some infant (especially neonatal) deaths, but scholarship has continued to use vital registration statistics, apparently under the assumption that the omissions have been infrequent or acceptably constant across regions and over time.[7] On the whole, it seems reasonable to proceed as if infant mortality estimates derived from Chilean vital registration records were fairly complete and accurate from 1960 to 1995. A careful review and reconciliation of statistics based on census data, national life tables, and vital registration records indicates that Chilean infant mortality was 118 per 1000 in 1960 and 11 per 1000 in 1995.[8] These figures are almost identical to those derived exclusively from vital registration records (Table 1).

In 1995 Chile's infant mortality rate was 11.1 per 1,000 and its life expectancy at birth was 74.9 years (Table 1). These figures placed Chile in the top 25 percent of countries on each indicator. From 1960 to 1995 Chile ranked 6th of 183 countries on percent decline of infant mortality, and 9th of 179 on percent rise in life expectancy.[9] Compared to other countries, then, Chile from 1960 to 1995 reduced mortality very steeply, to a remarkably low level.

In 1964, when Eduardo Frei Montalva, a Christian Democrat, became president of Chile, the infant mortality rate was still 104 per 1000, about the same as in 1953 (105 per 1000). By the end of Frei's six-year presidency (1964–1970) it had fallen to 82 per 1000, and by the end of Salvador Allende's presidency (1970–1973) it had declined to 66 per 1000.[10] Other indicators of premature mortality also improved from 1964 to 1973.[11] Although the rapid fall of infant mortality under military rule has received more attention, these figures show very respectable progress on a wider range of mortality indicators under a competitive political system from 1964 to 1973.

The decline of infant mortality under military rule occurred almost entirely between 1973 and 1984, when the rate, according to vital registration, fell from 65.8 to 19.6 per 1000, one of the sharpest sustained drops on record in any country ever. From 1985 to 1990, however, despite faster economic growth than in the first decade of the military regime, infant mortality fell

Table 1.
Chile: Mortality Indicators, 1960–1995.

Year	Infant mortality, vital registration	Infant mortality, vital registration, mean annual % decline over previous 5 years	Life expectancy at birth, World Bank	Life expectancy at birth, World Bank total % rise over previous 5 years
1960	119.5		57.3	
1965	97.3	−4.0%	59.6	8.3%
1970	82.2	−3.3%	62.4	11.0%
1975	57.6	−6.9%	65.7	14.6%
1980	33.0	−10.5%	69.3	18.7%
1985	19.5	−10.0%	71.9	16.6%
1990	16.0	−3.9%	73.7	13.7%
1995	11.1	−7.1%	74.9	10.5%

Sources, Definitions, and Notes:

Infant mortality: Infant (0–1) deaths per 1000 live births based on vital registration statistics. Data for 1960–1975 are from Banco Central, *Indicadores*, 428; Data for 1980–1995 are from Chile. INE, *Anuario de Estadísticas Vitales 2000*, 53. Mean annual percent decline is calculated by the formula =RATE(5,- IMR60, IMR65), and so on for successive periods, in Microsoft Excel. *Life expectancy at birth*: World Bank, *World Development Indicators 2008*. Percent rise is calculated as (LifeXendyear–LifeXstartyear)/ (85–LifeXstartyear). The result of this quotient may be pictured as the proportion of distance traveled by the last year in the period from the life expectancy in the initial year of the period toward a stipulated maximum of 85 years.

only from 19.5 to 16.0 per 1000. Rapid decline resumed after democracy returned in 1990. It took only eleven years, from 1990 to 2000, for Chile to cut infant mortality from 16.0 to 8.9 per 1000. By comparison, it took the United States seventeen years, from 1975 to 1991, to reduce it from 16.1 to 8.9 per 1000.[12] What needs to be explained, then, is why infant mortality was so high in Chile in 1960, and why a rapid decline began in the mid-1960s, accelerated during the first decade of the military regime, slowed in the late 1980s, and sped up again after democracy returned in 1990.

Affluence, Inequality, Poverty, and Mortality

Higher GDP per capita can contribute to lower premature mortality by giving individuals more income to spend on food and other basic needs, or by giving governments more revenues to spend on social services. In Chile, such effects appear to have been attenuated. Chile from 1960 to 1995 outpaced all but a handful of countries at raising life expectancy and reducing infant mortality. Its GDP per capita growth was unexceptional, however, averaging 2.3 percent a year from 1960 to 1995, only 45th among 110 countries with available data, and 39th among 70 outside sub-Saharan Africa.[13] From 1960 to 1985, moreover, infant mortality plunged from 120 per 1000 to 20 per 1000, even though GDP per capita rose only from US$3,853 to $4,986 (Tables 1 and 2). From 1960 to 1985, accordingly, Chile achieved a fast decline of infant mortality despite slow economic growth, whereas from 1985 to 1990 it registered a slow decline of infant mortality despite fast economic growth. Only after 1990 did the pace of economic growth and infant mortality decline begin to coincide.

Chilean governments from the mid-1950s to the early 1970s engaged in the single-minded pursuit of premature heavy import substitution, depending on copper revenues to finance imports of needed machinery.[14] The economic problems created by this development model, together with expectations generated by promises of land reform and income redistribution, created growing tension by the end of the 1960s. In 1970 Dr. Salvador Allende, a Socialist, won the presidency with only 36 percent of the vote. Undaunted by this frail mandate, Allende announced a transition to socialism and began to nationalize copper companies, raise the minimum wage,

Table 2.
Chile: Socioeconomic Indicators, 1960–1995.

	GDP per capita	GDP per capita, average annual growth in preceding 5-year period	Gini index of income inequality	Percent of population receiving less than $1 per day	Percent of population receiving less than $2 per day	Total fertility rate
1960	3,853					5.5
1965	4,100	1.3%				4.8
1970	4,794	3.3%	46.0	5.2	20.6	4.0
1975	4,172	−2.4%				3.1
1980	5,412	5.4%	53.2	7.7	23.5	2.7
1985	4,986	−1.4%	54.9			2.7
1990	6,148	4.3%	55.1	8.1	31.0	2.6
1995	8,488	6.7%	54.8	4.4	23.5	2.3

Sources, Definitions, and Notes:

GDP per capita: In 1996 parity purchasing power US dollars, according to a chain index. Heston, Summers, and Aten, *Penn World Table Version 6.1*, variable RGDPCH. Annual growth calculated with the RATE function in Microsoft Excel. Average annual growth in the preceding five-year period is the mean of the annual growth figures of the indicated and four preceding years (e.g., 1961–65). *Gini index*: WIDER 2007. Surveys from 1971, 1980, 1985, 1990, and 1996. Selection criteria described in McGuire, *Wealth, Health, and Democracy*, Web Appendix B1. *% of population receiving less than $1 or $2 per day*: In 1985 parity purchasing power US dollars. Londoño and Székely, "Persistent Poverty," 40. The figure for $2 poverty includes $1 poverty. *Total fertility rate*: World Bank, *World Development Indicators 2008*.

expand the scope of land reform, and boost social spending. Transitions from capitalism to socialism (or vice-versa) incur huge transitional costs, and this one did too. Imports of food and consumer goods rose and foreign exchange dried up, exacerbated by a drop in copper prices. By 1973, the fiscal deficit reached 25 percent of GDP. The United States ended foreign aid to Chile, pressured international financial institutions to stop lending to the Allende government, forced Chilean companies to pay cash for spare parts and other imports, and financed newspapers and organizations opposed to the government. Land seizures, factory occupations, and strikes burgeoned, while inflation rose to 78 percent in 1972 and 353 percent in 1973.[15] On September 11, 1973, Allende was overthrown in a military coup, ending 42 years of regular elections and continuous civilian rule.

The ensuing military regime (1973–1990) was one of the harshest in modern Latin American history. Security forces under Pinochet killed or "disappeared" at least 2000 persons and arrested and abused many more.[16] The military authorities shut down parties and unions, censored the press, purged universities, and stifled artistic expression. Meanwhile, they replaced the import substitution model with a new free-market one, privatizing 400 state firms, cutting tariffs, weakening laws protecting workers and unions, and selling or returning to former owners most of the land distributed under Frei Montalva and Allende.[17] Cuts in import tariffs and the recessionary impact of other economic policies destroyed hundreds of previously protected industrial firms, contributing to a 16 percent drop in GDP per capita in a single year, 1975. Despite this sharp contraction, the free-market reforms raised confidence among more competitive or otherwise favored entrepreneurs and emboldened them to borrow heavily from foreign banks, which were bursting with petrodollars and eager to lend.[18] Excessive borrowing led to another economic crisis. In 1982/83, GDP per capita fell by 18 percent and unemployment rose to 20 percent.[19]

The first crash in 1975 got rid of much of Chile's inefficient industry; the second in 1982/83 provided some sobering lessons about over-borrowing and speculation. Businesses that survived these catastrophes were likely to be viable, given an upturn in the business cycle and an environment of cautious macroeconomic policies, which the government proceeded to enact. As the economy recovered in the mid-1980s, the finance ministry replaced the radical neo-liberalism of the 1970s with a more pragmatic variant.[20] To raise revenue, improve the balance of trade, and protect recovering industries, the economic team in 1984 raised import tariffs from 20 to 35 percent.[21] To promote exports, the finance ministry in the mid- and late 1980s kept the peso undervalued (it had been highly overvalued in the late 1970s) and raised subsidies for non-copper exports like timber, fruit, wine, and seafood. To reduce the destabilizing impact of hot money, ministry officials in the late 1980s imposed taxes and reserve requirements on short-term foreign capital. These policies, some of which resembled South Korea's and Taiwan's in the 1960s and 1970s, helped to raise GDP per capita from US$4,611 in 1983 (down from $4,963 in 1974) to $6,068 in 1989.[22]

In 1988, with economic growth soaring and under international pressure to step down, General Pinochet called a plebiscite in which Chileans were asked to vote for or against his continuation in office for another eight years. Some 55 percent voted "no," against 43 percent in favor. In the 1989 elections the Concertación coalition, mostly the Christian Democrats and Socialists, won the presidency, a majority in the Chamber of Deputies, and a plurality of elected senators (military-designated senators prevented a majority). Concertación also won the 1994, 2000, and 2006 elections, defeating rightist candidates who drew votes from supporters of the military regime. The Christian Democrats Patricio Aylwin (1990–1994) and Eduardo Frei Ruiz-Tagle (1994–2000) served the first two terms of the new democracy, and the Socialists Ricardo Lagos (2000–2006) and Michelle Bachelet (2006–2010) served the next two.

With the transfer of office in March 1990, the Concertación coalition inherited a growing economy. Macroeconomic indicators were favorable, and conditions were ripe for an inflow of foreign capital. Populist-type policies had failed in the 1980s in Argentina, Brazil, and Peru (as well as in Chile itself in the mid-1960s and early 1970s), and enthusiasm for free-market reform was sweeping the world. In this context, the Concertación leaders decided that the pre-1973 import-substitution model was no longer viable.[23] Accordingly, although discarding the radical free-market orientation of the mid and late 1970s, they maintained the pragmatic free-market orientation of the mid and late 1980s, which featured cautious macroeconomic policies, export promotion, and openness to foreign trade and long-term foreign investment. The economy responded with rapid GDP growth, averaging 6.4 percent a year (4.9 percent per capita) from 1990 to 1999, and inflation fell from 26 percent in 1990 to 3 percent in 1999.[24]

Chile achieved rapid infant mortality decline from 1960 to 1995 despite high and rising income inequality, which has been found to be associated with higher premature mortality even controlling for absolute poverty.[25] Chile's Gini index from 1960 to 1990 averaged 51.8, 16th highest among 106 countries with available data.[26] Income inequality in the Santiago metropolitan area, which had remained steady from 1960 to 1973, rose sharply under military rule from 1973 to 1990, when the fastest infant mortality decline occurred.[27] Partly because the Concertación continued the military government's free-market orientation, income inequality changed little from 1990 to 1996, while infant mortality resumed a rapid decline after stagnating in the late 1980s (Tables 1 and 2). In 1996 Chile's Gini Index was 54.8, highest among the top 67 countries on the UNDP's Human Development Index, on which Chile ranked 38th.[28] Accordingly, Chile calls into question such claims as "a society with a highly unequal distribution of income . . . can never meet the basic needs of many of its people."[29] Despite high income inequality, Chile from 1960 to 1995 did better than most other developing countries at meeting some important basic needs.

A lower income-poverty headcount means that a larger share of the population has adequate resources with which to purchase food, housing, health care, and other basic needs, which should reduce the risk of early death, particularly among vulnerable people. From 1960 to 1968 urban poverty fell sharply, and new laws and policies during the late 1960s almost certainly reduced rural poverty as well.[30] Then, from 1970 to 1990, $2 per day poverty rose from 21 to 31 percent of the population. Income poverty and infant mortality thus evolved with quite different tempos from 1960 to 1990. In the 1960s income poverty fell steeply while infant mortality fell slowly, whereas in the 1970s and 1980s infant mortality plunged while income poverty rose (Tables 1 and 2).

To what extent, then, do GDP per capita, income inequality, and income poverty explain Chile's low level of infant mortality in 1995, its steep decline of infant mortality from 1960 to 1995, or the tempo of its infant mortality decline within that period? On level, Chile among 92 developing countries in 1990 had the sixth largest negative residual in a regression of infant mortality on GDP per capita and income inequality, indicating much lower infant mortality than these income-related indicators predicted.[31] On progress, Chile from 1960 to 1995 registered one of the fastest infant mortality declines in the world, despite slow economic growth and rising income inequality. On tempo, infant mortality fell sharply from 1967 (95 per 1000) to 1983 (22 per 1000), even though GDP per capita barely rose (by only U.S. $68, from $4,543 to $4,611) and income inequality and income poverty soared (Table 2).[32] From 1960 to 1995, then, the pace and tempo of change in income-related indicators was entirely out of phase with the pace and tempo of infant mortality decline. The public provision of basic social services does better than income-related indicators at explaining the pattern and pace of infant mortality decline in Chile from 1960 to 1995.

Education, Nutrition, Family Planning, Water, Sanitation, and Mortality Decline

Literacy and schooling, especially of women, are widely found to contribute to lower infant and child mortality.[33] Several mechanisms mediate this effect. Women with more education know more about nutrition, sanitation, and health; tend to be more assertive in demanding food and health care for children; and are more likely to use modern health facilities and child care practices that improve health.[34] Male education is also associated with lower child mortality, but not as strongly as female education.[35] Chile had little gender bias in basic education during the period under study. In 1970, adult (15+) literacy was slightly higher among males than among females (89 vs. 86 percent), but youth (15–24) literacy did not differ by gender, and female enrollment was at least as high as male enrollment at both the primary and secondary levels in both 1970 and 1995.[36]

The Chilean state began to fund primary education in 1860. By 1875 about 23 percent of the population was literate and about 17 percent of primary-school aged children were enrolled in school.[37] Literacy rose to 44 percent in 1900 and to 75 percent in 1930, helped along by a 1920 law that made primary education obligatory. From 1930 to 1960 literacy gains slowed; at the end of the period the literacy rate stood at only 84 percent.[38] The Christian Democratic government of Eduardo Frei Montalva (1964–1970) reinvigorated the educational system, doubling spending on scholarships and school loans and raising school enrollment from 1.8 million to 2.9 million.[39] As in most Latin American countries, however, education spending was top-heavy. In the late 1960s Chilean universities, which enrolled only 3 percent of the country's students (mostly from middle- and upper-class families), received 27 percent of public education spending, whereas primary schools, which enrolled 70 percent of students, received only 36 percent of such spending.[40]

Soon after the 1973 coup, "the new rector of the University of Chile parachuted down to the campus, as if landing in enemy territory." Meanwhile, the military government revamped the curricula of primary and secondary schools to reflect the conservative values of its leaders. A 1979 law shifted the administration of public schools to municipalities, and in 1980 the government began to subsidize tuition-free private schools at the same rate as state-run municipal schools. It is hard to assess the impact of "the world's farthest reaching neoliberal experiment in education," but one study concluded that it "did not dramatically improve education."[41] Nevertheless, mean years of schooling and secondary enrollment continued to rise under the military regime (Table 3).

Table 3.
Chile: Education, Nutrition, Family Planning, Water, and Sanitation, 1960–1995.

	Literacy (15+)	Mean years of school (15+)	Secondary enrollment (gross)	% children under 6 malnourished	Family planning effort	% with access to improved water source	% urban pop. with access to improved sanitation
1960	84.0	5.21	24	5.9			
1965		5.04	34			41.8	25.4
1970	88.2	5.65	37	3.5	53	58.5	31.1
1975	90.0	5.61	47			68.2	43.5
1980	91.6	6.42	53	1.6	44	82.5	67.4
1985	93.0	6.69	67			90.7	75.1
1990	94.1	6.97	74	0.3	58	93.6	80.6
1995	94.9	7.25	70		55	95.7	85.0

Sources, Definitions, and Notes:

Literacy: World Bank, *World Development Indicators 2001*, except 1960, from World Bank, *World Development Report 1980*, 154–155. In the population aged 15 and older. *Mean years of schooling*: Barro and Lee, *International Data*. In the population aged 15 and older. *School enrollment*: World Bank, *World Development Indicators 2002*. *% children under 6 malnourished*: Monckeberg, "Prevención de la desnutrición," Table 2. Children more than 2 standard deviations below the normal weight for age. *Family planning effort*: Ross and Mauldin, "Family Planning Programs," 146. Mean expert rating of family planning effort as a percent of the maximum attainable score. "1970"=1972; "1980"=1982; "1990"=1989; "1995"=1994. Mean effort in the respective years for 83–104 countries: 20, 29, 46, and 48. *% with access to improved water and sanitation*: Mesa-Lago, *Market, Socialist, and Mixed Economies*, 165 ("1995"=1993). Where separate estimates for access to safe water were provided for urban and rural areas, a national figure was calculated using data on proportion rural (World Bank, *World Development Indicators 1998*) in that year.

The Aylwin government (1990–1994) continued to subsidize tuition-free private institutions and to allow municipalities to run public schools, but launched a drive to improve the quality of education, resulting in a rise in test scores, and appealed successfully to Congress to raise the value-added tax to finance more education spending.[42] Moreover, the Aylwin and succeeding Frei Ruiz-Tagle (1994–2000) governments expanded preschool education, improved primary schools in poor areas, gave scholarships to needy students, and introduced work-study programs for impoverished high-school students who had to work.[43] Another progressive reform, continued from the period of military rule, was to halve the share of public education spending devoted to universities, from 36 percent in 1980 to 18 percent in 1996.[44] Chile thus made good progress on education from 1960 to 1995, and education must be counted as a factor that contributed to Chile's rapid mortality decline under authoritarian as well as democratic governments.

Adequate nutrition lowers mortality by increasing resistance to disease and by making it easier for an afflicted person to recover from illness.[45] Most Chileans did well on the nutritional front throughout the period analyzed.

Calorie availability was adequate and was actually higher in 1971 than in 1992.[46] Complementing adequate food availability were public milk distribution and school feeding programs that began in 1924 and expanded steadily thereafter, particularly during the mid-1960s, such that by 1967 about 50 percent of children aged less than five were receiving milk. From 1960 to 1970 the share of children under six suffering from moderate or severe malnutrition fell from 5.9 to 3.5 percent, while the proportion suffering from mild malnutrition fell from 31 to 16 percent.[47] The Popular Unity government of Salvador Allende stepped up the free milk program, tripling the amount distributed by raising eligibility to include children aged 7–14 as well as all pregnant women and nursing mothers. As much as 70 percent of this target population may have been reached under Allende. Between December 1970 and October 1973, malnutrition among children under six fell by about 17 percent.[48]

The military government ended the policy of distributing free milk to children aged 7–14 and halved the number of school meals.[49] Food consumption fell sharply in the years after the 1973 coup, particularly among low-income families, but government food programs partly offset the difficulty of acquiring food in the private market. The amount of milk provided in 1974, although below the level reached during the Allende period, was above its 1967 level, and the military government increased the caloric content of the milk.[50] Maintaining the integration of nutrition and health programs, the Pinochet government began nutrition monitoring that put more than one million children under the age of six (70 to 75 percent of such children in Chile) under surveillance at stations set up by the Ministry of Health, and provided intensive care for children with signs of malnutrition.[51] After the return to democracy, the Aylwin government continued the monitoring policies inherited from the military regime, while improving school-based nutrition assistance.[52] These policies helped to reduce the share of infants suffering from malnutrition from 7.4 percent in 1990 to 5.2 percent in 1993.[53] As with education, then, nutrition programs—which for infants and young children improved during Pinochet's presidency—contributed significantly to Chile's rapid infant mortality decline from 1960 to 1995.

Effective planning programs reduce fertility, which contributes to lower infant and child mortality by increasing birth spacing, by lessening the number of higher-order parities, by diminishing the share of births to very young and old mothers, by permitting parents to devote more attention to each child, and by reducing the burden on obstetric and pediatric services. Although lower fertility implies a higher proportion of first births, which some evidence suggests are riskier to infants than other low-order parities, that does not seem to have been the case in Chile, where first-born infants, at least in the 1970s, died in lower proportions than infants born subsequently.[54] Lower fertility can also reduce adult mortality, both directly by reducing a woman's lifetime risk of dying from pregnancy-related causes, and indirectly by reducing the burden on health, education, family planning, water supply, and sanitation services.[55]

Between 1960 and 1995 the total fertility rate fell sharply in Chile, from 5.5 to 2.3 expected children per woman of child-bearing age (Table 2). This 55 percent decline placed Chile 38th among 167 countries for which the World Bank provided data.[56] Modernization during this 35-year period contributed to the fall of desired fertility, while family planning aided the decline of unwanted fertility, especially in the late 1960s and early 1970s.[57] In 1962, the private Chilean Association for Family Protection (APROFA) launched a family planning program aimed at reducing Chile's high abortion rate. Three years later, APROFA and the Ministry of Health began to provide family planning information and services in National Health Service facilities.[58] In 1967 the government launched an integrated national family planning program, again aimed mostly at reducing the incidence of abortion and related maternal mortality.[59] After contraceptive delivery began, hospitalization for complications of abortion fell swiftly,[60] and the estimated maternal mortality ratio fell from 279 per 100,000 live births in 1965 to 131 per 100,000 in 1970.[61] By 1972 Chile had the third-strongest family planning effort rating in Latin America, behind only Costa Rica and Panama. Family planning effort fell under military rule, both in absolute terms (Table 3) and relative to other Latin American countries,[62] although fertility continued to fall swiftly, partly because impoverished Chileans decided to put off having children when unemployment surged during the mid-1970s and early 1980s.[63] One study found that fertility-related factors accounted for about 25 percent of the decline in infant mortality from 1974 to 1982; another found that such factors were responsible for about 30 percent of the infant mortality decline from 1972 to 1982.[64] Family planning effort rebounded between 1982 and 1989, but fertility decline slowed, falling only from 2.8 in 1980 to 2.6 in 1990. Fertility then dropped to 2.3 in 1995, aided by a plunge in the marriage rate, which, after holding steady at 7.5 per 1000 from 1970 to 1990, fell to 4.4 per 1000 in 2000.[65] Hence, whereas family planning programs made an important contribution to fertility decline during the 1960s, other factors, including high unemployment and a falling marriage rate, seem to have been more important after 1973. In general, then, Chile's record on family planning was not quite as strong as its record on education or nutritional intervention.

Piped water reduces the costs of washing and reduces the risk of contamination from unsafe water storage in wells and containers. Adequate systems of waste disposal also reduce the risk of contamination. Access to safe water and adequate sanitation rose steadily after the mid-1960s (Table 3), even during the military regime (1973–1990), when the government instructed health workers to build latrines and improve refuse disposal in the countryside.[66] Pooling annual observations over nine years (1974–1982) for Chile's 13 regions, one study found that the share of households with access to adequate sanitation was among the strongest predictors of the infant mortality level, controlling for other variables.[67] Experts identify the expansion of access to safe water and adequate sanitation as an important contributor to the rapid decline of infant mortality from 1974 to 1983.[68] Progress continued in both areas after the return to democracy. Access to improved water sources rose modestly in both urban and rural areas from 1991 to 1997, and access to sanitation in cities rose from 81 percent in 1990 to 96 percent in 2002.[69]

Chile thus did well from 1960 to 1995 on education, nutritional assistance, and the expansion of access to water and sanitation, and moderately well on family planning, especially before 1973. Democratic governments took the initial steps in each of these areas, but except in some areas of family planning (e.g., a 1989 law forbidding abortion even to save the life of the mother), progress continued under military rule from 1973 to 1990. It appears, then, that social service provisioning did more than GDP per capita, inequality, or poverty to shape the pattern and pace of mortality decline in Chile from 1960 to 1995. The evolution of the health care system lends support to this conjecture.

Health Care Policies and Mortality Decline

Health care, both curative and preventive, contributes directly to the decline of premature mortality. In Chile, the year 1924 was a watershed for public involvement in health care. In September, Congress passed a law providing for health, disability, accident, retirement, and burial insurance for blue-collar workers (*obreros*, a category that originally included some peasants, domestic workers, and low-income self-employed). A month later, fulfilling a promise made by the recently deposed president, Arturo Alessandri, a military junta issued a decree creating a Ministry of Labor, Hygiene, Assistance, and Social Welfare, the ancestor of the current Ministry of Health. Another wave of health-care related legislation came in 1938, when Congress required the blue-collar fund to give workers preventive care in the form of a yearly examination for tuberculosis and other diseases, to provide free treatment for any illness thus discovered, and to extend maternal and infant care to female contributors and to male contributors' wives. Four years later, Congress passed a law requiring the Servicio Médico Nacional de Empleados (SERMENA) to provide preventive care to white-collar workers and civil servants.[70] By the end of World War II, a significant share of the Chilean labor force was covered by health insurance.

The 1924 law creating a social security fund for blue-collar workers also provided for rural health posts supervised by a non-resident physician and staffed by nurses and lay health workers. In 1936, doctors associated with the blue-collar fund, noting that infant mortality had not declined much since the creation of the rural health posts, created a Mother and Child Department within the fund to expand the provision of prenatal, delivery, and postpartum care. The new Department also provided milk for mothers and infants and checkups for babies under age two. To gain access to these services, the mother or her husband had to belong to the fund.[71] This expanded program of mother and child health care, scholars have argued, helped to reduce infant mortality.[72] The Preventive Medicine Law, passed in 1938, also applied only to persons associated with the blue-collar fund, but it facilitated the wider distribution of newly invented antibiotics and paved the way for a campaign against tuberculosis, which also accelerated the pace of mortality decline.[73]

The administration of public health care underwent a major reform in 1952, when Congress passed a law that divided the blue-collar fund into a health care branch (the Servicio Nacional de Salud, SNS) and a pension branch. The SNS, or National Health Service, was funded by both general tax revenues and payroll deductions from blue-collar workers. It took charge of sanitation, epidemiology, and general public health; centralized the administration of the various regimes into which the original blue-collar fund had subdivided; and consolidated control over all of the country's medical facilities, including provincial and local health services, hospitals previously run by charities, and outpatient clinics previously run by the blue-collar fund. The new legislation tripled the share of the population covered by health insurance to 65 percent, including wives of affiliated workers (who had previously been covered only during pregnancy), children of affiliated workers up to age 15 (previously age 2), and the indigent uninsured.[74]

Despite these dramatic changes, infant mortality, which was 122 per 1000 in 1952, fell only to 120 per 1000 in 1960.[75] The slow pace of decline "created great consternation among the country's health authorities and within academic public health circles" and "gave special cause for increased concern to maternal and child health services."[76] Economic stagnation contributed to the slow decline of infant mortality during the 1950s, but so did the inaccessibility of health care to the poor. In 1966 only 55 percent of agricultural workers were insured, and even agricultural workers who contributed to the SNS faced formidable obstacles to obtaining adequate medical care.[77]

The Frei Montalva government (1964–1970) tried to correct some of these inequities. Soon after taking office it drew up Chile's first national health plan, putting more resources into maternal and child care.[78] Whereas GDP rose only about 30 percent from 1964 to 1970, public spending on health care rose 80 percent.[79] During this period, "the material and resources of the National Health Service . . . were redistributed clearly in favor of mothers, infants, children, and adolescents." The government also promoted the organization of mothers' centers and neighborhood councils.[80] The share of deaths with medical certification, indicating access to medical care during a health crisis, rose from 61 percent in 1964 to 82 percent in 1970. Meanwhile, although the number of doctors per capita stagnated during this period, nurses per capita rose by 32 percent and nurse auxiliaries per capita rose by 20 percent.[81] From 1965 to 1970 the share of births attended by professionals rose from 74 to 81 percent, while the number of public outpatient facilities rose from 613 to 918 (Table 4). Smallholders, tenant farmers, and agricultural laborers began to organize, often with the help of Socialist and Communist activists. Such organization helped them to overcome obstacles to using the health insurance benefits to which they were legally entitled.[82] In 1968 Congress passed a law giving white-collar employees access to curative care, freeing up National Health System resources for more impoverished Chileans.

Elected to succeed Frei as president of Chile (incumbents were not allowed to run for re-election) was the Socialist Salvador Allende, a physician and former health minister (1939–1942). Allende instructed the National Health Service to shift resources from hospitals to community health centers, whose opening hours were extended significantly. The government also required public-sector physicians to spend at least a quarter of their time practicing in such centers, and expanded compulsory service in health centers from three to five years after the student received a medical degree.[83] During Allende's presidency (1970–1973), the share of births attended by professionals rose from 81 to 85 percent while infant mortality fell from 82 to 66 per 1000.[84] Allende tried to unify the health system by shifting to the National Health Service a share of the contributions destined for the white-collar fund. This measure antagonized white-collar workers, who feared that their health care would deteriorate, and physicians with private practices, who feared a loss of customers.[85] Doctors were also annoyed by the decision to shift

Table 4.
Chile: Health Care, 1960–1995.

	Health spending, public, % GDP	Health spending, total, % GDP	Public outpatient facilities	Doctors per 10,000 population	Midwives working for National Health Service	Percent of births with professional care	Immunization, DPT3	Immunization, MCV
1960				5.6		66.9		
1965			613	4.7	761	74.3		
1970			918	4.6	1101	81.1		
1975				4.3	1377	87.4		
1980	2.1	5.5		5.2	1832	91.4	85	99
1985	1.9	5.3	2402	8.2		97.4	90	92
1990	2.0	5.5		11.0		98.4	99	82
1995	2.4	5.6	2336	10.8		100.0	94	97

Sources, Definitions, and Notes:

Health spending: PAHO, *PAHO Health Accounts Data* ("public" includes "social insurance's health spending"). *Public outpatient facilities*: 1965–1970: Livingstone and Raczynski, "Análisis Cuantitativo," 43. "1985" (=1987): Chile. ODEPLAN, *Evolución de la salud*, 6. 1995: Chile. INE, *Compendio Estadístico 2001*, 165. *Doctors per 10,000 population*. World Bank, *World Development Indicators 2001* ("1980"=1979, "1985"=1984). Figure for 1975 is from Mesa Lago, *Market, Socialist, and Mixed Economies*, 161, drawing on the WHO World Health Statistics Annual. *Midwives working for the National Health Service*: Raczynski and Oyarzo, "¿Por que cae la tasa?" 76, except 1980, from Scarpaci, "Restructuring Health Care Financing," 426. *% births with professional care*: Chile. Banco Central, *Indicadores económicos y sociales*, 424 ("1990"=1988). Figure for 1995 is from World Bank, *World Development Indicators 2001*. *Immunization, MCV and DPT3*. WHO/UNICEF, *Estimates of National Immunization Coverage*. *% of children under 12 months*. DPT3 means three doses of the antigens against diphtheria, pertussis, and tetanus; MCV is measles-containing vaccine.

resources from tertiary to primary care, and by a 1971 decree that shifted authority on Community Health Councils from physicians to health-worker unions and community associations. In October 1972, about 60 percent of the members of the Chilean Medical Association went on strike against the government, and in August 1973, the Association called a general strike and asked for Allende's resignation as president of Chile. The next month, Allende was overthrown in a military coup.[86]

After the coup, 9 doctors were executed, 11 "disappeared," and hundreds went into exile. The military government cut the budget of the University of Chile's School of Public Health by 75 percent and fired or imprisoned 82 of its 110 faculty members.[87] From 1974 to 1983, when the sharpest infant mortality decline occurred, the government slashed public spending on health care by 28 percent, with the biggest cuts coming in the area of public investment in the health sector.[88] By 1990 Chile's public health care system had lost many of its best professionals, half of the country's ambulances had broken down, and many public hospitals lacked sheets and bandages.[89] Crucially, however, the military government allocated a greater share of its reduced health care spending to inexpensive programs designed to improve the health of infants, young children, and expectant and new mothers, using a "map of extreme poverty" to target the poorest areas of the country.[90] From 1973 to 1979 the number of midwives rose sharply, as did the numbers of maternity beds and prenatal visits per live birth. The share of births attended by trained personnel also rose.[91] A time-series analysis suggests that trained attendance at birth, maternity bed availability, and the number of prenatal visits contributed heavily to the decline of infant mortality from 1965 to 1979.[92]

The military government complemented its improvement of mother and child health services with an expansion of mother and child nutrition programs, including weighing and monitoring, supplementary feeding, and nutritional rehabilitation for infants and children. The programs were linked: to receive free milk and food, parents had to bring children to a health center for observation.[93] These local facilities gained new staff even as overall spending on health personnel fell by 15 percent. Chile's public health service laid off 300 doctors in the late 1970s, but hired 900 nurses, 700 midwives, and 200 nutritionists.[94] These reforms coincided with a steep drop in infant mortality, from 65 per 1000 in 1974 to 22 per 1000 in 1983.[95]

Although the military government targeted health services to mothers and young children, it neglected other basic health activities. Cases of hepatitis and typhoid multiplied as the number of food inspections by health officials dropped. By 1983 Chile, with only 2 percent of the Western Hemisphere's population, had 25 percent of its typhoid cases.[96] From 1975 to 1985, even as plunging infant mortality generated soaring life expectancy at birth, life expectancy at age one rose only from 70.3 to 71.9, less than half the annual rate for 1965–75.[97] Neglect of health sector investment during the earlier years of the military regime may help to explain why infant mortality fell more slowly from 1985 to 1990 than in previous or subsequent five-year periods (Table 1). Note that percent decline, unlike absolute decline, is insensitive to the baseline level of infant mortality (using the percent decline indicator, a drop from 10 to 9 per 1000 gets exactly as much credit as a drop from 100 to 90 per 1000: 10 percent in each case).[98]

The military government in 1979 replaced both SERMENA (the white-collar health fund) and the funding branch of the SNS (National Health Service) with FONASA, a single National Health Fund whose revenue stream came from general taxes, payroll deductions from blue-collar and white-collar workers, and copayments from middle- and upper-income clients.[99] It thus managed for the first time to unify the public health system, a project that Frei Montalva and Allende had each attempted and abandoned in the face of resistance from white-collar workers and physicians. The military government also increased the role of the private sector in health care financing and delivery. A government decree in 1981 gave persons subject to payroll deductions for health care the option of channeling their contributions not to FONASA, but rather to Instituciones de Salud Previsional (ISAPREs), which operated like health maintenance organizations in the United States.[100] The proportion of Chileans enrolled in an ISAPRE rose from 2 percent in 1983 to 13 percent in 1989 to 27 percent in 1997.[101] The ISAPREs attracted the rich, young, and healthy, whereas FONASA retained the poor, old, and illness-prone. In addition, many ISAPRE members continued to use the public system for some (often expensive) procedures, draining its scarce resources.[102] In 1987 ISAPREs served only 11 percent of Chileans, but collected more than half of mandatory health care contributions and disbursed almost 38 percent of health care spending.[103] The steep decline of infant mortality between 1974 and 1983 cannot be traced, as has been claimed,[104] to such privatization. In 1983 only 2 percent of Chileans, almost all of them rich, belonged to an ISAPRE, and as the ISAPREs gained members, infant mortality decline slowed. If there is a lesson to be learned from the military government's health care policies, it is not to privatize health insurance, but rather to improve the quality and accessibility of publicly funded primary care.

The democratically elected government of Patricio Aylwin (1990–1994) inherited a public health system that worked well for the rich and for impoverished mothers and infants, but not for many others. To change this situation, the government raised public health spending by 75 percent between 1989 and 1994 and increased the number of doctors employed by the public health service from 5,438 in 1989 to 8,704 in 1993.[105] It also doubled the budget for primary health care in disadvantaged urban and rural communities, built new health posts, increased the staff and extended the hours of existing facilities, improved the quality of pre-natal and infant care, launched new programs for pregnant teenagers, and improved school-based nutrition assistance to children.[106] Infant mortality, which had stagnated from 1984 to 1989, began to fall rapidly again, from 17.1 per 1000 in 1989 to 8.9 per 1000 in 2000.[107] Rapid economic growth and poverty decline contributed to the renewed plunge in infant mortality after the transition to democracy, but so did the Concertación government's social welfare policies, particularly in the area of public health.

Political Determinants of Social Policies in Chile

Competition for votes, as well as pressure from unions and other interest groups, were the driving forces behind the creation and expansion of the Chilean welfare state.[108] As of 1960, however, this welfare state had performed poorly at reducing a high level of premature mortality, not least because, before the 1960s, those who ran the highest risk of early death were rarely among those who voted or pressured. Public policies reflected instead the political influence of a loose but powerful urban formal-sector coalition that included the rich, the middle classes, and unionized workers, but not destitute people in urban slums or rural areas.

Chile in 1960 had a union density (union members divided by the total labor force) of 16 percent,[109] which was high for a developing country at the time. Strong unions, along with groups representing the urban middle and upper classes, often induce governments to enact urban and formal sector-biased policies that contribute to the neglect or even to the further impoverishment of the very poor.[110] In Chile, organized labor until the late 1960s was reported to be "virtually the exclusive referent" of leftist political parties. A left party leader called the demands of other popular sector groups a "secondary structural contradiction," and union leaders tended to advocate policies and forge alliances that allowed them to stay in a position of relative privilege.[111] Meanwhile, a large "bottom stratum" at the margin of economic activity had weak organizational ties and little political clout.[112] This distribution of political resources helps to explain why Chilean economic and social policies at the end of the 1950s were biased toward relatively privileged groups.

The strength of the Chilean labor movement reduced the welfare of the very poor by allowing successive governments to undertake the obligatory gestures toward "the people" by attending to the demands of unionized workers, university students, and middle-class groups, while neglecting the interests of less articulate segments of the population, including the very poor and destitute. On the other hand, payroll taxes paid by blue-collar workers financed health facilities and services that poor people used, especially in cities; and the provision of social policies to the urban formal-sector coalition created a more congenial environment for the evolution of a belief that the state had an obligation to guarantee a minimum level of well-being to all citizens. Union pressure for social welfare benefits thus helped to expand and normalize the involvement of the state in social welfare activities. Whether this impetus toward the expansion of welfare benefits would overcome countervailing factors (lack of funds, antipathy to "socialism," etc.) depended in part on whether parties and politicians had incentives to court the votes of the poor and destitute.

Although Chile held regular and competitive elections from 1931 to 1973, the political regime was not fully democratic. Women received the vote only in 1949; the Communist Party was banned from elections from 1948 to 1958 (although it participated in electoral fronts with the Socialists in the presidential elections of 1952 and 1958); no secret ballot existed in the countryside until 1958; and voting was restricted by a literacy clause until 1970 (Allende was elected while the literacy clause was still in effect). The absence of a secret ballot in rural areas was particularly critical to shaping public policy. Before 1958, each party in Chile printed its own ballot. To vote, a citizen obtained a ballot from a local party representative and cast it at a place close to the voter's residence. This system permitted some anonymity in cities, but in rural areas it enabled landlords to coerce or cajole many of the poor into voting for the candidates that powerful local notables preferred.[113] This system began to break down in 1957, when a Christian Democratic Party was formed. The next year, the Communist Party was legalized and the Australian ballot (a uniform ballot printed and distributed by the government) was introduced in the countryside. These reforms intensified competition among right, center, and left parties, encouraging each to try to attract new or previously "captive" rural voters. The Christian Democrats appealed particularly to sharecroppers and tenant farmers, while the Socialists and Communists courted landless laborers and shanty-town inhabitants. Voter mobilization by the Christian Democratic Party, whose Catholic roots helped its doctrines and militants unravel the clientelist networks that bound the rural poor to conservative politicians, helped its candidate, Eduardo Frei Montalva, win the presidency in 1964.

Party competition among Christian Democrats, Socialists, and Communists gave politicians incentives to appeal to previously excluded groups, a process that intensified during the Allende presidency (1970–1973). The resulting "hypermobilization" of the population increased problems of governance,[114] but contributed to the extension of social services to previously excluded groups. During the 1970 presidential campaign, for example, each of the three major candidates courted votes by promising to expand nutrition programs. The winner, Salvador Allende, implemented a program to distribute a half-liter of milk per day to expectant and nursing mothers and to every child under fifteen (up from the previous age limit of six). A survey after the municipal elections of April 1971 revealed that this initiative was Allende's single most popular program.[115]

After the 1973 coup, the military government expanded Chile's health care, nutrition, safe water, and sanitation policies in poor areas, contributing heavily to the 70 percent decline of infant mortality from 1974 to 1983. The expansion of such services presents a puzzle. As Dréze and Sen note, "General Pinochet does not have a reputation of being a soft-hearted do-gooder." Government agents killed or "disappeared" more than 2000 people from 1973 to 1990, and top policy makers espoused until the mid-1980s a rigidly free-market ideology that stressed a minimal role for the state in the economy and in society. These observations raise "the intriguing question of why a government that had no hesitation in resorting to the most brutal political repression to protect the privileges of the dominant classes was so interested in looking after child health and extreme poverty."[116]

A review of available evidence provides at least five answers to Dréze and Sen's question, focusing respectively on international reputation, protest deterrence, state paternalism, market failure, and technocratic leadership. The international reputation and protest deterrence explanations imply that top government policy makers had no special desire to improve child health or to reduce extreme poverty, but enacted policies dedicated to these goals for instrumental reasons, either to improve the regime's reputation in the international community, or to defuse potential domestic protest. The state paternalism, market failure, and technocratic leadership explanations imply that at least some policy makers in the military government sincerely wished to improve child health and reduce extreme poverty, and were successful in designing and implementing policies conducive to these goals. The two broad lines of interpretation are not incompatible. That many people serving the military regime were involved in torture and murder does not preclude the possibility that others (or even, conceivably, some of the torturers and murderers) may have been sincerely committed to improving child health and reducing extreme poverty. Even those who did not share such a commitment may have supported policies beneficial to the poor on the grounds that such policies could deter protest or improve the government's international reputation.

Some observers believe that the military government's mother and child health policies were designed in part to win support (or reduce hostility) from foreigners. Collins and Lear observed that "at international conferences, where Pinochet's human rights record invariably came under attack, defensive Chilean officials would boast of Chile's falling infant mortality rate (IMR), which since the 1970s had become internationally recognized as a key indicator of socially positive economic development." Valdés argued that "the reason for the focus on mothers and children is clear: [infant mortality is] . . . considered internationally to be an indicator of development. It was . . . an indicator that would show how to evaluate the Pinochet government."[117]

Others stress the role of protest deterrence in motivating the government's mother and child health care policies. Drèze and Sen argue that the policies may be viewed in certain respects as "a strategy for checking popular discontent at a time of political repression, economic instability, and diminished general social provisioning . . . the expansion of targeted nutrition and health programmes [has a] populist ring in a country where popular expectations of public provisioning are very high . . . We cannot but observe the part that political pressure and a search for a popular mandate may play even in a country with an authoritarian political atmosphere," especially in a country with "a long tradition of democratic and pluralist politics."[118] Taucher concurs that one of the reasons why the military government maintained effective mother and child health care policies was that "people had already learned that they had a right to health."[119] Raczynski observes that Chilean mothers before the 1973 coup had built up a "belief in their entitlement to well-baby check-ups and supplementary feeding," and notes that protest from mothers helped to scuttle a 1985 plan to substitute rice for milk as a nutritional supplement.[120] Chile's long history of competitive elections and civil liberties, in this interpretation, along with the expectations generated by decades of welfare-state policies enacted partly in response to electoral competition and interest group pressure, were partly responsible for the military government's health care policies benefiting mothers and children. A variant on this interpretation would be to view these policies as a "payoff" to the poor: an attempt to deflect criticism about the main health care objectives of the government, which were to privatize health insurance and strengthen the role of the private sector in health service delivery.

The other broad line of interpretation holds that Pinochet and his allies improved maternal and child health care not for instrumental reasons, but because of a conviction that such improvement was just and appropriate. One variant of this interpretation focuses on state paternalism. In this perspective, the government improved maternal and child health care because its leaders regarded women and their children as helpless and in need of charity. Authoritarian leaders often endorse such views. Italian Fascists, for example, proclaimed that "women were to be wives, mothers, and nurturers," and in 1925 created the National Organization for the Protection of Motherhood and Infancy to improve maternal and child health care, especially in rural areas.[121] In 1974, General Pinochet stated that "a woman should become a mother and expect nothing of the material world; she should seek and discover in her child the culmination of her life, her single treasure, and the goal of all her dreams." According to Molina, "the government exalted the need to protect mothers" and "promoted the image of Pinochet as a stern father, as a protector and a provider. This made sense to many women in terms of their own life experiences, in which these attributes were viewed as the characteristics that a good father should display in the household. It was the most conservative expression of the model of the traditional patriarchal family."[122]

The market failure interpretation focuses not on a paternalistic obligation to help the weak, but on the benefits that such aid may bring to the task of promoting economic growth by making markets more efficient. Top government policy makers during the Pinochet era embraced the idea of a "subsidiary state" that would "assume only those duties that individuals or intermediate bodies are incapable of carrying out."[123] According to a 1979 National Planning Office document, these duties comprised only "national security, the administration of justice, and the implementation of social policy in favor of the most defenseless (*desvalidos*)."[124] Another government document advocated providing nutritional supplements to malnourished mothers and children because their hunger impeded the "socio-economic development possibilities of the country."[125]

The "committed technocrat" interpretation, like the "market failure" and "state paternalism" views, accepts that government policy makers were sincerely interested in helping the poorest, and focuses on the dedication and efficacy of a small group of government planners in charge of maternal and child health care. Central to this interpretation is Miguel Kast, a Chicago-trained economist who returned to Chile in 1974 to work in the National Planning Office. Kast headed the team that created the "Map of Extreme Poverty" by which the government targeted health, nutrition, education, and other social policies to the poorest Chileans.[126] According to his biographer, Joaquín Lavín—a conservative politician who narrowly lost the 2000 presidential election to the Socialist Ricardo Lagos—Kast took a special interest in poverty because of "the difficult years his family had spent after arriving in Chile." Kast's father, an officer in the German Army who had risen through the ranks during the Nazi era, surrendered to U.S. troops in April 1945, but escaped from custody and made his way back to his home town. Shortly after Miguel Kast's birth in 1948, his parents, "like many other families in post-war Germany, decided to seek out new opportunities in America." The Kast family lived on a small farm outside Santiago in a mud house without electricity or running water, where they grew crops and raised chickens. During this era Miguel Kast not only experienced poverty, but also "developed strong anti-communist feelings," after hearing stories from his father about "what had happened in Germany after the [Soviet] communists came to power . . . how they took away basic freedoms."[127]

Kast was attracted to Christian Democracy while studying economics at the Universidad Católica, but the dalliance ended with Frei's agrarian reform, which he opposed. After spending the Allende years at the University of Chicago on a Ford Foundation fellowship earning a master's degree in economics, Kast joined the National Planning Office a few months after the September 1973 coup. A "mystical Catholic who saw his work as a moral mission—and would stop at nothing to achieve it," Kast soon earned a reputation as persuasive, relentless, and hard-working. One of his collaborators noted a "strong sense of teamwork" at the agency, and another reported that "we became part of a crusade to build a modern, efficient economy to combat poverty . . . to us, it was a revolution. We had terrible salaries, but a great deal of mystique."[128] In April 1975 Kast became Deputy Director of the National Planning Office, a post that allowed him to meet regularly with General Pinochet, with whom he often spoke about social policies. He received the Directorship, a post with ministerial status, in 1978, and later served as Labor Minister and as president of the Central Bank before dying of cancer in 1983.[129]

More historical research is needed to weigh the various explanations for the expansion of maternal and infant health care during the military regime, and to incorporate other factors as well. The goal here is less to pit the explanations against one another—each provides a plausible account, and none seems inconsistent with any of the others—than to inventory possible motives for the military government's mother and child health care policies. Some of the explanations, especially the one focusing on protest deterrence, suggest ways in which Chile's long history of democracy may have affected policy making even during the military regime. Democracy may also have influenced the utilization of the services provided (the "demand side") in ways that reduced infant mortality.

The military government in 1980 changed the constitution to allow it to name nine of Chile's 38 senators. Just before exiting in 1990, it juggled electoral districts to over-represent conservative rural areas and created a two-seat-per-district electoral system for the lower house in which a minority party (presumably of the right in most districts) could win one of the seats with as little as 33 percent of the vote.[130] These amendments made the legislative right strong enough during the 1990s to block efforts to repeal them. The resulting sclerosis constrained social policies after 1990, but the economy continued to grow, the government channeled resources to social services in poor areas, and infant mortality began to fall steeply again after stagnating in the late 1980s.

The abolition of the literacy clause in 1970 and the weakening of unions under military rule made it easier for Concertación governments to favor the very poor without jeopardizing their re-election chances or risking massive protest from the not-so-poor. In 1998, taking into account both financing and expenditure, the poorest fifth of the Chilean population received 56 percent of public health spending; the next-poorest fifth received 30 percent; and the richest fifth paid a net subsidy, "receiving" –9 percent. Public education spending was also progressive: the poorest fifth received 35 percent; the next-poorest fifth received 26 percent, and the richest fifth received 6 percent.[131] As Ruiz-Tagle argues, "the return of democracy allowed for implementation of social policies clearly favourable to the lower income sectors, who were an important segment of the voting population which all parties wanted to attract to their ranks."[132] Good leadership in the social policy area, learning from past mistakes, and views prevailing in international agencies like the United Nations Development Programme, the World Bank, and the World Health Organization, also encouraged the Concertación governments to enact policies that helped the very poor as well as the not-so-poor.

Conclusion

What, then, does Chile tell us about how political democracy affects basic health care policies, and about how basic health care policies affect mortality decline? The years of military rule show that inexpensive public health care, nutrition, water, and sanitation programs can produce a steep decline in infant mortality. To design and implement these programs, however, the military government drew on infrastructure, expertise, and expectations that had emerged in the context of a welfare state encompassing an ever-widening share of the population.[133] Electoral competition and interest group activity contributed to the emergence of this welfare state, which popularized the idea that people have a right to social services. From 1964 to 1970 under Frei Montalva, and from 1970 to 1973 under Allende, adversarial politics and the mobilization of excluded groups in urban slums and rural areas helped to extend welfare state programs to the very poor.

The expectations generated by long experience with a welfare state and with a democratic or proto-democratic regime meant that the military had to use harsh repression to silence political parties and labor unions and to withdraw high wages, severance pay, retirement pensions, and other benefits from blue- and white-collar formal-sector workers. Maternal and infant health care and nutrition services thrived during the military regime, however, in part because they were much less expensive than most traditional welfare state benefits, and in part because the paternalism of the military leaders and their civilian allies made it harder for them to withdraw life-preserving services from mothers and children than to slash the wages, benefits, and job security of a largely adult male formal-sector labor force. Moreover, decades of democratic or proto-democratic experience not only generated expectations that militated against the withdrawal of social services, but also helped to produce the expertise and infrastructure on which these services drew, and increased the propensity of impoverished households to utilize services that survived the cutbacks. Even under Pinochet, then, Chile's democratic experience helped in various ways to reduce infant mortality.

Although Chile's authoritarian government (1973–1990) implemented public maternal and infant health care and nutrition policies that contributed to a rapid decline of infant mortality, it would be unwise to conclude from this experience that authoritarianism systematically encourages social policies that reduce the risk of infant death. Infant mortality, which fell rapidly during the first ten years of the military regime, fell slowly during the next five years; and even during the first ten years of military rule the pace of infant mortality decline was not radically faster than during the competitive political regimes of 1960–1973 and 1990–2006. Furthermore, life expectancy at age one, an indicator that reflects mortality in all age groups except infants, rose more slowly under military rule than during the elected Frei Montalva and Allende administrations. Moreover, to design and implement their maternal and infant health care and nutrition policies, technocrats in the military regime's Planning Office operated with human and physical resources and popular expectations inherited from the previous democratic era. Such expectations affected not only the provision of basic social services, but also their utilization. No strident demands by destitute rural people or shantytown inhabitants wrested pro-poor social policies out of the military regime, but expectations that the state would intervene to help the very poor meet basic needs exerted a quiet and steady pressure on government technocrats whose own worldviews had been shaped in part by democratization and social mobilization from 1958 to 1973. Combined with state paternalism, the goal of making markets more efficient, and the hope of improving the military regime's international reputation, popular expectations and technocratic worldviews originating in more democratic times shaped and constrained the military regime's maternal and infant care policies. Chile thus provides evidence to support, as well as to question, the claim that democracy on balance is conducive to social policies that reduce infant mortality.

Notes

* An earlier version of this paper was presented at the conference on "Living Standards in Latin American History," David Rockefeller Center for Latin American Studies, Harvard University, April 8–9, 2005. It was revised in January 2006 response to suggestions from the editors, commentator, and other conference participants. Additional revisions were made March 2009. The chapter overlaps with Chapter 4 of my *Wealth, Health, and Democracy in East Asia and Latin America* (New York: Cambridge University Press, 2010). The American Council of Learned Societies, the Harvard Center for Population and Development Studies, and the Woodrow Wilson International Center for Scholars provided generous support for this research. I am grateful to Lily Oster for research assistance, and to the editors of the volume and the participants in the conference for suggestions that improved the chapter. I am responsible for any errors of fact or interpretation.

1. Infant mortality from Hill et al., *Trends in Child Mortality*; life expectancy from World Bank, *World Development Indicators 2002*.
2. McGuire and Frankel, "Mortality Decline in Cuba," 85.
3. Chile figure from PAHO, *Health Situation*; USA figure from United States, *Statistical Abstract*, 64.
4. Data from Hill et al., *Trends in Child Mortality*.
5. Filmer and Pritchett, "The Impact of Public Spending"; Pritchett and Summers, "Wealthier is Healthier."
6. Gallegos Ulloa et al., "Mortalidad infantil en Chile"; Hill et al., *Trends in Child Mortality*, 56, 66; Raczynski, "Social Policies," 33; Taucher, "Mortalidad infantil en Chile," 3–5.
7. Hojman, *Chile*, 208 n. 9; Raczynski and Oyarzo, "¿Por que cae la tasa?" 70; Taucher, Albala, and Icaza, "Adult Mortality," 255; Taucher and Jofré, "Mortalidad infantil en Chile," 1226–1227. On the underreporting of infant, especially neonatal, deaths, see Chile. INE, *Anuario de Estadísticas Vitales 2000*, 26; De Kadt, "Aspectos distributivos," 149; and Mamalakis, *Historical Statistics of Chile*, 45.
8. Hill et al., *Trends in Child Mortality*, 56–57.
9. Data from World Bank, *World Development Indicators*, 2002.
10. Mamalakis, *Historical Statistics of Chile*, 40–41.
11. From 1964 to 1973 maternal mortality fell from 238 to 123 per 100,000 live births, while life expectancy at age 1 rose from 66.0 to 69.3 years. Chile. Banco Central, *Indicadores*, 405, 424.
12. Chile: Chile. INE, *Anuario de Estadísticas*, 53; USA: United States, *Statistical Abstract*, 64.
13. Comparative data from Heston, Summers, and Aten, *Penn World Table Version 6.1*. All figures in 1996 international dollars at parity purchasing power according to a chain index.
14. Cardoso and Helwege, "Import Substitution Industrialization"; Johnson, "Problems of Import Substitution." From 1960 to 1973 Chile increased its dependence

on copper, which rose from 68 to 78 percent of export revenue. Meller, "El cobre chileno," 17.

15. Cardoso and Helwege, "Populism," 52–54; Stallings, *Class Conflict*, 125–153. Fiscal deficit figure for 1973 from Paus, "Economic Growth," 37; inflation figures from Programa de Economía del Trabajo, *Series de indicadores*, 37.

16. Chile. CNVR, *Report of the Chilean National Commission*. Disappearance figure from Appendix II.

17. Constable and Valenzuela, *Nation of Enemies*, 166–246; Jarvis, *Chilean Agriculture*, 5, 26.

18. Roddick, *Dance of the Millions*.

19. Graham, *Safety Nets*, 33–42.

20. Silva, *State and Capital in Chile*, Chapters 5 and 7.

21. Mesa-Lago, *Market, Socialist, and Mixed Economies*, 87. The finance ministry reduced import tariffs to 15 percent in 1987.

22. GDP per capita from Heston, Summers, and Aten, *Penn World Table Version 6.1*, variable RGDPCH.

23. Weyland, "Growth with Equity"; Weyland, "Economic Policy."

24. IADB, "Chile: Basic Socio-Economic Data."

25. Eibner and Evans, "Relative Deprivation"; Kennedy, Kawachi, and Prothrow-Stith, "Income Distribution and Mortality"; Wilkinson, *Mind the Gap*.

26. Income inequality data from Deininger and Squire, "A New Data Set," 574–577.

27. Larrañaga, "Distribución de ingresos," 305; Marcel and Solimano, "Distribution of Income," 219. Later data for the country as a whole are taken from Table 2.

28. Comparative data from UNDP, *Human Development Report 2002*.

29. MacEwan, *Neoliberalism or Democracy?* 149–150.

30. Altimir, "Long-Term Trends," 138; Borzutzky, *Vital Connections*, 110–111.

31. Residuals from Model 2-2, Table 2, in McGuire, *Wealth, Health, and Democracy*, 44–45.

32. Infant mortality and GDP per capita from the sources cited in Tables 1 and 2.

33. Caldwell, "Routes to Low Mortality," 187–191; Hill and King, "Women's Education"; Schultz, "Returns to Women's Education," 68–78; Subbarao and Raney, "Social Gains."

34. Caldwell and Caldwell, "Women's Position"; Mellington and Cameron, "Female Education," 217.

35. Mosley and Chen, "Analytical Framework," 34–35; Murthi, Guio, and Drèze, "Mortality, Fertility, and Gender Bias."

36. Data from World Bank, *World Development Indicators 2002*.

37. Collier, "From Independence," 25–26; Gauri, *School Choice*, 15.

38. Astorga and Fitzgerald, "Standards of Living," 32.

39. Molina Silva, *El proceso de cambio*, 88.

40. Raczynski, "Social Policies," 41.

41. Gauri, *School Choice*, 76–77, 103.

42. Gauri, *School Choice*, 84–89; Ruiz-Tagle, "Balancing," 354–355.

43. Martin, "Integration and Development," 322–327; Mena and Belleï, "The New Challenge"; Nash, "Chile Advances"; Raczynski, "Social Policies," 102–103.
44. Gauri, *School Choice*, 53.
45. Fogel, *Escape from Hunger*, 44–46; Harris, *Public Health*; McKeown, *The Modern Rise of Population*.
46. FAO, "State of Food Insecurity"; Wilkie, Alemán, and Ortega, *Statistical Abstract*, 200.
47. Monckeberg, *Prevención de la desnutrición*, Table 2.
48. Hakim and Solimano, *Development, Reform and Malnutrition*, 6–12, 37–40, 51–52; Wilkie, Alemán, and Ortega, *Statistical Abstract*, 200
49. Castañeda, *Combating Poverty*, 71; Foxley and Raczynski, "Vulnerable Groups," 238–239; Hakim and Solimano, *Development, Reform and Malnutrition*, 40.
50. Hakim and Solimano, *Development, Reform and Malnutrition*, 40.
51. Castañeda, *Combating Poverty*, 70–79; Foxley and Raczynski, "Vulnerable Groups," 238–239; Raczynski and Oyarzo, "¿Por que cae la tasa?" 60–66.
52. Raczynski, "Social Policies," 101.
53. Ruiz-Tagle, "Balancing," 347.
54. Bongaarts, "Does Family Planning Reduce Infant Mortality Rates?" On first births in Chile see Raczynski and Oyarzo "¿Por que cae la tasa?," 72, and Taucher, "Impact of Fertility Decline," 296–297.
55. Graham and Campbell, "Maternal Health."
56. World Bank, *World Development Indicators 2001*.
57. Taucher, "Impact of Fertility Decline," 289.
58. Romero, "Planificación familiar"; Viel and Campos, "Historia Chilena."
59. Gall, "Births"; Livingstone and Raczynski, "Análisis cuantitativo," 31 n.1.
60. Taucher, "Impact of Fertility Decline," 289.
61. FRS/RSMLAC, "Atención Humanizada," 24. Maternal deaths per 100,000 live births. The actual figure is probably higher than vital registration statistics suggest.
62. Comparative data from Ross and Mauldin, "Family Planning Programs," 146.
63. Hojman, "Neoliberal Economic Policies," 94, 103; Taucher and Jofre, "Mortalidad infantil," 1230.
64. Foxley and Raczynski, "Vulnerable Groups," 233; Taucher and Jofré, "Mortalidad infantil," 1229.
65. Chile. INE, *Anuario*, 53.
66. Castañeda, "Contexto socioeconomico," 109; Giaconi, Montesinos, and Schalchli, "Rural Health Care," 74.
67. Castañeda, "Contexto socioeconómico," 61, 64.
68. Raczynski, "Social Policies," 81.
69. Safe water figures from WHO/UNICEF, "Access to Improved Drinking Water Sources"; sanitation figures from Table 3 (for 1990) and PAHO, *Health Situation* (for 2002).
70. Borzutzky, *Vital Connections*, 48–49, 61–63; Mesa-Lago, *Social Security,* 25–26; Raczynski, "Social Policies," 29.

71. Raczynski, "Social Policies," 7, 28–29; Rodríguez, "Estructura y características," 66.

72. Borzutzky, *Vital Connections*, 61–62; Rodríguez, "Estructura y características," 68.

73. Cabello, "Demography of Chile," 245; Hakim and Solimano, *Development, Reform and Malnutrition*, 12; Raczynski, "Social Policies," 7, 29; Rodríguez, "Estructura y características," 68.

74. Borzutzky, *Vital Connections*, 63, 104–105; Hakim and Solimano, *Development, Reform and Malnutrition*, 28–29; Mesa-Lago, *Social Security*, 27; Raczynski, "Social Policies," 30.

75. Mamalakis, *Historical Statistics*, 40–41.

76. First quotation from Taucher, "Mortalidad infantil," 1–2; second from Hakim and Solimano, *Development, Reform and Malnutrition*, 34.

77. See Taucher ("Mortalidad infantil," 1–2) on the contribution of economic stagnation. The figure for agricultural workers is from Mesa-Lago (*Social Security*, 45). Obstacles to agricultural workers receiving medical care are discussed in Borzutzky, *Vital Connections*, 51–55.

78. Borzutzky, *Vital Connections*, 104.

79. Ascher, *Scheming*, 125.

80. Alexander, *Tragedy of Chile*, 116–117.

81. Livingstone and Raczynski, "Análisis cuantitativo," 9, 11, 12, 43.

82. Borzutzky, *Vital Connections*, 81–87; Mesa-Lago, *Social Security*, 29.

83. Navarro, "What Does Chile Mean?" 107.

84. Chile. Banco Central, *Indicadores*, 424, 428.

85. Borzutzky, *Vital Connections*, 143.

86. Stover, *Open Secret*, 38–41.

87. Ibid., 42–51.

88. Foxley and Raczynski, "Vulnerable Groups," 229; Raczynski, "Social Policies," 71.

89. Collins and Lear, *Chile's Free-Market Miracle*, 101–104; Oppenheim, *Politics in Chile*, 262; Raczynski, "Social Policies," 101; Weyland, "'Growth with Equity,'" 44.

90. Chile. ODEPLAN, *Mapa extrema pobreza*; Constable and Valenzuela, *Nation of Enemies*, 230–231; Foxley and Raczynski, "Vulnerable Groups."

91. Chile: Banco Central, *Indicadores*, 422–424.

92. Raczynski and Oyarzo, "¿Por que cae la tasa?" 58–60.

93. Foxley and Raczynski, "Vulnerable Groups," 235–236.

94. Scarpaci, "Restructuring," 426.

95. From vital registration figures according to the sources cited in Table 1, note 2.

96. Scarpaci, "Restructuring," 427.

97. Chile. Banco Central, *Indicadores*, 405.

98. McGuire and Frankel, "Mortality Decline in Cuba," 85–86.

99. González Rossetti, Chuaqui, and Espinosa, *Enhancing the Political Feasibility*, 36; Mesa-Lago, *Market, Socialist, and Mixed Economies*, 56.

100. Barrientos, "Getting Better after Neoliberalism."

101. Barrientos, "Health Policy in Chile," 447; Miranda, Scarpaci, and Irarrázaval, "A Decade of HMOs," 54.

102. Barrientos, "Getting Better after Neoliberalism,"103; Barrientos, "Health Policy in Chile," 452–453; Raczynski, "Social Policies," 101; Ruiz-Tagle, "Balancing," 349; Titelman, "Reformas," 273.

103. Raczynski, "Social Policies," 69.

104. Cifuentes, "Sector Salud," 88.

105. Ruiz-Tagle, "Balancing," 348.

106. Raczynski, "Social Policies," 100, 103; Weyland, "Growth with Equity," 45.

107. Based on vital registration. Chile. INE, *Anuario*, 53.

108. Arellano, "Social Policies" and *Políticas sociales*; Mesa-Lago, *Social Security*, 30–33; Raczynski, "Overcoming Poverty," 120–121.

109. Calculated from Programa de Economía del Trabajo, *Series de indicadores*, 52 (union members in 1960); Goldenberg, *Los sindicatos*, 127 (public sector employees in quasi-union organizations in 1960), and ILO, *Laborista Database* (labor force in 1960).

110. McGuire, "Labor Union Strength."

111. Oxhorn, *Organizing Civil Society*, 48–49.

112. Ascher, *Scheming*, 34.

113. Bauer, *Chilean Rural Society*, 223; Loveman, *Chile*, 293–294; Robinson and Baland, "Land and Power," 19–32; Scully, "Reconstituting Party Politics," 116–117.

114. Landsberger and McDaniel, "Hypermobilization in Chile."

115. Hakim and Solimano, *Development, Reform and Malnutrition*, 39–40.

116. Drèze and Sen, *Hunger and Public Action*, 230, 238.

117. Collins and Lear, *Chile's Free-Market Miracle*, 93; Teresa Valdés, interview with L. Oster, a research associate of the author, Santiago, Chile, June 27, 2002.

118. Drèze and Sen, *Hunger and Public Action*, 238.

119. Erica Taucher, interview with L. Oster, a research associate of the author, Santiago, Chile, June 10, 2002.

120. Raczynski, *Social Policy and Economic Change*, 35 (quotation); Raczynski, *Social Policies*, 80 n. 75.

121. Ipsen, *Dictating Demography*, 146, 150, 165–173.

122. Molina, "Propuestas políticas," 63 (Pinochet quote), 66.

123. Vergara, *Políticas hacia la extrema pobreza*, 37.

124. Quoted in Raczynski, "Reformas al sector salud," 6.

125. Chile. ODEPLAN, *Social Development Experiment*, 66.

126. Chile. ODEPLAN, *Mapa extrema pobreza*.

127. Lavín, *Miguel Kast*, quotations respectively from pp. 47, 9, 25. Lavín did not call attention to the irony of a Nazi officer complaining that the Soviets "took away basic freedoms."

128. Quotations respectively from Constable and Valenzuela, *A Nation of Enemies*, 187; Cecilia Milevcic, Executive Director, Fundación Miguel Kast, interview

with L. Oster, a research associate of the author, Santiago, Chile, May 2, 2002; and Cristián Larroulet, quoted in Constable and Valenzuela, *Nation of Enemies*, 187.

129. Lavín, *Miguel Kast*, 53.

130. Constable and Valenzuela, *Nation of Enemies*, 1991: 313–316.

131. Chile. MIDEPLAN, "Indicadores económicos y sociales."

132. Ruiz-Tagle, "Balancing," 342–343.

133. "The success of the health and nutritional intervention programs [under military rule] rested in great measure on the structure and coverage that Chile's public health sector had achieved in the past." Raczynski, *Social Policies*, 80.

References

Alexander, Robert J. *The Tragedy of Chile*. Westport: Greenwood Press, 1978.

Altimir, Oscar. "Long-Term Trends of Poverty in Latin American Countries." *Estudios de Economía* 28, no. 1 (June 2001): 115–155.

Arellano, José-Pablo. "Social Policies in Chile: An Historical Review." *Journal of Latin American Studies* 17, part 2 (May 1985): 397–418.

———. *Políticas sociales y desarrollo: Chile 1924–1984*. Santiago: CIEPLAN [Corporación de Investigaciones Económicas para Latinoamérica], 1985.

Ascher, William. *Scheming for the Poor: The Politics of Redistribution in Latin America*. Cambridge, MA: Harvard University Press, 1984.

Astorga, Pablo, and Valpy FitzGerald. "The Standard of Living in Latin America during the Twentieth Century." Centro Studi Luca D'Agliano – Queen Elizabeth House Development Studies Working Paper No. 117 (1998), St. Antony's College, University of Oxford.

Barrientos, Armando. "Getting Better after Neoliberalism: Shifts and Challenges of Health Policy in Chile." In *Healthcare Reform in Latin America*, ed. Peter Lloyd-Sherlock, 94–111. London: Institute of Latin American Studies, University of London, 1984.

Barrientos, Armando. "Health Policy in Chile: The Return of the Public Sector?" *Bulletin of Latin American Research* 21, no. 3 (July 2002): 442–459.

Barro, Robert J., and Jong-Wha Lee. "International Data on Educational Attainment: Updates and Implications." Working Paper No. 42, Center for International Development, Harvard University (April 2000). Appendix. Data Table. Accessed June 20, 2001, at http://www2.cid.harvard.edu/ciddata /barrolee/panel_data.xls

Bauer, Arnold J. *Chilean Rural Society: From the Spanish Conquest to 1930*. Cambridge: Cambridge University Press, 1975.

Bongaarts, John. "Does Family Planning Reduce Infant Mortality Rates?" *Population and Development Review* 13, no. 2 (June 1987): 323–334.

Borzutzky, Silvia. *Vital Connections: Politics, Social Security, and Inequality in Chile*. Notre Dame: University of Notre Dame Press, 2002.

Cabello, Octavio. "The Demography of Chile." *Population Studies* 9, no. 3 (March 1956): 237–250.

Caldwell, John C. "Routes to Low Mortality in Poor Countries." *Population and Development Review* 12, no. 2 (June 1986): 171–220.

Caldwell, John, and Pat Caldwell. "Women's Position and Child Mortality and Morbidity in Less Developed Countries." In *Women's Position and Demographic Change*, ed. Nora Federici, Karen Oppenheim Mason, and Sølvi Sogner. New York: Oxford University Press, 1993.

Cardoso, Eliana, and Ann Helwege. "Populism, Profligacy, and Redistribution." In *The Macroeconomics of Populism in Latin America*, ed. Rudiger Dornbusch and Sebastian Edwards, 45–70. Chicago: University of Chicago Press, 1994.

———. "Import Substitution Industrialization." In *Modern Political Economy and Latin America*, ed. Jeffry Frieden, Manuel Pastor Jr., and Michael Tomz, 155–164. Boulder: Westview Press, 2000.

Castañeda, Tarsicio. "Contexto socioeconómico y causas del descenso de la mortalidad infantil en Chile." Documento de Trabajo No. 38 (July 1984). Santiago: Centro de Estudios Económicos.

———. *Combating Poverty: Innovative Social Reforms in Chile during the 1980s.* San Francisco: International Center for Economic Growth, 1992.

Chile. Banco Central. *Indicadores económicos y sociales.* Santiago: Banco Central de Chile, 1989.

Chile. CNVR [Comisión Nacional de Verdad y Reconciliación]. *Report of the Chilean National Commission on Truth and Reconciliation.* Notre Dame: University of Notre Dame Press, 1993.

Chile. INE [Instituto Nacional de Estadísticas]. *Compendio Estadístico 2001.* Santiago: Instituto Nacional de Estadísticas, 2001. Accessed July 1, 2003, at http://www.ine.cl/20–compendio/i-compendio.htm

———. *Anuario de Estadísticas Vitales 2000.* Santiago: Instituto Nacional de Estadísticas, 2002.

Chile. MIDEPLAN [Ministerio de Planificación y Cooperación]. "Indicadores económicos y sociales 1990–2000: Gasto social." Santiago: MIDEPLAN, 2003. Accessed July 7, 2003, at http://www.mideplan.cl/sitio/Sitio/indicadores /htm/indicadores_gastos.htm

Chile. ODEPLAN [Oficina de Planificación Nacional]. *Mapa extrema pobreza.* Santiago: ODEPLAN, 1975.

———. *A Social Development Experiment in Chile: Report.* Prepared by the Chilean National Planning Office to be presented to the United Nations General Secretariat. Santiago: ODEPLAN, 1977

———. *Evolución de la salud en Chile.* Santiago: ODEPLAN, 1988.

Cifuentes C., Mercedes. "Sector Salud." In *Soluciones privadas a problemas públicos*, ed. Cristián Larroulet, 51–91. Santiago: Libertad y Desarrollo, 1991.

Collier, Simon. "From Independence to the War of the Pacific." In *Chile since Independence*, ed. Leslie Bethell, 1–31. New York: Cambridge University Press, 1993.

Collins, Joseph, and John Lear. *Chile's Free-Market Miracle: A Second Look.* Oakland: Institute for Food and Development Policy, 1995.

Constable, Pamela, and Arturo Valenzuela. *A Nation of Enemies: Chile under Pinochet*. New York: W. W. Norton, 1991.

De Kadt, Emanuel. "Aspectos distributivos de la salud en Chile." CEPLAN, with contributions by Emanuel de Kadt et al., *Bienestar y pobreza*. Santiago de Chile: Ediciones Nueva Universidad, Universidad Católica de Chile, Vicerrectoria de Comunicaciones, 1974.

Deininger, Klaus, and Lyn Squire. "A New Data Set Measuring Income Inequality." *World Bank Economic Review* 10, no. 3 (September 1996): 565–591.

———. "Measuring Income Inequality: A New Database." Washington, D.C.: World Bank, Policy Research Department, 1998. Accessed May 8, 2001, at http://www.worldbank.org/research/growth/deisqu2.zip

Drèze, Jean, and Amartya K. Sen. *Hunger and Public Action*. Oxford: Clarendon Press, 1989.

Eibner, Christine, and William N. Evans. "Relative Deprivation, Poor Health Habits, and Mortality." *Journal of Human Resources* 40, no. 3 (Summer 2005): 591–620.

FAO [Food and Agriculture Organization]. *The State of Food Insecurity in the World 2000*. Rome: FAO, 2000. Accessed June 28, 2001, at http://www.fao.org/docrep/x8200e/x8200e00.htm.

Filmer, Deon, and Lant Pritchett. "The Impact of Public Spending on Health: Does Money Matter?" *Social Science and Medicine* 49, no. 10 (November 1999): 1309–1323.

Fogel, Robert William. *The Escape from Hunger and Premature Death, 1700–2100: Europe, America, and the Third World*. Cambridge: Cambridge University Press, 2004.

Foxley, Alejandro, and Dagmar Raczynski. "Vulnerable Groups in Recessionary Situations: The Case of Children and the Young in Chile." *World Development* 12, no. 3 (March 1984): 223–246.

FRS/RSMLAC [Foro-Red de Salud y Derechos Sexuales y Reproductivos-Chile/Red de Salud de las Mujeres Latinoamericanas y del Caribe]. "Atención Humanizada del Aborto Inseguro en Chile." Santiago de Chile: Foro-Red de Salud/RSMLAC, 2003. Accessed January 8, 2006, at http://www.forosalud.cl/forosalud/revista/uploaded/atencion_%20humanizada.htm

Gall, Norman. "Births, Abortions and the Progress of Chile." *American Universities Field Staff Reports*, West Coast South America Series 19 No. 2 (1972). Accessed July 5, 2003, at http://www.normangall.com/chile_art1.htm

Gallegos Ulloa, Doris, María Luisa Garmendi Miguel, Carla Marina Paredes Reyes, and Manuel Suzarte Vilches. "Mortalidad infantil en Chile según algunos diferenciales en los trienios 1987–1989 y 1993–1995." Programa de Magister en Salud Pública, Escuela de Salud Pública, Universidad de Chile, 1997. Accessed July 27, 2000, at http://www.chilemed.cl/xxi/articulos/may99 and http://www.chilemed.cl/xxi/articulos/jun99

Gauri, Varun. *School Choice in Chile: Two Decades of Educational Reform*. Pittsburgh: University of Pittsburgh Press, 1998.

Giaconi Gandolfo, Juan, Nestor Montesinos Belmar, and Adriana Schalchli Villalobos. "Rural Health Care in Chile." *The Journal of Rural Health* 4, no. 1 (January 1988): 71–85.

Goldenberg, Boris. *Los sindicatos en América Latina.* Hannover: Verlag für Literatur und Zeitgeschehen, 1964.

González Rossetti, Alejandra, Tomás Chuaqui, and Consuelo Espinosa. *Enhancing the Political Feasibility of Health Reform: The Chile Case.* Latin America and Caribbean Regional Health Sector Reform Initiative Document No. 40 (July 2000). Cambridge, MA: International Health Systems Program, Harvard School of Public Health. Accessed July 10, 2003, at www.hsph.harvard.edu/ihsg /publications/ pdf/lac/PolicyChile1.pdf.

Graham, Carol. *Safety Nets, Politics, and the Poor: Transitions to Market Economies.* Washington, D.C.: Brookings Institution Press, 1994.

Graham, Wendy J., and Oona M. R. Campbell. "Maternal Health and the Measurement Trap." *Social Science and Medicine* 35, no. 8 (October 1992): 967–977.

Hakim, Peter, and Giorgio Solimano. *Development, Reform and Malnutrition in Chile.* Cambridge, MA: MIT Press, 1978.

Harris, Bernard. "Public Health, Nutrition, and the Decline of Mortality: The McKeown Thesis Revisited." *Social History of Medicine* 17, no. 3 (2004): 379–407.

Heston, Alan, Robert Summers, and Bettina Aten. Penn World Table Version 6.1. Center for International Comparisons at the University of Pennsylvania (CICUP), October 2002. Accessed October 20, 2002, at http://pwt.econ.upenn.edu.

Hill, M. Anne, and Elizabeth M. King. "Women's Education in Developing Countries: An Overview." In *Women's Education in Developing Countries: Barriers, Benefits, and Policies*, ed. Elizabeth M. King and M. Anne Hill. Baltimore: Johns Hopkins University Press, 1993.

Hill, Kenneth et al. *Trends in Child Mortality in the Developing World: 1960–1996.* New York: UNICEF [United Nations Children's Fund], 1999.

Hojman, David E. "Neoliberal Economic Policies and Infant and Child Mortality: Simulation Analysis of a Chilean Paradox." *World Development* 17, no. 1 (January 1989): 93–108.

———. *Chile: The Political Economy of Development and Democracy in the 1990s.* Pittsburgh: University of Pittsburgh Press, 1993.

IADB [Inter-American Development Bank]. "Chile: Basic Socio-Economic Data." 2000. Accessed October 29, 2000, at http://www.iadb.org/int/sta/ENGLISH /brptnct/cnglish/chlbrpt.htm

ILO [International Labour Office]. Laborsta database. Accessed December 4, 2002, at http://laborsta.ilo.org/cgi-bin/brokerv8.exe.

Ipsen, Carl. *Dictating Demography: The Problem of Population in Fascist Italy.* New York: Cambridge University Press, 1996.

Jarvis, Lovell S. *Chilean Agriculture under Military Rule: From Reform to Reaction, 1973–1980.* Research Series No. 59. Berkeley: Institute of International Studies, University of California, 1985.

Johnson, Leland J. "Problems of Import Substitution: The Chilean Automobile Industry." *Economic Development and Cultural Change* 15, no. 2 (part 1, January 1967): 202–216.

Kennedy, Bruce P., Ichiro Kawachi, and Deborah Prothrow-Stith. "Income Distribution and Mortality: Cross Sectional Ecological Study of the Robin Hood Index in the United States." *British Medical Journal* 312 (April 20, 1996): 1004–1007.

Landsberger, Henry A., and Tim MacDaniel. "Hypermobilization in Chile: 1970–1973." *World Politics* 28, no. 4 (July 1976): 502–541.

Larrañaga, Osvaldo. "Distribución de ingresos: 1958–2001." In *Reformas, crecimiento y políticas sociales en Chile desde 1973*, ed. Ricardo Ffrench-Davis and Barbara Stallings, 295–328. Santiago: CEPAL/Naciones Unidas/LOM ediciones, 2001.

Lavín, Joaquín. *Miguel Kast: Pasión de vivir*. 3rd ed. Santiago: Zig-Zag, 1987.

Livingstone, Mario, and Dagmar Raczynski. "Análisis cuantitativo de la evolución de algunas variables de salud durante el periodo 1964–1972." CEPLAN Documento No. 40 (July 1974). Santiago: Universidad Católica de Chile, Centro de Estudios de Planificación Nacional.

Londoño, Juan Luis, and Miguel Székely. "Persistent Poverty and Excess Inequality: Latin America, 1970–1995." Working Paper 357, Office of the Chief Economist, Inter-American Development Bank. October 1997. Accessed February 3, 2004, at http://www.iadb.org/res/publications/pubfiles/pubWP-357.pdf.

Loveman, Brian. *Chile: The Legacy of Hispanic Capitalism*. New York: Oxford University Press, 1979.

MacEwan, Aaron. *Neo-Liberalism or Democracy? Economic Strategy, Markets, and Alternatives for the 21st Century*. London and New York: Zed Books, 1999.

Mamalakis, Markos J., ed. *Historical Statistics of Chile: Demography and Labor Force*. Vol. 2. Westport, CT: Greenwood Press, 1980.

Marcel, Mario, and Andrés Solimano. "The Distribution of Income and Economic Adjustment." In *The Chilean Economy: Policy Lessons and Challenges*, ed. Barry P. Bosworth, Rudiger Dornbusch, and Raúl Labán, 217–256. Washington, D.C.: Brookings Institution Press, 1994.

Martin, María Pía. "Integration and Development: A Vision of Social Policy." In *Chile in the Nineties*, ed. Cristián Toloza and Eugenio Lahera, 309–347. Stanford: Stanford University Libraries, 2000.

McGuire, James W. "Labor Union Strength and Human Development in East Asia and Latin America." *Studies in Comparative International Development* 33, no. 4 (Winter 1999): 3–34.

———. *Wealth, Health, and Democracy in East Asia and Latin America*. New York: Cambridge University Press, 2010.

McGuire, James W., and Laura B. Frankel. "Mortality Decline in Cuba, 1900–1959: Patterns, Comparisons, and Causes." *Latin American Research Review* 40, no. 2 (June 2005): 84–116.

McKeown, Thomas. *The Modern Rise of Population*. New York: Academic Press, 1976.

Meller, Patricio. "El cobre chileno y la política minera." CEA Documento de Trabajo No. 142. CEA [Centro de Economía Aplicada], University of Chile, 2002. Accessed July 2, 2003, at http://www.cea-uchile.cl/pags/publicaciones/index.html

Mellington, Nicole, and Lisa Cameron. "Female Education and Child Mortality in Indonesia." *Bulletin of Indonesian Economic Studies* 35, no. 3 (December 1999): 115–144.

Mena, Isidora, and Cristián Belleï. "The New Challenge: Quality and Equity in Education." In *Chile in the Nineties*, ed. Cristián Toloza and Eugenio Lahera, 349–391. Stanford: Stanford University Libraries, 2000.

Mesa-Lago, Carmelo. *Social Security in Latin America: Pressure Groups, Stratification, and Inequality.* Pittsburgh: University of Pittsburgh Press, 1978.

———. *Market, Socialist, and Mixed Economies: Comparative Policy and Performance: Chile, Cuba, and Costa Rica.* Baltimore: Johns Hopkins University Press, 2000.

Miranda, Ernesto, Joseph L. Scarpaci, and Ignacio Irarrázaval. "A Decade of HMOs in Chile: Market Behavior, Consumer Choice and the State." *Health & Place* 1, no. 1 (1995): 51–59.

Molina, Natacha. "Propuestas políticas y orentaciones de cambio en la situación de la mujer." In *Propuestas políticas y demandas sociales*, Vol. 3, ed. Manuel A. Garretón and Cristián D. Cox, 61–80. Santiago: FLACSO, 1989.

Molina Silva, Sergio. *El proceso de cambio en Chile: La experiencia 1965–1970.* Santiago: Editorial Universitaria, 1972.

Monckeberg, Fernando. "Prevención de la desnutrición en Chile. Experiencia vivida por un actor y espectador." *Revista Chilena de Nutrición* 30, no. 1 (Diciembre 2003, Suplemento 1): 160–176.

Mosley, W. Henry, and Lincoln C. Chen. "An Analytical Framework for the Study of Child Survival in Developing Countries." *Population and Development Review* 10 (Supplement: Child Survival: Strategies for Research, 1984): 24–45.

Murthi, Mamta, Anne-Catherine Guio, and Jean Drèze. "Mortality, Fertility, and Gender Bias in India: A District-Level Analysis." *Population and Development Review* 21, no. 4 (December 1995): 745–782.

Nash, Nathaniel C. "Chile Advances in a War on Poverty, and One Million Mouths Say 'Amen.'" *New York Times* Section 1 (April 4, 1993): 14.

Navarro, Vicente. "What Does Chile Mean? An Analysis of Events in the Health Sector Before, During, and After Allende's Administration." *Milbank Memorial Fund Quarterly. Health and Society* 52, no. 2 (Spring 1974): 93–130.

Oppenheim, Lois Hecht. *Politics in Chile.* 2nd ed. Boulder: Westview Press, 1999.

Oxhorn, Philip D. *Organizing Civil Society: The Popular Sectors and the Struggle for Democracy in Chile.* University Park, PA: Penn State University Press, 1995.

PAHO [Pan American Health Organization] (2003). *PAHO Health Accounts Data Spreadsheets.* October. Accessed June 30, 2008, at http://www.iadb.org/sds /specialprograms/lachealthaccounts/CreatingHA/data_sources_en.htm

———. *Health Situation in the Americas: Basic Indicators 2005.* Washington, D.C.: Programa Especiál de Análisis de Salud, PAHO, 2005. Accessed January 10, 2006, at http://www.paho.org/english/dd/ais/coredata.htm

Paus, Eva. "Economic Growth through Neoliberal Restructuring? Insights from the Chilean Experience." *Journal of Developing Areas* 28, no. 1 (October 1994): 31–56.

Pritchett, Lant, and Lawrence H. Summers. "Wealthier Is Healthier." *Journal of Human Resources* 31, no. 4 (Fall 1996): 841–868.

Programa de Economía del Trabajo. *Series de indicadores económico sociales. Series anuales 1960–1991.* Santiago: Programa de Economía del Trabajo, 1992.

Raczynski, Dagmar. "Reformas al sector salud: Diálogos y debates." *Colección Estudios CIEPLAN* 10, no. 70 (June 1983): 5–44.

———. "Social Policy and Economic Change in Chile, 1974–1985: The Case of Children." *International Journal of Health Services* 21, no. 1 (1991): 17–47.

———. "Social Policies in Chile: Origin, Transformations, and Perspectives." Working Paper No. 4 (Fall 1994), Democracy and Social Policy Series, Kellogg Institute for International Studies, University of Notre Dame.

———. "Overcoming Poverty in Chile." In *Social Development in Latin America*, ed. Joseph S. Tulchin and Allison M. Garland, 119–148. Boulder: Lynne Rienner, 2000.

Raczynski, Dagmar, and César Oyarzo. "¿Por qué cae la tasa de mortalidad infantil en Chile?" *Colección Estudios CIEPLAN* 6, no. 55 (December 1981): 45–84.

Robinson, James, and Jean-Marie Baland. "Land and Power: Theory and Evidence." Paper No. 16, Economic History Seminar, University of California, Berkeley. April 11, 2005. Accessed January 12, 2006, at http://repositories.cdlib.org /berkeley_econ211/spring2005/16/

Roddick, Jackie. *The Dance of the Millions: Latin America and the Debt Crisis.* London: Latin America Bureau, 1988.

Rodríguez, Fernando. "Estructura y características del sector salud en Chile." In *Salud pública y bienestar social*, ed. Dagmar Raczynski, 65–82. Santiago: CEPLAN, 1976.

Romero, Hernán. "Planificación familiar en Chile." *Revista Médica Chilena* 105, no. 10 (October 1977): 724–730.

Ross, John A., and W. Parker Mauldin. "Family Planning Programs: Efforts and Results, 1972–94." *Studies in Family Planning* 27, no. 3 (May–June 1996): 137–147.

Ruiz-Tagle, Jaime. "Balancing Targeted and Universal Social Policies: The Chilean Experience." In *Social Development and Public Policy: A Study of Some Successful Experiences*, ed. Dharam Ghai, 323–360. London and New York: St. Martin's Press and United Nations Research Institute for Social Development, 2000.

Scarpaci, Joseph L. "Restructuring Health Care Financing in Chile." *Social Science and Medicine* 21, no. 4 (April 1985): 415–431.

Schultz, T. Paul. "Returns to Women's Education." In *Women's Education in Developing Countries: Barriers, Benefits, and Policies*, ed. Elizabeth M. King and M. Anne Hill, 51–59. Baltimore: Johns Hopkins University Press, 1993.

Scully, Timothy R. "Reconstituting Party Politics in Chile." In *Building Democratic Institutions: Party Systems in Latin America*, ed. Scott Mainwaring and Timothy R. Scully. Stanford: Stanford University Press, 1995.

Silva, Eduardo. *The State and Capital in Chile: Business Elites, Technocrats, and Market Economics.* Boulder: Westview Press, 1996.

Stallings, Barbara. *Class Conflict and Economic Development in Chile.* Stanford: Stanford University Press, 1978.

Stover, Eric. *The Open Secret: Torture and the Medical Profession in Chile.* July 1987. Washington, D.C.: Committee on Scientific Freedom and Responsibility, American Association for the Advancement of Science, 1987.

Subbarao, K.Y., and Laura Raney. "Social Gains from Female Education: A Cross-National Study." *Economic Development and Cultural Change* 44, no. 1 (October 1995): 105–128.

Taucher, Erica. "Mortalidad infantil en Chile." Paper prepared for the Organización Panamericana de la Salud Taller Regional sobre Estrategias de Atención Primaria y Mortalidad del Niño, 7–11 de Mayo 1984, Mexico, DF.

———. "The Impact of Fertility Decline on Levels of Infant Mortality." In *The Fertility Transition in Latin America*, ed. José Miguel Guzmán et al., 291–309. Oxford: Clarendon Press, 1996.

Taucher, Erica, Cecilia Albala, and Gloria Icaza. "Adult Mortality from Chronic Diseases in Chile, 1968–90." In *Adult Mortality in Latin America*, ed. I. M. Timaeus, J. Chackiel, and L. Ruzica, 253–275. Oxford: Clarendon Press, 1996.

Taucher, Erica, and Irma Jofré (1997). "Mortalidad infantil en Chile: el gran descenso." *Revista Médica de Chile* 125, no. 10: 1225–1235.

Titelman, Daniel. "Reformas al financiamiento del sistema de salud en Chile." *Revista de la CEPAL* 69 (December 1999): 181–194.

UNDP [United Nations Development Programme]. *Human Development Report 2002.* New York: Oxford University Press, 2002.

UNICEF [United Nations Children's Fund]. *State of the World's Children*, 1997 and 1998 editions. Accessed at http://www.unicef.org.

United Nations. *Child Mortality since the 1960s: A Database for Developing Countries.* New York: United Nations, Department of Economic and Social Development, Population Division, 1992.

United States. Bureau of the Census. *Statistical Abstract of the United States: 2006.* Washington, D.C.: Government Printing Office, 2005.

Vergara, Pilar. *Políticas hacia la extrema pobreza en Chile, 1973–1988.* Santiago: FLACSO, 1990.

Viel, Benjamín, and Waldo Campos. "Historia Chilena de mortalidad infantil y materna, 1940–1985." *Perspectivas Internacionales en Planificación Familiar* (Special Issue, 1987): 24–28.

Wang, Jia et al. *Measuring Country Performance on Health: Selected Indicators for 115 Countries.* Washington, D.C.: World Bank, 1999.

Weyland, Kurt. "'Growth with Equity' in Chile's New Democracy." *Latin American Research Review* 32, no. 1 (1997): 37–67.

———. "Economic Policy in Chile's New Democracy." *Journal of Interamerican Studies and World Affairs* 41, no. 3 (Autumn 1999): 67–96.

WHO [World Health Organization]. WHO Global Database on Child Growth and Malnutrition. World Health Organization, Department of Nutrition for Health and Development, 2002. Accessed July 12, 2002, at http://www.who.int /nutgrowthdb /p-child_pdf/index.html.

WHO/UNICEF [World Health Organization/United Nations Children's Fund]. "WHO/UNICEF Estimates of National Immunization Coverage, 1980–2003." Database updated September 24, 2004. Accessed June 3, 2005, at http://www .who.int/vaccines-surveillance/StatsAndGraphs.htm.

———. "Access to Improved Drinking Water Sources: Chile." Geneva: World Health Organization and New York: UNICEF, 2001.

Wilkie, James W., Eduardo Alemán, and José Guadalupe Ortega, eds. *Statistical Abstract of Latin America.* Vol. 35. Los Angeles: UCLA Latin American Center Publications, University of California, Los Angeles, 1999.

Wilkinson, Richard G. *Mind the Gap: Hierarchies, Health, and Human Evolution.* New Haven: Yale University Press, 2001.

World Bank. *World Development Indicators.* 1998 and 2001 editions on CD-ROM, 2002 and 2008 editions on line (accessed respectively February 22, 2002, and March 15, 2008). Washington, D.C.: World Bank.

———. *World Development Report 1980.* New York: Oxford University Press, 1980.

9

An Anthropometric Perspective on Guatemalan Ancient and Modern History

Luis Ríos and Barry Bogin

Introduction

Human growth in height is an indicator of food intake, exposure to disease, and life expectancy, so the stature of children and adults may be used as a cumulative record of the nutritional and health history of the population and often reflects the economic, social, and political environment in which those people lived.[1] Determination of the stature of past and modern populations can be approached through the study of living and skeletal samples, both during the growth period and in the adult stage.

Child growth is considered by researchers[2] and international organizations[3] not only as an appropriate indicator of the welfare of children, but as an adequate measure of the standard of living of the society. In the words of one author, "the growth of children . . . reflects rather accurately the material and moral conditions of that society."[4] Adult stature, the final result of child growth, has been also widely used to evaluate the standard of living of various populations. First carried out in North America and some European countries, research on stature trends now includes diverse regions of the world. Thus in recent years there are more studies of height trends in relation to the economic, social, and political history of Latin American countries. Some of these works are produced and discussed by the authors in this volume.[5] For an assessment of the biological standard of living of past populations, we will engage the study of human skeletal remains. The study of human bones and teeth offer information about diverse aspects of the life cycle of both individuals and populations, including nutrition, health, lifestyle, social organization, and migrations.[6] The study of human skeletal remains has been fostered in the last decades by a new and more comprehensive approach to the study of the living standards in human history, which has brought together social scientists interested and even specialized in human biology, and human biologists interested in the social sciences.[7]

In the present work we will offer an overview of the living standards of the Guatemalan population from the perspective of biological anthropology. We will make use of anthropometric data from three different but complementary sets of observations about the size (stature) and shape (body proportions) of the Guatemalan population: child growth, adult stature, and osteological studies of archaeological and forensic samples. The work is organized in four sections. The first discusses the prevalence of malnutrition in Guatemalan children at global, regional, and national levels. The second focuses on the clear association between socioeconomic and biological variations and will show the plasticity or growth potential of the Guatemalan child population. The third section reviews data on the adult stature of the Guatemalan population during the twentieth century and summarizes some data from archaeological and modern forensic samples that will serve to place the question of stature change in a long-term perspective. In the final section we will synthesize all these anthropometric data to draw some broader implications about the living standard of the Guatemalan population.

Child Malnutrition in Guatemala: Global, Latin American, and Central American Contexts

An important resource to monitor global and regional trends in children's growth is the "WHO [World Health Organization] Global Database on Child Growth and Malnutrition." A brief history, description of the methodology, and applications of this database have been detailed elsewhere.[8] This database was initiated in 1986 to compile, standardize, and disseminate results of nutritional surveys performed worldwide. Monitoring secular trends in child growth, including underweight (low weight-for-age), overweight (high weight-for-height), wasting (low weight-for-height) and stunting (low height-for-age), is one of the specific objectives of this project.

A review of the major results of the WHO project will help us to place Guatemala in a global, Latin American, and Central American context. We will consider stunting or low height-for-age, a measure that reflects long-term cumulative effects resulting from inadequate diet and/or recurring illness.[9] Specifically, we will consider the prevalence of low height-for-age, defined as the proportion of children that fall below −2 standard deviations (SD) of the United States National Center for Health Statistics/WHO international reference median value (NCHS/WHO).[10] Although new growth standards are currently being prepared owing to some drawbacks observed in the NCHS/WHO results, a constant comparison with this reference allows us to monitor positive, negative, or absence of change in stunting since the 1980s at the global and regional levels.[11]

De Onis and his co-workers reviewed cross-sectional data from 241 nationally representative surveys of preschool children (under 5 years) from 106 nations included in the WHO database.[12] They used the statistical technique of multilevel modeling to analyze the data, and their general results show a trend of decrease in stunting in developing countries from 47.1% in 1980 to 33% in 2000, although the authors emphasize that this progress has been uneven according to the region considered, as can be seen in Figure 1. We observe that the Latin American region presents the lowest prevalence of stunted children, with a decline from 25.6% in 1980 to 12.6% in 2000, but again, if we look at the change of stunting in the different Latin American regions, we note significant differences in the rate of improvement and in the lowered prevalence of stunted children (Figure 2). The estimated prevalence of stunting in Latin America and the Caribbean declined from 25.6% in 1980 to 12.6% in 2000, but the rates of improvement were 0.54% for the Caribbean, 0.79% for South American and 0.10% for Central America. In

Figure 1.
Trends in Stunting for the Developing Countries by Region for the Period 1980–2000.

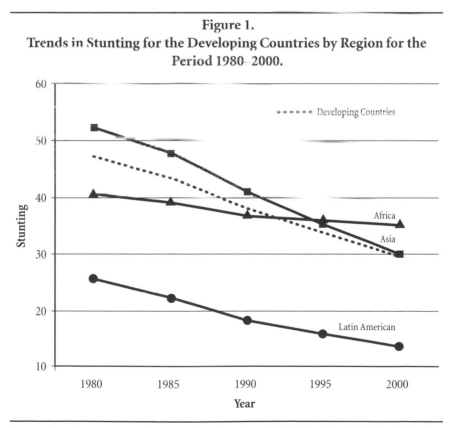

Sources: Data for 1980, 1985, and 1990 are from de Onis et al., "Is Malnutrition Declining?"; data for 1995 and 2000 are from de Onis et al., "Methodology for Estimating."

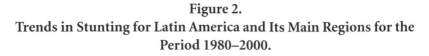

Figure 2.
Trends in Stunting for Latin America and Its Main Regions for the Period 1980–2000.

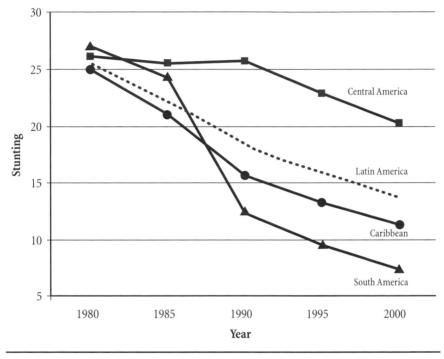

Sources: Data for 1980, 1985, and 1990 are from de Onis et al., "Is Malnutrition Declining?"; data for 1995 and 2000 are from de Onis et al., "Methodology for Estimating."

a more recent work,[13] 388 national representative survey data points were available from 139 nations, covering 99% of the under-5-year-olds in developing countries. This new analysis showed that for the developing countries during the 1990s there was a decline in stunting from 37.9% to 29.6%. The estimated prevalence of stunting in Latin America and the Caribbean declined from 18.3% to 11.8%, but again the estimated rates of improvement were 0.40% for the Caribbean, 0.28% for South America, and 0.21% for Central America.

Latin America is the least affected region in terms of prevalence of stunting when compared with other regions, mainly Africa and Asia. The prevalence of stunted children declined from 25.6% in 1980 to 11.8% in 2000, but significant differences can be observed at the regional level inside Latin America: the prevalence of stunted children as well as its rate of improvement in Central America lag behind the figures for the Caribbean and South

America, regions with lower prevalence and more marked decline rates of stunting. Central America shows little improvement in the prevalence of stunting in preschool children during the 1980s and a moderate improvement during the 1990s. The data from the "WHO Global Database on Child Growth and Malnutrition" indicate that Guatemala is the most affected region of Latin America in terms of both prevalence of stunted children and lower rates of improvement.

Figure 3 shows the change in prevalence of low height-for-age children in six Central American nations. We observe contrasting rates of stunting among the Central American nations, and note that Guatemala presents the highest prevalence of stunting, with moderate improvement between 1987 and 2002. Table 1 summarizes the data on child malnutrition for Guatemala from three diferente sources: *Encuesta Nacional de Salud Materno Infantil* (ENSMI),[14] *Encuesta Nacional de Condiciones de Vida* (ENCOVI),[15] and *Censos Nacionales de Talla de Escolares de Primer Grado de*

Figure 3.
Trends in Stunting for Six Central American Nations.

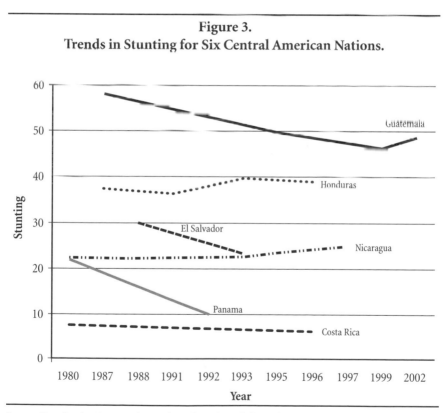

Source: Data for the six countries are from de Onis et al., "Is Malnutrition Declining?"; and de Onis et al., "Methodology for Estimating."

Table 1.
Rates of Stunting in Guatemala, 1987–2002.

		ENSMI 1987	ENSMI 1995	ENSMI 1998/99	ENCOVI 2000	ENSMI 2002
	Total	57.9	49.7	46.4	43.1	48.7
Residence	Urban	47.2	35.3	32.4	30.7	35.9
	Rural	62.1	56.6	54.4	49.1	54.9
Ethnicity	Ladino	–	36.7	–	31.4	35.7
	Maya	–	67.8	–	57	69.5
Literacy	Secondary or greater	30.2	14.7	12.7	–	18.4
	Primary	56.3	48	44.5	–	45.9
	Illiterate	68.6	63.8	64.4	–	64.8

Source: See text.

Primaria (CNT).[16] The data from ENSMI and ENCOVI refer to preschool children (under-5-year-olds) but there are data for older children from the CNT. This survey includes children between 6 years and 0 months to 9 years and 11 months. The sampling covered 70.4% of the children attending first grade of primary school in the 1986 census and 97.7% in the 2001 census. Again, children were classified in two categories by comparison with the NCHS/WHO reference: normal (–2 SD to 5 SD) and stunted (–5 SD to –2 SD). In the 2001 survey it was found that 48.8% of the children aged 6 to 10 were stunted or suffered chronic malnutrition. The prevalence of stunting for 1986 was estimated from the figures of the 1986 census published in the 2001 census, and this estimate was 50.38%. Because of the differences in coverage of the two censuses and the estimation of the 1986 figure, the comparison between the prevalence of stunted children is not accurate, but it can give us an idea of the high prevalence of stunting of the Guatemalan primary school children and the absence of a significant improvement in this indicator of chronic malnutrition between 1986 and 2001. In addition, the ENSMI-DHS, ENCOVI, and CNT report a clear association between stunting and residence, ethnicity, and education of the mother.

To sum up, Central America constitutes the most affected region of Latin America in terms of both prevalence of stunted children and low rates of improvement, and within this region, Guatemala presents the highest prevalence of stunted children as well as a moderate rate of improvement: almost half of the Guatemalan child population is stunted, and in a 15-year period (1986 to 2002), the prevalence declined from 57.9% to

48.7% for the preschool children and from 50.38% to 48.8% for the primary school children. The different levels of malnutrition observed in Table 1 lead us to explore these variations in the prevalence of stunting among diverse groups of Guatemalan children.

Socioeconomic Inequality and Biological Variability

In 2002, 57% of the Guatemalan population lived in conditions of total poverty, and 21.5% in conditions of extreme poverty.[17] As can be seen in Figure 4, total poverty affects especially the rural (74.49%) and Maya (77.32%) populations and there is a close association between these rates and the percentage of children with low height-for-age. In this section we will review the correlation between various measures of socioeconomic status and the growth status of the Guatemalan children.

Figure 4.
Stunting and Poverty Rates by Urban or Rural Residence and Ethnicity.

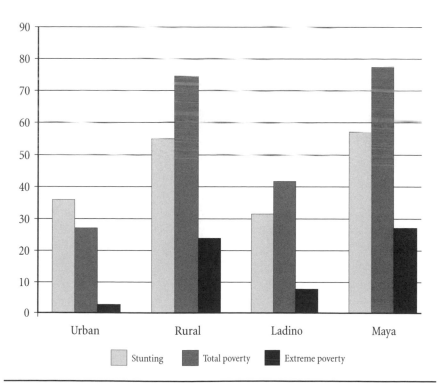

Sources: Data of poverty are from Instituto Nacional de Estadística, *Perfil de la pobreza,* 17. Data of stunting are from Instituto Nacional de Estadística, *Encuesta Nacional,* 39.

In the field of human biology and nutrition, Guatemala stands out because of the numerous studies undertaken about the growth and development of its child population. The main studies are: *Estudio Longitudinal del Desarrollo del Niño y del Adolescente* from Universidad del Valle,[18] in which one of the authors (B.B.) has been deeply involved during several years; the numerous and diverse projects of the *Instituto de Nutrición de Centroamérica y Panamá* (INCAP, see below); the aforementioned national surveys (ENCOVI, ENSMI, CNT), and the growth survey carried out by an international agreement between the Universidad de San Carlos de Guatemala and the Universidad Autónoma de Madrid (USAC-UAM), in which one of the authors (L.R.) was field anthropometrist.[19] The main results of these projects show the impact of diverse socioeconomic factors on biological variables like weight, height, head circumference, skinfolds, osseous development, as well as on the cognitive level, school achievement, working capacity, and, ultimately, the ability to generate capital as an adult.[20] We will review some of these results in order to clarify fully the association between socieconomic status, ethnicity, and the growth status of the Guatemalan children. First, we will describe the extent of the differences in height and body proportions among different groups of children and pay attention to the association between biological and socioeconomic status. Second, we will review the results of two studies that have estimated the impact of two factors upon the growth and development of children: a controlled nutritional supplement during the growth period, and migration to the United States, hence growing up in a different environment. The review of these results will allow us to understand the growth potential of the Guatemalan children. Finally, from a temporal perspective, we will see how the growth of children reflects the political, economic, and social environment.

Differences in Size and Shape among Diverse Groups of Guatemalan Children
The data we are going to review come from the growth survey by USAC-UAM, carried out between 1996 and 1999. In Figure 5 we can see the growth curve for height and body proportions[21] for three groups of children: a sample of children from rural communities, mostly of Maya ethnicity, and two urban samples from middle-class schools, mostly Ladino (mixed ethnicity), from Guatemala City and three other urban centers (Cobán, Jutiapa, and Quetzaltenango). For the 15-year-old boys there is a mean difference of 15.2 cm between the rural Maya and the urban Ladino from Guatemala City, while the boys from the other cities are 2.3 cm shorter than those from Guatemala City. The same applies to body proportions: at all ages, children from the rural communities have the shortest legs in relation to total height

(Figure 6). We can relate this difference in size and shape at 15 years of age to a variable that summarizes the general socioeconomic milieu experienced by these samples of children: the Human Development Index (HDI) associated to the Maya population (mostly rural) and to the population from the Department of Guatemala (mostly urban). The HDI is a composite measure of welfare that combines three variables: life expectancy, adult literacy rate plus the gross matriculation rate, and gross national product per capita, with the index's value ranging from 0 (absence of human development) to 1 (optimum human development). The HDI values for the department of Guatemala and for the rural Maya were obtained from the figures published in 1998 by the United Nations Program for Development in Guatemala.[22] Figures 7 and 8 show the correlation between HDI and height and body proportions at 16 years for the male sample.

Figure 5.
Stature Differences among Boys Aged 6 to 15 Years.

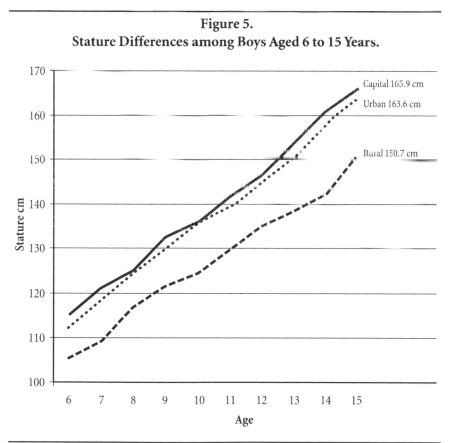

Source: Data from Ríos, unpublished.

Note. Capital: middle-class schools from Guatemala City. Urban: middle-class schools from Cobán, Jutiapa, and Quetzaltenango. Rural: schools from five rural communities.

Figure 6.
Body Proportions (Cormic Index): Differences among
Boys Aged 6 to 15 Years.

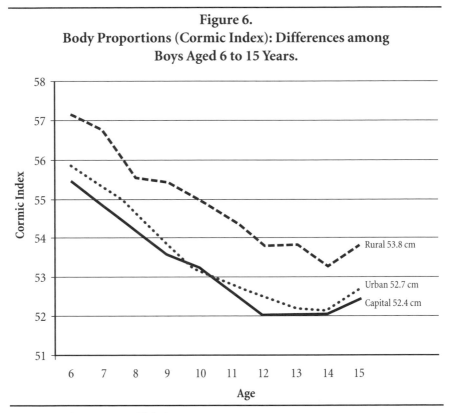

Source: Data from Ríos, unpublished.

Note: Capital: middle-class schools from Guatemala City. Urban: middle-class schools from Cobán, Jutiapa, and Quetzaltenango. Rural: schools from five rural communities.

Most of the differences in linear growth and proportionality between the samples can be attributed to the environmental effects summarized by this index acting upon the growth of these children. In fact, a closer and more specific look at the rural Maya sample also reveals differences in growth within this sample, depending on the socioeconomic status of the children. If we divide the male rural Maya sample according to the education of the mother, we observe differences in size and shape at most ages (Figures 9 and 10). This relationship between the education of the mother and the growth of children is well established and has been previously observed in Guatemala with regard to the prevalence of stunting (Table 1),[23] and in other ethnically and geographically diverse populations.[24] As described previously,[25] what figures 9 and 10 reveal is a continuum of body size and shape for the Guatemalan children paralleling the variation in living conditions: the differences in height and body proportions between the rural Maya and

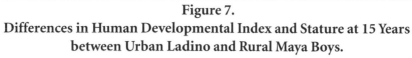

Figure 7.
Differences in Human Developmental Index and Stature at 15 Years between Urban Ladino and Rural Maya Boys.

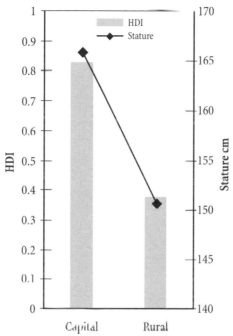

Sources: HDI values come from Programa de Naciones Unidas para el Desarrollo, *Guatemala: los contrastes*, 199. Stature data from Rios, unpublished.

urban Ladino samples decrease as the socioeconomic milieu of the rural Maya children improves.

Growth Potential of the Guatemalan Children: The INCAP and Migrant Studies

To date, the INCAP has done various studies of the short- and long-term effects of improved nutrition during the growth period in a Guatemalan Ladino population of low socioeconomic status.[26] In the Longitudinal Study (1969–77) from which most of the other studies developed, four Guatemalan Ladino villages were selected with social, economic, and demographic conditions representative of the general context of poverty and isolation of the rural Guatemalan towns. A protein-caloric drink called Atole (11.5 g of protein and 163 kcal/682 kj per 180 mL) was taken by the inhabitants of two villages while the inhabitants of the other two had a drink called Fresco (0 g of protein and 59 kcal/247 kJ per 180 mL). Children under

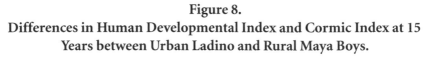

Figure 8.
Differences in Human Developmental Index and Cormic Index at 15 Years between Urban Ladino and Rural Maya Boys.

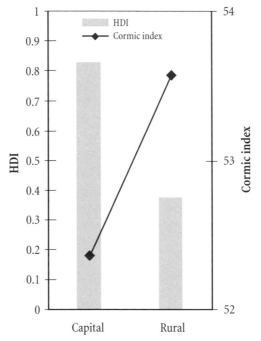

Sources: HDI values from Programa de Naciones Unidas para el Desarrollo, *Guatemala: los contrastes*, 199. Stature data from Ríos, unpublished.

7 and pregnant and breastfeeding mothers were monitored according to the drink provided (Fresco or Atole), and diverse anthropometric variables and motor and mental tests were recorded. The participants in this study were included in the Follow-up Study (1988–1989). These same samples and their offspring have been subsequently included in the Birth Weight Study (1991–1996), Intergenerational Effects Study (1996–1999), Risk Factors in Cardiovascular Disease Study (1998), and, finally, the Early Nutrition, Human Capital and Economic Productivity Study (2001–2006). Among the major effects of a protein-caloric supplement during the growth period were: a significant effect on infant mortality,[27] a decline of the prevalence of stunted children,[28] a greater adult stature and fat-free mass, particularly in females,[29] and improved work capacity in males.[30] It was also found that better nutrition during the prenatal and the first two years of life improved intellectual performance at ages 13 to 19 in boys and girls,[31] and educational achievement in adult women.[32] Moreover, the design of the

Figure 9.
Stature Differences between the Urban and Rural Male Samples.

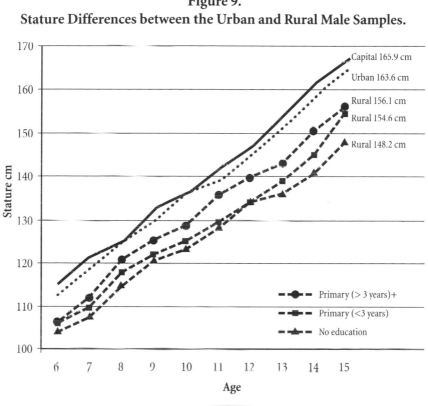

Source: Data from Ríos, unpublished.

Note: The rural sample is divided according to the education of the mother in three categories: no education; 1 to 3 years of primary school; at least 3 years of primary school, including secondary or higher.

INCAP projects has allowed us to study the generational effect of the nutritional supplement: the children born to women who received Atole were significantly taller and grew faster than the children whose mothers received Fresco.[33]

With regard to the migrant study, since 1992 Bogin and co-workers have been studying the growth of Maya children born and matured in the United States.[34] As explained elsewhere,[35] the study of migrants has a long tradition in human biology, as this "natural experiment" inserts similar individuals into diverse environments, allowing us to study the effect of this change upon the physical and physiological features of the migrant population and its offspring. Thousands of Maya fled Guatemala in the 1970s and 80s to escape the prevailing human rights violations and the deteriorated economic situation. Some groups of refugees arrived to the United States and

Figure 10.
Differences in Cormic Index between the Urban and
Rural Male Samples.

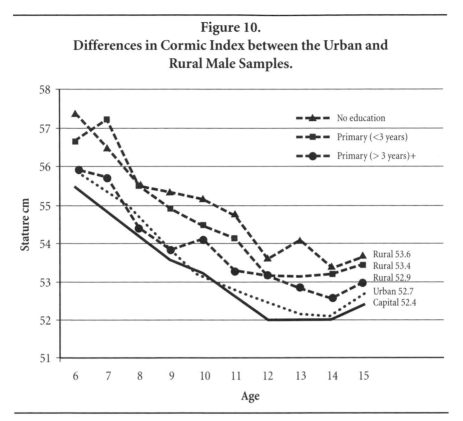

Source: Data from Ríos, unpublished.

Note: The rural sample is divided according to the education of the mother in three categories: no education; 1 to 3 years of primary school; at least 3 years of primary school, including secondary or higher.

settled in Indiantown, Florida, and Los Angeles, California. These migrants come from the Q'anjob'al-speaking area in northwest Guatemalan highlands, and the history and biocultural environment of these communities have been reported elsewhere.[36] These ethnographic works report that the Maya families in both U.S. locations are of generally low socioeconomic status, with many families below the U.S. poverty line. Two anthropometric surveys were carried out, in 1992 and 2000. The height and sitting height of 6- to 12-year-old children were recorded and compared to the aforementioned USAC-UAM growth survey from rural communities at home.[37] In Figure 11 we observe that at age 12, Maya-American children surveyed in 2000 are currently 12 cm taller, on average, than Maya rural children living in Guatemala. This positive trend in height has reduced the difference in size between the Maya and urban Ladino sample from Guatemala City to the degree that this difference at 12 years was only 1.9 cm for the migrant

Maya children measured in 2000. As can be observed in Figure 12, body proportions are also sensitive to this environmental change; the migrants are 6.8 cm longer-legged, on average, than Maya rural children living in Guatemala, and the cormic index of the migrant sample is closer to the Guatemala City children than to children of the rural Maya. Stated another way, these results show that one effect of growing up in the United States on the Maya-American children is that they are significantly taller than Guatemala Maya children and the effect on leg length is greater that the effect on sitting height (trunk height). A change in stature and body proportions of this magnitude in less than one generation is unlikely to have any genetic basis, and studies show that in most cases there is no physical selection in the migrant populations.[38] It is relief from poverty in Guatemala and the availability of better nutrition, clean water, and education in the United States that may explain a change in size (height) and shape (body proportions) of this magnitude for the infant population of Maya-American migrants. It is important to note here that some scholars have argued that the short stature of the Maya population is due to some genetic limitation or the result of an adaptation to reduced food supplies ("small but healthy").[39] The results we have just reviewed clearly show that the short stature of the Maya is the consequence of the negative environmental conditions that this population faces during the growth period. The "small but healthy" hypothesis is not supported by the evidence, which shows instead the long-term negative effects of chronic malnutrition during the growth period, of which the adult size is an index.[10]

A Negative Secular Trend in the Stature of Guatemalan Children

Given our previous analysis, it is now reasonable to search for secular trends in stunting, height, and body proportions of the infant population in recent Guatemalan history. We have seen that since the first national surveys in 1986 and 1987, although Guatemalan children have experienced a moderate improvement in their nutritional status, in 2002 approximately half of the infant population presented chronic malnutrition (Table 1). With regard to height, a negative secular trend in stature has been shown for children born between 1974 and 1985, a time of major decline in the quality of life as a result of economic deterioration and the armed confrontation and civil repression that spread throughout the country.[41] In this study, three groups of children were included, representing high, middle and very low socioeconomic status from Guatemala City and its surroundings.[42] Figure 13 displays a moving average of per capita GNP[43] and the mean height of the three samples of Guatemalan children born during the period 1974 to 1985 and aged 10 or 11 years. The negative trends in stature and in percent change of

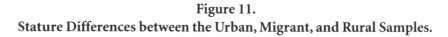

Figure 11.
Stature Differences between the Urban, Migrant, and Rural Samples.

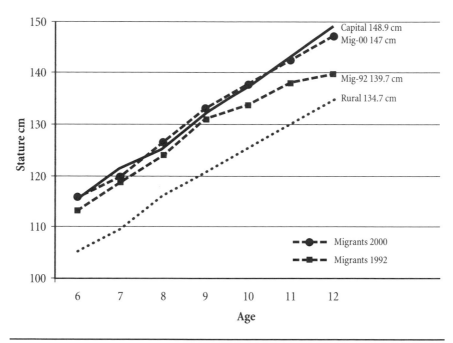

Source: See text.

Note: Capital: middle-class schools from Guatemala City. Migrants 2000 (Mig-00): offspring of
Guatemalan Maya migrants measured in 2000. Migrants 1992 (Mig-92): offspring of Guatemala
Maya migrants measured in 1992. Rural: schools from five rural communities.

per capita GNP are evident, and this change in the mean income of the
Guatemalan population summarizes the worsening of the economic, nutritional, and health situation during the growth period of these children.[44]

The studies reviewed in this section show the clear association of stunting, height, and body proportions with the environmental conditions experienced by Guatemalan children during the growth period, and the growth
potential of this population when relieved from these negative conditions.
With regard to secular trends, we have also observed a decrease in stature for
the children born during the period 1974 to 1985 in Guatemala City and its
surroundings. The data from the growth surveys of Guatemalan children
would allow a search for secular trends from 1953, date of the beginning of
the Universidad del Valle project, a study that still remains to be completed.
But in order to look further back for the presence of secular trends in height,
we would have to consider adult stature.

Figure 12.
Cormic Index Differences between the Urban, Migrant,
and Rural Samples.

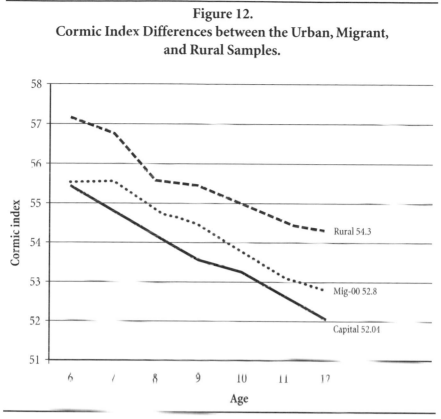

Source: See text.

Note: Capital: middle-class schools from Guatemala City. Migrants 2000 (Mig-00): offspring of Guatemalan Maya migrants measured in 2000. Rural: schools from five rural communities.

Adult Stature

Anthropometry and Historical Records of Height

The results of diverse studies about the nutritional and growth status of Guatemalan children indicate that the differences in body proportions and the retardation in linear growth (and therefore the prevalence of stunting) for the Guatemalan child population are related to the quality of the environment during the growth period. A consequence of this retardation in linear growth is the small size of the adult Guatemalan population. In Table 2 we have summarized the published data on the stature of Guatemalan adults that we have been able to find in the literature. During the first half of the twentieth century several anthropometric studies were carried out, most of them in samples of reduced size; subsequently, in the second half of the past century, the INCAP began to include adult stature in its research projects.

Figure 13.

Change in Real Per Capita National Income, and Mean Height of Guatemalan Children (ages 10 and 11) by Socioeconomic Status.

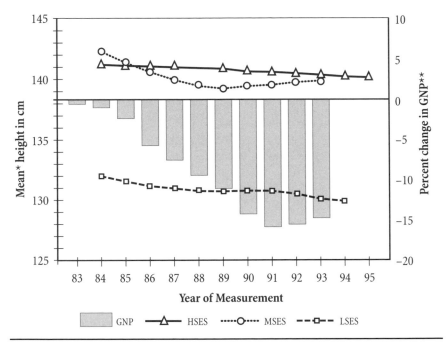

Source: Bogin and Keep, "Eight Thousand Years," 346.

Note: HSES, MSES and LSES stand for high, medium and low socioeconomic status.

From the 1980s onward, the ENSMI-DHS systematically included adult stature in the surveys, especially of females, and some other research projects also measured adult height. For the first half of the twentieth century, the mean height of twelve rural male samples ranged from 152.9 cm to 157.5 cm, with an average of 155 cm. The stature of five rural male samples measured in the second half of the twentieth century range from 154.8 cm to 160.7 cm, with an average of 158.44 cm. The stature of two female samples from the first half of the past century ranged from 143.1 cm to 144.2 cm (average of 143.65 cm), while the stature of three female rural samples from the second half of the past century ranged from 142.4 cm to 147.7 cm (average of 145.5 cm). These data suggest a positive trend in stature of approximately 2–3 cm for the period 1930 to 2000, but the differences in sampling, socioeconomic status, geographic location, and age (as well as possible differences in measurement protocols) among the various samples shown in Table 2 suggest a cautious approach to the interpretation of any temporal

Table 2.
Adult Mean Heights in Guatemala, 1931–2001.

Group	N	Stature cm	Year of survey	Reference
MALE				
Maya Indians	18	157.5	1931[a]	Shattuck and Benedict
K'iche'	45	152.9	1939[a]	D'Aloja[c]
Kaqchiquel	59	154.5	1939[a]	D'Aloja[c]
Mam	23	155.1	1939[a]	D'Aloja[c]
Ixil	22	153.7	1939[a]	D'Aloja[c]
K'iche'	216	154.9	1939[a]	Crile and Quiring
K'iche'	63	154.2	1947[a]	Stewart[c]
Kaqchiquel	72	155.3	1947[a]	Stewart[c]
Kaqchiquel	32	154.8	1947[a]	Stewart[c]
Q'anjob'al	74	154.8	1947[a]	Stewart[a]
Mam	91	155.9	1948[a]	Goff[l]
Q'anjob'al	37	156.3	–	La Farge-Byeres[c]
Western Highlands Maya	158	154.8	1959–1971[b]	Russell
South Coast Plantation	158	159.3	1975[b]	Immink et al.
Western Highlands Maya	664	157.5	1987[b]	Flegal et al.
Western Highlands	49	160.7	1991[b]	Díaz et al.
Guatemala City middle class	1057	172	1997[b]	Ríos, unpublished
Jutiapa middle class	130	169.5	1997[b]	Ríos, unpublished
Quetzaltenango middle class	92	165.7	1997[b]	Ríos, unpublished
K'eqchi	28	159.9	2002[b]	Ríos, unpublished
FEMALE				
K'iche'	117	143.1	1939[a]	Crile and Quiring
Mam	20	144.2	1948[a]	Goff[l]
South Coast Plantation	380	142.4	1981[b]	Martorell et al.
Urban Guatemala	12786	153	1984–1986[b]	Flegal et al.
Western Highlands	49	147.7	1991[b]	Díaz et al.
Guatemala City middle class	1057	159.2	1997[b]	Ríos, unpublished
Jutiapa middle class	139	158.1	1997[b]	Ríos, unpublished
Quetzaltenango middle class	104	154.2	1997[b]	Ríos, unpublished
K'eqchi	55	146.4	2001[b]	Ríos, unpublished
Maya	2355	145.3	2001[b]	ENSMI
Ladino	4990	151.1	2001[b]	ENSMI

Source: See text.

Notes: [a]Year of publication. [b]Year of measurement. [c]Data from Villanueva, "Las características físicas," 103.

change in height. These diverse data show that to date, with few exceptions, no systematic study has approached the question of temporal change in adult height in this Central American country.

The INCAP study of four Ladino villages in Guatemala found no secular trend in the age-adjusted height of adults born between 1905 and 1959.[45] The author concluded that, despite some improvements in global health and nutrition indicators that occurred in Guatemala during this period, improvements in environmental sanitation, health care, and food security at the household level appear to have been insufficient to produce a significant increase in adult stature over time. The results are summarized in Figure 14. To date, the most systematic collection of adult height data has been carried out by ENSMI. Table 3 shows the data from these surveys. Between 1995 and 2002 a general positive secular trend in height can be observed for the female Guatemalan population, with an average increase of 1.2 cm for this 7-year period. If we consider the stature trend according to basic geographic, social, and demographic variables, we find some interesting results. First, note the stature difference between the Guatemalan regions,

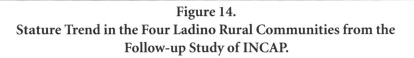

Figure 14.
Stature Trend in the Four Ladino Rural Communities from the Follow-up Study of INCAP.

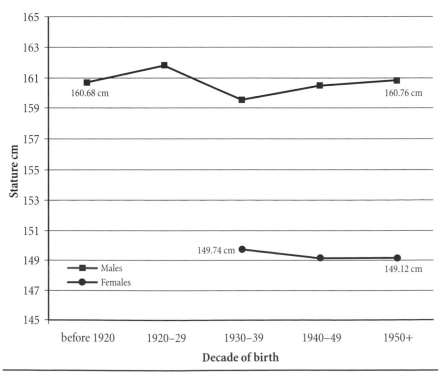

Table 3.
Female Statures Compiled from ENSMI.

| | 1995 | | 1998/99 | | 2002 | | Difference |
Department	Stature	N	Stature	N	Stature	N	1995–2002
Metropolitan	150	1488	150.1	814	151.5	2718	+ 1.5
North	146.1	470	146.5	186	146.6	538	+ 0.5
North-Orient	148.6	459	147.5	214	149.2	564	+ 0.6
South-Orient	150.5	517	150.3	222	149.7	360	− 0.8
Central	148.8	594	148.6	259	149.5	745	+ 0.7
South-Occident	146.3	1157	146.8	532	147.2	1429	+ 0.9
North-Occident	144.8	735	144.8	279	145.9	740	+ 1.1
Peten	–	–	148.2	78	149.6	250	+ 1.4
Total	148	5420	148.2	2585	149.2	7345	+ 1.2
Ethnicity							
Maya	144.7	2143	144.8	887	145.3	2355	+ 0.6
Ladino	150.1	3259	150	1698	151.1	4990	+ 1.0
Residence							
Rural	147	3538	147.2	1568	148.3	4880	+ 1.3
Urban	149.8	1882	149.8	1017	150.4	3159	+ 0.6
Education							
No education	145.7	1970	145.1	804	145.8	1873	+ 0.1
Primary school	148.2	2664	148.5	1336	148.7	3253	+ 0.5

Source: Instituto Nacional de Estadística, *Encuesta Nacional de Salud Materno-Infantil (ENSMI)*, 1995–2002.

which can be as high as 5.2 cm in 1995 and 5.6 cm in 2002 between the Metropolitan and North-Occident regions. In conjunction with the data in Table 2, it is clear that urban middle class women from the cities of Guatemala, Jutiapa, and Quetzaltenango were 5 to 15 cm taller than the rest of the women in other regions. Second, we can observe the absence of a significant change in height (0.1 cm) for the women without education between 1995 (145.7 cm) and 2002 (145.8 cm). Finally, it is interesting to note the negative secular trend of 0.8 cm observed for the South-Orient sample, whose mean stature decreased from 150.5 cm to 149.7 cm. No information is offered about the statistical significance of all these changes.

To discuss the presence or absence of secular trends in the stature of the adult population, we should take into account the distinctive features of the demographic, social, and economic history of the different Guatemalan regions, which requires a more consistent and systematic approach. Our current project is the study of the height records of the Guatemalan population using identification card records held in municipal archives. Every

Guatemalan citizen is required to have an identification card. At the moment of registration, the stature of every person is measured and information about place of birth, residence, literacy, and occupation is recorded. A copy of all these data is kept locally. This policy was implemented in Guatemala in the early 1930s, so there is a historical record of heights from that date to the present time that includes most of the adult population.

In Table 4 and Figure 15 we present a preliminary reconstruction of adult stature of men born between 1917 and 1982, who registered in the municipality of Cobán, located in the central region, about 60 miles north of Guatemala City. Only individuals whose occupation figured as *jornalero* or *agricultor* were included, most of them born in *fincas* or *aldeas* near this urban center. Here we show these preliminary data only for illustrative purposes. In future research we intend to refine the results of our analysis to examine the the ups and downs in the series in relation to cycles of economic and social variables, as well as to possible spurious effects. Figure 15 shows a trend toward higher stature for the male population registered at Cobán, with a mean difference of 3.6 cm between the samples born in 1917 (155.2 cm) and 1982 (158.8 cm). These figures are in agreement with the data previously shown in Table 2, which offered a mean height of 155 cm for the twelve rural samples from the first half of the twentieth century, and a mean height of 158.44 cm for the five rural samples measured in the second half of the past century (difference of 3.4 cm).

Table 4.
Adult Male Stature in Rural Areas near Cobán, 1917–1982.

Year of birth	N	Mean height	SD
1917	138	155.2	4.8
1922	202	154.9	5.0
1927	170	156.6	5.5
1932	206	155.6	4.6
1937	234	155.4	5.6
1942	251	156.9	5.1
1947	219	156.2	4.8
1952	214	155.8	5.0
1957	227	156	5.1
1962	245	158.3	5.3
1967	267	156.7	5.1
1972	215	157.5	5.4
1977	234	158.6	5.3
1982	262	158.8	5.0

Source: Municipal Archive of Cobán.

Figure 15.
Secular Trend of Adult Male Stature in Rural Areas Near Cobán,
1917–1982.

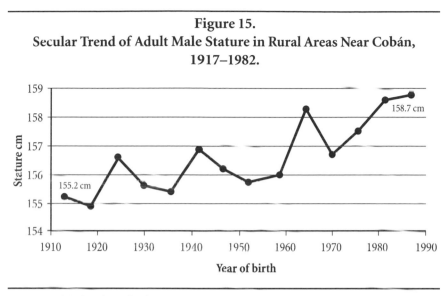

Source: Municipal Archive of Cobán.

The evidence shown in Table 2 and the data from the height series from Cobán suggest a positive change of approximately 3.5 cm in the stature of the Guatemalan male population for the period 1930 to 2000, with the increase centered in the last quarter of the 20th century. The study of INCAP indicates a lack of secular change in the mid-20th century for the rural villages sampled, and the ENSMI data indicate a positive change of 1.2 cm for some groups of Guatemalan women during the latter half of the 1990s. The evidence from geographically close Mesoamerican populations also indicates an absence of secular trend for rural populations during most of the past century. In his work about male samples from Yucatan,[46] McCullough found no evidence of secular trend in stature from 1895 (155.2 cm) to 1968 (155.1 cm); in another study of adult stature in Zapotec-speaking communities in the Valley of Oaxaca,[47] the authors also found negligible secular changes for this population for the period 1899 to 1978. Clearly, more research on bigger samples from the different Guatemalan regions is needed in order to verify our findings.

Osteology
Osteological evidence for adult height comes from archaeological and forensic samples. The study of human skeletal remains offers important information about diverse aspects of the life cycle of both individuals and populations, including nutrition, health, lifestyle, social organization, and

migrations.[48] Skeletons provide us with the only available material to explore the biological standard of living in ancient populations. We will focus on long bone length and estimated height from two sources: archaeological samples from the Mesoamerican area in the past and a forensic sample from contemporary Guatemala. The archaeological data come from two recent overviews of the state of ancient osteological research,[49] and the forensic data come from a database developed by Luís Ríos during his work with Guatemalan forensic teams. This database was developed to test and develop osteometric references for this population in order to increase the reliability of the forensic analysis.[50] The data are summarized in Tables 5 (stature) and 6 (long bone length). The mean stature and long-bone length of the forensic male and female samples are among the lowest in the historical osteological record. Several authors[51] warn us to be cautious in our interpretations, given the limitations and errors associated with stature estimation from long bone lengths with regression equations, small sample sizes representing broad time periods, sampling variation, and incomplete background information. With this limitation in mind,[52] the available data suggest a long-term shortening trend from the Pre-classic period to the present. Similar studies using smaller archaeological and living samples from the Valley of Oaxaca (Mexico) and Yucatán found negligible or negative change in the long run.[53]

Other osteological and dental markers of health status have been studied in contemporary Guatemalan samples. A recent study on the prevalence of porotic hyperostosis and anemia among the Maya of Central America reinterpreted previous conclusions in the light of the epidemiology of modern Maya populations and the prevalence of skeletal lesions of anemia in a forensic sample.[54] The rarity of porotic hyperostosis on the skulls of modern forensic skeletons (11% adult crania) may be due to a heavier burden of infectious disease, earlier weaning, and thus higher childhood mortality experienced by the Guatemalan rural population when compared to the ancient Maya condition. The authors conclude that childhood health is more compromised in the present that it was for the ancient Maya. Linear enamel hypoplasias (LEH), a non-specific marker of physiological stress, have also been studied in the Guatemalan rural population.

Conclusions

Data from the National Surveys provide an idea of the nutritional status of Guatemalan children and its change over the last 20 years. A decrease in stunting for preschool children was observed between 1987 and 1995 (from 57.9% to 47.9%), but since 1995 the nutritional status has not changed

Table 5.
Estimates of Height by Bone Samples, Preclassic through Modern.

	Male		Female	
	Stature	N	Stature	N
Preclassic				
Altar de Sacrificios	166.6	4	148.3	2
Tikal	161.7	6	144.4	4
Yucatán Maya	164.4	7	151.2	2
Average	164.2		147.96	
Classic				
Jaina	160.6	12	151	12
Altar de Sacrificios	159	3	–	–
Tikal	155.2	21	148.5	11
Xcaret	164.5	2	154	3
Copán urban	162.8	36	155.5	46
Copán rural	160.1	9	154.9	13
Yucatán Maya	162.1	22	151.8	14
Average	160.6		152.61	
Postclassic				
Yucatán Maya	161.5	25	148.4	5
Colonial Maya				
Tipu	160.3	149	148.3	106
Xcaret	157.3	15	145.5	31
Average	158.8		146.9	
Modern Maya				
Forensic[a]	158.01	70	145.52	53
Anthropometry	158.44	1057	145.3–151.5	7345

Sources: See text. The anthropometry averages for males and females are based on Table 2 and Instituto Nacional de Estadística, *Encuesta Nacional 2002*, respectively.

Notes: [a]Estimation from maximum length of the femur using the Genovés equation.

Table 6.
Long Bone Length (Femur and Tibia).

	Male				Female			
	Femur	N	Tibia	N	Femur	N	Tibia	N
Preclassic	43.51	11	37.33	7	39.13	3	33.05	2
Classic	41.62	22	36.16	32	38.99	17	33.26	14
Postclassic	42.87	29	35.88	25	38.2	11	32.02	5
Modern forensic								
(Western Highlands)	41.65	70	34.65	62	37.94	53	30.91	50

Sources: See text. Data from archaeological and forensic samples.

significantly and the percentage of stunted children remains disturbingly high (Figure 3, Table 1). Moreover, these figures should be considered in light of the results of other studies on the growth and development of the Guatemalan child population. We have examined the impact of socioeconomic variables on the growth of children in groups of different socioeconomic status, residence, and ethnicity (Figures 5 to 8), and documented a continuum of body size and shape paralleling the variation in living conditions (Figures 9 and 10). The results of the INCAP Follow-up study reveal the significant results, in the short and long term, that can be achieved with a moderate nutritional improvement in the first years of life, and the migrant study illustrates the plasticity or growth potential of the Maya population (Figures 11 and 12), potential that this population fails to reach owing to socioeconomic forces holding back growth in Guatemala, and not because of genetic limitation. From the point of view of child growth, the standard of living in Guatemala during the last 20 years has not improved significantly.[55]

An obvious consequence of these poor living conditions of the Guatemalan child population is the short stature of the adult population. The available evidence points to no change in stature during most of the twentieth century, and to a recent positive trend during the last quarter of the past century, at least for some population groups. Although this suggestion should be considered with caution due to the aforementioned drawbacks (diverse geographic locations, small sample sizes, different age distributions, etc.), these data do provide a general idea of the low height of an important segment of the Guatemalan population at the turn of the twentieth century: below 160 cm for males and below 150 cm for females. The continuum of body size paralleling living conditions observed for children can be seen in the adult population. The comparison of archaeological and forensic samples allows us to speculate, with caution, about an unfavorable trend in height from the Pre-classic period to modern times, with the modern Guatemalan rural forensic sample presenting the lowest stature estimations, as well as femoral and tibiae lengths (a proxy for leg length), in comparison with the archaeological samples. In future research we hope to contribute more comprehensive and systematic evidence of adult stature change over the last century and over the very long run.

The proximate causes of the worrying growth status and short adult stature of an important segment of the Guatemalan population are the critical situation of poverty and inequality under which this population lives. The most recent data summarize this critical situation. In the 2005 Human Development Report,[56] Guatemala ranks at number 117 out of

177 nations surveyed for the HDI, making it the second least developed country in the Americas (only Haiti presents a worse situation), while the Gini index for inequality in income or consumption indicates that Guatemala, together with six other nations (Brazil, Swaziland, Central African Republic, Sierra Leona, Botswana, and Namibia), presents the most unequal income distribution of the world.[57] But as others have stated, "while it has become relatively common to associate biological variation with socioeconomic variation, it is rare that the context or roots of the socioeconomic variation are addressed."[58] There is no doubt that these proximate causes (poverty and inequality) of the high levels of malnutrition and the short stature of the Guatemalan population are the consequences of the political, economic, and social history of this Central American country. The literature on nutrition and development offers some complementary ideas that illuminate this issue.

Scholars have argued that adverse agricultural conditions, difficult communications and land tenure regimes are behind the wide regional disparities in adult height, stunting, and poverty rates in Guatemala and neighboring countries.[59] The commercialization of agriculture from 1966 to 1980 increased land concentration and unemployment, reducing food consumption and child nutrition and resulting in deteriorating living standards.[60] Overall, it is clear that national and regional dynamics of land availability and tenure, type of employment, wage rates, ethnicity and social class are major causes of malnutrition and short adult stature.[61]

A recent work which included studies carried out in Brazil, India, Philippines, South Africa, and Guatemala found that adults with low human capital (including school achievement and economic productivity) were shorter on average and were more likely to have suffered stunting as children.[62] In Guatemala, infants and toddlers who received Atole supplements as part of the INCAP Follow-up program were more likely to earn higher hourly wages as adults (a 46% increase in average wage).[63] Cognitive skills probably improve with better nutrition (of which adult stature is an indicator), resulting in higher wages in adult life.[64] Hence, one of the key reasons to increase investment in nutrition programs at early ages is that "they drive long-term economic growth by leading to healthier and more productive adults,"[65] and that "many investments in nutrition are in fact very good economic investments."[66] However, it is necessary to bear in mind that in order to transfer an improvement in individual skills into an increase in productivity at the individual and national levels, society must be able to make an effective use of those skills, and all of this depends on economic demands and social organization.[67]

Extreme poverty and inequality are forms of structural violence that has dominated Guatemalan history. Following Galtung, one of the founders of modern peace studies, "violence is present when human beings are being influenced so that their actual somatic and mental realizations are below their potential realizations."[68] The studies about the growth and development of Guatemalan children clearly show that their observed somatic realizations are below their potential, and it is the poor environment during the growth period and not any genetic limitation that is the cause of this failure. At the same time, the ongoing forensic projects document the periods of direct violence exerted against the Guatemalan civil population.[69] Combining data from different sources researchers have estimated that the numbers of persons killed or disappeared as a result of these violent periods reached a disturbing total of over 40,000.[70] Moreover, both kinds of violence are related. According to the World Bank, "lasting peace and faster growth require not only the cessation of violence, but addressing Guatemala's poverty and social inequality,"[71] and the United Nations Development Programme for Guatemala stated recently that the deteriorated living standard was at the root of the insurgencies and subsequent repression of the last decades, and that despite recent progress the structural causes of the civil war still remain present.[72]

In conclusion, biological anthropology documents the pattern of structural violence exerted against an important segment of the Guatemalan population during the recent history of this Central American nation, and this discipline has significant intellectual resources that could modestly contribute to a peaceful change toward social justice and durable peace.

Notes

1. Fogel, "Anthropometric History"; Steckel, "Stature and the Standard."
2. Ulijaszek et al., *The Cambridge Encyclopedia.*
3. Organización Mundial de la Salud, *El estado físico.*
4. Tanner, "Growth as a Mirror," 3.
5. Bogin and Keep, "Eight Thousand"; López-Alonso y Porrás, "The Ups and Downs"; Meisel and Vega, "The Biological Standard of Living"; Salvatore, "Stature, Nutrition."
6. Larsen, *Bioarcheology.*
7. Steckel, "Health and Nutrition."
8. De Onis and Blossner, "The World Health."
9. Mascie-Taylor, "Nutritional Status."
10. Organización Mundial de la Salud, *El estado físico,* 266.
11. De Onis et al., "Time for a New"; de Onis et al., "The WHO Multicentre."
12. De Onis et al., "Is Malnutrition Declining?"

13. De Onis et al., "Methodology for Estimating."

14. Instituto Nacional de Estadística, *Encuesta Nacional*.

15. Instituto Nacional de Estadística, *Perfil de la pobreza*.

16. Ministerio de Educación, *Segundo Censo*.

17. Programa de Naciones Unidas para el Desarrollo, *Guatemala: Una Agenda*, 228. As explained in Banco Mundial, *La Pobreza en Guatemala*, 36, extreme poverty is defined as income insufficient to meet the annual cost of a *canasta básica de alimentos* (basic food basket) needed to cover a minimum daily caloric intake of 2172. The line of extreme poverty in 2002 was U$245 per capita. In turn, total poverty is defined as the income needed to meet nutritional and non-nutritional basic needs; it was estimated at U$554 per capita.

18. For a brief but detailed history of this project see Bogin, *Patterns of Human*, 45.

19. Universidad de San Carlos de Guatemala, *Curvas de Crecimiento*.

20. Bogin, *Patterns of Human*, 268; Martorell, "Results and Implications." Currently, a multidisciplinary team of biomedical investigators and economists is studying the data from a follow-up study in 2002–04 of a cohort of fully adult young men and women, who participated as young children in the nutrition supplementation carried out from 1969–77. See below and Martorell et al., "Rationale for a Follow-up."

21. Much evidence supports the idea that the quality of the nutritional and health environment affects not only height but also body proportions, see Bogin et al., "How Genetic," 205 and references therein, and see below. In this analysis we are going to use the cormic index, defined by the formula (sitting height* 100/ stature). This index is a measure of the relative contribution of leg length to total stature; the lower the cormic index, the longer-legged is the population under study. Therefore, this index is a measure of body proportions or body shape. It is an interesting measure in human biology, as the decrease in adult height due to child malnutrition usually affects leg length.

22. Programa de Naciones Unidas para el Desarrollo, *Guatemala: los contrastes*, 199. The figure for the department of Guatemala was obtained from table 1 (Statistical appendix). The figure for the Maya group was obtained by averaging the HDI from the four ethnic groups included in table 6 (Statistical appendix).

23. See also Gragnolati, *Children's Growth*, 32.

24. De Onis, "Commentary: Socioeconomic."

25. Johnston et al., "Growth Status."

26. The results of these studies were published in several studies cited below. A web portal to studies originated in these data is at http://bvssan.incap.org.gt /php/index.php.

27. Rose et al., "Infant Mortality."

28. Martorell, "Results and Implications."

29. Rivera et al., "Nutritional Supplementation."

30. Haas et al., "Nutritional Supplementation."

31. Pollit et al., "Nutrition in Early."

32. Li et al., "Effects of Early."
33. Stein et al., "Prospective Study"; Stein et al., "Comparison of Linear."
34. Bogin, "Plasticity in the Growth"; Bogin and Loucky, "Plasticity, Political"; Bogin et al., "Rapid Change."
35. Mascie-Taylor and Little, "History of Migration."
36. Bogin and Loucky, "Plasticity, Political"; Loucky, "Central American"; Loucky, "Maya Americans."
37. For this analysis, the data for boys and girls were combined, given the absence of statistically significant differences by sex across ages 6–12 within the migrant, urban, and rural samples in the anthropometric variables, and in order to increase the sample size from the migrant community.
38. Kaplowitz et al., "Selection for Rural"; Malina et al., "Childhood Growth."
39. From economists like Seckler, "Malnutrition: An Intellectual"; "Small but Healthy"; to anthropologists who assume this widespread version, such as like Rojas Lima, *Los Indios de Guatemala*, 257, who writes: "Hay rasgos físicos o genéticos (producto de las tendencias endógamas) que distinguen a los grupos: el color de la piel, el cabello, la estatura, entre los principales."
40. Stinson, "Nutritional Adaptation."
41. Bogin and Keep, "Eight Thousand."
42. For more detailed information about these samples see ibid., 342.
43. This moving average was calculated for the percent change in the per capita GNP of Guatemala from year to year, expressed as the average of the previous ten years.
44. See Pan-American Health Organization's country profile for Guatemala, www.paho.org; Instituto Nacional de Estadística, *Encuesta de Salud*; USAID, *USAID/Guatemala*.
45. Martorell, "Results and Implications."
46. McCullough, "Secular Trend."
47. Malina et al., "Adult Stature."
48. Larsen, *Bioarchaeology*.
49. Marquez Morfin and del Angel, "Height among"; Storey et al., "Social Disruption."
50. Ríos et al., "Crecimiento y desarrollo"; Ríos, "Estimación de la estatura"; Ríos, "Determinación métrica."
51. Marquez Morfin and del Angel, "Height among," 61.
52. Storey et al., "Social Disruption," 303.
53. Malina et al., "Adult Stature"; McCullough, "Secular Trend."
54. Wright and Chew, "Porotic Hyperostosis."
55. A new National Height Census was published in 2009 with updated information on children's anthropometrics (Ministerio de Educación, *Tercer Censo*). A total of 459,808 children were included in the database, with coverage above 95% of the primary school population. These new data were compared with the recently available new growth reference from the WHO (De Onis et al., "WHO growth standards," 47–53) and it was found that 45.6% of the children sampled were stunted. The comparison of the figures from the three national height censuses

with the new WHO reference indicates a prevalence of stunting of 51.1%, 49.7% and 45.6% for the 1986, 2001 and 2008 studies respectively. In a twenty two years period, prevalence of stunted Guatemalan school children has diminished by 5.5%. As stated in the report, in spite of some decrease in the prevalence of stunting, the figure is still very high and requires interventions in order to reduce chronic malnutrition in a systematic and accelerated manner; see Ministerio de Educación, *Tercer Censo*, 17).

56. United Nations Development Program, *Human Development*, 271.
57. The Gini index for Guatemala was 59.9, the highest value, 70.7, was reported for Namibia. A value of 0 represents perfect equality and a value of 100 perfect inequality.
58. Goodman and Leatherman, "Traversing the Chasm," 32.
59. Loyola et al., "Situación del retardo," 13; Pebley and Goldman, "Social Inequality."
60. Brockett, "Malnutrition, Public," 477. However, Pebley and Goldman find that plantations may offer improved employment opportunities that result in better nutritional levels.
61. For a recent compendium of these variables in Guatemala's history see Adams and Bastos, *Las relaciones étnicas*, and references therein.
62. Victora et al., "Maternal and Child Undernutrition," 354.
63. Hoddinott et al., "Effect of a Nutrition Intervention," 414.
64. Behrman et al., "Does It Pay to Become Taller?"
65. Hoddinott et al., "Effect of a Nutrition Intervention," 411.
66. Alderman et al., "Economic and Nutritional Analyses," 2.
67. Martorell et al., "Malnutrition, Work Output."
68. Galtung, "Violence, Peace," 168. For a similar approach for the Guatemalan situation see Preti, "Guatemala: Violence."
69. The total number of skeletons recovered by one forensic team for the period 1992 to 2004 is 2,982, see information at www.fafg.org.
70. Comisión para el Esclarecimiento Histórico, *Guatemala Memoria*, 17.
71. World Bank, *Guatemala: Investing*, 14.
72. Programa de las Naciones Unidas para el Desarrollo, *Guatemala: una agenda*, xxxv, Anexo Especial.

References

Adams, Richard N., and Santiago Bastos. *Las relaciones étnicas en Guatemala, 1944–2000*. Guatemala: Centro de Investigaciones Regionales de Mesoamérica, 2003.

Alderman, Harold, Jere R. Behrman, and John Hodinott. "Economic and Nutritional Analyses Offer Substantial Synergies for Understanding Human Nutrition." *Journal of Nutrition* 137 (2007): 537–544.

Aufderheide, Arthur C., and Conrado Rodríguez-Martín. *The Cambridge Encyclopedia of Human Paleopathology*. Cambridge: Cambridge University Press, 1998.

Ball, Patrick, Paul Kobrak, and Herbert F. Spirer. *State Violence in Guatemala 1960–1996: A Quantitative Reflection*. Washington, D.C.: American Association for the Advancement of Science, 1999.

Banco Mundial. *La pobreza en Guatemala*. Washington, D.C.: Banco Internacional de Reconstrucción y Fomento, Banco Mundial, 2003.

Behrman, Jere H., John Hoddinott, John A. Maluccio, and Reynaldo Martorell. *Does It Pay to Became Taller? Or Is What You Know All That Really Matters?* Philadelphia: University of Pennsylvania Press, 2005.

Blanco, Ricardo A., Roy M. Acheson, Cipriano Canosa, and Joao B. Salomon. "Height, Weight and Lines of Arrested Growth in Young Guatemalan Children." *American Journal of Physical Anthropology* 40 (1972): 39–48.

Brockett, Charles D. "Malnutrition, Public Policy, and Agrarian Change in Guatemala." *Journal of Interamerican Studies and World Affairs* 26 (1984): 477–497.

Bogin, Barry. "Plasticity in the Growth of the Mayan Children Living in the United States." In *Human Variability and Plasticity*, ed. C. G. N. Mascie-Taylor and B. Bogin. Cambridge: Cambridge University Press, 1995.

———. *Patterns of Human Growth*. 2nd ed. Cambridge: Cambridge University Press, 1999.

Bogin, Barry, and James Loucky. "Plasticity, Political Economy, and Physical Growth Status of Guatemala Maya Children Living in the United States." *American Journal of Physical Anthropology* 102 (1997): 17–32.

Bogin, Barry, and Raymond Keep. "Eight Thousand Years of Economic and Political History in Latin American Revealed by Anthropometry." *Annals of Human Biology* 26 (1999): 333–351.

Bogin, Barry, Matthew Kapell, Maria Inés Varela Silva, Bibiana Orden, Patricia K. Smith, and James Loucky. "How Genetic Are Human Body Proportions?" In *Perspectives in Human Growth, Development and Maturation*, ed. P. Dasgupta and R. Hauspie. Dordrecht: Kluwer Academic Publisher, 2001.

Bogin, Barry, Patricia Smith, Bibiana Orden, Maria Inés Varela Silva and James Loucky. "Rapid Change in Height and Body Proportions of Maya American Children." *American Journal of Human Biology* 14 (2002): 753–761.

Comisión para el Esclarecimiento Histórico. *Guatemala, Memoria del Silencio. Conclusiones y Recomendaciones del Informe de la Comisión para el Esclarecimiento Histórico*. Guatemala: Comisión para el Esclarecimiento Histórico, 1999.

De Onis, Mercedes. "Commentary: Socioeconomic Inequalities and Child Growth." *International Journal of Epidemiology* 32 (2003): 503–505.

De Onis, Mercedes, Cutberto Garza, and Jean-Pierre Habicht. "Time for a New Growth Reference." *Pediatrics* 100 (1997): E8.

De Onis, Mercedes, Edward A. Frongillo, and Monika Blössner. "Is Malnutrition Declining? An Analysis of Changes in Levels of Child Malnutrition since 1980." *Bulletin of the World Health Organization* 78 (2000): 1222–1232.

De Onis, Mercedes, and Monika Blössner. "The World Health Organization Global Database on Child Growth and Malnutrition: Methodology and Applications." *International Journal of Epidemiology* 32 (2003): 518–526.

De Onis, Mercedes, Monika Blössner, Elaine Borghi, Richard Morris and Edward A. Frongillo. "Methodology for Estimating Regional and Global Trends of Child Malnutrition." *International Journal of Epidemiology* 33 (2004): 1260–1270.

De Onis, Mercedes, Cutberto Garza, Cesar G. Victora, Adelheid W. Onyango, Edward A. Frongillo, and Jose Martines. "The WHO Multicentre Growth Reference Study: Planning, Study, Design, and Methodology." *Food and Nutrition Bulletin* 25 (2004): 515–526.

De Onis, Mercedes, Cuthberto Garza, Adelheid W. Onyango, M F Rolland-Cachera. "WHO Growth Standards for Infants and Young Children." *Archives de Pédiatrie* 16, no. 1 (2009): 47–53.

Díaz, Erik, Teresa González-Cossío, Juan Rivera, Maarten D.C. Immink, Rubén Darío Mendoza, and Rafael C. Flores. "Body Composition Estimates Using Different Measurement Techniques in a Sample of Highland Subsistence Farmers in Guatemala." *American Journal of Human Biology* 3 (1991): 525–530.

Flegal, Katherine, Lenore J. Launer, Barry I. Graubard, Edgard Kestler, and Jorge Villar. "Modeling Maternal Weight and Height in Studies of Pregnancy Outcome among Hispanic Women." *American Journal of Clinical Nutrition* 58 (1993): 145–151.

Fogel, Robert W. "Anthropometric History: Notes on the First Two Decades of a New Field of Research." In *Essays on Auxology*, ed. R. Hauspie, G. Lindgren, and F. Faulkner. Welwyn Garden City: Castlemead Publications, 1995.

Galtung, Johan. "Violence, Peace and Peace Research." *Journal of Peace Research* 6 (1969): 167–191.

Goodman, Alan H., and Thomas L. Leatherman. "Traversing the Chasm between Biology and Culture: An Introduction." In *Building a New Biocultural Synthesis. Political-Economic Perspectives on Human Biology*, ed. A. H. Goodman and T. L. Leatherman. Ann Arbor: University of Michigan Press, 1999.

Haas, Jere, Elkin J. Martínez, Scott Murdock, Elizabeth Conlisk, Juan Rivera, and Reynaldo Martorell. "Nutritional Supplementation during the Preschool Years and Physical Work Capacity in Adolescent and Young Adult Guatemalans." *Journal of Nutrition* 125 (1995):1078S–1089S.

Hoddinott, John, John A. Maluccio, Jere A. Behrman, Rafael Flores, and Reynaldo Martorell. "Effect of a Nutrition Intervention during Early Childhood on Economic Productivity in Guatemalan Adults." *Lancet* 371 (2008): 411–416.

Infante, Peter A., and George M. Gillespie. "An Epidemiologic Study of Linear Hypoplasia of Deciduous Anterior Teeth in Guatemalan Children." *Archives of Oral Biology* 19 (1974): 1055–1061.

Instituto Nacional de Estadística. *Encuesta Nacional de Salud Materno Infantil 1987.* Guatemala: Instituto Nacional de Estadística, 1988.

———. *Encuesta Nacional de Salud Materno Infantil 1995.* Guatemala: Instituto Nacional de Estadística, 1996.

———. *Encuesta Nacional de Salud Materno Infantil 1998/99.* Guatemala: Instituto Nacional de Estadística, 2000.

———. *Encuesta Nacional de Salud Materno Infantil 2002.* Guatemala: Instituto Nacional de Estadística, 2003.

———. *Perfil de la pobreza en Guatemala.* Guatemala: Instituto Nacional de Estadística, 2002.

Johnston, Francis E., Setha M. Low, Yetilu de Baessa, and Robert B. MacVean. "Growth Status of Disadvantaged Urban Guatemalan Children of a Resettled Community." *American Journal of Physical Anthropology* 68 (1985): 215–224.

Kaplowitz, Haley Jo, Reynaldo Martorell, and Patrice Engle. "Selection for Rural to Urban Migrants." In *Urban Ecology and Health in the Third World*, ed. L. Schell and A. Bilsborough. Cambridge: Cambridge University Press, 1993.

Larsen, Clark S. *Bioarchaeology. Interpreting Behaviour from the Human Skeleton.* Cambridge: Cambridge University Press, 1997.

Li, Haojie, Giman X. Barnhart, Aryeh D. Stein, and Reynaldo Martorell. "Effects of Early Childhood Supplementation on the Educational Achievement of Women." *Pediatrics* 112 (2003): 1156–1162.

López-Alonso, Moramay, and Raúl Porras. "The Ups and Downs of Mexican Economic Growth: The Biological Standard of Living and Inequality, 1870–1950." *Economics and Human Biology* 1 (2003): 169–186.

Loucky, James. "Central American Refugees: Learning New Skills in the U.S.A." In *Contemporary Anthropology*, edited by M. C. Howard. 4th ed. New York: Harper Collins, 1993.

Loucky, James. "Maya Americans: The Emergence of a Transnational Community." In *Central Americans in California*, ed. N. Hamilton and N. Chinchilla. Los Angeles: Center for Multiethnic Studies and Transnational Studies, University of Southern California, 1996.

Loyola, Enrique, Patricia Nájera, Ramón Martínez, Manuel Vidaurre, et al. "Situación del retardo severo del crecimiento entre escolares de primer grado de países de Centroamérica alrededor del año 2000." *Boletín Epidemiológico de la Organización Panamericana de Salud* 25 (2004): 9–13.

Malina, Robert, Peter Buschang, and Wendy L. Aronson. "Childhood Growth Status of Eventual Migrants and Sedentes in a Rural Zapotec Community in the Valley of Oaxaca." *Human Biology* 54 (1982): 709–716.

Malina, Robert M., Henry A. Selby, Peter H. Buschang, Wendy L. Aronson, and Richard G. Wilkinson. "Adult Stature and Age at Menarche in Zapotec-speaking Communities in the Valley of Oaxaca, Mexico, in a Secular Perspective." *American Journal of Physical Anthropology* 60 (1983): 437–449.

Marquez Morfin, Lourdes, and Andres del Angel. "Height among the Prehispanic Maya of the Yucatán Peninsula: Reconsideration." In *Bones of the Maya*, ed. S. Whittington and D. Reid. Washington, D.C.: Smithsonian Institution Press, 1997.

Martorell, Reynaldo. "Results and Implications of the INCAP Follow-up Study." *Journal of Nutrition* 125 (1995): 1127S–1138S.

Martorell, Reynaldo, Hernán L. Delgado, Víctor Valverde, and Robert E Klein. "Maternal Stature, Fertility and Infant Mortality." *Human Biology* 53 (1981): 303–312.

Martorell, Reynaldo, and Guillermo Arroyave. "Malnutrition, Work Output and Energy Needs." In *Capacity for Work in the Tropics*, ed. K. J. Collins and D. B. Roberts. Cambridge: Cambridge University Press, 1988.

Martorell, Reynaldo, Jere J. Behrman, Ricardo Flores, and Aryeh D. Stein. "Rationale for a Follow-up Study Focusing on Economic Productivity." *Food and Nutrition Bulletin* 26 (2005): S5–S14.

Mascie-Taylor, C. G. Nicholas. "Nutritional Status: Its Measurement and Relation to Health." In *Applications of Biological Anthropology to Human Affairs*, ed. C. G. N. Mascie-Taylor and G. W. Lasker. Cambridge: Cambridge University Press, 1991.

Mascie-Taylor, C. G. Nicholas, and Michael A. Little. "History of Migration Studies in Biological Anthropology." *American Journal of Human Biology* 16 (2004): 365–378.

May, Richard L., Alan H. Goodman, and Richard S. Meindl. "Response of Bone and Enamel Formation to Nutritional Supplementation and Morbidity among Malnourished Guatemalan Children." *American Journal of Physical Anthropology* 92 (1993): 37–51.

McCullough, John. "Secular Trend for Stature in Adult Male Yucatec Maya to 1968." *American Journal of Physical Anthropology* 58 (1982): 221–225.

Meisel, Adolfo, and Margarita Vega. "The Biological Standard of Living (and Its Convergence) in Colombia, 1870–2003: A Tropical Success Story." *Economics and Human Biology* 5 (2007): 100–122.

Ministerio de Educación. *Segundo Censo Nacional de escolares de primer grado de primaria de la República de Guatemala.* Guatemala: Ministerio de Educación, 2002.

———. *Tercer Censo Nacional de escolares de primer grado de primaria de la República de Guatemala.* Guatemala: Ministerio de Educación, 2009.

Organización Mundial de la Salud. *El estudio físico: uso e interpretación de la antropometría.* Madrid: Organización Mundial de la Salud, 1995.

Pebley Anne R. and Noreen Goldman. "Social Inequality and Children's Growth in Guatemala." *Health Transition Review* 5 (1995): 1–20.

Pollit, Ernesto, Kathleen S. Gorman, Patrice L. Engle, Juan A. Rivera, and Reynaldo Martorell. "Nutrition in Early Life and the Fulfilment of Intellectual Potential." *Journal of Nutrition* 125 (1995): 1111S–1118S.

Preti, Alessandro. "Guatemala: Violence in Peacetime—a Critical Analysis of the Armed Conflict and the Peace Process." *Disasters* 26 (2002): 99–119.

Programa de Naciones Unidas para el Desarrollo. *Guatemala: los contrastes del desarrollo humano.* Guatemala: Sistema de Naciones Unidas en Guatemala, 1998.

———. *Guatemala: una agenda para el desarrollo humano.* Guatemala: Sistema de Naciones Unidas en Guatemala, 2003.

Ríos, Luis. "Estimación de la estatura a partir de restos óseos en las exhumaciones forenses en Guatemala: problemas metodológicos." Presented at the XVII Simposio de Investigaciones Arqueológicas en Guatemala. Museo de Arqueología, Guatemala City, Guatemala, 2003.

———. "Determinación métrica del sexo en las exhumaciones forenses en Guatemala." Presented at the XVI Simposio de Investigaciones Arqueológicas en Guatemala. Museo de Arqueología, Guatemala City, Guatemala, 2002.

Ríos, Luis, Mario Vasquez, and Lourdes Penados. "Crecimiento y desarrollo del esqueleto en una muestra forense guatemalteca." Presented at the XVIII Simposio de Investigaciones Arqueológicas en Guatemala. Museo de Arqueología, Guatemala City, Guatemala, 2004.

Rivera, Juan A., Reynaldo Martorell, Marie Ruel, Jean-Pierre Habicht, and Jere Hass. "Nutritional Supplementation during Preschool Years Influences Body Size and Composition of Guatemalan Adolescents." *Journal of Nutrition* 125 (1995): 1078S–1089S.

Rojas Lima, Flavio. *Los Indios de Guatemala.* Madrid: Fundación Mapfre, 1992.

Rose, Donald, Reynaldo Martorell, and Juan A. Rivera. "Infant Mortality Rates before, during, and after a Nutrition and Health Intervention in Rural Guatemalan Villages." *Food and Nutrition Bulletin* 14 (1992): 215–220.

Ruel, Marie T., Juan Rivera, Hilda Castro, Jean-Pierre Habicht, and Reynaldo Martorell. "Secular Trends in Adult and Child Anthropometry in Four Guatemalan Villages." *Food and Nutrition Bulletin* 14, no. 3 (Sept. 1992). www.unu.edu /unupress/food/8F143e/8F143E0n.htm.

Russell, Marcia. "Parent-child and Sibling-sibling Correlations of Height and Weight in a Rural Guatemalan Population of Preschool Children." *Human Biology* 48 (1976): 501–515.

Salvatore, Ricardo. "Stature Decline and Recovery in a Food-rich Export Economy: Argentina 1900–1934." *Explorations in Economic History* 41 (2004): 233–245.

Seckler, David. "'Malnutrition': An Intellectual Odyssey." *Western Journal of Agricultural Economics* 5 (1980): 219–227.

———. "Small but Healthy: A Basic Hypothesis in the Theory, Measurement and Policy of Malnutrition." In *New Concepts in Nutrition and Their Implications for Policy*, ed. P.V. Sukhatme. Pune: Maharashtra Association for the Cultivation of Science Research Institute, 1982.

Steckel, Richard. "Stature and the Standard of Living." *Journal of Economic Literature* 23 (1995): 1903–1940.

———. "Health and Nutrition in Pre-Columbian America: The Skeletal Evidence." *Journal of Interdisciplinary History* 36, no. 1 (2005): 1–32.

Stein, Aryeh D., Huiman X. Barnhart, Morgen Hickey, Usha Ramakrishnan, Dirk G. Schroeder, and Reynaldo Martorell. "Prospective Study of Protein-energy Supplementation Early in Life and of Growth in the Subsequent Generation in Guatemala." *American Journal of Clinical Nutrition* 78 (2003): 162–167.

Stein, Aryeh D., Huiman X. Barnhart, Meng Wang, Moshe B. Hoshen, et al. "Nutritional Adaptation." *Annual Review of Anthropology* 24 (1992): 143–170.

Storey, Rebecca, Lourdes Marquez Morfin, and Vernon Smith. "Social Disruption and the Maya Civilization of Mesoamerica." In *The Backbone of History*, ed. R. Steckel and J. Rose. Cambridge: Cambridge University Press, 2002.

Sweeney, Edward A., Jorge Cabrera, Juan Urrutia, and Leonardo Mata. "Factors Associated with Linear Hypoplasia of Human Deciduous Dentition." *Journal of Dental Research* 48 (1969): 1275–1279.

Tanner, James M. "Growth as a Mirror for the Condition of Society: Secular Trends and Class Distinctions." In *Human Growth: A Multidisciplinary Review*, ed. A. Demirjian. London: Taylor and Francis, 1986.

Ulijaszek, Stanley, Francis E. Johnston, and Michael A. Preece. *The Cambridge Encyclopedia of Human Growth and Development*. Cambridge: Cambridge University Press, 1998.

United Nations Development Programme. *Human Development Report 2005. International Cooperation at a Crossroads: Aid, Trade and Security in an Unequal World*. Geneva: United Nations, 2005.

Universidad de San Carlos de Guatemala. *Curvas de crecimiento de niños urbanos de Guatemala de 6 a 16 años*. Guatemala: Universidad de San Carlos de Guatemala, Dirección General de Investigación, 1998.

USAID. *USAID/Guatemala-Central American programs. Program Overview: Guatemala*. Washington, D.C.: United States Agency for International Development, 1995.

Victora, Cesar A., Linda Adair, Caroline Fall, Pedro C. Hallal, Reynaldo Martorell, Linda Richter, Harshpal Singh Sachdev (Maternal and Child Undernutrition Study Group). "Maternal and Child Undernutrition: Consequences for Adult Health and Human Capital." *Lancet* 371 (2008): 340–357.

Villanueva, Maria. "Las características físicas de algunos grupos indígenas mayas de las zonas centro y sur en territorio mexicano y guatemalteco." In *Dinámica Maya. Los Refugiados Guatemaltecos*, ed. M. Messmacher, S. Genovés, M. Nolasco, et al. México: Fondo de Cultura Económica, 1986.

Wright, Lori and Francisco Chew. "Porotic Hyperostosis and Paleoepidemiology: A Forensic Perspective on Anemia among the Ancient Maya." *American Anthropologist* 100 (1998): 924–939.

World Bank. *Guatemala: Investing for Peace*. Washington, D.C.: World Bank, 1997.

Contributors

Luis Bértola has a Ph.D. in Economic History (University of Gothenburg), and is Professor at the Economic and Social History Program (Universidad de la República, Uruguay) and director of the M.A. and Ph.D. programs in Economic History. He has been visiting professor and taught postgraduate courses at several universities. He is editor of the *Revista de Historia Económica/Journal of Iberian and Latin American Economic History*. His main field of research and publications is comparative long-run development of the Latin American economies.

Barry Bogin is currently at the Centre for Human Development and Ageing, Loughborough University (U.K.), where he teaches courses in human biology, physical anthropology, and nutrition. His research area is human physical growth and development. Among other projects on human growth, since 1992 Bogin has been working with Guatemalan Maya children, and their families, living in the United States. He has more than 100 books, articles, book chapters, and popular essays, including *The Growth of Humanity* (2001, Wiley).

María Magdalena Camou has a Ph.D. in Economic History from the Universidad de la República, Uruguay, where she is a professor at the Economic and Social History Program. Her main research lines are labor markets during industrialization, international comparative wages, living standards, and gender inequality.

Amílcar E. Challú is Assistant Professor of History at Bowling Green State University. He was the recipient of the Economic History Association's Gerschenkron Prize for the best economic history dissertation on an international topic (2009) and a National Endowment for the Humanities Fellowship (2010–11). His research deals with the political economy of hunger in Mexico in the late colonial period.

John H. Coatsworth is the Dean of the School of International and Public Affairs and Professor of International and Public Affairs and of History, at Columbia University. He coedited the *Cambridge Economic History of Latin America*, and is the author or editor of seven books and many scholarly articles on Latin American economic and international history. He is a former president of the American Historical Association and of the Latin American Studies Association.

Moramay López-Alonso is an economic historian and Assistant Professor of History at Rice University. Her research on biological well-being in Mexico has been published in *Economics and Human Biology* and the *Journal of Latin American Studies*.

Silvana Maubrigades holds a master's degree and is a Ph.D. candidate in economic history (Universidad de la República, Uruguay). She is a research assistant at the Economic and Social History Program. Her main research fields are gender, education, and development.

James W. McGuire is Professor in the Department of Government at Wesleyan University. He specializes in comparative politics with a regional focus on Latin America and East Asia and a topical focus on democracy and public health. He is the author of *Peronism without Perón: Unions, Parties, and Democracy in Argentina* (Stanford, 1997) and of *Wealth, Health, and Democracy in East Asia and Latin America* (Cambridge, 2010).

Adolfo Meisel is the Director of the Centro de Estudios Regionales (CEER) of the Colombian Central Bank in Cartagena, Colombia. His interests include fiscal and monetary policy of the late colonial and early national periods, regional development, and biological well-being. His research has been published in journals such as *Economics and Human Biology*, *Revista de Historia Económica/Journal of Iberian and Latin American Economic History*, and in edited books.

Natalia Melgar is an Assistant Professor at the Department of Economics, Universidad de la República, Uruguay, and a Ph.D. candidate at the University of Granada (Spain).

Leonardo Monasterio is an economist at the Instituto de Pesquisa Econômica Aplicada (IPEA) in Brazil. His research has been mainly concerned with the application of quantitative methods to Brazilian economic history and long-term regional issues. He is currently researching the evolution of human heights in Southern Brazil between 1889 and 1980.

Luiz Paulo Ferreira Nogueról is a historian at Universidade de Brasilia (UnB) in Brazil. Currently he studies the slave trade from Rio de Janeiro to Rio de la Plata between 1770 and 1830. His broader research is the complexity of slavery in the South Americans Spanish colonies.

Luis Ríos received his Ph.D. in Anthropology in 2010. He is a lecturer at Universidad Autónoma de Madrid (Spain), where he teaches courses in physical anthropology and human osteology. His research area is human physical growth and the applications of physical anthropology to forensic science. He has worked on human growth projects, and in archaeological and forensic projects, in Guatemala and Spain. He has published his research in the *American Journal of Physical Anthropology, Forensic Science International, American Journal of Human Biology,* and *Revista de Historia Agraria.*

Ricardo D. Salvatore is Professor of History at Universidad Torcuato Di Tella in Buenos Aires. He is the author of *Wandering Paysanos* (2003) and *Imagenes de un Imperio* (2006), and coeditor of *Crime and Punishment in Latin America, Close Encounters of Empire,* and, more recently, *Los lugares del saber.* His research on biological well-being in Argentina has been published in *Social Science History, Explorations in Economic History, Historia Agraria,* and *Revista de Historia Económica/Journal of Latin American Economic History.*

Claudio D. Shikida obtained a doctorate degree at the Universidade Federal do Rio Grande do Sul (UFRGS). Currently he is a Professor and Researcher of Economics at Ibmec Minas Gerais, in Brazil. His main interests are: public choice, Brazilian economic history, and economics of conflict.

Margarita Vega is an economist based in Colombia. Her research on biological well-being, in collaboration with Adolfo Meisel, has been published in *Economics and Human Biology* and publications in Colombia.